Consuming Cultures, Global Perspectives

Cultures of Consumption Series

Series Editor: Frank Trentmann

ISSN 1744-5876

Previously Published Titles

The Making of the Consumer
Knowledge, Power and Identity in the Modern World
Edited by Frank Trentmann

Forthcoming Titles

Fashion's World Cities
Edited by Christopher Breward and David Gilbert

The Khat Controversy
Stimulating the Debate on Drugs
David Anderson, Susan Beckerleg, Degol Hailu and Axel Klein

Governing Consumption
New Spaces of Consumer Politics
Clive Barnett, Nick Clarke, Paul Cloke and Alice Malpass

Alternative Food Networks
Reconnecting Producers, Consumers and Food?
Moya Kneafsey, Lewis Holloway, Laura Venn, Rosie Cox,
Elizabeth Dowler and Helena Tuomainen

The Design of Everyday Life
Elizabeth Shove, Matthew Watson and Jack Ingram

Consuming Cultures, Global Perspectives

Historical Trajectories, Transnational Exchanges

Edited by
John Brewer and Frank Trentmann

Oxford • New York

English edition
First published in 2006 by
Berg
Editorial offices:
1st Floor, Angel Court, 81 St Clements Street, Oxford OX4 1AW, UK
175 Fifth Avenue, New York, NY 10010, USA

Berg is the imprint of Oxford International Publishers Ltd.

This book has been produced with the support of the
Economic and Social Research Council and the Arts and Humanities Research Council

Library of Congress Cataloging-in-Publication data
Consuming cultures : global perspectives, historical trajectories, transnational
exchanges / edited by John Brewer and Frank Trentmann.
    p. cm.—(Cultures of consumption series)
    Includes bibliographical references and index.
    ISBN-13: 978-1-84520-246-0 (hardback)
    ISBN-10: 1-84520-246-5 (hardback)
    ISBN-13: 978-1-84520-247-7 (pbk.)
    ISBN-10: 1-84520-247-3 (pbk.)
    1. Consumption (Economics)—Social aspects. 2. Culture—Economic aspects.
3. Material culture. I. Brewer, John, 1947- II. Trentmann, Frank. III. Series.

    HC79.C6C665 2006
    306.3—dc22

                                                                    2006009547

British Library Cataloguing-in-Publication data
A catalogue record for this book is available from the British Library.

ISBN-13 978 1 84520 246 0 (Cloth)
         978 1 84520 247 7 (Paper)

ISBN-10 1 84520 246 5 (Cloth)
         1 84520 247 3 (Paper)

Typeset by JS Typesetting Ltd, Porthcawl, Mid Glamorgan
Printed in the United Kingdom by Biddles Ltd, King's Lynn

www.bergpublishers.com

Contents

List of Illustrations

Acknowledgements

Consuming Cultures, Global Perspectives grew out of efforts to explore new narratives of consumption. Over the last two decades there has been an explosion of work on 'consumer culture', 'consumer society' and 'consumer revolutions'. Most of this work has been governed by a story of modernity firmly located in the West. What narratives emerge if the global diversity of consuming cultures is taken into consideration or consumption practices that do not easily fit a 'modern' picture of the individual consumer, choice and hedonism? What stories do the politics of consumption and attention to power tell about the trajectories of consumption? We invited international experts from a range of disciplines to collectively think about new perspectives.

Most chapters in this volume developed out of papers first discussed at the conference 'Consumption, Modernity, and the West', which we convened at the California Institute of Technology, in Pasadena, in April 2004. We are grateful to the other participants and commentators who contributed so much to the intellectual momentum and focus of this project: Craig Clunas, Liz Cohen, Jean Comaroff, Deborah Davis, Margot Finn, Ken Pomeranz and Nigel Thrift. Special thanks must go to Susan Davis for her support of the project, to Sabrina Boschetti for her help with the organization and logistics of the conference, and to Stefanie Nixon for her help in preparing the final manuscript. For their generous support we should like to thank the Division of the Humanities and Social Sciences at Cal Tech, the Economic and Social Research Council and the Arts and Humanities Research Council (L142241003). Finally, we should like to thank everyone at Berg, and Laura Bevir for preparing the index.

John Brewer and Frank Trentmann

List of Contributors

David M. Anderson is University Lecturer in African Studies, University of Oxford, and a Research Fellow of St Antony's College, Oxford. Recent publications include *Histories of the Hanged: Britain's Dirty War in Kenya and the End of Empire* (New York, 2005) and *Eroding the Commons: Politics of Ecology in Baringo, Kenya, 1890–1963* (Oxford, 2000).

Adam Arvidsson is Assistant Professor in the Department of Film and Media Studies, University of Copenhagen. Recent publications include *Brands: Meaning and Value in Postmodern Media Culture* (London, 2005) and *Marketing Modernity: Italian Advertising from Fascism to the Postmodern* (London, 2003).

Robert Batchelor is Assistant Professor of Modern British History at Georgia Southern University. His research has focused on Britain and China, transcultural technologies and national identity. His publications include 'Concealing the Bounds: Imagining the British Nation through China', in F. Nussbaum (ed.), *The Global Eighteenth Century* (Baltimore, 2003).

John Brewer is Eli and Edye Broad Professor of Humanities and Social Sciences and Professor of History and Literature at California Institute of Technology. His many books include *The Pleasures of the Imagination: English Culture in the 18th Century* (London, 1997) and *Sentimental Murder: Stories of Love and Madness in the 18th Century* (London, 2004).

Neil Carrier is an ESRC Postdoctoral fellow at the University of Oxford. His PhD and forthcoming publications focus on the farming, trade and consumption of Kenyan khat.

Sheldon Garon is Professor of Modern Japanese History at Princeton University. He is the author of *Molding Japanese Minds: The State in Every-day Life* (Princeton, NJ, 1997) and the editor (with Patricia Maclachlan) of the forthcoming collection of essays *The Ambivalent Consumer: Questioning Consumption in East Asia and the West* (Ithaca, NY).

Sheryl Kroen is Associate Professor in the Department of History and a member of the Paris Research Centre at the University of Florida. Her publications include *Politics and Theater: The Crisis of Legitimacy in Restoration France* (Berkeley, CA, 2000).

Bronwen Morgan is Professor of Socio-legal Studies in the School of Law at the University of Bristol. Recent publications include *Social Citizenship in the Shadow of Competition: The Bureaucratic Politics of Regulatory Justification* (Aldershot, 2003).

Michael R. Redclift is Professor of Geography at King's College London. Recent publications include *Chewing Gum: The Fortunes of Taste* (New York, 2004) and *The Frontier Environment and Social Order: The Letters of Francis Codd from Canada West* (Chichester, 2000).

Roberta Sassatelli is Associate Professor at the University of Bologna, where she lectures in cultural sociology and social theory. Recent publications include *Consumo, Cultura e Società* (Bologna, 2004).

Frank Trentmann is Senior Lecturer in Modern History at Birkbeck College, University of London, and Director of the Cultures of Consumption research programme funded by the UK Economic and Social Research Council (ESRC) and the Arts and Humanities Research Council (AHRC). Recent publications include the volumes of essays *Worlds of Political Economy: Knowledge and Power 1700 to the Present* (London, 2004, edited with Martin J. Daunton) and *The Making of the Consumer: Knowledge, Power and Identity in the Modern World* (Oxford and New York, 2006).

Richard Wilk is Professor of Anthropology and Gender Studies at Indiana University. Recent publications include *Globalization and the Environment*, with Josiah Heyman (series editor) (Lanham, MD, 2002) and *Home Cooking in the Global Village: Caribbean Food from Buccaneers to Ecotourists* (Oxford and New York, 2006).

–1–

Introduction

Space, Time and Value in Consuming Cultures
John Brewer and *Frank Trentmann*

Consumption in the modern world encompasses a rich and diverse set of practices, tastes and values. It ranges from people chewing gum in American cities to those chewing khat in Addis Ababa or in South London. It includes luxury goods, like the richly decorated bowls of porcelain that began to circulate in Asia and Europe in the sixteenth and seventeenth centuries, as well as more mundane, everyday routines like drinking water or taking a bath. Consumption can be deeply symbolic, charged with social meanings about justice, order and the good life, as in campaigns for balancing saving and restraining consumption in post-war Japan or in current movements such as ethical consumerism. Or it can be more individualistic, for example in the production of self and identity through brands in the commercial sector. People do a lot of consuming without necessarily thinking about themselves as consumers, but at certain historical moments they can also acquire a voice and identity as consumers, as in battles over food and water in Victorian England or in contemporary politics over privatization in South Africa and Latin America.

If the complexity of the subject reflects the unprecedented amount and velocity of consumption in the modern world, it also poses a challenge for analysis and interpretation. How to talk about such a diverse set of practices and settings? What framework and what questions can be usefully employed that shed light on shared themes and developments without losing sight of the specificity of particular kinds of consumption? Which older narratives fail the test of handling the global complexity of consumption? Which can be revised to add new perspectives? This volume takes up this challenge by placing different sites, commodities and contests over consumption alongside each other. It examines the dialogue between norms and practices of consumption that occurred at different times and in different spaces, deploying a variety of disciplinary approaches and perspectives. In this introductory chapter we offer several overarching perspectives to foster that dialogue and to develop a new set of shared concerns and emerging questions.

Our aim is to develop an analysis that avoids the temptation of talking about consumption either in terms of globally advancing homogeneity or in richly detailed terms of local specificity.[1] Much of the latter, practised to good effect in what has become a cottage industry of deeply contextualized ethnographic studies, was a healthy reaction to grand if simplified stories of consumerism, Americanization or globalization. At the same time, such micro-studies also carry the risk of losing the multiple levels across time and space which influence consuming cultures on the ground.

Perhaps the dominant way of talking about these long-term trends that emerged in the post-war world has been one or another version of Americanization. Such was the enormous expansion of material culture in the golden age of affluence in the 1950s and 1960s that the United States became the exemplary model of imagining and measuring the nature and pace of consumption, creating its own language and symbolism of what it meant to be a 'consumer society'.[2] Other consuming cultures now became measured by their proximity and distance to the American model. And its dominance came to marginalize or distract our attention from other forms of consumption. Thus historical investigation of consumption quickly became dominated by the search for the origins or birth of this sort of consumer society.[3] The missionary energy of the American model in the era of the Cold War meant that it had an inbuilt momentum that saw consumption in terms of expansion and convergence. The story of 'modern' consumption therefore became the story of an advancing, seemingly unstoppable wave of a certain form of materialistic and individualistic 'consumerism' that spilled over from the centre into the periphery, thereby transforming the more 'traditional' hinterlands of consumption with their own distinctive local cultures.

Recent research by anthropologists and geographers in particular locales inside and outside the West has raised doubts about the merit of this model of Americanization and of its successor, globalization, in describing material culture today.[4] Centre and periphery, modernity and tradition are not fixed and have no preassigned meanings. Reciprocal flows and the simultaneous presence and interaction of diverse cultures – whether global, national, local, or ethnic and religious – encourage us to broaden and rethink historically the nomenclature of older narratives, to question the particular positions that time, space and value occupy in the model of Americanization.

The Americanization story gained cultural and political purchase hand in hand with its powerful twin in economic theory and public policy: neoclassical economics. Both share a focus on the individual and the act of purchase, making it possible to calculate, aggregate and compare consumption across groups and regions in terms of demand.[5] Consumption becomes an index of measurable satisfaction and pain. Spatially, the model favours a unilinear view that looks outwards from centre to periphery. Questions of value are not at the forefront of the analysis – purchasing decisions are measured in terms of utility not judged for their ethical worth. A distinct view of value, however, informs the background knowledge on which the public appeal of the model is based: the more individual consumption (whatever its particular motivation), the greater the public benefit.

This introduction and the chapters that follow develop a different approach to time, space and value. In our account, the act of purchase occupies only a particular moment in the timeline of consumption. People have dreams and desires of consuming long before they reach a shop counter to purchase a particular item. After purchase, goods are used, manipulated, disposed of and recycled. Even so-called consumer goods come to have complex meanings, uses and attachments that move far beyond their original 'value' as purchased commodities. All sorts of consumption take place outside the presumed model of shopping. Having a shower is consumption, as is eating out with friends, but it would be simplistic to reduce such practices and experiences to one of money changing hands. Individuals and groups, as well as commodities, have life cycles – desires and habits are shaped over time. And, from a broader perspective, we need to question the changing historical dynamics of consumption. Whereas the old model, with its binary of tradition versus modernity, imagined change in terms of a 'take off' (Rostow),[6] a more variegated approach raises the question of which forces have accelerated or inhibited the flow of consumption in different contexts.

Such contexts need to be defined in terms of space as well as time. In examining the complex networks that characterize so much consumption, our approach emphasizes not unilinear but multidirectional flows of goods and their meanings. Even where there are asymmetries of wealth, power and economic development, movement is rarely just in one direction. In addition to the circulation of goods, a spatial approach is concerned with reconnecting their consumption with their production. It has become a cliché that one of the features of modern consumption is the distancing, both physical and imaginative, of production from consumption. But such distancing is not a separation and should not be treated as such. Consumer goods and services are not the product of immaculate conception. Thinking about the connections between different sites of consumption and between production and consumption requires attention to physical, material places as well as to virtual ones, to the forests in which labour gangs risk their lives in the making of tropical commodities as well as to the conceptual and discursive realms that produce labour and utility, as in recent brand management.

Broadening the temporal and spatial dimensions of consumption inevitably prompts questions about value. Much of the scholarly literature on consumption has taken a moralistic attitude towards consumption, sometimes positive, but more usually negative – as in the frequently expressed anxiety that consumption turns active citizens into passive dupes.[7] In this it reflects rather than analyses the public debate about the ethics of consumption. This is not to argue that such discussions should be ignored. On the contrary, we need to analyse the immensely important role that consumption has come to play as a system of values, not just for individuals but also for states and social movements. Instead of falling back on pronouncements about the moral hazards of consumption, or seeking to evacuate the terrain of values, we should think about the changing moral landscape of consumption. This landscape includes the social significance attached to acts of consumption – is using a particular good virtuous or corrupting?; the norms governing consumption – should a society encourage its members to spend freely for their personal pleasure or direct them to think about matters of national or human welfare?; and the rights and responsibilities of consumers – what makes a consumer 'ethical' or selfish? Indeed, these questions about values connect with the fundamental question of how the consumer acquired voice and identity in the modern period.

In all these three dimensions – time, space and values – power and politics are at work. The unprecedented expansion of consumption in the last three centuries occurred in a period of a more general transformation of power. The organization and distribution of power changed with the expansion of the market, the rise of nation-states and empires, and political mass mobilization fuelled by new ideologies. Put simply, consumption did not flow effortlessly but was channelled through organizations and ideologies that shaped the spaces, rhythms and values of its current. And, in due course, these institutions of power – the market as well as state, civil society and international organizations – became themselves sites of contest over the meaning of consumption.

After the 'Consumer Revolution'

The historical salience and political power of the American 'consumer society' model were twin products of the Cold War era. For champions of economic development at the time, like the American economist Walt Rostow, an open society was a crucial precondition for successful growth. For the academic study of consumption, this association left its biggest imprint as a concern to trace the origins of consumer society as a revolutionary system of capitalist modernity, an analysis made famous in Neil McKendrick's influential thesis in the seminal book on consumption in eighteenth-century Britain, *The Birth of a Consumer Society* (1983).[8] Since its publication, historians have made it a sport to trace elements of consumerism in ever earlier and more varied settings, from fifteenth and sixteenth-century Italy to the seventeenth-century Netherlands.[9]

But this predominantly Western view, focused on Europe and its Atlantic colonies, has recently been challenged by comparative research which has pointed to the spectacular increase in the consumption of exotic goods and textiles in China, and by analyses of parts of the Southeast Asian economy which make the European case seem less singular than was once thought.[10] Nevertheless, it would be dangerous to duplicate the error of the Americanization debate and simply compare and measure non-Western developments against a British or European norm. Rather, comparative perspectives alert us both to the unevenness of the expansion of consumption in the West and to the multiple and multidirectional fields of exchanges through which consumption passes.

Robert Batchelor's discussion of porcelain in seventeenth and eighteenth-century China and Britain illustrates the shift in perspective this entails.[11] Instead of focusing on origins or measuring societies against each other – who consumed more porcelain or valued it more – his chapter looks at the different yet interrelated fields of exchange that developed. Porcelain expanded as a medium as well as a commodity. A bowl could be used and read in different ways. Different print cultures interacted with different cultures of consumption. Porcelain had performative powers, and these were significantly shaped by different regional networks of print and production – the typographic regime of the Atlantic world centred on London and Amsterdam, the calligraphic regime in Southeast Asia and old Islamic trading networks, and the xylographic network of coastal China. In all these regions, porcelain circulated ever more freely. But what we see here is ultimately not a story of the same article reaching ever more consumers in different parts of the world. Rather, it is about the different genres of representations, systems of production and habits of reading through which porcelain passed in each of these regimes. Instead of viewing a commodity like porcelain in isolation, Batchelor shifts our attention to its place in exchange networks and to the connected cultural media, sensibilities and perspectives which gave the commodity a distinct meaning.

If it had been relatively silent about developments beyond the Atlantic world, the literature on the consumer revolution had something to say about the moralities of consumption. Here, reinforcing a view of consumerism as giving birth to a distinctly Western modernity, the story has been that of the creation of a new kind of human sensibility and behaviour that broke through and ultimately eroded older moralities. In the so-called luxury debates of the eighteenth century a new defence emerged for unrestrained consumption against an older paternalistic critique: private pleasures could produce public benefits.[12] The calculating spirit of an increasingly rich middling sort in mercantile societies carried elements of what later became known as economic man. Individual hedonism was further boosted by the romantic imagination. Perhaps individuals had a natural drive to seek pleasure?

These new cultural tendencies certainly gave consumption a novel position in private and public life, but they do not amount to a watershed leading to the hegemony of hedonistic consumers. The material flow of goods and the identity of consumers have all too easily been conflated. By the late eighteenth century most people in the Atlantic world had become deeply engaged in a commercial system of consumption, but few saw themselves or their neighbours as 'consumers'. This puzzle is the starting point for Frank Trentmann's search for the origins of the consumer.[13] As his account of the genealogy of the consumer shows, the consumer initially gained purchase as a civic identity, tied to increasingly ambitious demands of citizens framed in particular political traditions, not as a description of new individual desires in the language of hedonism. The unfolding and strength of the new language of the consumer was uneven. Political traditions could favour the take-up of the identity of this new social actor – as in Victorian Britain – or they could retard this identity formation – as in countries like China or Germany, where the consumer appeared a marginal or selfish category alongside the larger claims of land, nation or production. Two general and provocative ideas emerge from this revisionist intervention that find echoes in several of the other contributions to this volume. First, it suggests the need to decouple the consumer, consumer culture and consumption, three large phenomena often lumped together, and, instead, to consider more carefully their changing material and discursive connections. Second, it points to the significance of political traditions or languages in creating what Trentmann calls a synapse that stabilizes the idea and identity of the consumer by connecting it with favourable views of society and politics.

Instead of a breakthrough of one particular mode of individualistic consumerism, then, modernity appears marked by the gaps and tensions between consumption as practice, the identity of the consumer, and social systems and values. Instead of a linear convergence, we continue to see parallel moralities at work and an ongoing battle between rival moral and political systems seeking to claim consumption and the consumer for their own cause. For the United States, Lizabeth Cohen has recently argued that the second half of the twentieth century should indeed be seen as a narrowing of an earlier, more public-oriented view of consumption into an increasingly privatized, individualistic regime.[14] A look at other societies shows how other trajectories have been able to coexist with this American story, even at the time of America's greatest influence after the Second World War. If the American language of the consumer as quintessential citizen found a receptive audience in a defeated and occupied country like Germany, the story was a different one in France and Britain. Here, as Sheryl Kroen shows in her discussion of post-war Europe, American Marshall Plan initiatives to advertise consumer society were constrained and influenced by local political traditions and circumstances.[15] In France, communist suspicion was strong and the American portrayal of the *Vrai Visage* focused much on productivity and the need for harmonious labour relations. In Britain, the image of the consumer and consumption was filtered through the politics of austerity that informed Labour's policy of 'fair shares' after the Second World War.

Parallel moralities of consumption also continued to be actively entwined in the public policy and discourse of a rapidly modernizing society like Japan. In post-war Japan, a country to which the United States significantly did not extend Marshall Aid, consumption was part of a very different experiment of modernity from that conventionally associated with consumer culture. Instead of a simple divide between consumerism and anti-consumerism, Shel Garon's chapter highlights the dynamic relationship between the desire to consume and discourses, practices and policies seeking to restrain it.[16] In the prosperous 1950s and 1960s, Japanese people simultaneously began to spend more and save more; by 1961 the household savings rate reached a stunning 19 per cent.

It is one of the curiosities of the large literature on consumption that questions of money have received relatively little attention.[17] Garon shows how assumptions about money were intricately woven into a particular culture of consumption. This took the form of directing investment but also of shaping the temporal nature of consumption more generally. Thus considerable value was placed on forgoing immediate pleasures for the future welfare of family and nation. In line with such goals, the trajectory of consumption in post-war Japan was heavily influenced by savings policies and widespread educational efforts to socialize Japanese consumers, especially housewives. The aim was to rationalize their habits and control 'wasteful' expenditure for the sake of the national interest by containing inflation and boosting production. Importantly, this was not a homegrown, isolated campaign, but part of a broader set of transnational exchanges of ideas and policies. British austerity and European networks of savings banks, not the American Dream, were the main points of orientation for Japanese policy-makers, bankers and social movements. It may be tempting to suspect statist or paternalistic motives at work. But this would be simplistic. The savings campaigns also energized a large network of women's associations. After generations of patriarchal submission, women acquired a new public role and became responsible for the sound finance and welfare of family and nation. The call for rationalizing consumption went hand in hand with other progressive initiatives in public health and family planning. The progressive elements of such a vision of restrained consumption run counter to the transgressive, free floating and dream-like qualities often associated with modern consumerism.

Conversely, it is also interesting to think afresh about the origins of more unrestrained tastes and habits normally associated with consumerism. Garon's discussion of restrained consumption in post-war Japan can creatively be read alongside Rick Wilk's account of periodic bouts of extreme consumption practised by workers in extractive industries at the margins of the world system.[18] The story of a consumer revolution has tended to focus on bourgeois or elite consumption. As far as they have featured at all, workers and the poor have entered this story as creatures responding to dynamics unleashed by their social superiors, seeking to climb up the ladder of modern consumption in a race for distinction where the rules, tastes and customs are defined by the elite. In this account, the less affluent especially fall victim to what has recently been called 'luxury fever'.

Wilk's focus on binge consumption and wild seasonal spending patterns amongst loggers in Belize retrieves a forgotten strain of modern consumerism. The rhythmic pattern between excess and restraint, between the release and control of emotional energy that is a characteristic pattern of contemporary consuming cultures with their lavish seasonal parties and commercialized gift-giving extravaganza, like Christmas, is here related to the distinctive organization of the work and group life of pirates, mahogany loggers and gold miners. What may be at the margin of the modern capitalist system in terms of production and exchange here moves back to the centre as far as elements of consumerist lifestyle are concerned. Together, accounts like those of post-war Japanese saving or bingeing in Belize reveal the multiple rationalities at work in consuming cultures. If it was rational for the Japanese housewife to save for family and nation, it was no less rational for a man in the mahogany work gang to treat his workmates to champagne and oysters. Work was risky and lonely, without an effective cash economy. Bouts of consumption were an essential way of building the social solidarity vital for human survival in these harsh conditions.

Contemporary societies continue to involve competing, parallel moralities of consumption. Single narratives of a paradigm shift, of one morality or lifestyle replacing another, as in grand stories of the consumer revolution or the triumph of postmodern lifestyles, founder when judged against the evidential record. This is partly because consumption itself continues to include a diversity of practices, some routine, some spontaneous, some involving regulation, repetition and control, others favouring short-term release or excessive display. The routine of eating breakfast and reading the paper comes with a different form of rationality and consciousness than a once-in-a-lifetime trip or cruise or a holiday visit to a casino.[19] While some routines appear mundane, others, such as the season ticket holder's weekly support of an English Premier League football club, follow cycles of deep emotional intensity. Arguably, what distinguishes contemporary cultures of consumption is not the qualities of the moralities and habits involved, but the range and intensity of these as people consume more and as consumption is discursively thematized more intensely in expanding spheres of everyday life.

Far from seeing the triumph of a particular liberal version of the consumer, then, these parallel moralities have also fuelled a contest over the nature of the consumer. The synergies between different ideas and languages of the consumer are the theme of Roberta Sassatelli's discussion of critical consumerism.[20] Fair trade and ethical consumerism here are of interest less for their direct impact on purchasing patterns than for their influence in shaping the idea and identity of the consumer. In other words, critical consumerism is not just a response to a dominant form of consumer culture but actively boosts the growing public significance attributed to the consumer. The discourse of the critical consumer frames a particular mode of rationality. Rejecting the liberal notion of the individual with a right to choose freely for his or her private satisfaction, the discourse circulating in 'alternative' movements looks to a consumer defined in terms of public duties. As Sassatelli emphasizes in her analysis of British, Italian and American movements, the discourse of critical consumerism is about a diverse mix of norms and values, not a simple opposition between renouncing consumerism and free choice. Rather than viewing these discourses as a sharp break made possible by postmodernity, it is possible to see here a reconnection with older notions of civic consumers and socially responsible consumption discussed elsewhere in this volume. Once again, the idea and language of the consumer affords opportunities for cutting across and connecting spheres like state, market and civil society. Consumers regain an element of political agency.

Topographies of Power

Politics has been a crucial conduit through which the values, practices and identities of consumption have been shaped. The last decade especially has seen an increasingly assertive and highly publicized return of a politics of consumption, stretching from local community actions to global civil society. Perhaps the dominant scholarly response to this phenomenon has come from political scientists.[21] Their studies of political consumerism are primarily driven by an interest in the changing forms and spaces of the political. At a time of a much-debated decline of older formal forms of political activity and engagement, such as through parties, consumption offers an alternative arena for political expression and agency through a wide range of practices, ranging from consumer boycotts to buying Fairtrade products. This volume offers a rather different perspective, one less concerned with consumption as a form of political expression than with the politics of consumption itself. Political ideas and discourses, political institutions and political economy channel and shape consumption and consumers.

That states shape the realm, amount and velocity of consumption through their policies, such as tax and social security systems, has of course long been recognized. In an influential discussion, Victoria de Grazia has emphasized the role played by social welfare systems that set European societies, with their emphasis on social participation and equality of rights, apart from the more commercial and individualistic post-war American version of consumer sovereignty that celebrated freedom of choice.[22] Chapters in this volume extend this perspective by situating consumption in very different political contexts, from those of citizenship to commercial notions of governance, from the national organization of production to global regimes of regulation.

We have already noted the ways in which the consumer was favoured by particular political traditions which were concerned with the citizen as taxpayer, questions of accountability, rights and representation. In a society like late nineteenth-century Britain, where democratic politics expanded dramatically, liberal and radical traditions turned to the consumer as an answer for problems of governance – in order to make monopolies like the London water companies responsive to the needs of citizens. In recent years, the expanding networks of critical consumerism similarly turn to the consumer as a figure with the capability of regulating and reforming the flow of goods, an additional unit of governance outside the formal institutional channels of regulation and control. States have not been idle either in looking to consumers to shoulder responsibility and initiative, attempts that have probably as much to do with mobilizing consumers in times of war and for the purpose of economic development as with the recent consumerist initiatives of 'advanced liberalism'.[23]

As the diverse responses of consumers to recent food scares in different European societies have shown, assumptions about the appropriate politics of consumption and the relative role to be played by state, civil society and market take distinctive national forms. But emphasizing the relative power of the nation-state and national sets of practices and values does not mean they can be viewed in isolation from international and global developments in governance. With a few exceptions, historians have been slow to follow the lead given by anthropologists, geographers and lawyers working at the interface of local and global developments.[24]

The tension and interaction between competing local and global narratives of consumption are the focus of David Anderson and Neil Carrier's chapter on khat.[25] An indigenous crop of East Africa, khat is a mild social stimulant that offers an interesting way of connecting areas of the globe that rarely feature in the same analytical frame of 'consumer society', linking consumers and producers in Kenya and Yemen with emigrant communities and police authorities in Europe and North America. Partly, the discussion echoes an older concern, familiar to early modernists, about the multiple meanings of an object that in some communities functions as a commodity chewed as part of a leisure routine, in others as a prohibited drug. Significantly, however, these local routines and battles over classification are placed in the context of competing global narratives of khat informed by Western fears of immigration, drugs and the war on terror. While narratives of khat consumption in East Africa continue to reflect the influence of indigenous religious and cultural factors, the debate in a society like Ethiopia has also increasingly been coloured by the global representation of khat as a drug linked to criminal and violent behaviour.

Global developments can shape local cultures of consumption and give them greater visibility by projecting anxieties onto local practices. But the reverse process has been equally important in the modern flow of consumption. How spatial relations between production and consumption have been rearranged and made invisible in the evolution of commodity culture is the theme of Michael Redclift's discussion of chewing gum.[26] Chewing gum, that quintessential commodity symbolizing modern consumption, was initially made of *chicle* from *chicozapote* trees in the Yucatan and in Central America. Patterns of production and consumption were part of a tenuous geopolitics in an area divided by the Caste War; into the 1930s rebel Mayan leaders used friendly relations with gum manufacturers like Wrigley's to fund their armed struggle. The rise of synthetic production transformed not only the commodity but also spatial and power relations. With *chicle* production in decline, the Mexican state now asserted its power further into the jungle of the Yukatan and sought to socialize production. Chewing gum became a global commodity. Its earlier physical and spatial connections to the Yukatan and a brutal world of production have been forgotten, replaced today by coastal eco-hotels.

Local–global relations are shaped by the uneven playing field of political economy. In growing areas of consumption they have also been transformed by the new architecture of global governance that has been erected, especially in the last decade. Global water provision is a central feature of this emerging regulatory space. As Bronwen Morgan shows in her discussion comparing politics in South Africa and New Zealand,[27] this new space is far from homogeneous and is filled by different political ideas and strategies of activism. Instead of a stark dichotomy between appeals to consumer rights and appeals to human rights, Morgan highlights the shifts in discursive strategies used by activists. The global regime of water welfarism, with its pressure to liberalize and commodify goods and services like water, creates more or less space for certain discursive and political strategies over others. Thus, the global regime's influence is much stronger in a less developed society like South Africa than in a country like New Zealand which already has virtually universal access to water. Global water regulatory politics acts as a transmitter of corporate knowledge into local settings, providing, for example, educational directives to create more 'responsible consumers'. The effectiveness of these initiatives depends in no small part on existing national institutional structures. In New Zealand, a country far less dependent on global institutional assistance, local governments have strong fiscal autonomy, providing a national bulwark against global pressures on commodification. In South Africa, a country that has given a rare constitutional commitment to a human right to water, by contrast, municipal governments have been far poorer and more vulnerable to pressure to give private water providers greater influence.

Emphasis on the individual consumer is far from being solely a political matter, but is also nourished by discursive and managerial developments in capitalism itself. How the consumer became re-envisaged as a productive subject in contemporary brand management is the topic of Adam Arvidsson's chapter.[28] Brand management undermined an older distinction between production/wage labour and consumption/leisure. Instead of the concern with reorganizing and disciplining consumption characteristic of modern marketing in the inter-war years, brand management has absorbed the consumer into the very heart of the creation of value and productivity. The use-value of a brand has become dependent on what consumers can make with it. Consumers, in this view, are productive communicators who create the social world in which the brand thrives. As Arvidsson notes, there is a certain Faustian bargain here between brand management and consumer. For brand management is premised on the seductive charm of the consumer as a free subject.

Conclusion

We began this chapter by commenting on the remarkable richness and diversity of modern consumption and on the difficulty of accommodating such variety within a single interpretative framework. The growing historical importance of the consumption of an ever-increasing number of goods and services and the proliferation of consumer practices and identities have meant that consumption has multiple meanings and has produced many, sometimes contradictory, values and views. No single narrative of consumption, no single typology of the consumer and no monolithic version of consumer culture will suffice. Contemporary consumption processes and the values that give them meaning have a complex historical genealogy that cannot be reduced to the global story of the growth (and triumph) of neoliberal consumerism. Our understanding of their diversity and complexity depends, as we have tried to show, on a number of approaches and research strategies. First, our definition of consumption has to extend beyond the acquisition of the sorts of goods associated with 'consumerism', so as to include the most mundane and prosaic of commodities. Even more importantly, the processes of consumption and their different meanings can only be properly recovered if we analyse the links that connect (and feed back into) the different places (physical and conceptual) in which goods are produced, distributed, purchased or consumed and given meaning. We need, in other words, to trace consumption along axes of time as well as space, identifying points of convergence, divergence and rupture. An effective analysis has to take into account the position of different actors and institutions along these axes, examining the power relations and the different discourses and values that give meaning to consumers' actions and the goods and services they consume. Finally, it has to recognize that markets are necessarily embedded within complex political and cultural matrixes that give acts of consumption their specific resonance and import. Only then will we be able to do justice to modern consumption in all its power and plenitude.

Notes

1. G. Ritzer, *Explorations in the Sociology of Consumption: Fast Food, Credit Cards and Casinos* (London, 2001); P.N. Stearns, *Consumerism in World History: The Global Transformation of Desire* (London, 2001); D. Miller (ed.) *Acknowledging Consumption: A Review of New Studies* (London, 1995); M.K. Hogg (ed.), *Consumer Behaviour I: Research and Influences, vol. I: Consumer Behaviour as a Field of Study* (London, 2005); D. Miller, P. Jackson, N. Thrift, B. Holbrook and M. Rowlands (eds), *Shopping, Place and Identity* (London, 1998). M. Alfino, J.S. Caputo and R. Wynyard (eds), *McDonaldization Revisited: Critical Essays on Consumer Culture* (London, 1998).

2. V. Packard, *The Hidden Persuaders* (Harmondsworth, 1960); G. Katona, *The Mass Consumption Society* (New York, 1964); C. Lasch, *The Culture of Narcissism* (London, 1979). For further discussion see D. Slater, *Consumer Culture and Modernity* (Cambridge, 1997); D. Horowitz, *The Anxieties of Affluence: Critiques of American Consumer Culture, 1939– 1979* (Amherst, MA, 2004).

3. J. Brewer, *The Error of Our Ways*: *Historians and the Birth of Consumer Society*, Working Paper 12, June 2004, www.consume.bbk.ac.uk.

4. P. Jackson, 'Local Consumption Cultures in a Globalizing World', *Transactions, Institute of British Geographers*, 29(2) (2004), pp. 165–78; A. Appadurai (ed.), *The Social Life of Things: Commodities in Cultural Perspective* (Cambridge, 1986); T. Burke, *Lifebuoy Men, Lux Women: Commodification, Consumption, and Cleanliness in Modern Zimbabwe* (London, 1996); D. Miller and D. Slater, *The Internet: An Ethnographic Approach* (Oxford, 2000); D. Howes (ed.), *Cross-cultural Consumption: Global Markets, Local Realities* (London, 1996); M.B. Gillette, *Between Mecca and Beijing: Modernization and Consumption among Urban Chinese Muslims* (Stanford, CA, 2000); L. Beng-Huat (ed.), *Consumption in Asia: Lifestyles and Identities* (London, 2000); H.-G. Haupt, *Konsum und Handel: Europa im 19. und 20. Jahrhundert* (Göttingen, 2002); P. Maclachlan and S. Garon (eds), *The Ambivalent Consumer* (Ithaca, NY, forthcoming); Viviana Zelizer, 'Culture and Consumption', in N.J. Smelser and R. Swedberg (eds), *The Handbook of Economic Sociology* (second edn, Princeton, NJ, 2005), pp. 331–54.

5. B. Fine, *The World of Consumption: The Material and Cultural Revisited* (London, 2002).

6. W.W. Rostow, *The Stages of Economic Growth: A Non-Communist Manifesto* (3rd edition, Cambridge, 1990).

7. J. Habermas, 'Konsumkritik – Eigens zum Konsumieren', *Frankfurter Hefte. Zeitschrift für Kultur und Politik*, 12(9) (1957), pp. 641–5; S. Ewen, *Captains of Consciousness: Advertising and the Social Roots of the Consumer Culture* (New York, 1976). See also Adam Curtis's BBC documentary 'The Century of the Self' (2002).

8. N. McKendrick, J. Brewer and J.H. Plumb, *The Birth of a Consumer Society: The Commercialization of Eighteenth-century England* (London, 1983).

9. S. Schama, *The Embarrassment of Riches* (Berkeley, CA, 1988); J. Brewer and R. Porter (eds), *Consumption and the World of Goods* (London and New York, 1993); J. De Vries, 'The Industrial Revolution and the Industrious Revolution', *The Journal of Economic History*, 54(2) (1994), pp. 249–70; C. Walsh, 'Social Meaning and Social Space in the Shopping Galleries of Early Modern London', in J. Benson and L. Ugolini (eds), *A Nation of Shopkeepers: Five Centuries of British Retailing* (London, 2003), pp. 52–79; L. Jardine, *Worldly Goods* (London, 1996); M. North, *Genuss und Glück des Lebens: Kulturkonsum im Zeitalter der Aufklärung* (Cologne, Weimar and Vienna, 2003).

10. K. Pomeranz, *The Great Divergence: China, Europe, and the Making of the Modern World Economy* (Princeton, NJ, 2000); P. Parthasarthi, 'The Great Divergence,' *Past and Present*, 176(1) (2002), pp. 275–93; M. Berg, *Luxury and Pleasure in Eighteenth-Century Britain* (Oxford, 2005); C.A. Bayly, 'The Origins of Swadeshi (home industry): Cloth and Indian Society, 1700–1930', in A. Appadurai (ed.), *Social Life of Things*, pp. 285–321; C.A. Bayly, '"Archaic" and "modern" Globalization in the Eurasian and African Arena, c. 1750–1850', in A.G. Hopkins (ed.), *Globalization in World History* (London, 2002), pp. 47–73; C. Clunas, *Superfluous Things: Material Culture and Social Status in Early Modern China* (Chicago, 1991).

11. R. Batchelor, 'On the Movement of Porcelains: Rethinking the Birth of Consumer Society as Interactions of Exchange Networks, 1600–1750', in this volume.

12. C.J. Berry, *The Idea of Luxury: A Conceptual and Historical Investigation* (Cambridge, 1994); M. Berg and E. Eger (eds), *Luxury in the Eighteenth Century: Debates, Desires and Delectable Goods* (Basingstoke, 2003); M. Berg and H. Clifford (eds), *Consumers and Luxury: Consumer Culture in Europe 1650–1850* (Manchester, 1999).

13. F. Trentmann, 'The Modern Genealogy of the Consumer: Meanings, Identities and Political Synapses', in this volume. See also F. Trentmann (ed.), *The Making of the Consumer: Knowledge, Power and Identity in the Modern World* (Oxford and New York, 2005).

14. L. Cohen, *A Consumers' Republic: The Politics of Mass Consumption in Postwar America* (New York, 2003).

15. S. Kroen, 'Negotiations with the American Way: The Consumer and the Social Contract in Post-war Europe', in this volume.

16. S. Garon, 'Japan's Post-war "Consumer Revolution", or Striking a "Balance" between Consumption and Saving', in this volume.

17. L. Calder, *Financing the American Dream: A Cultural History of Consumer Credit* (Princeton, NJ, 1999); M.C. Finn, *The Character of Credit: Personal Debt in English Culture, 1740–1914* (Cambridge, 2003).

18. R. Wilk, 'Consumer Culture and Extractive Industry on the Margins of the World System', in this volume.

19. J. Gronow and A. Warde (eds), *Ordinary Consumption* (London, 2001); E. Shove and A. Warde, 'Inconspicuous Consumption: The Sociology of Consumption, Lifestyles and Environment', in R. Dunlap (ed.), *Sociological Theory and the Environment* (Colorado, 2002); E. Shove, *Comfort, Cleanliness and Convenience: The Social Organisation of Normality* (Oxford, 2003).

20. R. Sassatelli, 'Virtue, Responsibility and Consumer Choice: Framing Critical Consumerism', in this volume.

21. M. Micheletti (ed.), *Political Virtue and Shopping: Individuals, Consumerism, and Collective Action* (Basingstoke, 2003); M. Boström, A. Føllesdal, M. Klintman, M. Micheletti and M.P. Sørensen, *Political Consumerism: Its Motivations, Power, and Conditions in the Nordic Countries and Elsewhere* (Copenhagen, 2005).

22. V. de Grazia, 'Changing Consumption Regimes in Europe, 1930–1970', in S. Strasser, C. McGovern and M. Judt (eds), *Getting and Spending: European and American Consumer Societies in the Twentieth Centuries* (Cambridge, 1998), pp. 59–83; V. de Grazia, *Irresistible Empire: America's Advance through 20th-century Europe* (Cambridge, MA, 2005).

23. N. Rose, *Powers of Freedom: Reframing Political Thought* (Cambridge, 1999).

24. But see Burke, *Lifebuoy Men*; B. Morgan, 'Water: Frontier Markets and Cosmopolitan Activism', *Soundings: A Journal of Politics and Culture*, Issue 27 on 'The Frontier State' (Autumn 2004), pp. 10–24; S.K. Vogel, *Freer Markets, More Rules: Regulatory Reform in Advanced Industrial Countries* (Ithaca, 1996).

25. D. Anderson and N. Carrier, '"Flowers of Paradise" or "Polluting the Nation"? Contested Narratives of Khat Consumption', in this volume.

26. M. Redclift, 'Chewing Gum: Mass Consumption and the "Shadowlands" of the Yucatan', in this volume.

27. B. Morgan, 'Emerging Global Water Welfarism: Access to Water, Unruly Consumers and Transnational Governance', in this volume.
28. A. Arvidsson, 'Brand Management and the Productivity of Consumption', in this volume.

−2−

The Modern Genealogy of the Consumer
Meanings, Identities and Political Synapses
Frank Trentmann

Consumers have been elusive characters, for scholars as much as for producers and marketeers. Some twenty years ago the sociologist Claus Offe stressed that consumers do not form a 'clearly delimitable and organizable complex of individuals. Rather they do constitute an abstract category which defines certain aspects of the social actions of almost all individuals. Everyone and at the same time no one is a "consumer".'[1] This chapter takes this sociological observation in a historical direction and asks how and when this category evolved and why at certain historical moments (but not others) some groups (but not others) managed to arrive at a distinct sense of themselves as consumers. What are the historical processes that have promoted or retarded the formation of consumer identity, for actors and their observers?

'Consumption' has become widely recognized as a central, even dominant, dimension in many societies – 'the vanguard of history' in Daniel Miller's phrase.[2] Donald Quataert has presented modernity as marked by the 'ascendancy of the consumer over the producer'.[3] But who is this consumer? Three approaches dominate, which, for all their differences, have tended to minimize the historically contingent, uneven and incomplete processes involved in the evolution of the identity and knowledge of the consumer. The first pictures the consumer as a universal economistic category. The second treats consumers simply as the natural product of a commodity culture that expanded from the eighteenth century onwards. A third, more recent approach sees the 'active consumer' as the product of postmodernity or of an advanced type of liberal governmentality associated with neoliberal capitalism and public sector reform.

These approaches share an essentialist, under-historicized view of the consumer. The existence of people as consumers has mainly been taken as given. Acts of consumption or preferences have all too easily been tied to the persona of the consumer, blurring the process of identity and knowledge formation. Neoclassical economics and political and commercial organizations influenced by it have presented the abstract figure of the consumer as a rational utility-maximizing individual; the consumer here is little more than a 'noiseless servant named Demand ... bled white of all personality and urgency', as Robert S. Lynd, the American consumer advocate, complained in 1936.[4] Most commentators in the social sciences and humanities have, of course, been critical of this individualist utilitarian model, but their alternative presentation of the consumer has been no less problematic. One approach has been to presume that consumers emerge as the natural by-product of the expanding world of consumption that swept across the transatlantic world from the late seventeenth century. Attention to the distribution, display and handling of goods – in the marketplace and the home, in advertisements, exhibitions and stores– is accompanied by references to actors involved in these processes as simply 'consumers'.[5] As comparative ethnography has shown, such an instrumental view of identity formation is problematic. Users of new technologies like the Internet, for example, incorporate their consumption practices into their identities in different ways in different cultures.[6] This is not to suggest that commodification does not influence social relations and identities, merely that consumption does not in and of itself tell us about the specific sense of self and collective identities attached to goods and their use. If consumption is a universal aspect of human culture, it also involves extremely disparate types of practices that have been tied to a multitude of identities. To *describe* purchasers or users as consumers in different settings might be convenient shorthand, but it does not *explain* how, when, where and which actors began to conceive of themselves or others as consumers.

This chapter offers a new, historicized narrative. It seeks to problematize and loosen the rise of the consumer from the history of commodity culture and the study of consumption as practice. Here we will encounter the 'dog that did not bark', for the early modern transformation of the world of goods did not automatically generate a new identity of the consumer. Nor, as we shall see, was the consumer the preserve of liberal knowledge systems, typically associated with liberal economics. Knowledge regimes sceptical of market society, such as national and historical economics, could also turn to the consumer. Instead of a straight line from market and commodity to consumer and consumer society, and unlike narratives of global convergence or Americanization, then, the chapter argues for the uneven and contested evolution of the consumer, highlighting the role of agency and political conflicts that energized the consumer in some societies in the nineteenth and early twentieth centuries, but not in others.

The configuration of consumers required political synapses, that is, political traditions and languages through which actors were able to connect material experiences to a sense of belonging, interest and entitlement. We shall examine the contribution of these political synapses in two conjunctures in which the political status of 'necessaries' became pivotal in the course of the nineteenth century. The first was the battle over accountability, access and representation in nineteenth-century Britain that turned groups of users into articulate, organized and increasingly demanding 'water consumers'. The second was global: rising economic nationalism, imperial tension and a growing concern about the survival of national culture in an age of advancing globalization at the turn of the twentieth century. It was the synapses of political traditions, rather than just state power or material interests, that determined whether this mobilization of consumption led to a stronger vision of consumers (Free Trade Britain), was diluted by prior collective traditions of producers (Imperial Germany) or became a means for fostering alternative identities, such as the patriotic citizen (Republican China). The First World War and inter-war years saw the consolidation of different traditions of consumers, a process shaped from within civil society (as much as by the state or business) through discourses of ethics and citizenship (rather than neoclassical economics) and around questions of the social and political values guiding consumption (rather than just affluence or an unreflective pursuit of commodities). By the early/mid-twentieth century, commercial culture was able to employ and build on diverse and fertile images of the consumer, but it was far from being its sole or even primary creator.

This genealogy of the consumer raises questions about the periodization of conventional narratives of consumer society and their teleological model of convergence around American 'consumerism'. It is unhelpful to envision some ideal-typical American model of affluence as the starting point for critical enquiry or to see the American model of consumer society as the natural end point of development for modern societies. Instead, we unfold here an alternative genealogy of the consumer that points to contingency and diversity and to the centrality of political tradition, civil society and ethics through which agents discovered themselves as active consumers.

The Dog That Did Not Bark

The rich historiography on the 'consumer revolution' of the early modern transatlantic world is a natural starting point in a search for the consumer. If viewing the upsurge in consumption as a uniquely 'Western' phenomenon has become debatable,[8] there can be little doubt that the commercial world of goods expanded quantitatively and qualitatively in unprecedented fashion. By the mid-eighteenth century there were forty-two people per shop in Britain.[9] The working classes bought virtually all their food through markets and worked longer hours to enable them to buy more goods.[10] Exotic articles like tea, coffee and tobacco had become 'mass consumer' goods reaching more than 25 per cent of the population in Britain and the American colonies. The consumption of cultural artefacts and services transformed the subjectivity of the middling sort and shaped a cult of civility and sensibility.[11] In the very year that Adam Smith laid down the famous dictum that 'consumption is the sole end of all production,'[12] American colonists declared their independence after a struggle that had begun with a series of non-consumption protests. In Europe the old century ended and the new began with a series of bread and flour riots.

It is against this background that many commentators have argued for the rise of the consumer. In a complete reversal of Karl Marx's analysis of the dialectic of modernity in splitting human identity into public citoyen and private bourgeois,[13] recent authors have presented consumption and the consumer as crucial forces in forging a new link between personal and political identities. The American Revolution, T.H. Breen has argued, grew out of a consumer revolution. The boycotts of tea and other commodities were 'rituals of non-consumption' through which political independence was discovered: '[n]o previous rebellion had organized itself so centrally around the consumer'.[14] Consumer goods created a new 'shared framework of consumer experience' among colonialists, he argues, allowing them to 'situate a universal political discourse about rights and liberties, virtue and power, within a familiar material culture'.[15] The problem with Breen's argument is that it rests on an essentialist ascription of the consumer, deduced from a shared material culture, rather than on the colonists' self-understanding. Organizers of boycotts rallied their fellow 'countrymen', 'honest industrious patriot[s]', 'freemen' or 'Americans'. The language of 'consumers' was almost never used. The principal group identity invoked by John Dickinson, in his influential *Late Regulations*, was that of 'the reputable freeholder', while it was 'our merchants and the lower ranks of people' who were immiserated by the stamp duty. America was turning into a nation of debtors who needed to learn 'strict frugality and industry, [so] we may render ourselves more independent of the merchants'.[16] American colonists had two choices: they could supply more manufactures of their own or they could practise what is today called 'slow consumption', that is keep foreign manufactures longer in use. Here indeed was a moment of political consumerism, but acts of consumption were mobilized to generate the shared identity of Americans and freemen, not that of a consumer. Far from unleashing 'the consumer' on the world of politics, the American Revolution impeded its arrival; it was a battle between frugal patriots and Empire. Republicanism advertised an organic nationhood in which the imperative of home production and self-sufficiency muffled any sense of the independent existence, rights or identities of consumers.

In eighteenth-century Europe and America the meanings and practices of consumption remained embedded in older social identities defined by craft, land, trade and production.[17] The consumer makes an occasional appearance as a synonym for purchaser, as in Daniel Defoe's writings at the beginning of the eighteenth century or in Sieyès' *Qu'est-ce que le Tiers Etat?* towards its end,[18] but these rare references carried little weight in relation to collective interests endowed with recognized social or constitutional meanings. Defoe, who in 1728 compared the 'large, populous, rich, fruitful' state of England and its 'large, luxurious, vain and expensive' 'way of living' to the austere Dutch, limited his references to 'the consumer' to discussions of the value paid to a retailer.[19] Malachy Postlethwayt notes that, to be satisfied, the 'various humours and caprices of consumers' need skilful workmen, but in his *Universal Dictionary of Trade and Commerce*, much cited not least by American revolutionaries, he does not even reserve a category for these consumers, nor for consumption. The consumer was virtually absent from eighteenth-century discourse. Significantly, it only appears in seven of the 150,000 works of the eighteenth-century collections on line – twice as private customer (Defoe's 'last consumer'), once as the consumer paying an import duty on colonial goods, once as the customer suffering from traders' high prices and the excessive profits of stockowners, and, more metaphysically, twice with reference to time 'the speedy consumer of hours'.[20] Even after the French Revolution, when deputies in Restoration France considered consumers' interests, it was only to render them insignificant compared to people's social station and larger national interests represented by land, production and trade.[21]

The many battles over basic provision and 'just price' in food riots or complaints against corrupt traders in eighteenth and early-nineteenth century Europe developed equally without a notion of the consumer. In France food rioters were 'the people', 'the poor' and 'workers', 'petits laboureurs' or 'women of the people'.[22] Britons complaining about fraudulent weights and measures invoked the 'good of the public' or 'the poor people'.[23] As late as the 1840s, Germans referred to the 'lamentation of the people', 'the public' or 'rabble'. Where they disaggregated these identities, it was by profession (e.g. clothmakers) or by age and gender ('old people, boys, apprentices, fellows, girls and old women').[24]

Although industrial relations on the shop floor were increasingly understood as market exchanges in the late eighteenth and early nineteenth centuries,[25] the primary social categories of emancipation remained rooted in the independent farmer and the independent artisan (versus the wage 'slave').[26] In early socialist thought, consumption was subordinate to the primacy of productive welfare: good consumption was collective consumption.[27] There was little room for the consumer as a separate identity in the increasingly masculine productivist language of independence and community,[28] or in gendered notions of women's domestic sphere unsullied by the market. Women's boycotts against slave goods thus invoked a sympathetic femininity with its '"purely human" sympathy unpolluted by commercial desires'.[29]

The resilience of older social identities and categories, then, was one reason why the material culture of consumption found it difficult to generate a more active sense of 'consumer' identities. Raymond Williams in a classic, short text on the consumer notes how, in the course of the eighteenth century, the consumer emerges as a less negative, more neutral term in writings on political economy[30] – a new science which has often been accorded a crucial part in legitimating the spread of market society. Yet, why only 'less negative'? Put differently, why did the well-recorded appreciation of consumption as a source of wealth and civilization not trigger a more wide-reaching transvaluation and embrace of the 'consumer'? Instead of following a fluid transition from luxury (goods and sensations) to consumer (identity) to consumer society (social system), the virtual absence of the 'consumer' and 'consumer society' should give us pause to think about the particular ways in which contemporaries situated consumption with respect to identities.

Attitudes to luxury oscillated between new positive understandings of consumption as an engine of wealth and civilization (Barbon, Mandeville, Hume, Smith) and condemnations of extravagance and greed leading to an enslaved self, dependent on appearance and the opinion of others (Rousseau, Smollett).[31] Most societies have competing moral value systems, so the question remains why the positive strand of the transvaluation of luxury did not do more to publicly elevate the consumer? At the level of economic thought, the answer may have to do with the short-lived dominance of the new Enlightenment appreciation of consumption as social investment which 'vanished like a comet'.[32] Far from being defeated, the long-standing fear of goods resurfaced during the Industrial Revolution. And a new generation of economic writers – the classical school – again saw workers' increased consumption as removing resources from investment and from development.

A more general answer may lie with the internal and domestic direction of the new culture of consumption. Consumption was an act of discovering and cultivating the self. Dutch consumption patterns in the Golden Age, Jan de Vries has argued, 'brought into being a distinctive material culture in which the luxuries were directed towards the home more than the body, and adorned the interior – of both home and body – more than the exterior. They tended to achieve comfort more than refinement.'[33] Instead of directly contesting an older moral discourse warning of the public decadence stemming from personal vice and providing a new public language, the new lifestyle of luxury turned inwards.

If the Dutch Golden Age has been characterized as the first consumer society, it is also a prime example of the contingent nature of transmission between material and political cultures. As de Vries notes, 'the Dutch did not fashion its bits and pieces of religious and republican thought into a new discourse to describe and theorise the new reality'.[34] This was left to English and Scottish writers of the next three generations. The now leading interpretations focus on the redescription of luxury as the pursuit of personal pleasure with unintended public benefits as a decisive step in the positive and now conscious embrace of a 'consumer society'.[35] Indeed, late mercantilist and Enlightenment writers put a new emphasis on the role of productive consumption in the moral and material progress of societies. Instead of leading to idleness and decline, increasing the consumption of producers would improve human welfare, pleasure and productivity. Increasing the consumption of workers, by which Enlightenment thinkers meant better education and skills as well as higher wages, led to an increase in human capital. But what was the imagined place of the consumer in this society?

David Hume's *Essays* (1742) provide one entry point for thinking about this failure to connect the process of consumption with a consumer identity. It highlights how consumption needs to be situated within the overarching tradition through which actors make sense of themselves and their society. Britain was a commercial society, not a consumer society. The primary dynamic, the engine of wealth, civilization and national strength, was commerce. Commerce 'rouses men from their indolence' and presents the richer members of society with 'objects of luxury' previously undreamed of.[36] 'The individuals reap the benefit of these commodities, so far as they gratify the senses and appetites; and the public is also a gainer, while a greater stock of labour is, by this means, stored up against any public exigency.'[37] Luxury is defended for promoting industrious, creative dispositions and for refining the mental capacities of the members of a commercial, law-based society.

Here, then, unlike the inward Dutch domestication of consumption, is an outward justification for material culture as central to public life. But, significantly, the defence of luxury as a public good operated in a vision of commercial society where the decisive actors and identities that were legitimated were merchants. Other groups in society benefited from the luxury circulating in commercial society, but, as recipients, there was no need for Hume to elevate them to a shared category of consumers. '[W]here luxury nourishes commerce and industry,' Hume concludes, 'the peasants, by a proper cultivation of the land, become rich and independent: while the tradesmen and merchants acquire a share of the property, and draw authority and consideration to that middling rank of men, who are the best and firmest basis of public liberty.'[38] Consumers did not need to be named separately because (as a collective group) they did not yet play a shared part in the imagined drama of an unfolding civil society.

Will the Real Consumer Please Stand Up?

The conceptual evolution of 'the consumer' before the nineteenth century, then, was limited, carrying yet little significance for social and political identities. Isolated instances of the consumer as wasteful shopper can be traced to the sixteenth century.[39] Well into the nineteenth century, however, the 'consumer' mainly appeared with reference to particular physical or metaphysical processes of use, waste and destruction. Consumers were individuals who used up energy resources or basic utilities (water, gas, coal, electricity)[40] or who were affected by particular consumption taxes, such as excise duties. German statutes for tobacco 'consumption-factories', for example, regulated the prices traders and shopkeepers could charge 'the consumer and common man'.[41] Next to this, an older use survived of referring to consumers in the metaphysical sense of devourers, likening them to time and death, 'the two consumers of the whole world'.[42] Disraeli speculated in *Coningsby* (1844) that 'he is a sagacious statesman who may detect in what form and in what quarter the great consumer will arise' that may destroy Parliament just as Barons, Church and King 'have in turn devoured each other', a usage that shows the survival of the early modern 'the consumer of thy Dukedome' or 'kingdome'.[43]

A more wide-ranging use of the consumer as a category of social order emerged only slowly in the eighteenth and early nineteenth centuries, and then with highly uneven influence on broader social and political discourse. In his essay on social order (1772), Isaac Iselin, discussing François Quesnay's *Tableau économique*, wrote that all of society consisted only of the following pairings: 'purchasers and sellers, consumers and producers or workers'.[44] In general, however, the status of the 'consumer' remained ambiguous, as the precise relationship between consumption and production, between private and public activities and between material and non-material acts of consumption remained subjects of ongoing debate amongst social and economic writers in nineteenth and early-twentieth century Europe.[45] J.B. Say was one of the few political economists to accord consumption a special section. Alongside private end-use he included the 'reproductive consumption' of goods in factories.[46] This concern with production in the analysis of consumption had implications for the analysis of individuals who did the consuming. Enlightenment thinkers had drawn a vital distinction between the productive consumption of the middle classes, whose moderate luxury reflected and stimulated peace, commerce and civil society, and the unproductive consumption of the aristocracy, whose excessive and ostentatious lifestyles destroyed investment and impeded development. By the turn of the eighteenth to the nineteenth century, as the conservative reaction to the French Revolution gathered steam, these roles were once more revalued. Thomas Malthus thus distinguished between 'productive consumers' and 'non-productive consumers', the latter being the worker, the former reserved for the 'consumption or destruction of wealth by capitalists with a view to reproduction'.[47] To avoid his much-feared glut of commodities, Malthus believed it was necessary to increase the 'unproductive consumption' of landlords. Consumers, in other words, were not one collective group but differentiated by their more or less productive functions.

If Adam Smith is now remembered for his famous maxim on the priority of the interests of consumers over those of producers, it is interesting to note how limited the space was that the following generations of so-called classical economists accorded to this actor and practice. Unorganized consumers needed to be protected against organized monopoly, but beyond this defensive position there was little of a more positive focus on the consumer and consumption. David Ricardo and J.S. Mill have been seen as marking 'a retreat rather than advance in conceptions of the role of consumption' by focusing on cost rather than demand, making 'the role of the "unfortunate" consumer in classical economics … not markedly different from that of the "servile" consumer in mercantilism'.[48] Mill, indeed, went so far as to deny that consumption was a worthy subject for the science of political economy: 'We know not of any laws of the consumption of wealth as the subject of a distinct science: they can be no other than the laws of human enjoyment.'[49] For Mill, an interest in consumption was associated with Malthus and Sismondi and signalled (in his view) altogether erroneous and politically dangerous diagnoses of under-consumption. The consumer began to play a more prominent role in the French school of utility theorists and, in Frédéric Bastiat's popular writings, became linked to a vigorous defence of property rights and free markets. But from a Ricardian position of exchange value, this weaving together of the consumer with a normative defence of *laissez-faire* was deeply flawed, neither good politics nor sound theory.[50] Put simply, the critique of utility theory meant that consumers were of greater interest as occasional victims of artificial monopoly and in conditions of market failure than as central players in a supposedly natural and harmonious market economy. Mill's critic John Ruskin was someone who took consumption very seriously, but he linked it to a concern about the welfare and happiness of producers and communities without requiring the development of a distinct category of 'consumers'.[51] As late as 1910, the eleventh edition of the *Encyclopaedia Britannica* only found it necessary to have a short entry on 'consumption', defined as wasting away in a physical sense or as a 'technical term' in economics about the destruction of utilities. There was no entry on 'the consumer'.

If it is problematic to draw a straight line from commodity culture to the consumer, then, it is similarly debatable to presume a neat correlation between the rise of the consumer and the rise of liberal knowledge systems premised on markets, exchange and rational utility-maximizing individuals. In the story of the consumer, the place of liberal knowledge is one of dissonance and discontinuities, not a unidirectional force converging towards neoliberalism. Recent scholars of governmentality have argued how, in 'advanced liberalism', consumer choice has come to play a central role in the formation of individual autonomy and selfhood.[52] Early and mature liberal culture, however, lacked an essentialist individualist consumer. From the 1870s to 1880s the marginal revolution and its individualist theory of consumer behaviour would introduce key categories like consumers' rent and consumer surplus. These would come to dominate twentieth-century economics and marketing,[53] but it is easy to exaggerate their influence on social and political discourse at the time, including the public attitude of neoclassical writers themselves. Jevons famously argued that 'the theory of economics must begin with a correct theory of consumption'.[54] Yet, neoclassical writers continued to treat the satisfaction of human needs more as a 'fundamental datum or premises [sic] of the science' than as the starting point for an exploration of consumption and consumers on a par with the laws of production, distribution and exchange, as J.N. Keynes pointed out in 1891 in a rare English discussion of whether consumption should receive a more distinct treatment.[55] Significantly, the technical, measurable apparatus introduced by the marginal revolution, which in the last few decades has been applied to all sorts of activities and goods, was defined along a narrow group of subjects, namely food and clothing.[56] If positivist interpersonal utility comparisons found their way into the textbooks of the new economic science, its doyen, Alfred Marshall, nonetheless kept alive a normative voice condemning morally and socially 'suspect' forms of consumption.

When the intellectual pursuit of the consumer took off in the 1890s, it was driven as much by a dialogue between public intellectuals and reformers outside or at the margins of liberal economics as by neoclassical economists: national economists in Germany, the radical liberal Hobson in England, the progressive Patten in the United States, and the cooperator Charles Gide in France. Hobson invoked a 'citizen-consumer' whose material acts and desires would increasingly be informed by civic values.[57] Likewise, Gide, who devoted an entire book in his *Cours d'économie politique* to consumption, focused on collective action amongst consumers to advance the interests of society. Patten saw selfish individuals as atavistic survivors of a past age of scarcity who would give way to the socialized generosity of an age of abundance. Here was a new appreciation of the pleasure economy, and the contribution of cinema, theatre and sport to wealth and welfare. But rather than couched in a positivist emphasis on individual consumer choice and satisfaction or measurable quantity and demand, Patten's vision was about increasing the quality of consumption and seeking to reconcile desire and restraint in a way that advanced communal welfare.[58] For all their differences, consumers in these reformist visions were mobilized for their civic and collective characteristics, not some inherent economic individualism.

Rather than adhering to a conventional Anglo-American liberal story line that traces the rise of the consumer from neoclassical economics and the marketplace of the commercial domain to recent episodes of neoliberalism and globalization, then, it may also be refreshing to ask about other, alternative biographies and birthplaces of the consumer. Historical or national economics is one such alternative site of knowledge. Intriguingly, the *Encyclopaedia Britannica* refers English readers to Wilhelm Roscher's *Nationaloekonomie* (1874), not to Jevons and Marshall.[59] In historical economics, interest in the consumer was driven by a concern with national power and resources and with social welfare and mores. Styles and levels of consumption were a marker of national character, and thus integral to an understanding of the historical evolution of national economies. Already in 1840 Moritz Carl Ernst von Prittwitz had added a whole section on consumption in his *Die Kunst reich zu werden*, a study of the wealth of nations. Here consumption concerned individuals using up commodities, art, holidays and personal services. And it extended to the consumption by organizations, like associations and the state itself.[60] Roscher, writing a generation later, distinguished between *Erwerbsgebrauch* (acquisition consumption) and

Genussgebrauch (enjoyment consumption). Interest went far deeper than the act of purchase and the immediate preferences and satisfaction associated with it. Consumption continued with the use of commodities – for Roscher, a person who bought a coat had only consumed it and the capital spent on it when the coat was finally worn out.

If national economics did not produce a theory of consumption, it certainly widened the scope of discussion. One connection was between consumption, waste, national character and civilization. Discussion of the waste of national resources was now decoupled from an earlier critique of luxury. The more civilized a nation, Prittwitz and Roscher believed, the less would it tend to destroy value – advanced nations would reuse more of their left-over food and old clothes.[61] As civilization progressed, luxury was directed towards 'the real, healthy and tasteful enjoyment of life, rather than inconvenient display'. Modern England and Holland proved the possibility of combining 'salutary luxury' with frugality and an appreciation of nature symbolized by the country house. Only in declining nations did luxury assume an 'impudent and immoral character'.[62] Here was an appreciation of advancing middle classes creating more conscientious consumers, a line of thought that carried echoes of the Enlightenment defence of moderate luxury and productive consumption. 'To enjoy more meant to live more, to be more human', Prittwitz concluded.[63] At the same time, the normative place of consumers in the social order depended not on the individuals as such but on the collective purpose and consequence of their actions. Motivation and social action remained inseparable in historical economics, much more so than in the eighteenth-century recognition of the virtuous public benefits from the sometimes not so virtuous stimulus behind private consumption behaviour. The danger lay not with consumption but with excessive, thoughtless or repetitive consumption that made consumers forget about their family, neighbours and community. Consumption made national strength and civilization possible, the family an escalation of personal wants or desire bearable. 'Without the demands of family life regarding sacrifice and commitment that distract us from our personal consumption purposes, consumption would be as unbearable for us as it was for single young men', Karl Oldenberg argued in 1910, whose views highlight the dialectical role of consumption in social evolution.[64] Consumption was nature's cunning: even where an increase in desire did not produce enhanced satisfaction, it nonetheless forced people to exert their energies, thus bringing the 'lazy mass' into the realm of civilization. Unlike for Adam Smith, where these social benefits had been seen as a process of individual deception, German national economists now tied a growing demand for more and more consumption to a growing sense of other-regarding actions and collective national virtues: 'the consumer appreciated the value of his [sic] consumption not only differently in different ages but at different levels of his ethical education [*sittliche Erziehung*]. Whether he places consumption in the services of transcendental obligations, or personal education or social considerations: his satisfaction of his wants is only an end in itself at the most primitive, non-reflexive stage of culture.' Instead of peace and harmony, the advance of consumption now pointed to national power and domination. Consumption, Oldenberg emphasized, cultivated 'strong people and strong nations, which can rule over others and imprint their characteristics on them'.[65]

From Users to Consumers

The growing attention given to the consumer in different intellectual traditions in the late nineteenth century did not occur in a vacuum but followed from a discursive and sociopolitical strengthening of the consumer as a category of identity and social praxis, and a persona with legal and political rights. In literature, politics and public discussion, the consumer gradually became a more frequent point of reference, but as a social identity its formation remained fractured and uneven across the advanced societies of Western Europe.

Consumer cooperatives spread from the 1840s across Europe, though membership of societies did not automatically create a collective identity of consumers and was mediated by different traditions. Significantly, German cooperatives did not call themselves *Konsumentenvereine* but *Konsumvereine*; here consumption was object, not identity, which remained centred in production or class categories, as in the big *Konsum, Bau- und Sparverein 'Produktion'* in Hamburg Altona.[66] In France the centrality of labour in political discourse and the emphasis on the mutual dependence between consumption and production hampered the coming of a distinct consumer identity until the 1880s. As with the Rochdale pioneers in England, cooperation here was firstly concerned with emancipating workers from the control of middlemen and producers. Consumption was a medium for strengthening a brotherhood of workers.[67]

Even in Britain, where the consumer gained the greatest resonance and legitimacy, the meaning and social universe of the consumer were in flux and contested. Giving attention to the consumer raised questions about who the consumer was and who represented the consumer interest. William Gladstone, who early on in his career, in the debate about the corn laws in 1842, urged contemporaries to 'consider the consumer', had no problem in identifying intermediary socioeconomic groups as speaking for the consumer. In 1883 he hoped to conclude the negotiations about canals 'with a fair regard to the views and interests of the mercantile community, who in this case represent the consumer, that is to say the world'.[68] By the time of the First World War the consumer had not yet narrowed to the private end-user. In 1913 accounts of the London taxicab drivers' strike still spoke of 'consumers' as the users of petrol, not the passengers.[69] And while battles over tariffs could sharpen a new sense of antinomy between social groups – 'the producer and the consumer'[70] – the growing debate about the consumer also produced visions of an organic life, in which consumption and production were reunited, as in the work of the feminist socialist Teresa Billington Greig.[71]

It was in Victorian England more than anywhere else that the ideological barriers to collective identity and action would be overcome and the political synapses of consumer politics sprang into action. Commercial traditions had left more discursive openings for the formation of collective consumer identities than traditions that privileged production or the land. It was languages of citizenship and battles over taxation that provided the political synapses for an increasingly articulate and assertive consumer identity. Debates about free trade and empire inserted 'the consumer' into an expanding range of political relationships and material goods. Instead of a universal category, a subject with preferences for an infinite number of goods and services in general, consumers here emerged as bounded figures in particular material and political contexts, with reference to particular goods, especially utilities (water, gas, coal) and crucial and highly emotive foodstuffs (bread and sugar). It was taxation and debates about the rights and responsibilities of citizens which connected these different material zones and created long-lasting openings for a more general breakthrough of the language and identity of the consumer. In the 1790s abolitionist groups on both sides of the Atlantic began to appeal to conscientious consumers in the fight against slavery: if consumers abstained from slave-grown sugar and bought 'free produce', there would be no more slaves. The ingestion of slave sugar literally threatened to contaminate the consumer's body.[72] The battle over sugar duties sharpened a sense of shared grievance and identity. Thus *The Consumers of West India Sugar* made their case against slavery and duties in Britain in 1828.

The conflict between tariffs and free trade that shaped Victorian and Edwardian politics led more generally to an increased circulation of the consumer. Fiscal debates began to extend the use of the term to all individuals affected by duties, a trend that can be traced in literature as well as politics. James Fenimore Cooper in *The Crater, or, Vulcan's Peak* (1847), for example, referred to 'true free trade' as meaning no taxation or restrictions whatsoever, not even free ports, since 'the consumer' would still have to pay 'customary impositions'.[73] Just as in the sphere of international trade, the consumer as taxpayer was also the link that mobilized citizens as ratepayers in local government. Victorians spoke of the 'consumer' as the 'occupier' who bore the local tax on the value of the house. Let us now briefly examine two historical settings in which the politics of citizenship and taxation provided an important synapse for the consumer as a social actor and public voice – first, battles over access, control and the payment of water in Victorian London; and second, a more global–local conjuncture in which anxieties over trade energized consumption as a question of national identity and citizenship around the turn of the twentieth century.

The conflict between users and natural monopolies in Victorian Britain produced a seminal point of connection between material needs and collective consciousness and action. This early synapse of consumer politics was initially fused by propertied and commercial users through notions of access, public accountability and representative government, rather than choice or universal consumer democracy. In the case of a utility like gas, those who defended their interests as 'consumers' were almost exclusively merchants, shopkeepers and industrialists.[74] When a 'Gas Consumer' asked in a pamphlet of 1849: 'Are the Citizens of London to have better Gas, and more of it, for Less Money?', the writer presented himself as a 'plain tradesman'. The consumer was mobilized in a battle against monopoly for cheaper and safer service, and to make companies accountable in a way that was analogous to the Westminster model of parliamentary representation. Liberal thinkers and commercial users alike feared that utility companies were evolving into a new breed of private monopolies like the East India Company and corrupting the public spirit.[75] When asked how the monopoly would be avoided by 'forming a Company comprised of consumers for the supply of the City [of London]', the gas consumer's answer is revealing. 'The citizens [of the City] will have a double security; in the first place the consumers will elect their own Directors.'[76] Second, they will have a fixed maximum price, with dividends on profits reducing the price further. In short, the consumer acquired shape through a model of citizenship: accountability via representation went hand in hand with consumer protection in the form of lower and stable prices.

Water was the single most fiercely contested good in nineteenth-century London politics and the site of a widening social identity of consumers.[77] Water users became articulate consumers whose growing self-confidence sparked a network of consumer defence leagues and consumer boycotts. By the 1880s and 1890s, the social category of consumers had widened from propertied rate-paying private and commercial users to include the public more generally. Water carried a high cultural capital as 'the first necessary of life', a significance reinforced by the politics of public health in the early Victorian period.[78] While local councils after mid-century were required to provide a clean and adequate supply of water, the supply in London and many other cities remained in the hands of private monopolies.[79] It was 'an article, as necessary to existence as light and air', which, in the words of early reformers, could not be left safely in the hands of 'monopolists' and 'these jobbers in one of God's choicest blessings' who were treating 'customers ... like so many Negroes'.[80]

The 1875 Public Health Act required local councils to ensure an adequate and clean water supply. Some commercial users paid for a metered amount of water consumed, but, unlike in cities such as Berlin, water to private users was not metered in London. Instead, water was paid for through rates, a local tax on property. In the eyes of local government, water companies and taxpayers, 'consumers' were ratepayers – that is, property owners, owner-occupiers and tenants above a certain rent who paid their rates directly. Consumers were not just anyone using water (women, children and poorer tenants were initially not included). It was the more privileged section which first agitated as consumers for greater accountability and representative powers. Complaints about supply, access, quality and price escalated as water companies' costs rose and consumers became more vocal about companies raising water rates at a time of falling commodity prices. It was in this pressure cooker of increasing rates and rising norms of personal comfort and hygiene – water closets and bathtubs were subject to additional water rates – that the consumer acquired an increasingly assertive voice; continuous supply was introduced in the 1880s and 1890s. In 1882–3 the barrister Archibald Dobbs brought a successful legal challenge to the water companies' rating policy on his modest home. He became the hero of the 'rate-paying public' and began a crusade to secure the same advantage for 'every water consumer in London'.[81] A network of Water Consumers' Defence Leagues sprang up all over London. They set up advice bureaus, circulated posters with 'Instructions to Consumers', organized boycotts, and provided legal support for aggrieved consumers.[82]

At first, consumer rights remained tied to property rights as the basis of citizenship and representation. Dobbs charged that the water companies had led an 'invasion of the property of water consumers ... a confiscation of the statutory rights of ratepayers'.[83] Without a system of regulation, however, the battle over rights, rates and accountability quickly developed into a contestation of the nature of the 'consumer' and the rights and responsibilities that came with a legal entitlement to an 'adequate' supply of water for 'domestic use'. Commercial users in the city tried to mobilize these categories in their battle for lower rates. The water companies sought to drive a wedge through a consolidating consumer interest, but in the process gave the consumer even greater currency through a massive counter-campaign that blamed irresponsible and 'wasteful consumers' for the water shortages, dirt and increased prices experienced by honest consumers.[84] The discovery of the propertied consumer with rights went hand in hand with the discovery of the 'apathetic consumer'.[85]

In the expanding political culture of late Victorian Britain, ratepayer activism expanded the social universe and public imagery of the consumer. Mobilization could be spontaneous, triggered by the experience of scarcity against a backdrop of rising norms and consumption practices assisted by better and more constant supply, and fuelled by a distrust of monopoly communicated through a broadly liberal tradition of freedom. For all its ebbs and flows, consumer activism was not the matter of an instant – a bubble that would burst when pricked because of the amorphous nature of consumers' interests. For the contestation of water left behind an enriched sense and symbolism of the consumer as representing the public interest. In the early nineteenth century the debate between supporters and critics of the private water companies invoked the 'rate-paying public' or the 'health of the public'.[86] By the late nineteenth century a shared language of the consumer began to be invoked by householders as well as users more generally, from affluent property owners in Belgravia to mechanics in rental accommodation in the East End and female tenants.

The mobilization of the consumer reached its peak during the so-called 'water famines' of the mid-1890s, in which, after a cycle of droughts and frost, the East London Water Company reintroduced intermittent supply. The East London Water Consumers' Defence Association pressed for municipal control of the water monopoly and called on consumers to boycott local taxes for water not supplied. Radical imagery showed the water monopoly as a rocky skull propped up by 'capitalism' and 'government acts', with helpless men, women and children squashed by cholera and typhoid, waiting for Moses to lead them from private monopoly to municipal control. 'Moses 2nd' is cheered on by a worker whose side-pocket holds a telling paper: 'Public Opinion'.[87]

The formative history of the consumer in local water politics is important because it was marked by features not conventionally associated with 'consumer society'. Water combined a popular sense of a 'necessary' with the civilizing properties of bodily comfort and hygiene. As a scarce good that was easily lost or exhausted, it raised questions of waste, not abundance.

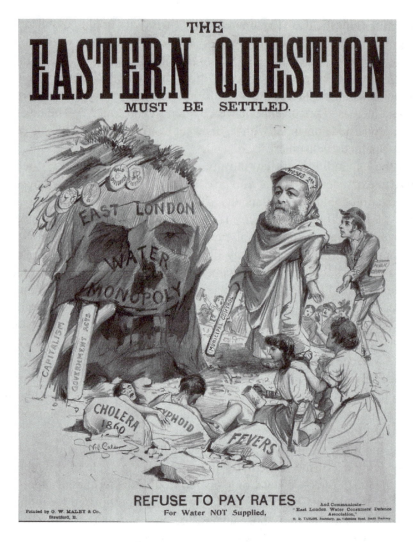

Figure 1 Water Consumers, 1898

Source: PRO, COPY 1, 143 folio 165.

Water was not sold and bought on the market but provided by private monopolies; nor was the price determined by the volume of consumption. Users turned into consumers protesting about conditions of supply as well as price, and demanding civic rights and public control – not individual choice in the marketplace. Consumers, in short, acquired their voice in an arena of consumption that lay outside the widening universe of commodity culture.

Consumption, International Trade and National Power

Trade and imperial rivalries added a more intense national and global dynamic to such local and particular mobilizations of the consumer, particularly from the 1890s. Against the background of an increasingly global circulation of food and commodities, and a shifting balance between town and country, consumption became a contested site in debates about agricultural and trade policy, social reform, racial strength and the relationship between citizenship and nationhood. The agitation about Free Trade in Britain, protectionism in Germany and alien commodities in China can be seen as part of this global conjuncture. The degree to which consumer identities were mobilized in these debates, however, differed according to traditions of citizenship and social and national solidarities. Whereas the consumer became a firmly established political and social voice in Britain before the First World War, that voice remained underdeveloped in Imperial Germany and was stillborn in the Chinese case of commodity nationalism.

It was the popular politics of Free Trade that firmly established the consumer as an identity and actor in Britain, especially in the Edwardian campaigns (1903–10).[88] References to the consumer had not altogether been absent from the earlier anti-corn law movement or debates about the public exhibition of commodities,[89] but they played a marginal, descriptive role that never acquired the broader, inclusive normative appeal of 'the people' or the status of the merchant spreading the civilizing 'douceur' of commerce. Popular editions of Bastiat's *Sophismes* went some way towards disseminating an image of consumers as that of humanity.[90] Yet it was Edwardian politics that made 'the consumer' an altogether more active, ubiquitous character. Between the general elections of January and December 1910, for example, one Free Trade body alone organized 6,000 public meetings, magic-lantern lectures and travelling exhibits, offering lessons on how an import duty adversely affected consumers. Alongside, women's groups like the Women's Cooperative Guild, which spoke on behalf of the 'women with the basket', invoked the civic rights and contributions of their members as consumers.

Consumption was a gendered subject, but, as evidence of the male propertied gas and water consumers suggests, this did not mean that the identity of the consumer was a female preserve. The gendered make-up of the consumer was much more fluid and contested than earlier scholarly models of a sexual division of labour and sharp divide between public and private spheres would suggest. Contemporaries debated the moral properties and civic status of male as well as female consumers.[91] The political debate, too, remained open for national and male representations. In a depiction of the vulnerable

Figure 2 The Male Consumer, 1909

Source: Bristol University Archive, DM 669 Free Trade Union, Leaflet no. 328, 24 Nov. 1909.

position of the consumer under protectionism, the Free Trade Union showed a troubled middle-class shopper standing in front of a shop window with leather goods at higher prices under tariff reform.[92]

The strength of Free Trade rested partly on its ability to incorporate older and newer images of the consumer. Free Traders moved beyond a fixation with necessities (the cheap loaf) to a broader display of goods, including branded goods (Quaker Oats and Lea and Perrin sauce) and clothing for different social groups (the bowler hat as well as the worker's cap). At the same time, discussions on how duties were paid by the 'home consumer' rather than the foreigner grouped all Britons together. Free Trade businessmen, like the leading chemical industrialist Alfred Mond, emphasized how industries were consumers too. In contrast to the earlier, more bounded tradition of the consumer, with its persona of the propertied ratepayer and its emphasis on specific utilities, the consumer had become an integral part of society.

There was nothing inevitable about the coming together of this synapse of consumer politics. Mass politics and debates about the standard of living and trade regulation existed in many societies at the time without producing an equally strong identity or discourse of the consumer. Across Europe the consumption and saving habits of different social groups became a central topic of social investigation.[93] In Imperial Germany the public agitation about price increases fuelled opposition to agricultural tariffs. Milk wars, butter boycotts and protests against meat prices between 1905 and 1912 articulated a new sense of entitlement amongst blue and white-collar workers and parts of the middle classes. Initially the mobilization was led by the social democrats and by women's groups, but by 1912 the Christian trades unions, too, had swung from earlier support to oppose the protectionist regime. Social democrats increasingly tried to address consumer as well as producer issues, but political parties in general were slow to adopt a unifying language of the consumer. Politicians bemoaned the 'pure consumer point of view' of the lower middle classes. Even national-liberal advocates for this group separated salaried employees ('first of all consumers') from the rest of the middle classes rather than stressing a shared, public consumer interest.[94] The consumer was a sectional interest, far from representing the nation, let alone humanity as a whole, as it did for popular liberals in Britain. Consumer and shopping leagues set up to promote better working conditions also spread to Imperial Germany from Britain, France and America. But here, too, a more inclusive identity of the consumer remained underdeveloped. The emphasis was on developing socially responsible habits of consumption amongst middle-class 'consumers' to improve the social conditions of 'workers'.[95] Tellingly, the German housewives' association (*Hausfrauenverein*) remained sceptical of the category of the consumer and, instead, presented itself as a corporate organization of women in charge of managing and preparing goods as much as purchasing them.[96]

In China consumption moved to the centre of popular politics in the context of weak state power and militant patriotism. From 1900 until 1931 there was a steady series of campaigns for the recovery of sovereign rights, directed first against Russia and the United States and later against Japan, which involved anti-imperialist boycotts and exhibits promoting the use of national products. In a state that had lost the power to control imports, the regulation of consumption became a substitute for state sovereignty. For bodies like the National Products Preservation Association, as Karl Gerth has recently shown, 'material culture such as fabrics and clothing styles played a direct role in connecting individuals to the nation: individual bodies were key sites of a national symbology and hence for the construction of modern Chinese nationalism as such'.[97] The use of goods as national symbols has of course played an integral part in consumption debates in many other settings, not least the patriotic iconography of the British white loaf of freedom at the time. Yet while the British consumer's interest was tied to the cheapness and purity of the article rather than its origin (foreign wheat), in China the campaign after the 1911 Revolution focused on product-nationality (not style or price). Reforming consumption styles, by organized resistance to foreign goods and by promoting national products, was seen as essential to overcoming national humiliation and building strong Chinese citizens. In Groups of Ten for National Salvation, members pledged their lives to forgo the consumption of all imports. Economic nationalism was promoted by students and shopkeepers, as well as producers, who used boycotts to increase their market share.[98] Governments elsewhere in the inter-war years also introduced marketing and cultural initiatives to boost the purchase of home or imperial products, but these were dwarfed by the scale of the Chinese movement; Hangzhou's West Lake Exhibition, for example, had eighteen million visitors in 1929.[99] The wise consumption of national products was seen as the duty of all citizens fighting for national survival, but especially of women. The 'determined use of national products' raised women's status in the household to the equivalent of a battlefield commander 'kill[ing] the enemy for the country', as organizers of the Women's National Products Year of 1934 put it.[100] Building a strong Chinese nation required more conscious habits of consumption, but the subject addressed was not the consumer but the 'citizen,' 'compatriot', 'Chinese People' or 'masses'. Groups promoting commodity nationalism formed Citizens' Associations, not consumer associations.[101]

The contrasting forms in which consumption was politicized point to the contingent and diverse trajectories of the consumer in modernity. Commodity culture played an increasingly important role in all three societies in this earlier period of globalization, but it was negotiated through different social and political traditions that mapped consumption practices onto different social identities. One favourable condition for the creation of a consumer identity, these cases suggest, was the comparatively early erosion of rival social identities based on estates, work or corporation. By the late nineteenth century, workers in Britain and America had largely accepted the reality of wage labour and given up earlier ideals of artisanal, corporate or republican independence.[102] In this indirect way, the early commercialization of society created greater elbow room for the consumer. In Britain Free Trade created a more inclusive, universal sense of consumers with a stake in society and polity. Where corporate, producer and landed identities remained stronger and were seen as commensurate with the national interest or republican citizenship, by contrast, the space for the consumer was more limited. In Germany it was not until after the defeat of Nazism that the consumer became an attractive cultural vehicle of national refashioning.[103]

Early twentieth century Japan, Korea and India offer different variations on this theme.[104] In Korea national product promotion campaigns sought to instil a new sense of moral and national self-sufficiency to overcome Japanese colonial domination. In a strong state like Japan, too, consumption remained culturally ambivalent and contested; even as urban Japanese were expanding their consumption habits and using new forms of consumer credit, the state and social movements attacked the consumption of imported goods as leading to moral and national dependence. It was the saver in Japan who was mobilized as the pillar of economic and military strength, in contrast to Britain, a similarly export-oriented economy, where a liberal tradition linked the national interest with urban and industrial consumers' interest in an open economy. In India the campaign to promote khadi turned to indigenous craft and consumption practices for moral and sexual cleansing to create conscious nationals; here was an extreme version of self-sufficiency that rejected the modernity of commodity culture as such and prescribed less consumption altogether. Whereas Free Traders and members of the cooperative movement projected the consumer as an internationalist link between societies, the politicization of consumption in nationalist traditions favoured identities of citizens in territorially bounded states.

Attention to social and political traditions suggests the degree of commodification might account less for the strength of the consumer in the modern period than conventionally thought. The campaigns over water and gas provision indicate that the formation of consumers need not take place in commercial competitive market settings; rather, the failure (real or perceived) of monopolies might act as a catalyst. Paradoxically, too, it was Free Traders' ambivalence towards consumerism that provided the 'citizen-consumer' with public legitimacy. The initial focus on necessaries and taxed goods was crucial in the British case because, in a liberal tradition of the tax-paying citizen, it allowed the construction of an organic public interest around taxpayers; it created a virtuous distance from a morally more ambiguous 'consumerism' or charges of selfishness. Radical and progressive traditions were subsequently able to build on this liberal foundation and invoke the civic, community-oriented outlook of a citizen-consumer. Politics, of course, was not immune from the expanding world of consumption, which through new commercial spaces, like department stores and tea rooms, facilitated middle-class women's entry into public spaces.[105] At the same time, the identity of the consumer in political culture remained largely distinct from that in commercial culture. The consumer here was a citizen with a social conscience and with shared basic needs, not the *flâneur* or *flâneuse* exploring infinite desires, nor the utility-maximizing individual of neoclassical economic theory. The consumer in Britain was thus largely able to withstand the charge, so overwhelming on the European continent and in Asia, of being a selfish, apatriotic individual whose obsessions with universal cheapness eroded the collective good. In fact, materialism, millionaires and social polarization came to be associated in Free Trade Britain as the natural products of tariff regimes abroad, typified by the United States and Germany. The non-threatening image of the consumer as a public interest (rather than a sectional interest) was underwritten by a self-denying view of state power. British liberals and radicals saw the House of Commons as a kind of virtual representation for all consumers, representing all taxpayers (including women) irrespective of whether they had the vote or not. Consumers thus did not corrupt the much idealized 'purity of politics'. The organizational base of consumers remained civil society. It was here that consumer organizations like the cooperatives saw their main area for moralizing the market and creating a higher social conscience amongst consumers.[106]

Instead of picturing a natural synergy between the consumer, individualism and liberal economics, it is vital to retrieve this earlier moment of an association between civil society, citizenship and the consumer. Next to the citizen-consumer in Free Trade, we can also think here of the consumer leagues that sprang up in America and continental Europe in the 1890s, with their emphasis on the social responsibility of consumers to shop wisely. These leagues strove to improve the welfare of workers and small traders by refraining from shopping after 8 p.m., by paying in cash, by planning ahead, and by taming the impulse to buy shoddy, fashionable goods made by sweated labour.[107] The identity of consumers and the mentalities and responsibilities ascribed to them here are worlds apart from the universe of hedonism, unlimited choice and the city as 24-hour mall.

Social Ethics and Political Empowerment: Consumers between State and Civil Society

The populist consummation of the consumer happened in the First World War, driven forward by the state as well as civil society. Scarcities and inflation produced consumer boycotts and demands for representation. Equally significantly, state planning led to state-sponsored recognition and institutionalization, as in the war committees of consumer interests (*Kriegsausschüsse für Konsumenteninteressen*) set up in Germany in December 1914.[108] Debates about economic controls and rationing set in motion a process that would provide states and consumers with a much more transparent view of the economy and businesses, all the way down to detailed accounts of the prices, profits, supplies and distribution of particular commodities. Subjects graduated from the war with an elementary education of themselves as consumers and citizens. Within the state, rationalization and campaigns for thrift highlighted the vital economic role of consumers in national survival.

The war thus placed new social, ethical and political responsibilities on the consumer, even or especially in producer-oriented national traditions. Consumers were identified as vital, if compliant, partners in the state's project of a more rational and equitable allocation of resources. 'Consumption', the German industrialist, politician and thinker Walther Rathenau argued, 'was not a private affair but an affair of the community, the state, ethics and humanity.'[109] Citizens needed to overcome their 'crazy hunger for commodities' that was responsible for a misallocation of natural resources. Overcoming waste – through a mixture of consumption taxes and import controls – would create more conscientious consumers and a more productive nation that, in turn, would allow for greater public spending on social welfare and on 'higher' forms of cultural consumption.

For organized consumers across Europe, the suffering and responsibilities placed on them during wartime led to a new focus on the state. The demand for consumer councils and an attack on profiteering corporations and middlemen was its political articulation.[110] The demand for state controls to provide consumers with a stable supply of commodities was its policy implication.[111] In Britain consumers now advocated secure provision and regulation, instead of cheapness and freedom of trade.

The maturing of the consumer during and after the First World War was inextricably tied to the development of welfare policies, 'social citizenship' and the state's challenge to civil society. As nineteenth-century battles

over the public control of basic goods suggest, this twentieth-century story
had historical antecedents, but the consumer politics of war and welfare
also began to diverge in fundamental ways from those of gas and water
socialism. The consumer was increasingly only an individual citizen or
private end-user. The earlier inclusion of commercial or collective users
became rare (though still traceable in Weimar corporatism). State planning
projected socioeconomic rights onto a universal private consumer. In the
1930s advocates of a middle way between socialism and capitalism such as
Britain's future prime minister Harold Macmillan, for example, argued for
a minimum standard of living for all households, 'whether the consumer is
in or out of work', as part of economic reconstruction.[112] At a local level, the
British Council for Art and Industry urged education authorities in 1936 to
remember, 'even where it conflicts with a strict economy ... that they are
educating the future consumer; and may be setting a standard for industry
in the next generation'.[113] At a global level, internationalists turned to
consumers as key instruments in the programme of 'economic appeasement'
and international peace. Advocates of international planning sensed an
epochal shift in history: if the nineteenth century had been preoccupied with
production, the twentieth century needed to look at consumption. Future
international growth and harmony were now seen to depend on creating
better-off consumers who could absorb excess production.[114]

The growing prominence of the consumer as a pillar of wealth, welfare
and peace was reinforced not only by the material challenge prompted by the
world depression (1929–32) but also by the spread of totalitarian ideologies.
The consumer advanced into an attractive alternative pillar of social order,
an antidote to the temptations of fascism and communism alike. This turn
perhaps had more to do with social norms and political ideas and less with
economic arguments about market efficiency and 'consumer welfare' than
might be expected, including for economic writers. In Britain and America
advertisers positioned themselves as guardians of democracy by embracing
the consumer as king. Tellingly, the concept of 'consumer sovereignty',
which William Hutt, a British economist teaching in South Africa, began
to circulate in the mid-1930s, was introduced to explain the favourable
mechanisms of social harmony and political consent in a market society in
which consumers were able to exercise their power through demand.[115] In a
totalitarian society, producers were dependent on the state and constrained
by regulations and identifiable networks of power. In a functioning market
society, by contrast, producers were dependent on consumers, a diffuse and far
less identifiable group. There were echoes here of an older critique of vested
interests that united Free Trade liberals with eighteenth-century writers.

This diffuseness, Hutt argued, was a vital precondition for social harmony and political legitimacy in a complex and dynamic modern society. In short, producers who lost out in a market society or had difficulties in adjusting to changing tastes and demand found it much more difficult to pin their grievances on a particular social group or the state. Consumer sovereignty mixed a sense of freedom for consumers with an atmosphere of restraint for producers; Hutt was clear that this freedom often was little more than an illusion and that much consumption was not the result of short-term rational choices but of long-term routines and traditions. Consumer sovereignty might not necessarily make for the maximum allocation of resources, Hutt argued, but it did favour conditions of political consent and a minimum base of toleration. Effectively, this was an argument that fused consumer power with civil society, updated for an age of ideologies; consumer sovereignty taught people to learn to live with difference. The state and producers did not seek to steer or dictate consumption but accepted that society was a mix of different, even conflicting, tastes and preferences. The argument for 'consumer sovereignty' did not even require that consumers knew what was best for them. It was the acceptance of difference that mattered. Consumer sovereignty defused potential conflict between different interests and ways of life.

To some liberals, consumers advanced into the last defence against total-itarianism. In the United States, Horace Kallen, in 1936, took the argument so far as to present human history as a gradual process of alienation from an original consumer state of existence. Human beings were born consumers and only became producers under coercion. To preserve humanity it was necessary to develop the full personality of consumers, for their 'cultural spirit, their personal disposition, their social attack, their economic method must oppose themselves in unmistakable contrast to those of the *duces*, *Fuehrers*, and *commissars* of the Fascist, Nazi and Communist cults as well as those of the captains of industry and finance of the capitalist economy'.[116] Here was an ethical conception of the trinity of consumption, freedom and American leadership before it mutated into a material defence of a 'consumers' republic' that became an American export-staple during the Cold War.[117]

The unprecedented attention given to the consumer in questions of citizen-ship and economic policy was part of a larger social and cultural trend that associated the consumer with an expanding and increasingly diversified field of practices, goods and services. Already in the late nineteenth century, Charles Gide, the French economist and a strong supporter of the cooperatives, extended the consideration of consumption to include 'houses, gardens, money, furniture, curios'.[118] The consumer's interest moved beyond food, gas and water, though this did not automatically point to consumerism. Gide urged recycling, for example, and imagined an ideal state of consumption where goods never wore out; in the United States, Patten equally looked towards a wiser use of natural resources in an age of affluence. The consumer interest expanded in social class and social practice, encompassing health, housing, leisure and collective forms of consumption. Cooperatives in France spoke of 'consumers of health' in the 1920s and included free holidays for children and families as 'consumer' activities; consumers now encompassed bourgeois and petit-bourgeois groups as well as workers and farmers.[119] By 1936 the British Institute of Adult Education was investigating 'The Consumer's View of Adult Education'.[120] In the United States, college and secondary school courses on consumption addressed questions of medical care and the purchase of services, automobiles and electrical appliances, as well as food and clothing.[121] Within the federal government, the newly established Consumers' Division identified housing as a critical issue for 'John Public – the consumer'.[122]

The enrichment of the social body and practice of the consumer, then, was well under way by the time J.M. Keynes in his *General Theory of Employment, Interest and Money* (1936) accorded the consumer a central role in the creation of wealth and full employment. Two years earlier, in 1934, the British satirical magazine *Punch* (only slightly) caricatured consumers' new public status that placed them on a par with workers, indeed went as far as presenting the pursuit of consumption as a form of work itself. When asked by a 'kind old Bishop' how he intended to 'help Society's plan', the 'bright-haired lad replied': 'I want to be a Consumer ... I've never had aims of a selfish sort, / For that, as I know, is wrong, / I want to be a Consumer, Sir, / And help the world along ... I want to be a Consumer / And work both night and day, ... There are too many people working / And too many things are made. / I want to be a Consumer, Sir, / And help to further Trade.'[123]

The growing attention given to the consumer in society, culture and political economy in the inter-war years, however, was not uniformly positive everywhere. Consumers and consumption remained ambivalent, even troubling, categories in many Asian societies. In Europe and the United States, too, the liberal upgrading of the consumer worked in tandem with progressive debates about the civic nature and limits of consumers. The father of Keynesianism was deeply critical of the kind of mass consumer society with which his theory is sometimes associated. Abundance, Keynes hoped, would eventually be enjoyed by people who 'cultivate into a fuller perfection, the art of life itself and do not sell themselves for the means of life', recognizing the 'love of money' as a 'somewhat disgusting morbidity'.[124] Other progressives began to ask how the growing emphasis on individual choice and demand could be reconciled with the universal principles of citizenship or the ethics informing social solidarities. Two divergent responses deserve attention here.

In one response, 'social citizenship' began to question the organic union of the 'citizen-consumer' imagined by earlier radicals. Modern society had been marked by the parallel growth of associations of consumers and associations of citizens. Would this development lead towards symbiosis or end in a conflict of identities and solidarities? 'There may be significance', the British Fabian Beatrice Webb observed in 1928 in *The Discovery of the Consumer*, 'in the fact that during the same century in which these voluntary organizations of consumers have taken so great and so widespread a development, the compulsory organization of citizens that we know as government has largely changed in form and in function, so as to approximate, more or less, to an Association of Consumers.' Old states had been based on vocational castes and tended towards military aggression requiring 'arbitrary taxation'. In the course of democratization, by contrast, 'the nation comes very near to becoming ... an Association of consumers', as 'the central government, carrying out the common will of the citizens, conveys their letters and parcels; transports their goods and themselves by railway, canal or steamship; provides for them news and entertainment by "wireless"; supplies for them a thousand and one common requirements, from medical attendance at birth to burial at death, together with museums, libraries, picture galleries, music, and dramatic performances during life.'[125]

The question was: how much could the state come to resemble an association of consumers, like the cooperatives, before eroding itself as a community of citizens? Webb had long appreciated the contribution of the cooperatives in stimulating civic culture and in nursing a practice of 'democratic self-government'.[126] Yet would there be a similar flow of strengthened democratic sentiment and practice, if consumer representation was placed at the centre of the state? Partly this was a problem of size: it was wishful thinking that millions of people sending letters 'could be marshalled into effective democracy for controlling the management of the post'.[127] Partly, most social services involved a problem of asymmetry: a minority used them while the whole community paid for them.[128] Social democracy required areas of public life where citizenship overruled the voluntary principles of consumer organization: '[t]he suppression of nuisances, the enforcement of universal schooling, and the general convenience of making some services free (which involves payment by compulsory levies irrespective of the use of such services) seem to require an association not of consumers, but of citizens, adhesion to which cannot be left merely optional'. There had to be an enforceable standard of a 'national minimum of civilized life' for the community as a whole. Municipal government was 'advantageous for the election of representatives and the levying of taxation'. It also provided citizens with a fixed sense of belonging. Webb could not see how it would be possible to 'endow obligatory associations of citizens with the freedom and elasticity of co-operative societies without leading either to injustice and oppression or to endless litigation'.[129]

In the United States, the New Deal, too, created a very different political synapse for citizens and consumers from earlier traditions, combining an economic model of growth through increased purchasing power with a democratic model of mobilizing consumers as citizens supported by the state. Whereas in Free Trade the public identity of the consumer was anchored in a basic range of goods, the New Deal expanded it to cover everything from food quality to inefficient machines and corporate structure. And instead of an idealized purity of politics where consumers had no direct connection to the state, the New Deal used state power to mobilize consumers directly. In the course of the 1930s the economic power of consumers became a vehicle for a public project of safeguarding the general good, in competition with what Liz Cohen has called the more individualist commercial project of the 'purchaser consumer' that came to dominate after the Second World War.[130] Historians have paid attention to the rise of consumer rights and activism and new state support of the 'citizen consumer' via consumer advisors in federal government and consumer committees in the localities.[131] A second strand of scholarship has traced the more technocratic concept of the rational consumer that began to circulate through organizations like Consumers' Research.[132] Here I want to briefly tease out an ethical dimension that informed this public accreditation of individual purchasing.

The development of the rational consumer had as much to do with an ethical conception of how individual consumers made their decisions as with material interest or an institutional critique of corporations. For the burgeoning home economics and consumer education movement, ethics and choice were symbiotic. Established in 1899, the American Home Economics Association had 12,000 members by the 1930s. Colleges, secondary schools and women's clubs carried an ever-increasing number of courses and study guides; already by 1928 there were 322 four-year degree granting programmes producing 37,619 majors. One author of key texts was Hazel Kyrk, the influential home economist at the University of Chicago.[133] For Kyrk the goal was to teach the consumer to 'consult his individual need, to form his own judgements, to desire for himself and to respect in others a creative, experimental attitude toward the various means that are offered him for the enhancement of his health and comfort, or the enrichment of his experience'. 'Wise consumption choices' led to greater mental stimulation and sociability as well as to a higher level of personal comfort and safety. Kyrk made a crucial distinction between a 'consumer' and a 'buyer'. These were not rival social models but different stages in the individual practice of consumption. The first, the stage of the consumer, was about the evaluation of choices and the setting of standards, the second, that of the buyer, concerned efficient purchasing decisions. The 'buyer' was about the 'technology of consumption': exercising choice, saving money and time, and securing a fair price necessary to keep labour and capital fully employed. The consumer was about cultivating tastes and forming new concepts of need. Choice, then, was not just a neutral mechanism to allow individuals to pursue their previously formed preferences but a much more active and moral instrument, involving 'questions of motives, of values, of ends'.[134]

Kyrk's work reflects how broad and diverse the intellectual and cultural sources were that pushed the consumer to the centre of public discourse in the inter-war years. In her prize-winning *Theory of Consumption* (1923), Kyrk demolished W.S. Jevons' theory of economics as a mere theory of exchange value that failed to offer any understanding of the attitudes that lay behind choice.[135] Individuals did not have free choice, nor were they rational maximizers; but neither were they passive minds. In her critique of the utility-maximizing individual in neoclassical economics, Kyrk drew on philosophy, social and functional psychology and, in particular, on John Dewey's philosophy of knowledge through practice. Dewey was a key influence on many consumer advocates. Through the League for Independent Political Action (established in 1929) he stressed the affinities between consumer and citizen. Empowering consumers needed to begin with reflections on higher values and new ideals and purposes. Freedom of choice would let individuals develop higher social and personal ethics. All psychical life was 'in some sense a choosing'. Values and actions determined each other. Value was not a question of the magnitude of feelings, as in neoclassical economics, nor was it located in the object. It was about individual will and the social organization of values. By the 1930s questions of value, the position of the consumer in society and educational theory were as familiar in consumer education as labelling, quality and price. A culture of thrift was being eroded, but, instead of simply being swamped by a culture of materialist individualism, choice was also being channelled into a social ethics of consumption.

Conclusion

Kyrk's concern with the moral dimension of consumer choice brings us back to the problem of the elusive consumer with which we began. Consumers, she emphasized, were no easily identifiable separate group: 'consumers are simply the general public'. 'Try to lay your hands upon the general public and it has disappeared or is non-existent. The consumer from being every one seems to be no one.'[136] Much more so than academics, consumer advocates together with states and businesses have reflected on the slippery nature of the consumer, seeking to mould, modify and contest the identity and interests of this person. This chapter has pursued the consumer as a social identity and as a category of knowledge and ascription in the making. Taking the consumer seriously as a historical actor and category raises larger questions for standard interpretations of modern 'consumer society'. They challenge causation, chronology and convergence.

Most interpreters of 'consumer revolutions' and commodity culture have instinctively relied on an essentialist category of the consumer. While this may yield insights into goods, symbols, their distribution and economic consequences, it reveals far less about the self-identification and ascription of the actors themselves. To follow the consumer as an evolving category of knowledge and identity, we must jettison the instinctive assumption that any user of commercial commodities and services naturally is a consumer. This assumption says more about us than about past actors. Arguably, it is a result of the historical evolution of the consumer (not its explanation). The consumer, like 'class', 'citizen' or 'nation', is no natural or universal category but the product of historical identity formations, in which actors through available traditions make sense of the relationship between material culture and collective identity.

Importantly, the birth and maturing of the consumer are principally a nineteenth and early-twentieth century story. It sits uneasily between the early modern consumer revolutions – with their emphasis on exotic goods, luxury and a cult of sensibility – and the mid-twentieth-century stories of mass consumption or consumer society – with their fixation on affluence, advertising, mass produced durables and visions and dystopias of consumerism. The material culture of consumption and the political culture of the consumer do not map onto each other neatly. In Britain utilities and taxed necessaries were the consumer's domain – not the growing number of commercially traded goods and services. Taxpayers, especially propertied male householders and commercial users of utilities, were the first to speak up as consumers. Property was a vital ingredient in the consumer's initial self-definition. The mobilization of the consumer in mid- and late Victorian

Britain reveals the centrality of political synapses, in this case the liberal and radical traditions through which material relations were connected to collective identities and a sense of rights and accountability. Cooperatives added a popular dimension to the expanding social universe of consumers, but the continued importance of commercial consumers cautions against seeing the evolution of the consumer as a simple story of democratization. Equally, it questions the dominant tendency in the social sciences to turn first to business, liberal economics, advertising and states to account for the rise of the consumer.[137] These agencies, indeed, came to compete for the consumer's soul and money, but it was actors in civil society who first breathed life into this identity in Europe and America by mobilizing as consumer defence leagues, shopping leagues, Free Trade groups and consumer education movements.

Modernity created different openings for consumers in different political and cultural spaces, depending on the role of nation, state, traditions of citizenship and social identities. There is no universal history of the consumer, just as there is no essentialist consumer. The prominence of the consumer as citizen in Edwardian Britain was a particular developmental stage in the genealogy of the consumer in a liberal radical tradition. In societies with corporate traditions and nation or producer-oriented discourses of citizenship, like Imperial Germany, the consumer was more marginal and more easily seen as a special interest. In societies where the control of consumption became a means of overcoming weak statehood, as in China, or of promoting economic modernization, as in Japan, the consumer did not emerge as an actor and identity because national consumption became the responsibility of patriotic citizens. Modern liberal traditions (though not republicanism) allow for an easier development of consumer identity because of a less territorially or corporately bounded sense of citizenship. In societies like early-twentieth-century Japan, users or purchasers found it difficult to imagine themselves and agitate as consumers, being preoccupied instead with the imperative of strengthening themselves as a nation (*kokumin*). The resulting identity of producer and patriot – more than the negative cultural connotations of consumption (*shōhi,* referring to extinction and waste) – explains the historical weakness of Japanese consumer identity. After all, it was around the waste of finite resources that consumers found a voice in nineteenth-century Britain and continued to do so in the late twentieth century in pursuit of sustainable consumption.

The genealogy of the consumer is not a linear story, nor does it converge. To be sure, we observe in the early twentieth century the expansion of the social body and set of practices (including social services) appropriated by consumers that foreshadows the controversial inflation of the consumer in recent neoliberal public policy. Citizenship and consumption became more frequently linked, but actors in different settings created different configurations working within different social and political traditions. Viewing the evolution of the consumer from multiple positions opens up some constructive perspectives for current debates over the place of consumers. Much of the debate in Europe, America and Asia has become stuck in the civic costs or benefits of neoliberal consumerism. Supporters present the introduction of market-style rational consumers in public services as a way of empowering citizens and democratizing public institutions, as well as of creating choice and efficiency. Critics warn that consumerism will unravel the sources and solidarities of citizenship themselves. It is tempting to see the twentieth century as a fall from grace of an earlier more civic-minded age of consumers, eroded by the power of profit, markets and individualism.

The modern genealogy of the consumer suggests a more cyclical and contingent story. There is no zero-sum game between market and politics. Starting the comparison between past and present in the mid-nineteenth century, for example, would reveal the importance of a small group of propertied men whose self-interest fused with a sense of public accountability in bounded spheres of consumption. Their agitation contrasts with a much larger spectrum of social movements that today speak out on a vast range of consumer interests, from nutrition to the environment, and from disadvantaged consumers to choice and media regulation. Starting the story in Britain before the First World War would highlight a dominant consumer interest much more committed to freedom of trade than the current landscape of consumer movements. Similarly, in the inter-war United States freedom of choice would appear to be part of a social ethics of civic consumption – not necessarily selfish consumerism. Starting the story elsewhere, however, say in early-twentieth-century China and Japan, might suggest not the fall but the recent rise of active consumers willing to speak their name. A multicentred understanding of the genealogy of the consumer not only sheds doubt about a US-centred story of convergence but also offers a more realistic view of the potential synapses between consumption and citizenship so often ignored by Western critics of consumerism.

Acknowledgements

Earlier versions of this chapter were presented at Cal Tech, the SSRC/ ABE workshops in New York and Tokyo, and the Institute of Historical Research (London). Thanks to all participants for discussion. For additional comments I should like to thank Mark Bevir, John Brewer, James Livesey, John Styles, Vanessa Taylor and Donald Winch, as well as colleagues in the Cultures of Consumption programme. Support from ESRC-AHRC grant no. L143341003 is gratefully acknowledged.

Notes

1. C. Offe, *Contradictions of the Welfare State* (Cambridge, 1984), p. 228.
2. D. Miller, 'Consumption as the Vanguard of History', in D. Miller (ed.), *Acknowledging Consumption* (London, 1995), pp. 1–57. For the vast and expanding literature, see also V. Zelizer, 'Culture and Consumption', in N.J. Smelser and R. Swedberg (eds), *The Handbook of Economic Sociology* (second edn, Princeton, NJ, 2005), pp. 331–54; M.K. Hogg (ed.), *Consumer Behaviour I: Research and Influences; vol. I: Consumer Behaviour as a Field of Study* (London, 2005); and the bibliography at: www.consume.bbk.ac.uk/publications.html.
3. D. Quataert (ed.), *Consumption Studies and the History of the Ottoman Empire, 1550–1922* (Albany, 2000), p. 1.
4. R.S. Lynd, 'Democracy's Third Estate: The Consumer', *Political Science Quarterly*, 51(4) (Dec. 1936), p. 496. A recent critique is B. Fine, *The World of Consumption* (London, 2002), second edn.
5. T.H. Breen, '"Baubles in Britain": The American and Consumer Revolutions of the Eighteenth Century', *Past and Present*, 119 (1988), pp. 73–104; Thomas Richards, *The Commodity Culture of Victorian Britain: Advertising and Spectacle, 1851–1914* (London, 1991); P.H. Hoffenberg, *An Empire on Display: English, Indian, and Australian Exhibitions from the Crystal Palace to the Great War* (Berkeley, 2001); C. Jones speaks of readers of local newspapers (*Affiches*) as consumers, 'The Great Chain of Buying: Medical Advertisement, the Bourgeois Public Sphere, and the Origins of the French Revolution', *American Historical Review*, CI(1) (Feb. 1996), pp. 13–40.
6. Recent research shows, for example, that Trinidadians are more likely to use the Internet as a 'cool' consumerist service that connected their Trinidadian identity to a sense of global culture, whereas Sri Lankans tend to view it more as an educational investment; D. Miller and D. Slater,

The Internet: An Ethnographic Approach (Oxford, 2000); D. Slater, 'Modernity under Construction: Building the Internet in Trinidad', in P. Brey, T. Misa and A. Rip (eds), *Modernity and Technology: The Empirical Turn* (Cambridge, MA, 2003).

7. To emphasize, the critical line of enquiry here focuses on how the consumer emerged as a category of identity and knowledge, through what traditions actors mobilized and established this category, regarding what claims, practices and relationships. The aim is to trace this developing reflexivity amongst actors. It shares Colin Campbell's plea to take actors' consciousness and the meaning of consumption for them more seriously than do studies which read back from consequences to intentions. However, because 'expressive goods' were important to the Romantic sensibility does not mean that these historical actors saw themselves as consumers; C. Campbell, *The Romantic Ethic and the Spirit of Modern Consumerism* (Oxford, 1987); C. Campbell, 'Understanding Traditional and Modern Patterns of Consumption in Eighteenth-century England: A Character-action Approach', in J. Brewer and R. Porter (eds), *Consumption and the World of Goods* (London, 1993), pp. 40–57. As recent sociologists of 'ordinary consumption' have shown, many forms of consumption have been and continue to be routine practices on which subjects do not reflect, or do not reflect as consumers. My concern here is to stimulate greater discussion about the history of how and when connections or disconnections between practice and identity and reflexivity occur. The impact of state policies or company policies on people's consumption behaviour or, vice versa, the political and economic consequences of people's consumption are equally legitimate but different types of enquiry. From the large literature, good starting points are V. de Grazia with E. Furlough (eds), *The Sex of Things: Gender and Consumption in Historical Perspective* (Berkeley, CA, 1996); M. Daunton and M. Hilton (eds), *The Politics of Consumption: Material Culture and Citizenship in Europe and America* (Oxford, 2001); H.-G. Haupt, *Konsum und Handel: Europa im 19. und 20. Jahrhundert* (Goettingen, 2002); E.D. Rappaport, *Shopping for Pleasure: Women and the Making of London's West End* (Princeton, NJ, 2000); S. Strasser, C. McGovern and M. Judt (eds), *Getting and Spending: European and American Consumer Societies in the Twentieth Century* (Cambridge, 1998). Just as consumption does not automatically create consumers, so the study of the politics of consumption needs to be differentiated from the study of self-conscious consumer politics, where the historically contingent potential of actors to understand themselves and others as consumers is switched on.

8. K. Pomeranz, *The Great Divergence: China, Europe and the Making of the Modern World Economy* (Princeton, NJ, 2000); R. Bin Wong, 'The Search for European Differences and Domination in the Early Modern World: A View from Asia', *American Historical Review*, 107 (2002); P. Parthasarthi, 'The Great Divergence', *Past and Present*, 176(1) (2002), pp. 275–93; M. Berg, 'In Pursuit of Luxury: Global History and British Consumer Goods in the Eighteenth Century', *Past and Present*, 181(1) (2004), pp. 85–142.

9. C. Shammas, *The Pre-industrial Consumer in England and America* (Oxford, 1990), pp. 111, 145ff., 224ff. See also C. Walsh, 'Social Meaning and Social Space in the Shopping Galleries of Early Modern London', in J. Benson and L. Ugolini (eds), *A Nation of Shopkeepers: Five Centuries of British Retailing* (London, 2003), pp. 52–79.

10. H.-J. Voth, 'Work and the Sirens of Consumption in Eighteenth-century London,' in M. Bianchi (ed.), *The Active Consumer: Novelty and Surprise in Consumer Choice* (London, 1998), pp. 143–73, and his *Time and Work in England 1750–1830* (Oxford, 2000).

11. J. Brewer, *Pleasures of the Imagination: English Culture in the Eighteenth Century* (New York, 1997); A. Vickery, *The Gentleman's Daughter: Women's Lives in Georgian England* (New Haven, 1998); M.C. Moran, 'The Commerce of the Sexes', in Frank Trentmann (ed.), *Paradoxes of Civil Society* (Oxford, second edn, 2003), pp. 61–84; M. North, *Genuss und Glück des Lebens: Kulturkonsum im Zeitalter der Aufklärung* (Cologne, Weimar and Vienna, 2003).

12. A. Smith, *The Wealth of Nations* (1776), BK. IV, VH. VIII, ed. E. Cannan (Chicago, 1904/1976), Vol. II, pp. 179.

13. K. Marx, 'On the Jewish Question' (1843), *Selected Essays*, trans. H.J. Stenning (London, 1926), pp. 75–85.

14. T.H. Breen, 'Narrative of Commercial Life: Consumption, Ideology, and Community on the Eve of the American Revolution', *The William and Mary Quarterly*, 50(3) (1993), pp. 471–501, cit. at p. 486. See now also T.H. Breen, *The Marketplace of Revolution: How Consumer Politics Shaped American Independence* (New York, 2004).

15. Breen, '"Baubles in Britain"', cit. at p. 76.

16. [J. Dickinson], *The Late Regulations Respecting the British Colonies on the Continent of America Considered* (London, 1766).

17. M. Sonenscher, *Work and Wages: Natural Law, Politics and the Eighteenth-Century French Trades* (Cambridge, 1989); J.A. Jaffe, 'Commerce, Character and Civil Society', *European Legacy*, VI(2) (April 2001), pp. 251–64; J. Bronstein, 'Land Reform and Political

Traditions in Nineteenth-century Britain and the United States', in M. Bevir and F. Trentmann (eds), *Critiques of Capital in Modern Britain and America: Transatlantic Exchanges* (London, 2002), pp. 26–48.

18. E.J. Sieyès, *Qu'est-ce que le Tiers Etat?* (1789).
19. D. Defoe, *A Plan of the English Commerce, Being a Compleat Prospect of the Trade of this Nation, as well the Home Trade as the Foreign* (1728; Oxford, 1928), pp. 144, 154.
20. M. Postlethwayt, *Britain's Commercial Interest Explained and Improved* (London, 1757), vol. 2, p. 411; *The Universal Dictionary of Trade and Commerce with Large Additions and Improvements, Adapting the Same to the Present State of British Affairs in America, since the Last Treaty of Peace Made in the Year 1763, incl. Savary's Dictionary* (London, 1766). Daniel Defoe, *The Complete English Tradesman: Directing him in the Several Parts and Progressions of Trade, from his First Entering upon Business, to his Leaving Off...*, 2 vols (London, 1738; London 1745); note Defoe once extends this characterization from purchaser to wearer or user of cloth, see 1738 edn, Vol. 1, p. 160. Bryan Edwards, *The History Civil and Commercial, of the British Colonies in the West Indies* (London, 1799). Anon., *Patriotic Competition against Self-interested Combination, Recommended; by a Union between the Nobility, the Landed, and Independent, Interest, the Clergy, and Consumer: with a View of Reducing Commodities from their Money, or Market Price, to their Real, or Labour, Price* (London, 1800). Nicholas Ling, *Antiquity; or the Wise Instructer* (York, 1770; York 1773); Nicholas Ling, *Wits Common-wealth: or, a Treasury of Divine, Moral, Historical and Political Adomonitions, Similies and Sentences* (London, 1722). The searchable 'Eighteenth-century Collections Online' contain over 150,000 English-Language works or 33 million pages of text.
21. D. Todd, 'Before Free Trade: Commercial Discourse and Politics in Early Nineteenth Century France,' in M. Daunton and F. Trentmann (eds), *Worlds of Political Economy* (London, 2004), pp. 54–7.
22. C.A. Bouton, *The Flour War: Gender, Class, and Community in Late Ancient Regime French Society* (University Park, 1993), pp. 83–5, 109; for exceptions (Terray in the 1770s), see S.L. Kaplan, *Bread, Politics and Political Economy in the Reign of Louis XV* (The Hague, 1976), 2 vols.
23. A.D. Leadley, 'Some Villains of the Eighteenth-century Market Place', in J. Rule (ed.), *Outside the Law: Studies in Crime and Order 1650–1850* (Exeter, 1982), p. 27.

24. 'Klage des Volkes', 'Publikum', 'Poebel'; 'Wir armen Arbeitsleute'; 'Junge', 'Etablierte', 'Greise, Knaben, Gesellen, Burschen, Maedchen und alte Weiber', from sources cit. in M. Gailus, *Strasse und Brot: Sozialer Protest in den deutschen Staaten unter besonderer Berücksichtigung Preussens, 1847–1849* (Göttingen, 1990), pp. 220, 242, 246, 255, 266ff., 271ff.

25. J.A. Jaffe, *Striking a Bargain: Work and Industrial Relations in England, 1815–1865* (Manchester, 2000).

26. J. Bronstein, *Land Reform and Working-class Experience in Britain and the United States, 1800–62* (Stanford, 1999); Bronstein, 'Land Reform and Political Traditions', in Bevir and Trentmann, *Critiques of Capital*, ch. 2.

27. See N. Thompson, 'Social Opulence, Private Asceticism: Ideas of Consumption in Early Socialist Thought', in Daunton and Hilton (eds), *The Politics of Consumption*, ch. 3.

28. G. Stedman Jones, 'Rethinking Chartism', in G. Stedman Jones, *Languages of Class: Studies in English Working Class History, 1832–1982* (Cambridge, 1983); G. Claeys, 'The Origins of the Rights of Labor: Republicanism, Commerce, and the Construction of Modern Social Theory in Britain, 1796–1805,' *Journal of Modern History*, 67(2) (1994), pp. 249–90; A. Clark, *The Struggle for the Breeches: Gender and the Making of the British Working Class* (London, 1995).

29. K. Davies, 'A Moral Purchase: Femininity, Commerce and Abolition, 1788–1792', in E. Eger and C. Grant (eds), *Women, Writing and the Public Sphere, 1700–1830* (Cambridge, 2001), p. 150.

30. R. Williams, 'Consumer', in *Keywords* (London, 1976), pp. 78f. Cf. R. Porter, 'Consumption: Disease of the Consumer Society?', in Brewer and Porter, *Consumption and the World of Goods*, pp. 58–81.

31. M. Berg and H. Clifford (eds), *Consumers and Luxury: Consumer Culture in Europe 1650–1850* (Manchester, 1999); M. Berg and E. Eger (eds), *Luxury in the Eighteenth Century: Debates, Desires and Delectable Goods* (Basingstoke, 2003). For the continuing ambivalence towards commercial consumption, see M. Finn, 'Working-class Women and the Contest for Consumer Control in Victorian County Courts', *Past and Present*, 161 (1998), pp. 116–54; M. Hilton, 'The Legacy of Luxury: Moralities of Consumption since the Eighteenth Century', *Journal of Consumer Culture*, 4(1) (2004), pp. 101–23; Erika Rappaport, *Shopping for Pleasure*, chs 2 and 3; P. Maclachlan and F. Trentmann, 'Civilising Markets: Traditions of Consumer Politics in Twentieth-century Britain, Japan, and the United States', in M. Bevir and F. Trentmann (eds),

Markets in Historical Contexts: Ideas and Politics in the Modern World (Cambridge, 2004), pp. 170–201.

32. C. Perrotta, *Consumption as an Investment I: The Fear of Goods from Hesiod to Adam Smith* (London, 2004), p. 240.
33. J. de Vries, 'Luxury in the Dutch Golden Age in Theory and Practice', in Berg and Eger, *Luxury*, p. 51. For a different interpretation of the attitudes to luxury, stressing Calvinism, see S. Schama, *The Embarrassment of Riches* (Berkeley, CA, 1988). See also Campbell, *Romantic Ethic.*
34. De Vries, 'Luxury', p. 53.
35. For the demoralization of luxury, see C.J. Berry, *The Idea of Luxury: A Conceptual and Historical Investigation* (Cambridge, 1994), pp. 108ff.
36. D. Hume, *Essays, Moral, Political and Literary* (1742, OUP 1963 edn), p. 270.
37. Hume, *Essays*, p. 269.
38. Hume, *Essays*, p. 284.
39. E.g., A. Daye, *The English Secretorie Wherein is contained a pefect Method, for the inditing of all manner of Epistles and familiar Letters* (1586), p. 225: Warning to a young man that in a City 'so ordinarilye frequented as is that City wherein you are, and being in fellowship with so many and diuers sorts of men as you now be, conuersing also with the innumberalbe multitudes of persons, of all estates, condictions and faculties, as you there doe, It is no difficult thing for a young youth of your birth and qualitie to be led into lewdness, of a wanton to become dissolute, of a spender to be made a consumer, nor of a towardly Gentleman, to be framed to an untowarde companion'.
40. *The Coal Traders and Consumers Case* (c. 1692); L. Duckworth, *The Consumer's Handbook of the Law Relating to Gas, Water, and Electric Lighting* (London, 1903).
41. *Preiss-Satzung, Nach welcher die aus denen Churfuerstl. Taback-Consumptions-Factorien zur Abnahm vorgelegte Sorten von denen Handels-Leuthen und craemeren hinwiderumben an den Consumenten und gemeinen Mann in Minuto abzugeben seynd* (1745). Excise duties and *consumptions-accise* were often used synonymously in the eighteenth century; see U. Wyrwa, 'Consumption and Consumer Society', in Strasser *et al.* (eds), *Getting and Spending*, pp. 432f., a discussion that unfortunately muddles the history of 'consumption' in Germany with that of 'consumer society'. Cf. J. Brewer, 'The Error of Our Ways: Historians and the Birth of Consumer Society' (2003) at: www.consume.bbk.ac.uk/publications.html.

42. S. Rowlands, *A Terrible Battell Betweene the Two Consumers of the Whole World: Time, and Death* (London, 1606). See also J. Clare, the poet (1793–1864): 'I am the self-consumer of my woes.'

43. Disraeli, *Coningsby* (1844), p. 174. Cf. R. Greene, *Gwydonius* (1584); J. Hind, *Eliosto Libidinoso* (1606). In France consumption had a less destructive meaning; there are early-nineteenth-century references to the 'consommateur' as someone who perfects things, see E. Furlough, *Consumer Cooperation in France: The Politics of Consumption, 1834–1930* (Ithaca, 1991), p. 200.

44. I. Iselin, *Versuch ueber die gesellige Ordnung* (Basle, 1772), 'aus Kaeufern und Verkaeufern, aus Verbrauchern oder Verzehrern und Herrvorbringern oder Arbeitern'.

45. The multiple and competing meanings of consumption in the econ-omic literature continued to be a subject of complaint into the 1920s; H. Mayer, 'Konsumtion', in *Handwoerterbuch der Staatswissen-schaften*, L. Elster, A. Weber and F. Wieser (eds), fourth edn (Jena, 1923), vol. V, pp. 867–74.

46. J.B. Say, *Traité d'économie* (Paris, 1841), III, ch. 2.; an inclusion that had its supporters until the turn of the twentieth century, e.g. W. Lexis, G. Schönberg (ed.), *Handbuch der politischen Oekonomie* (Tübingen, 1890), Vol. I, Part 2, ch. XII, p. 750; F.B.W. Herrmann, *Staatswirt-schaftliche Untersuchungen* (Munich, 1870); K. Apelt, *Die Konsumtion der wichtigsten Kulturlaender in den letzten Jahrzehnten: eine statistisch-volkswirtschaftliche Studie* (Berlin, 1899). In the late nineteenth century Charles Gide spoke out against the frequent fusing of consumption and production, as when Jevons saw eating as production for a worker, C. Gide, *Cours d'économie politique*, third edn, Eng. trans. *Political Economy* (London, 1914), p. 694. Nineteenth-century concepts derived from the analysis of production and land would also inform neoclassical concepts, such as consumers' rent.

47. T. Malthus, *Principles of Economics* (1820), vol. 8, p. 119. Cf. J.S. Mill, *Principles of Political Economy*, section V, ch. 3, and the discussion in M. Blaug, *Economic Theory in Retrospect* (Cambridge, fifth edn 1997), pp. 168–75.

48. M.J. Bowman, 'The Consumer in the History of Economic Doctrine', *American Economic Review*, 41(2) (1951), pp. 1–18.

49. J.S. Mill, *Essays on Some Unsettled Questions of Political Economy* (London, 1844), p. 132.

50. For this underlying difference in theories of value, see D. Winch, 'The Problematic Status of the Consumer in Orthodox Economic Thought',

in F. Trentmann (ed.), *The Making of the Consumer: Knowledge, Power and Identity in the Modern World* (Oxford and New York, 2006), pp. 34–8.

51. J. Ruskin, *'Unto This Last': Four Essays on the First Principles of Political Economy* (Orpington, 1877), esp. pp. 153, 170ff.

52. N. Rose, *Powers of Freedom: Reframing Political Thought* (Cambridge, 1999). The diversity of images of the consumer created is recognized by P. Miller and N. Rose, 'Mobilizing the Consumer: Assembling the Subject of Consumption', *Theory, Culture and Society*, 14(1) (1997), pp. 1–36. Contemporary citizens have been more critical, resistant or apathetic to the public discourse of the consumer than is often presumed, see J. Clarke, N. Smith and E. Vidler, 'Consumerism and the Reform of Public Services: Inequalities and Instabilities', in M. Powell, L. Bauld and K. Clarke (eds), *Social Policy Review 17* (Bristol, 2005).

53. For a survey of work on consumption in micro- and macro-economic work, see A. Deaton's entry on consumers' expenditure, *New Palgrave*, pp. 592–607. In contrast to standard modern consumer theory, Marshall had a distinct sense of the consumer as a dynamic individual whose activities created new wants (not vice versa) and as a social actor whose pursuit of distinction was in part shaped by peer groups, *Principles of Economics* (London, 1895), book III, ch. 2; see G.M.P. Swann, 'Marshall's Consumer as an Innovator', in S.C. Dow and P.E. Earl (eds), *Economic Organization and Economic Knowledge, I* (Cheltenham, 1999), pp. 98–118.

54. W.S. Jevons, *Theory of Political Economy* (London, 1879), p. 43.

55. J.N. Keynes, *The Scope and Method of Political Economy* (London, 1904, third rev. edn, first 1891), p. 111. Note professional economics was still divided on this question in the inter-war years, see P.T. Homan, 'Consumption', in *Encyclopedia of the Social Sciences* (New York, 1930; 1949 repr.), p. 295, an entry that shows how far utility theory still was from having attained hegemony.

56. R.H. Inglis Palgrave (ed.), *Dictionary of Political Economy* (London, 1894), Vol. I, entry on consumers' goods; there is no separate entry for consumer.

57. M. Freeden (ed.), *Reappraising J. A. Hobson* (London, 1990); F. Trentmann, 'Commerce, Civil Society, and the "Citizen-Consumer"', in *Paradoxes of Civil Society*, pp. 312–15. Altruism and other-regarding motives also played a more significant role amongst professional economists than is often recognized, see H. Pearson, 'Economics and Altruism at the Fin de Siècle', in Daunton and Trentmann (eds), *Worlds of Political Economy*, pp. 24–46.

58. S.N. Patten, *The Consumption of Wealth* (Philadelphia, 1889) and *The Theory of Prosperity* (New York, 1902). For Patten, as for German historical economists, the state had an obligation to discourage the waste of national resources, a position that led him to support tariffs to reduce 'inefficient consumption'. For all his attention to consumption, the consumer is not yet a master category for Patten, who prefers to speak of 'the people' or 'society'. See also D.M. Fox, *The Discovery of Abundance: Simon N. Patten and the Transformation of Social Theory* (Ithaca, 1967); D. Horowitz, *The Morality of Spending: Attitudes Towards the Consumer Society in America, 1875–1940* (Chicago, 1992), pp. 30–49; A.R. Schäfer, 'German Historicism, Progressive Social Thought, and the Interventionist State in the US since the 1880s', in Bevir and Trentmann (eds), *Markets in Historical Contexts*, ch. 8.

59. John Neville Keynes had read Roscher.

60. M. v. Prittwitz, *Die Kunst reich zu werden, oder gemeinfassliche Darstellung der Volkswirtschaft* (Mannheim, 1840), pp. 471–552. Significantly, he speaks for the first time of 'Consumenten' in the context of state expenditure and taxes.

61. W. Roscher, *Principles of Political Economy*, vol. II, trans. J.J. Lalor (New York, 1878), trans. of thirteenth German edn of 1877, pp. 185f., 230ff.; Prittwitz, *Kunst*, pp. 488f.

62. Roscher, *Principles*, pp. 191, 230, 241.

63. Prittwitz, *Kunst*, p. 485. See also Roscher: 'The act of saving, if the consumption omitted was a productive one, is detrimental to the common good.' Yet to let consumers rule everything would mean 'utmost cheapness ... universal superfluity', *Principles*, section CCXVIII.

64. K. Oldenberg, 'Die Konsumtion', ch. III, in *Grundriss der Sozialökonomie, II: Die natuerlichen und technischen Beziehungen der Wirtschaft*, eds Fr. Von Gottl-Ottlilienfeld, H. Herkner, A. Hettner, R. Michels, P. Mombert and K. Oldenberg (Tübingen, 1914), pp. 103–64, cit. at p. 123; my translation. Oldenberg, who feared Germany's growing dependence on agricultural states like the United States and China, took the leading Anglophile liberal Lujo Brentano to task for not adequately highlighting the significance of patriotism and religion in shaping people's needs. Significantly, Brentano wrote his *Versuch einer Theorie der Beduerfnisse* (Munich, 1908) without an analytical category of the consumer. While he shared Gossen's and Marshall's emphasis on the unlimited nature of human needs, his discussion of the hierarchy of needs ends in a warning about the dangerous consequences of affluence and passive enjoyment, which lead to a numbing of the soul

and character, in contrast to self-fulfilment and social advance, which come from sacrifice and an act of will that cannot be purchased.

65. Oldenberg, 'Konsumtion', pp. 119, 124.

66. Similarly, miners' cooperatives, e.g. the Konsumverein rheinisch-westfaelischer Bergleute Glückauf; M. Prinz, *Brot und Dividende. Konsumvereine in Deutschland und England vor 1914* (Göttingen, 1996), esp. pp. 235ff. See also P. Gurney, *Co-operative Culture and the Politics of Consumption in England, 1870–1930* (Manchester, 1996); E. Furlough and C. Strikwerda (eds), *Consumers against Capitalism?* (Oxford, 1999).

67. See Furlough, *Consumer Cooperation in France*, esp. for the long influence of Fourier.

68. *The Gladstone Diaries*, ed. H.C.G. Matthew, vol. X, 30 June 1883 (Oxford, 1990), p. 467.

69. *The Times* (London), 2 January 1913, p. 8.

70. *Justitia, The Queen and the Constitution, the Producer and the Consumer, or Protection, What Is It, and Where to Put It* (London, 1851). *Brockhaus* (1852); note Grimm's *Woerterbuch*, Vol. 12 (1886) still did not have an entry on *Verbraucher* or *Konsument*.

71. T. Billington Greig, *The Consumer in Revolt* (London, 1912).

72. L. Glickman, 'Buy for the Sake of the Slave: Abolitionism and the Origins of American Consumer Activism', *American Quarterly*, 56(4) (2004), pp. 889–912; C. Sussman, *Consuming Anxieties: Consumer Protest, Gender and British Slavery, 1713–1833* (Stanford, CA, 2000).

73. J. Fenimore Cooper, *The Crater, or, Vulcan's Peak* (1847), p. 123. In *Homeward Bound* (1838) he speaks of 'factors' as regular agents between 'common producer and the common consumer', p. 54; Cooper is still employing the older usage in *The Monikins* (1835), where Miss Poke is a 'desperate consumer of snuff and religion', p. 115. A. Trollope's novels show the expanding social canvas on which the consumer is projected in the mid-Victorian period, moving from basic provision of bread and corn to goods more widely. In *The Warden* (1855) the protagonist's worry that he might be seen as that 'unjust griping priest' articulated itself as the fear of being pointed at 'as the consumer of the bread of the poor'. In the *Eustace Diamonds* (1873) we find Greystock thinking of himself as a 'spender of much money and a consumer of many good things'; A. Trollope, *The Warden*, p. 140; *The Eustace Diamonds*, p. 115.

74. In Wolverhampton in 1847 over 80 per cent of gas consumption was for commercial use, with an additional 13 per cent used by streetlights,

and only 2 per cent used in (wealthier) households; percentages based on cubic feet cited in M. Daunton, 'The Material Politics of Natural Monopoly', in *Politics of Consumption*, p. 76.

75. See Daunton, 'Natural Monopoly', esp. pp. 70ff.; M. Daunton, *Trusting Leviathan: The Politics of Taxation in Britain, 1799–1914* (Cambridge, 2001), pp. 266ff.; D. Owen, *The Government of Victorian London, 1855–1889: The Metropolitan Board of Works, the Vestries, and the City Corporation*, ed. Roy MacLeod (Cambridge, 1982), pp. 140 ff.

76. Anon., *Are the Citizens of London to have better Gas, and more of it, for Less Money? A Dialogue between (C.P.) Mr. Charles Pearson and (G.C.) a Gas Consumer of the City*, 16 February 1849 (London, 1849), p. 5. See also J.F.B. Firth, *The Gas Supply of London* (London, 1874).

77. The following draws on F. Trentmann and V. Taylor, 'From Users to Consumers: Water Politics in Nineteenth-century London,' in Trentmann (ed.), *Making of the Consumer*, pp. 53–79.

78. C. Hamlin, *Public Health and Social Justice in the Age of Chadwick: Britain, 1800–54* (Cambridge, 1998).

79. See R. Millward, 'The Political Economy of Urban Utilities', in Martin Daunton (ed.), *The Cambridge Urban History of Britain, III: 1840–1950* (Cambridge, 2000), pp. 315–49.

80. [J. Wright], *The Dolphin: or, Grand Junction Nuisance* (London, 1827), pp. 6f. The complaint here was directed at the ways in which companies at the time of monopolistic consolidation in 1817 handed over customers to each other.

81. *The Times*, 20 December 1883, p. 6e.

82. Public Record Office (PRO), London, MH 29/6, Clapham, Stockwell and South Lambeth Water Consumers' Defence Association, Jan. 1884.

83. *The Times*, 7 May 1884, p. 5e.

84. PRO, MH 29/5, 'Notice to Consumers and Sanitary Authorities', East London Waterworks Company, 2 Aug. 1883. Note the recent battles over rights, waste and educating consumers in South Africa and New Zealand discussed by Bronwen Morgan in this volume.

85. PRO, MH 29/5, Monthly Report by Frank Bolton, July 1883, pp. 1f.

86. [J. Wright], *The Dolphin*, p. 8; W. Matthews, *Hydraulia: An Historical and Descriptive Account of the Water Works of London* (London, 1835), pp. 332f.

87. 'The Eastern Question Must Be Settled' (1898), East London Water Consumers' Defence Association, poster in PRO, COPY 1, 143 folio 165. The battle over water eventually led to the establishment of the Metropolitan Water Board in 1902, a Conservative triumph that

included representatives from outer and inner London on the board, with favourable terms of arbitration for the companies, defeating the hopes of liberal reformers who wanted municipal management of the water supply in the hands of the London County Council; see A.K. Mukhopadhyay, *Politics of Water Supply: The Case of Victorian London* (Calcutta, 1981), chs 3 and 4. For ratepayers' associations' growing rebelliousness, see A. Offer, *Property and Politics, 1870–1914: Landownership, Law, Ideology and Urban Development in England* (Cambridge, 1981), pp. 295ff.

88. See F. Trentmann, 'National Identity and Consumer Politics: Free Trade and Tariff Reform', in P.K. O'Brien and D. Winch (eds), *The Political Economy of British Historical Experience, 1688–1914* (Oxford, 2002), pp. 215–42.

89. *Speeches on the Questions of Public Policy by Richard Cobden* (London, third edn, 1908). The inventor Charles Baggage argued (in vain) for the display of prices at the Great Exhibition, noting that 'all men are *consumers*, and as such their common bond of interest is to purchase every thing in the *cheapest* market', *The Exposition of 1851 or, Views of the Industry, the Science, and the Government of England* (London, 1851), p. 44. Contemporaries sometimes talked of 'consuming nations', not individuals or social groups.

90. F. Bastiat, *Sophismes Économiques* (Paris, 1846), p. 49. Bastiat's *What is Seen and What is not Seen: or, Political Economy in one lesson* appeared in newspapers and book form in 1859; selections from his *Sophisms* and *Essays on Political Economy* went through several people's editions in the 1870s and 1880s. Famously, Bastiat's last recorded words on his deathbed in 1850 were: 'We must learn to look at everything from the point of view of the consumer.' As Charles Gide noted, such statements were politically stillborn since, after all, it was presumed that free competition would automatically make for consumers' greatest satisfaction: 'The consumer, like a king, has only to let himself be served.' Gide, *Political Economy* (*Cours d'économie politique*), p. 700.

91. See now L. Nead, *Victorian Babylon: People, Streets and Images in Nineteenth Century London* (New Haven, 2000); C. Breward, *The Hidden Consumer: Masculinities, Fashion and City Life 1860–1914* (Manchester, 1999). Cf. L. Auslander, *Taste and Power: Furnishing Modern France* (Berkeley, 1996), pp. 21, 277f.; S. Kroen, 'Der Aufstieg des Kundenbürgers? Eine politische Allegorie für unsere Zeit', in M. Prinz (ed.), *Der lange Weg in den Überfluss: Anfänge und Entwicklung der Konsumgesellschaft seit der Vormoderne* (Paderborn, 2003), pp. 540–51.

92. Bristol University Archive, DM 669 Free Trade Union, leaflet no. 328, 24 Nov. 1909. See also ibid., leaflet no. 310. Note that again the consumer here is not necessarily the end-user, as some of the gloves and shoes on display are ladies' articles. It is debatable whether, because of the language of separate spheres, the consumer became fixed on women, as Furlough has argued, *Consumer Cooperation*, pp. 20 ff., 219 ff.; note, e.g., the 1893 cooperative illustration of the male *pauvre consommateur* crushed by the weight of overcharging retailers and wholesalers, ibid., p. 87. In France, Hubertine Auclert argued in 1908 *(Le Vote des femmes)* that women as producers and consumers should have the vote because they were taxed, see Auslander, *Taste and Power*, p. 296. Similarly, in the United States J.W. Sullivan, *Markets for the People: The Consumer's Part* (New York, 1913), addresses male and female consumers. See also the photos of the man examining a shirt, representing the 'American consumer', in *Building America*, II, 6 (March 1937), p. 3.

93. B.S. Rowntree, *Poverty: A Study in Town Life* (London, 1901); *Erhebung von Wirtschaftsrechnungen minderbemittelter Familien im Deutschen Reiche. Bearb. Im Kaiserlichen Statistischen Amte* (Berlin, 1909) (Reichs-Arbeitsblatt, 2. Sonderheft); M. Halbwachs, *La Classe ouvrière et les niveaux de vie* (Paris, 1912); M. Bulmer, K. Bales and K.K. Sklar (eds), *The Social Survey in Historical Perspective, 1880–1940* (Cambridge, 1991); R. Spree, 'Knappheit und differentieller Konsum während des ersten Drittels des 20. Jahrhunderts in Deutschland', in Hansjörg Siegenthaler (ed.), *Ressourcenverknappung als Problem der Wirtschaftsgeschichte*, Schriften des Vereins für Socialpolitik, Vol. 192 (Berlin, 1990), pp. 171–221.

94. 'Nurkonsumentenstandpunkt', 'erster Linie Konsumenten', Albrecht Patzig, 1905, cit. in C. Nonn, *Verbraucherprotest und Parteiensystem im wilhelminischen Deutschland* (Düsseldorf, 1996), pp. 76, 78; see now also C. Torp, *Die Herausforderung der Globalisierung: Wirtschaft und Politik in Deutschland, 1860–1914* (Göttingen, 2005), pp. 245–51. As late as 1934 Arthur Feiler noted that '[f]or a long time, in Germany at least, the best means of discrediting some measure of economic policy in the opinion of the public was to argue that it was "consumer's policy" only. Such an argument is still effective to a great extent', 'The Consumer in Economic Policy', *Social Research*, 1:1/4 (1934), p. 287.

95. E. von Knebel-Doeberitz, 'Die Aufgabe und Pflicht der Frau als Konsument', in *Hefte der Freien Kirchlich-Sozialen Konferenz*, Heft 40 (Berlin, 1907), p. 41. For a similar disjunction of identities in France,

see M.-E. Chessel, 'Women and the Ethics of Consumption in France at the Turn of the Twentieth Century: The *Ligue Sociale d'Acheteurs*', in Trentmann (ed.), *Making of the Consumer*, pp. 81–98.

96. B. Strauß, *Die Konsumtionswirtschaft: Ihre Parallelentwicklung mit der Frauenberufsfrage* (Leipzig, 1929), pp. 59–62.

97. This paragraph draws on K. Gerth, *China Made: Consumer Culture and the Creation of the Nation* (Cambridge, MA, 2003), cit. at p. 118, albeit with a different interpretation. Thanks to Karl Gerth for additional discussion.

98. S. Cochran, *Big Business in China: Sino-Foreign Rivalry in the Cigarette Industry, 1890–1930* (Cambridge, MA, 1980), pp. 68–77.

99. By comparison, the pavillon of the Empire Marketing Board at the Cardiff Empire Exhibition in 1928 was visited by a record 70,833; S. Constantine, 'Bringing the Empire Alive', in J.M. MacKenzie, *Imperialism and Popular Culture* (Manchester, 1986), p. 207.

100. Cit. in Gerth, *China Made*, p. 296.

101. Cit. in Gerth, *China Made*, pp. 103, 105, 139, 175, 239, 253. 'Consumer' (*xiaofeiren*) was rarely used.

102. L.B. Glickman, *A Living Wage: American Workers and the Making of Consumer Society* (Ithaca, 1997).

103. E. Carter, *How German Is She? Postwar West German Reconstruction and the Consuming Woman* (Ann Arbor, 1997). The new cultural ascendancy of the consumer in the 1950s, however, did not create any institutionalized recognition of the consumer as political actor, as Ludwig Erhard relied on markets and competition policy; H. Schröter, 'Konsumpolitik und "soziale Marktwirtschaft"', in H. Berghoff (ed.), *Konsumpolitik: Die Regulierung des Privaten Verbrauchs im 20. Jahundert* (Göttingen, 1999), pp. 113–33.

104. L. Nelson, *Measured Excess: Status, Gender, and Consumer Nationalism in South Korea* (New York, 2000), pp. 110ff.; S. Garon, 'Luxury Is the Enemy: Mobilizing Savings and Popularizing Thrift in Wartime Japan', *Journal of Japanese Studies*, 26(1) (2000), pp. 41–78; L. Trivedi, 'Visually Mapping the "Nation": Swadeshi Politics in Nationalist India, 1920–1930', *The Journal of Asian Studies*, 62(1) (2003), pp. 11–41; S. Garon and P.L. Maclachlan (eds), *The Ambivalent Consumer: Questioning Consumption in East Asia and the West* (Ithaca, NY, forthcoming 2006). See also the chapter by Garon in this volume.

105. Rappaport, *Shopping for Pleasure*.

106. See F. Trentmann, 'Commerce, Civil Society, and the "Citizen-consumer"', pp. 307–19.

107. K.K. Sklar, '"The Consumers" White Label Campaign of the National Consumers' League, 1898–1918', in Strasser *et al.* (eds), *Getting and Spending*, pp. 17–35; Chessel, 'Women and the Ethics of Consumption in France'. For the recent revival of ethical consumerism, see R. Sassatelli in this volume.

108. R. Schloesser, *Konsumentenkammern* (Cologne, 1916); for him the consumer was not everyone but referred to people who had an overwhelming interest in consumption. The transformation of the consumer into the private individual end-user was not yet complete in Weimar Germany, where industrial users and coal dealers, for example, posed as a consumer interest in the Coal Council; Feiler, 'The Consumer in Economic Policy', p. 296.

109. W. Rathenau, *Von Kommenden Dingen* (Berlin, 1917), pp. 39, 90, 131ff.

110. An advisory council was introduced in Britain in the latter stages of the war. Consumers (including industrial consumers) were represented on the National Economic Council in post-war Germany, while consumer organizations also gained representation at state level, as in Hamburg in 1923. For conflict during the war, see B.J. Davis, *Home Fires Burning: Food, Politics, and Everyday Life in World War 1 Berlin* (Chapel Hill, NC, 2000). For the anti-Semitic attack on profiteers in Germany, see M.H. Geyer, 'Teuerungsprotest, Konsumentenpolitik und soziale Gerechtigkeit waehrend der Inflation: Muenchen, 1920–1923', *Archiv fuer Sozialgeschichte*, 30 (1990), pp. 181–215. The anti-corporate bias of consumer groups in the United States in the 1930s also fed on war and post-war grievances against profiteering. For consumer protests in Spain, see T. Kaplan, 'Female Consciousness and Collective Action: The Case of Barcelona, 1910–1918', *Signs: Journal of Women in Culture and Society*, 7(3) (1982), pp. 545–66.

111. F. Trentmann, 'Bread, Milk and Democracy: Consumption and Citizenship in Twentieth-Century Britain', in Daunton and Hilton (eds), *Politics of Consumption*, pp. 129–63; C. Nonn, 'Vom Konsumentenprotest zum Konsens', in Berghoff, *Konsumpolitik*, pp. 30ff.

112. H. Macmillan, *The Middle Way: A Study of the Problem of Economic and Social Progress in a Free and Democratic Society* (London, 1938).

113. *The Times*, 24 Dec. 1936, p. 9. M.J. Dollard, 'Developing the Intelligent Consumer of Art', *Design*, 37(7) (Jan. 1936), p. 28.

114. *Final Report of the Mixed Committee of the League of Nations on the Relation of Nutrition to Health, Agriculture, and Economic Policy* (League of Nations Document No. A. 13. 1937. II. A.); E.M.H. Lloyd, *Stabilisation: An Economic Policy for Producers and Consumers*

(London, 1923); C. Delisle Burns, 'The Need for National and International Planning', in *The Problems of Peace: Lectures Delivered at the Geneva Institute of International Relations at the Palais des Nations, August 1932* (London, 1933).

115. See W.H. Hutt, *Economists and the Public: A Study of Competition and Opinion* (London, 1936), and the discussion in J. Persky, 'Consumer Sovereignty', *Journal of Economic Perspectives*, 7(1) (Winter 1993), pp. 183–91. Hutt was a critic of Keynesianism.

116. H.M. Kallen, *The Decline and Rise of the Consumer: A Philosophy of Consumer Cooperation* (New York, 1936), pp. 14f., 94. In Germany neoliberals' reaction to totalitarianism also upgraded the positive contribution of the 'consuming desires of consumers' – like Kallen, Röpke in 1942 saw the danger of totalitarian states in their attempt to emancipate themselves from consumers, *Die Gesellschaftskrise der Gegenwart* (Zurich, 1942).

117. L. Cohen, *A Consumers' Republic: The Politics of Mass Consumption in Postwar America* (New York, 2003); Kroen, 'Aufstieg des Kundenbürgers?', pp. 554–64; M. Hilton, *Consumerism in Twentieth-century Britain: The Search for a Historical Movement* (Cambridge, 2003). See now also V. de Grazia, *Irresistible Empire: America's Advance through 20th-century Europe* (Cambridge, MA, 2005), and S. Kroen's chapter in this volume.

118. Gide, *Political Economy*, pp. 700f.

119. Furlough, *Consumer Cooperation in France*, pp. 275ff. See also G. Cross, *Time and Money: The Making of Consumer Culture* (London, 1993).

120. W.E. Williams and A.E. Heath, *Learn to Live: The Consumer's View of Adult Education* (London, 1936), a study of students at Ruskin College and the WEA, co-funded by the Carnegie Corporation.

121. H. Harap, 'Survey of Twenty-eight Courses in Consumption', in *The School Review* (Sept. 1937), pp. 497–507; J.E. Mendenhall and C. Maurice Wieting, 'Consumer Education through the Curriculum', *Journal of Educational Sociology*, XI(7) (March 1938), pp. 398–404.

122. *The Consumer*, no. 3 (15 November 1935): 11. 1/5 to ¼ of 'everyman's income' went on housing. This broader public definition of the consumer went alongside an explicit rejection of an older tradition in women's movements to present the consumer as the women with the basket.

123. *Punch, or the London Charivari*, 25 April 1934, p. 467.

124. J. Maynard Keynes, 'Economic Possibilities for Our Grandchildren' (1930), in *Essays in Persuasion* (London, 1984), pp. 328f.

125. B. Webb, *The Discovery of the Consumer* (London, 1928), pp. 4f.
126. Webb, *Discovery*, p. 22.
127. Webb, *Discovery*, p. 23.
128. Webb's example, it may be interesting to note, was healthcare, a subject that under New Labour is now moving fast in the direction of markets, consumers and choice.
129. Webb, *Discovery*, pp. 25f.
130. Cohen, *Consumers' Republic*.
131. M. Jacobs, '"How About Some Meat": The Office of Price Administration, Consumption Politics, and State Building from the Bottom Up, 1941–1946', *The Journal of American History*, 84(3) (1997), pp. 910–41, and now M. Jacobs, *Pocketbook Politics: Economic Citizenship in Twentieth-century America* (Princeton, NJ, 2005).
132. L. Glickman, 'The Strike in the Temple of Consumption: Consumer Activism and Twentieth-century American Political Culture', *The Journal of American History*, 88 (2001), pp. 99–128; H. Rao, 'Caveat Emptor: The Construction of Nonprofit Consumer Watchdog Organizations', *American Journal of Sociology*, 103(4) (1998), pp. 912–61; C. Beauchamp, 'Getting Your Money's Worth: American Models for the Remaking of the Consumer Interest in Britain, 1930s–1960s', in Bevir and Trentmann, *Critiques of Capital*, pp. 127–50; M. Hilton, 'The Fable of the Sheep, or, Private Virtues, Public Vices: The Consumer Revolution of the Twentieth Century,' *Past and Present*, 176(1) (2002), pp. 229ff.; Hilton, *Consumerism*.
133. F.W. Inenfeldt, 'Teaching Consumer Buying in the Secondary School', *Journal of Home Economics*, 26(5) (1934), p. 280; M. East, *Home Economics: Past, Present, and Future* (Boston, 1980), p. 48; L. Bader and J.P. Wernette, 'Consumer Movements and Business', *The Journal of Marketing*, III(1) (July 1938), p. 10.
134. H. Kyrk, *Economic Problems of the Family* (1929; New York, 1933), pp. 396, chap. 5, 19, 22, 23, cit. at 393, 396.
135. H. Kyrk, *A Theory of Consumption* (London, 1923), which won the first prize, $1,000, offered by Messrs Hart, Schaffner and Marx of Chicago.
136. Kyrk, *Theory of Consumption*, pp. 1f.
137. R. Williams, *Keywords: A Vocabulary of Culture and Society* (1976; London, 1983), pp. 78f.; T.W. Adorno and M. Horkheimer, *Dialectic of Enlightenment* (London, 1979); S. Ewen, *Captains of Consciousness: Advertising and the Social Roots of the Consumer Culture* (New York, 1976).

−3−

Brand Management and the Productivity of Consumption

Adam Arvidsson

The distinction between 'production' and 'consumption' has been central to modern social theory. 'Production' has generally been identified with (mostly male) wage labour, while 'consumption' has encompassed reproduction, recreation and leisurely or hedonistic pursuits that have transpired beyond the command of the wage relation. It did not matter much whether these activities involved investments of energy or effort, or whether they actually produced things (as in the case of the toils of the housewife or the stylish productivity of youth culture). Consumption was in any case posited as the antinomy of production, the site where values were used up or destroyed. To the extent that the productive dimensions of consumer practice were actually recognized, they were generally seen as either residual elements of an earlier mode of production to eventually be rationalized away (as in the case of the reproductive labour of the housewife), or as irrational investments of productive energies into the escapist and ultimately passive pleasures of a commodified mass culture, as in the case of Richard Hoggart's 'Juke-box Boys'.[1] For both Marxists and non-Marxists it seemed obvious that the material production of commodities also produces value, while the circulation of commodities does not. That way, thinkers as diverse as John Kenneth Galbraith and Ernst Mandel could agree in denouncing investments in facilitating the circulation process, like advertising and 'the sales effort' in general, as wasteful and irrational.[2]

Today that distinction is crumbling. Sociologists have pointed at the productive dimensions of consumer practice since the impact of Cultural Studies in the mid-1970s. Anthropologists, historians, cultural geographers and, ultimately, academic marketing scholars have followed suit. Consequently, it has become standard practice to think of consumers as active and creative, and of consumption as a productive practice where immaterial use-values like identity, community and common meaning systems are created.[3] More importantly, there are also signs that many productive consumer practices have come to produce commercially realizable values in more or less direct ways. In these cases consumption is not just something that transpires outside of, or in opposition to, the capitalist production process – a place where, as Daniel Miller argues, the meaning and empowerment not available in the workplace can be found. Rather the production of immaterial wealth through consumer practices – the 'making love in supermarkets', to use Miller's fortunate term – has come to directly contribute to the self-valorization of capital; it has itself become part of its extended reproduction process.[4]

This tendency to extend the capitalist production process to include phenomena that were formerly thought to belong to leisure, private life or the 'domain of circulation', to use a Marxian term, is not limited to consumption. A similar fusion of 'production' and 'consumption' is visible in phenomena like the blurring of work and leisure that marks the lived reality of the new 'symbol analytical' professional classes, for whom the 'network sociality' of social events and the pursuit of 'culturally mobile' forms of consumption have come to feed directly into the 'entrepreneurial' production of a professional self with an attractive market position.[5] It is visible in aspects of the 'online economy' like dating sites or Massive Multiplayer Online Role-Playing Games (MMORPGs), where play, flirtation and other forms of user interaction are what actually produce the attractive content to which the sites in question sell access.[6] It is visible in the growing importance of lottery games and pyramid schemes, and new forms of direct valorization of the faith and religious belief, like the prosperity gospels or the other forms of 'money magic' that have become an important aspect of 'Millennial Capitalism'.[7] It is visible in the new strategic importance of intellectual property rights and the present tendency towards the appropriation and privatization of common resources, like genetic information or bio-diversity. There, in Morris-Suzuki's words, 'the direct exploitation of labour is becoming less important as a source of profit and the private exploitation of social knowledge is becoming more important'.[8] In all of these areas activities connected to the social circulation of commodities have come to contribute directly to both the production of wealth and the extraction of surplus value.[9] One prominent example of this tendency to posit consumption as an economically productive activity, as a form of labour, is contemporary brand management.

Before taking on the central argument of this chapter it might be worthwhile to embark on a short *excursus* on the complicated argument of value. The expansion of the capitalist production process to include a range of activities connected to the circulation and consumption of commodities tends to problematize central categories of political economy like 'consumption' and 'production', 'labour' and 'value'. This semantic insecurity is not only an academic matter but also grounded in a real contingency (or even crisis) of the value-form itself: to count as 'productive labour' (in the Marxian sense) an activity must not only produce use-value; it must also add to the reproduction of capital.[10]

But in so far as a greater amount of the value of commodities becomes based on activities that unfold outside of the direct command of capital (be this the self-organizing productive teams of contemporary knowledge-intensive labour, or, as I will describe in this chapter, the productive practices of consumers), then 'labour in the direct form has ceased to be the great well-spring of wealth, labour time ceases and must cease to be its measure and hence exchange value [must cease to be the measure] of use value'.[11] Capital loses its 'natural' command over the production process and a crisis of the value-form ensues. The result is a real drive to valorize productive practices by imposing a more or less artificial measure. The products of such essentially autonomous processes are appropriated and monopolized so as to conform to the capitalist value-form. It is this need to impose a measurable and propertied value-form on use-values that are essentially immeasurable and commonly available that lies behind present developments like the extension of the scope and duration of patents and copyrights, or the various attempts to outlaw measures that circumvent (or 'hack') artificial barriers to circulation inscribed in software code.[12] In short, the question of value becomes progressively separated from the question of production, and increasingly linked to the ability to impose a measure through extra-economic (juridical or technological) means. This artificial imposition of a value-form is also the logic that underlies the progressive attempts to valorize productive consumer practices in the form of propertied brands, which are the topic of this chapter.

Brands have acquired a growing economic importance in the post-war years, in particular since the 1980s.[13] At the same time, marketing has evolved from 'salesmanship' to take an increasing interest in the meanings and social relations that consumers produce by means of goods. In the form of brand management, marketing has become a matter of managing productive consumer practices. Also, the new financial importance of brands has made the business of producing and selling commodities take on many aspects of the 'attention economy' that was once particular to the culture industries. True marketing is still about selling goods, but it is also and increasingly about building brands that act as valuable assets on financial markets. In turn, the financial value of brands builds on calculations of the quantity and quality of consumer attention that the brand has accumulated. Brand management is thus about managing productive investments of affect on the part of consumers and translating these into quantifiable estimates of attention that underpin very real values, like share prices. Brands first developed as markers of distinction between functionally similar products. Since the 1970s the scope of brand management has expanded to become a paradigmatic form of economic governance, a new 'logos of the global economy' to use Celia Lury's phrase, and it is estimated that 95 per cent of the new products that arrive on the US market every year are launched as brand extensions.[14] Even though brand awareness was originally seen as a distinguishing element of the United States' 'affluent society', it has now become a motivating factor for consumer choice globally and in particular in the emerging Asian economies.[15] That brands have acquired a global presence, and, in many cases, brand management a global reach does not mean of course that the 'logos' of the brand governs all instances and aspects of consumer practice. (Rather, as I will argue in this chapter, it is the *excess* that consumers produce in relation to the steering efforts of brand managers that makes up the surplus that is the source of brand value.) On the other hand, it is probably difficult to indicate one form or area of consumer practice that is completely beyond the reach of brand management, or where brand awareness does not have some impact on consumer choice, motivation or modalities of use.[16] However, the scope of this chapter is not to estimate the reach and impact of the brand on global consumer practice, but rather to trace the historical development of brand management as a form of economic governance, and to describe the logic of its contemporary practice. Although most of my examples are taken from European and US markets, and although brand management in the contemporary sense developed as a response to the transformation of the US consumer society in the post-war years, the managerial principle of brand management has now acquired a global validity. It is implemented in diverse cultures and markets where its aim is precisely to translate such local difference into a common value-form.

I shall begin by arguing that brand management has evolved as a response to consumers' 'becoming productive', which in turn has been an outcome of the mediatization of consumption in general. I will then proceed to show how brand management takes productive consumption as its object, and how brand valuation translates consumer affect into commercially viable attention.

The Mediatization of Consumption

'Mediatization' has become a popular buzz word in Media Studies.[17] Like many buzz-words (globalization, postmodernity, etc.) it is often imprecise and ill-defined. To some extent all human communication is of course mediatized, at least to the extent that it makes use of a medium (be this spoken language or the language of gestures and bodily demeanour) that transforms or distorts the intended message of 'the sender'. Seen in this way, *communication* is not so much a matter of transmitting a message as a matter of making something common, of producing something new and shared. This way, mediatization stands behind the very intrinsic productivity of social interaction; because people cannot directly understand each other, they have to produce an intelligible world that they can have in common.[18]

However, within Media Studies, 'mediatization' generally refers to the diffusion of an industrial 'media culture', based on post-oral media technologies like writing and, in particular, electronic media, and its becoming an integral part of lived social relations.[19] One distinctive trait of this media culture is that, as the identity of the sender fades away, communications tend to be perceived less as relations between identifiable persons, and more as a series of events with more or less anonymous or abstract origins. This abstraction of language from lived social relations means that media culture acquires a general validity, 'language becomes wider than human experience', to use Hannah Arendt's words.[20] Media culture becomes part of the informational environment in which life transpires.[21] This, in turn, has two important consequences. First, media culture becomes a common resource that can be drawn upon to create something in common with strangers, with people whose concrete lived existence is different from your own. Mediatization thus heightens the communicative potential of social life. It enables, as Gabriel Tarde was among the first to notice, the emergence of coherent social formations, like 'publics' that stretch across geographical and cultural distance and involve individuals with widely different experiences and life positions.[22] Second, as a commonly available resource, as part of the informational ambience of life, media culture empowers people to relate reflexively to their actual lived experience. It tends to widen the horizons of social actors, and to introduce contingency into their lives. It becomes obvious, in a tangible way, that life could be lived differently. Media culture thus liberates the energies of the social towards the imagination of new forms of life.[23] Mediatization thus extends the productive potential of human sociality, its capacity to produce something in common. It does this both 'horizontally', by providing a more general medium that can be valid across a wider range of social situations, and 'vertically', by opening up deeper aspects of everyday existence for productive intervention and agency. The role of mediatization in stimulating the productivity of social life is particularly evident in the case of the mediatization of consumption. Indeed, the diffusion of modern consumer goods has been intimately linked to the mediatization of social life. As Chandra Mukerji has argued, it was the link to a common print culture that pioneered the new fashions and tastes that in turn enabled the diffusion of new consumer goods. Print, she argues, made 'material culture throughout Europe in the sixteenth and seventeenth centuries more cosmopolitan, at the same time that the economic system was becoming more international'.[24] More generally, the link to a common media culture is what enables the 'high turnover of criteria of appropriateness (fashion)' that guides modern consumers, in contrast to the more stable sumptuary laws of less complex societies.[25] In turn, material goods can give a tangible materiality to such new imagined symbolic and social relations. In most cultures, and perhaps particularly in modern societies, material objects serve to give a certain durability to social facts; they serve to give a materiality to culture.[26] With consumer goods it thus becomes possible to *fantasize realistically*, to produce new social identities and forms of community that have a more or less enduring material foundation. Indeed much of the use-value of consumer goods lies (and has lain) in their function as means of production that permit the creation of identities and forms of community that can acquire an independent reality. In the 1850s New York 'Bo-Hoys' used flamboyant clothing to give a tangible materiality to their newly constructed urban proletarian masculinity; at the same time, middle-class men used 'sartorial restraint' to materialize what set them off from the working classes; in the 1950s Italian migrants used refrigerators and modern kitchens not just as functional devices, but also as objects that marked a durable transition to urban modernity; in the 1970s punks used original forms of *bricolage* to erect the material foundations for a new urban life form, and so on.[27] These were real identities; with a refrigerator you actually became a modern person, you did not just think that you were one. Consumer goods, like other material objects, have the capacity to make fantasies real; like technology in general, they make 'society durable'.[28]

The productive potential of consumer goods thus lies in their ability to give tangible materiality to an imagination that has been enhanced by mediatization. This productive potential has increased in the post-Second World War years. There are several well-known reasons for this. First, class re-composition and structural transformation have destroyed many old socially anchored identities and world-views and made others inadequate. For many people, mediatized consumer goods have been the main alternative available for the construction of new forms of identity and community. This has perhaps been most evident in the case of post-war youth culture. However, consumption and media culture have played an important part also in the articulation of middle-class identity, particularly in the case of the new, managerial middle class.[29] Second, a new media environment and new 'means of consumption' that have accompanied it have combined to enhance the productivity of mediatized consumer goods. The new media ecology that developed around television in the post-war years created a pressure for greater audience differentiation and segmentation (in particular, for the magazine market, but soon enough for television too). This in turn spurred a greater inclusiveness on the part of the media industries: new consumer practices were actively sought out and transformed into market niches in a much more systematic fashion than before.[30] At the same time, styling of domestic appliances, emerging mass fashion and lifestyle marketing (in particular in the case of the automobile and tobacco industries that drew heavily on the new imaginary of youth culture) increased the expressive potential of consumer goods, to the point that 'self-codification through fashion statements' became a sort of natural middle-class attitude from the 1970s on.[31] Since the 1980s the growth and deregulation of the media and culture industries, the arrival of new media like networked computers, VCRs (then digital cameras) and mobile phones, and the greater integration between the consumer industries and the culture industries proper (visible in things like cross-promotions between Disney and McDonald's, between Pepsi and Britney Spears, etc.) have tended both to increase the mediatization of consumer goods and to further the integration of a mediatized consumer culture into everyday life to the point of ubiquity.[32]

If we believe the as good as unanimous results of academic consumer research, this has corresponded to the generalization of a 'producerly attitude' towards consumption and consumer goods.[33] Many argue that consumer goods now often function as a sort of means of production of sociality. They are 'linking devices' that serve to materialize social and communal ties.[34] This is true not only for various subcultures, like those of skydivers, fundamentalist Christians or health enthusiasts, but also for ordinary people (or at least Americans), who readily form communities around brands like Saab, Bronco or Macintosh.[35] These communities are significant social formations, maintained through investments in face-to-face and online interaction, and they generate moral ties and a sense of mutual commitment. Americans might 'bowl alone' but they create things in common by means of brands and consumer goods. Mediatized consumer goods have become a sort of medium by means of which new, less enduring and more 'nomadic' forms of sociality can be constructed in response to the flexibility demanded by a transitory and complex environment.[36]

Marketing

Marketing has discovered the productivity of consumers in the post-war years. When modern marketing first took a coherent and organized interest in consumer behaviour – some time in the 1920s – its project was to discipline and reorganize consumption. Modern marketing aimed at imposing an established set of rational, modern or desirable needs and preferences on what was perceived of as irrational, disorganized and incoherent consumer patterns. It was a re-educational and disciplinary project (in the Foucaultian sense of the term); its ethos has been aptly described by Anne McCarthy (in the case of 1930s in-store merchandizing) as 'taylorizing consumption with images'.[37] Modern marketing worked *against* the productivity of the social.

A volte-face occurred in the mid-1950s and had a complex assembly of causes. First, increasing standards of living and the emergence of a culturally influential new middle class transformed actual consumer practice. Second, industrial overcapacity created an increased pressure for market differentiation and for the discovery of new niches and possibilities. Third, the new media environment introduced new constraints and possibilities for advertising. Most importantly, however, the informational interface of marketing changed so that these very real transformations now became visible and possible to act on. The business of market research had expanded all through the 1950s, and in 1963 the turnover of the research business was estimated to be ten times (in current dollars) that at its inception some thirty years before.[38] The fact that there was now simply more information available meant that consumer practice and motivations began to appear as more complex than had previously been thought. This produced a declining faith in the adequacy of the ABCD typology that had structured the American advertising market since its adaptation by the Cooperative Analysis of Broadcasting's (CAB) nationwide ratings research in the 1930s (and later, in 1942, by the Nielsen ratings index).[39] Its key principle, that socioeconomic position correlated with the embrace of a particular package of needs and desires, now began to seem particularly dubious. Consequently, demographic variables began to lose their status as the privileged key to unlocking the secrets of consumer behaviour.[40]

The most important novelty was qualitative market research. Qualitative research had been introduced in the late 1940s in the form of 'motivation research' by pioneers like Ernest Dichter and Pierre Martineau. At the core of motivation research was the idea that people's real needs and desires differ from the ones that are socially established. Rather, people's real motivations are often unarticulated or even 'unconscious'.[41] Consequently, motivation researchers set about uncovering such 'unconscious motives' through in-depth interviews. This was the secret behind the commercial success of motivation research. The fact that Dichter and his associates actually talked to consumers meant that they got a wide range of new and unexpected results. This satisfied the need for new angles and niches that could support a tendency towards increasing market differentiation. Despite, or perhaps because of, Dichter's fundamental disregard for research methodology, his services were popular with business and his Institute for Motivation Research flourished. As one client put it: 'I don't care whether Dichter's chi-squares are everything they should be. I get more useful ideas in talking with Dichter for one day than I ever get out of a hundred tables in a survey report.'[42] What Dichter and his fellow motivation researchers discovered in their in-depth interviews was that people tend to use consumer goods as tools for the construction of social relations, of a sense of self or of a context for life in general. Goods have use-values that go beyond their established functionality, they work as means of production of a common social world. For example, Dichter argued that women do not so much use detergents to 'guarantee social acceptance and safety', as much as they use them to reassure themselves of their own social identity as modern and competent women. They like to 'be able to like themselves, to feel clean, to consider themselves smart beauty technicians'.[43] Similarly, furniture was used to 'put into practice an emerging – even if unformulated – philosophy of life', and domestic appliances worked to 'create the home as part of yourself'.[44] Cigarettes were instruments deployed to 'cope with life', and shopping was a constitutive experience in the construction of the suburban couple's way of life.[45] Dichter's idea that consumers used goods to produce their own self and its moorings in social relations and common experiences harmonized well with the Maslowian ideas of a coming post-materialistic age that were influential in the advertising and marketing business in the 1960s. Maslow had famously argued that increasing affluence would enable people to develop 'post-materialistic' desires that centred on the realization and expression of individuality. These ideas were taken on by psychologically inspired market researchers, like Pierre Martineau and Sidney Levy, and eventually developed into the 'Lifestyle' concept. The notion of lifestyle as a central principle of consumer behaviour began to gain momentum in the second half of the 1960s. This notion built on the idea that consumers 'scan, screen and process goods for their symbolic suitability, not only because the products can provide specific results, but because they become incorporated into the lifestyle of the person'.[46] 'Lifestyle' was in turn not perceived as the cause of consumer decisions (as in the case of the demographic categories of the ABCD typology), but as a *result* of such choices. 'A consumer's personality', Sydney Levy argued, 'can be seen as the peculiar total of the products he consumes.'[47] The status of the lifestyle concept was reinforced in the 1970s as viable methods of 'psychographic' market research, like the Yankelovich Monitor (1971), PRIZM (1974) and VALS (1978), became available.[48] These methods were based on an inductive clustering of a wide variety of variables (in turn made possible by advances in computer technology), and not on assumptions that one particular variable or set of variables (like socioeconomic standing) were determining *a priori*. This meant that psychographic research was capable of monitoring a changing and mobile consumer sociality (indeed, the very development of psychographics was often perceived as a reaction to the 'rapidly changing values' that marked the 1970s). Psychographics could monitor what consumers produced with goods and represent that productivity as an evolving set of 'lifestyles'.[49]

Brand Management

Brands have a long history that goes back, at least, to the origins of modern consumer culture, and recent scholarship has underlined the growing importance of brands within an emerging late nineteenth-century mass consumerism.[50] However, the principle of brand management, which implies the use of the brand as a managerial tool and not just the construction of a distinctive trademark, can be traced to developments within large US consumer goods companies in the 1930s (the figure of the brand manager was famously pioneered by Procter & Gamble). It developed through the renewed discussions of the brand that began within the United States marketing profession in the 1950s. At that time, the renewed importance of brands was directly linked to the availability of new market information. According to market researchers Sydney Levy and Burleigh Gardner (who published a seminal article on the concept of the brand in 1955), such new studies had shown that consumers no longer necessarily followed older socially institutionalized sets of motivations, like '(a) striving to be economical and (b) the desire to emulate people of higher status', but that actual motivations were far more complex and related to the local and particular circumstances of consumers' lived realities.[51] The fact that many of these motivations were psychological or social, that 'people buy things not only for what they can do, but also for what they mean', meant that the brand image as a symbolic entity now emerged as something clearly separated from the product itself.[52] 'A brand name is more than the label employed to differentiate among the manufacturers of a product. It is a complex symbol that represents a variety of ideas and attributes.'[53] To Gardner and Levy, and to other early 'branding gurus', the symbolic value of the brand was mainly articulated by the presence and role that it had acquired in media culture. The brand represented the media content of commodities, which was understood to play a new and powerful role in motivating consumer choice:

> Grandmother cherished her furniture for its sensible, practical value, but today people know that it is hardly the practical considerations which determine their choices between Post's and Kellogg's, Camels and Luckies, Oldsmobiles and Buicks, or Arpege and Chanel No 5. They know that package color, television commercials, and newspaper and magazine advertisements incline them toward one preference or another.[54]

The role of advertising and marketing was thus to build and maintain the brand as an enduring entity in media culture. This principle lay behind the kinds of 'lifestyle advertising' that developed in the 1960s.

If advertising copy in the inter-war years had tried to inscribe the product within a set of pre-given motivations and desires (avoiding social failure, living up to the role of the housewife etc.), to socialize products into an idealized simulacrum of middle-class life, advertising now began to place more emphasis on the construction of a brand image that contained needs, motivations and desires that were particular to the product itself. The brand image was to communicate a particular context of use for the product. The brand image communicated a certain ambience or 'feel' that suggested how the product could be used and with what results. It made up a kind of media extension of the product that anticipated what kinds of meanings or sensations the consumption of this particular brand could convey. This idea of the brand image as a media extension of the product clearly emerges from a 1969 Coca-Cola memorandum:

> Consumers see every ad or commercial for Coke as an extension of the product itself. Time and again in research studies people will comment, 'that's not Coca-Cola' when the ambience of the commercial or ad is not 'quality' or 'tasteful' or misses the way people see the product and how it fits the pulse of their daily lives. So it follows that a commercial for Coca-Cola should have the properties of the product itself. It should be a pleasurable experience, refreshing to watch and pleasant to listen to. It should reflect quality by being quality. And it should make you say, 'I wish I'd been there. I wish I had been drinking Coke with those people.'[55]

The brand in its modern sense thus came to stand for a context of use that is inscribed in the product. The brand image, represented by the logo, anticipated certain ways of feeling or acting with the brand, certain ways of relating to it. In contemporary brand management discourse this is also thought to be the most important dimension of the use-value that the brand provides. It is how you *feel with* the branded product, what kind of person it can make you become, that is what sets it apart from other branded products or unbranded generics.[56] Brand management is, then, the management of the particular context of action that the brand conveys.

During the 1960s and 1970s the management of such a context of action was mainly limited to caring for the brand image as a 'public object', as an entity in media culture. Lifestyle advertising relied on psychographic monitoring of consumer practices and sought to transform these into more or less coherent lifestyles that could work as contexts for the consumption of particular goods. The main medium remained advertising. In the 1980s this practice changed somewhat. The emerging new media landscape (multiple television sets, cable, remote controls and the VCR) was perceived to diminish the efficiency of advertising. At the same time, new media like video and computer games and the expanding toy and fast-food industries created new possibilities for product placements, cross-marketing and synergies. The kids' market was a pioneer in this respect (the first feature films to rely heavily on merchandizing and cross-promotions were *Star Wars* and *E.T.*). Already in the mid-1980s Nintendo licensed a wide range of gadgets around its successful core products, the videogames *SuperMario Bros.* and *Zelda*: T-shirts, watches, cereals, sleeping bags, dolls, magazines, cartoons, wallpaper, snacks and a film (*The Wizard*) that together constructed a context within which play could unfold, on and off the Gameboy screen.[57] During the 1990s the emergence of new media, together with ownership concentration in the media industries, intensified the use of product placements and cross-promotions and spread these techniques outside of the kids' segment. Advertising was no longer the only, or even the most important, medium for managing a brand image.

But the 1980s also brought on other developments in brand management. The availability of new kinds of consumer information (mined from bar-code scans, credit-card records and a variety of other sources) permitted a closer targeting of loyal customers. This facilitated investments in customer relations management. Through discounts, bonuses (frequent flyer miles in the case of airlines), investments in call centres and other forms of customer relations, and, in some cases, buyer's magazines, companies sought to build stronger and more enduring relations between the brand and a select, but presumably loyal, customer base.[58] Soon enough companies began to constitute these relations as a (more or less coherent) community.

British supermarkets like Tesco and Sainsbury's were among the pioneers in this respect. Both created ties to their customers through membership cards, special discounts, direct mailing and company publications. They make ties *between* customers possible through social events like cooking courses, gourmet dinners and wine tasting.[59] Some brands like Jeep and Harley Davidson routinely organize 'brandfests' where users can come together, improve their skills at using the product and, most importantly, socialize and create community ties. Harley Davidson has been particularly successful in creating a feeling of community around the brand, defined by a particular 'biker ethos' where true biker status is contingent on participation in a branded Harley gathering.[60] The ability to create such a communitarian 'feel' around the brand has been further empowered by new media like the Internet and mobile phones. Motorola recently launched an interactive game called PartyMoto where users use chat and SMS to acquire points from other users. These points would eventually give them the community status required to enter the PartyMoto virtual nightclub, where they could assume a wide variety of characters as the interactivity proceeded on a new level. Companies like Pepsi, IBM, Ford and Siemens have also used interactive 'advergames' to generate consumer interaction around their brands.[61] Another technique that has developed significantly during the 1990s has been the creation of brand spaces. Whether this be the 'superstores' of Nike, Ralph Lauren or Prada, where the architectural and design environment is created so as to produce an intense experience of the brand and what it stands for, or more mundane places like McDonald's or Starbuck's, where a particular way of consuming hamburgers or coffee is suggested by the environment as well as the heavily scripted behaviour of personnel ('baristas'), the idea is to turn the very physical environment itself into a branded context of action. More recently, techniques like 'real life placements', whereby a product is inserted into the social and symbolic networks of a particularly attractive subculture (Courvoisier cognac and rap music, Absolut vodka and the urban gay scene), or 'viral marketing', whereby the personal influence of a particular trendsetting elite is used to add to the make-up of the brand, use social relations themselves as a medium of brand management. During the 1990s these different techniques have expanded the object domain of brand management far beyond advertising and media visibility to reach far into the lived reality of consumers. Brand management now means governing a complex web of media, social and symbolic relations that anticipate a 'preferred' modality of consumption. It also means doing this in a dynamic and open-ended way that acknowledges the mobile and transitory status of consumer preferences. While it is important that brands are consistent, it is also important that they move with consumers, that they 'breathe with the market' and do not lose touch. Such continuous contact is ensured by the availability of a wide range of information services, from vast quantitative data-mining operations, through mixed techniques like trend indexes, to 'cool hunting' where anthropologists follow around certain influential consumer groups (like high-school kids) in their everyday lives. Indeed, contemporary brand management, conceived as the management of social relations and not just media content, has given birth to a new professional figure within the advertising industry: the account planner. The role of the 'planner' is to provide constant feedback to the creative team, using a wide variety of information sources. He or she is to function as the omnipresent 'voice of the consumer'.[62]

Brand Values

Since the 1980s brands have become more than just a 'public image'. They have become something of a premise for communication, interaction and experience – for human life itself. In turn, brand management has evolved into the management of the place that the brand occupies in the lived reality of consumers. The purpose of such extended intervention is to make consumer practice add value to the brand. Principally this can be done in two ways. First, the results of a relatively autonomous consumer practice can be appropriated and employed as an input into the actual production of the branded commodity. Trend scouting is an obvious example of this. By means of ethnographic research and a network of informants among 'cool' or 'trendsetting' people, autonomous consumer innovations can rapidly be appropriated. The messaging practice among Japanese teenage 'thumb tribes' (*oyayubisoku*) contributed to developing the SMS function on Nokia and Sony phones.[63] Nike and Reebok routinely submit new sneaker models to the scrutiny of 'cool' teenagers.[64] In both cases taste structures and consumption practices that have evolved autonomously, outside of the command of the wage relation, are used as a valuable input to the product or brand development process. Consumption becomes a kind of productive labour in the direct and obvious sense of that term. Trend scouting developed as a service for the fashion industry that needed to rapidly learn from the street. Now it is used by a wide range of mainstream companies in the communication, computer, fast-food, clothes and technology businesses. Similar practices are widely used on the Internet. The Lego sub-brand 'Bionicle' draws directly on users' online discussion to develop the product story and come up with new characters. Much of the value of the E-bay auction site builds on the trustworthiness that users themselves construct through an intelligent community-management system. Finally, our everyday surveyed flaneuring on and off the net (when we use our credit cards or purchase bar-coded goods in supermarkets, for example) generates massive amounts of data that feed into product development and targeting decisions. Through these techniques, the everyday life of consumers is directly subsumed as a productive force.

Most of contemporary brand management, however, consists in providing and managing a context in which the productivity of consumers is likely to evolve in a particular way, where consumers are likely to produce desir-able experiences of, or relations to, the brand, that in turn reproduce and strengthen the standing of a desirable brand image. Advertising, product placements in media discourses or in real life, the visibility of logos and the prevalence of branded spaces, brand communities and viral marketing all serve these purposes. These techniques are combined to construct a series of inter-textual links that anticipate what consumers are likely to do with or feel about the brand, and that discourage certain undesirable attitudes. It is important to stress that such branded contexts anticipate a possible experience or relation, but they do not supply this as a ready-made object simply to be consumed. Rather, they presume a certain productivity on the part of consumers. It is up to the consumer to fill in the blanks, to actually perform the value of the brand (be this a relaxing experience at Starbuck's or quality time with the kids at McDonald's). Brand management, like many other forms of 'advanced liberal' governance, works with the freedom of the subject.[65] Indeed it is generally understood that the use-value of the brand to consumers consists in what they can make with it: what kind of person they can become with it, what kinds of social relations they can form around it. 'The power of any brand is how it makes you feel.'[66]

The industry term for the standing of the brand in the minds of consumers, its productive potential, is 'brand equity'. In David Aaker's classic formula-tion, brand equity refers to the potential value that the context of consumption provided by the brand can add on to the commodity or service: 'Brand Equity is a set of brand assets and liabilities linked to a brand, its name and symbol, that add to or subtract from the value provided by a product or service to a firm and/or to that firm's customers.'[67] Today most branding theorists agree that the most important dimension of brand equity is what is known as 'customer based brand equity'. This term generally refers to 'the knowledge that has been created around the brand in consumers' minds from the investments in previous marketing programs' and 'the differential effect of brand knowledge on consumer response to the marketing of the brand'.[68] Such knowledge that makes a difference can be of a wide variety of kinds, from simple brand awareness and brand loyalty, via brand associations (what kinds of 'positive attitudes and feeling' that the brand can create), to identity-related or quasi-religious dimensions. For example, BBDO's (Batten, Barton, Durstine & Osborn) internal publication on Brand Equity Excellence defines the two highest dimensions of brand identity as 'self share: [how] the brand functions as manifestation of the self, as a tangible expression of self-image within the social environment' and 'legend share: [how] the brand shares in the existential search for meaning conducted by a consumer in a world enlightened to the point of meaning-lessness [sic] and takes on a virtually religious character'.[69] Brand equity stands for what consumers can do with the brand, the potential of the context of consumption that the brand encompasses: 'Knowing that a piece of jewellery came from Tiffany can affect the experience of wearing it: the user can actually feel different.'[70] From a financial point of view, brand management is the management of brand equity: it is about managing consumer practices so that they add on to the stock of positive associations, potential experiences or forms of identity that make up the productive potential of the branded context.

How, then, does brand equity add value to the firm? On a first and direct level, brand equity can facilitate the marketing effort and offer leverage for promotional campaigns. Brand equity can also translate directly into a premium price. It can produce a set of positive associations that can be directly valorized by consumers' willingness to pay extra for the branded item. That way the relative standing of different brands of sneakers in American high-school culture more or less directly translates into their market prices. More importantly, brand equity generates brand values that are directly realized on financial markets (and which encompass but exceed an estimate of the premium price that is attributable to the brand). Here, measurements of the attention invested by consumers in the brand are used to underpin share prices. The Interbrand method, for example, is based on an estimate of (among other things) 'stability' (the position that the brand occupies in the cultural universe of consumers) and 'trend' (the actuality of the brand in the culture of consumers). Measurements of brand values are important factors behind the price of shares. (And studies have shown correlations between the share prices of companies with strong brands and the standing of those brands in trend indexes.[71]) The idea here is that the social standing of the brand will aid the company in ways other than providing premium revenue. Brand equity will generate easier access to capital and facilitate relations with investors and other interested parties more generally. The attention and affect accumulated under the propertied symbol of the brand works as a kind of immaterial capital. Both channels of valorization – premium prices and financial brand values – appear in the accounting literature as values that are directly generated by the immaterial capital of brand equity. But they also derive from what consumers do with brand equity – with the productive potential of the context embodied by the brand – what meanings, experiences and relations they produce around it, what social standing they give to it in their lived reality. (This is also what is actually measured by methods of brand valuation.) The value-generating potential of brand equity consists in its capacity to put the productive sociality of consumers to work. The surplus value generated by brand equity is thus (at least in part) based on the surplus sociality generated by consumers around the brand.

Conclusion

Brand values build on a direct valorization of consumer attention and affect. This way the mediatization of consumption has made the business of producing and distributing consumer goods similar to the attention economy that originally characterized the culture industries. Indeed, brands with their ubiquitous logos are primary examples of how 'looking is posited by capital as labour'.[72] The value of attention in Dallas Smythe's original model of the attention economy consisted in its capacity to reproduce a particular consumption norm, 'the work which audience members perform for the advertiser to whom they have been sold is learning to buy goods and to spend their income accordingly'.[73] The value of brand equity as accumulated attention is rather its capacity to put the productive potential of social interaction to work in the creation of experiences, shared meanings and social relations, in producing the forms of affect that make up the lived social world itself. The source of brand value is thus the capacity on the part of consumers to create a social world through productive communication, to create a 'common' – in the sense of a shared resource – that gives substance to and 'realizes the promise' of the brand.[74] In Maurizio Lazzarato's words, surplus value is based on the ability to produce surplus community. Contrary to Smythe's idea of the role of the advertising producer, the brand manager does not control the actual productive practice of consumers. He or she might try to achieve this, but ultimately the forms of affect that consumers generate around the brand are (at least in part) unpredictable – and the more recent brand management literature acknowledges this.[75] This way, the capacity to generate surplus value on the part of brand managers does not primarily build on their direct control of a labour process (although this can also be a factor), but rather on their ability to appropriate values that derive from communicative and interactive processes that are beyond their direct command. The brand manager is thus an excellent example of what Maurizio Lazzarato claims has become the general model for the post-Fordist (informational) entrepreneur, what Max Weber called a 'political entrepreneur'. Weber used the term to refer to people who *live off* politics in a systematic way: 'like the condottiere or the holder of a farmed-out or purchased office, or like the American boss who considers his costs a capital investment which he brings to fruition through exploitation of his influence'.[76] As a corollary, brand management builds on an ability to control and steer the flows of human communication and to direct its capacity to construct a common in ways that contribute to the accumulation of brand value. Now this ability to create a common is precisely what Hannah Arendt identified as the foundation for political practice. Recently, this line of thought has been taken up again, first by Habermas and then by Michael Hardt and Antonio Negri. For the latter, it is in the communicative production of a common that exceeds the anticipatory control of the constituted order that we can find a potential for negation and alternatives: 'the surplus of the production of the common is what transforms the multitude into an antagonistic subject'.[77] To Hardt and Negri human communication in an age of 'hyper-mediation' has been empowered to the point of becoming a potential political force in its own right. It is precisely this political potential that forms the real foundation for brand values and the object of brand management.

Notes

1. 'The regular, increasing, and almost entirely unvaried diet of sensation without commitment is surely likely to help render its consumers less capable of responding openly and responsibly to life, is likely to induce an underlying sense of purposelessness in existence outside the limited range of a few immediate appetites', R. Hoggart, *The Uses of Literacy* (London, 1969 [1957]), p. 246.
2. J.K. Galbraith, *The Affluent Society* (London, 1958); E. Mandel, *Late Capitalism* (London, 1975).

3. For a useful overview see D. Miller (ed.), *Acknowledging Consumption: A Review of New Studies* (London, 1995).
4. D. Miller, *A Theory of Shopping* (Cambridge, 1998); cf. J. Fiske, *Reading the Popular* (London, 1989).
5. Cf. J. Hage and C.H. Powers, *Post-industrial Lives: Roles and Relationships in the 21st Century* (London, 1992); A. Wittel, 'Toward a Network Sociality', *Theory, Culture & Society*, 18(6) (1999), pp. 51–76; R.B. Reich, *The Work of Nations: Preparing Ourselves for the 21st Century* (New York, 1999); A. Gorz, *L'Immatériel* (Paris, 2003).
6. A. Arvidsson, 'Reality Love: Internet Dating as Immaterial Labour', Cultures of Consumption Working Paper 22, April 2005; R. Barbook, *The Digital Economy* (posted on Nettime 17/6/1997, www.nettime.org); M. Copier and J. Raessens (eds), *Level Up* (Utrecht, 2003).
7. J. Comaroff and J. Comaroff, 'Millennial Capitalism: First Thoughts on a Second Coming', *Public Culture*, 12(2) (2000), pp. 291–343.
8. T. Morris-Suzuki, 'Capitalism in the Computer Age', in J. Davis, T. Hirschl and M. Stack (eds), *Cutting Edge: Technology, Society and Social Revolution* (London, 1997), p. 64.
9. B. Lee and E. LiPuma, 'Cultures of Circulation: The Imaginations of Modernity', *Public Culture*, 14(1) (2002), pp. 191–213; Y. Moulier-Boutang (ed.), *L'età del capitalismo cognitivo* (Verona, 2002).
10. It does not matter whether the particular use-values produced are material or immaterial, solid or ephemeral. Indeed, 'for *labour to be designated productive*, qualities are required which are utterly unconnected with the *specific content* of the labour, with the particular utility of the use value in which it is objectified', K. Marx, *Capital*, Volume 1 (London 1976 [1867]), p. 1044. Rather a (necessary but not sufficient) condition for a practice to count as 'productive labour' is that its product is measurable in terms of the specific value-form of capitalism: the 'general equivalent' ultimately grounded in abstract labour time. As long as the main source of value is commanded labour – labour that by means of its enclosure within the time-space of the factory is already immanently measurable in terms of such a general equivalent – then this is not a problem.
11. K. Marx, *Grundrisse* (London, 1973 [1939]), p. 705. (The passage is also known as the 'fragment on machinery'; for a comment see P. Virno, 'Notes on the General Intellect', in S. Makdisi, C. Casarino and R. Karl (eds), *Marxism beyond Marxism* (London, 1996), pp. 265–72.
12. L. Lessig, *Free Culture: The Nature and Future of Creativity* (New York, 2004).

13. It is difficult to find exact figures on the economic weight of brands. Jan Lindemann of the Interbrand consultancy group estimates that the economic weight of tangible assets in non-financial businesses has decreased from slightly over 70 per cent in 1980 to slightly over 50 per cent in 2000. The corresponding increase in intangible assets includes things like patents and intellectual property rights, but since the relative weight of brands versus other intangibles has increased in the same period, a substantial share of this increase is attributable to the growing economic weight of brand values. In absolute terms the value of the world's 100 most valuable brands was estimated to be $434 billion in 2001, roughly 4 per cent of US GDP (at $10.400 billion in 2002), and roughly three times total US advertising expenditure (at $132 billion in 2000); J. Lindemann, 'The Financial Value of Brands', in R. Clifton and J. Simmons (eds), *Brands and Branding* (London, 2003).

14. J. Murphy, 'What is branding?', in S. Hart and J. Murphy (eds), *Brands: The New Wealth Creators* (Basingstoke, 1998); C. Lury, *Brands: The Logos of the Global Economy* (London, 2004).

15. L. Beng-Huat (ed.), *Consumption in Asia: Lifestyles and Identities* (London, 2000); D. Davies (ed.), *The Consumer Revolution in Urban China* (Berkeley, 2000); A. Rajagopal, 'Thinking through Emerging Markets: Brand Logics and the Cultural Forms of Political Society in India', *Social Text*, 17(3) (1999).

16. Even illicit drugs are now branded, as in the case of Ecstasy pills or the Dutch cannabis market, cf. L. Caramiello, *La droga della modernità. Sociologia e storia di un fenomeno fra devianza e culture* (Torino, 2003).

17. W. Schultz, 'Reconstructing Mediatization as an Analytical Concept', *European Journal of Communication*, 19(1) (2004), pp. 87–101.

18. Niklas Luhmann is famous for this argument. In his view, it is the fundamental insecurity provided by the double contingency inherent in all human communication that is the very origin of 'social facts' like languages, codes and institutions, cf. N. Luhmann, *Social Systems* (Stanford, CA, 1995).

19. D. Kellner, *Media Culture: Cultural Studies, Identity and Politics between the Modern and the Postmodern* (London, 1995).

20. H. Arendt, *The Human Condition* (Chicago, 1958), p. 3. Arendt of course took this as a sign of the fundamental alienation that marks the modern human condition.

21. T. Terranova, *Network Culture: Politics for the Information Age* (London, 2004); G. Boccia-Altieri, *I media-mondo: Forme e linguaggi dell'esperienza contemporanea* (Rome, 2004).

22. G. Tarde, 'The Public and the Crowd', in T. Clark (ed.), *Gabriel Tarde on Communication and Social Influence: Selected Papers* (Chicago, 1969 [1901]).

23. Indeed, Durkheim's concept of anomie can be read as pointing precisely at these intrinsically modern dangers of an excessive, media-enhanced imagination. Durkheim defined anomie as a situation in which one imagines forms of life for oneself that go beyond what is realistically possible or socially permissible. He argued that this occurs when the individual is suddenly put outside of the control exercised by the implicit laws and expectations of the social, like rapid social mobility (downwards but also upwards) and divorce. Durkheim thought that the specifically modern nature of anomie was connected to the mobility of modern life. But others, like Rosalind Williams, have argued that anomie as a particularly modern state of mind should also be connected to the enhanced fantasy life that comes with mass media and consumer culture. In other words, anomie is a consequence not just of a new social mobility (if there indeed was one), but also of the fact that modern people live in a social environment where mass media stimulate their imagination to the point of excess. Anomie is a result of a new mobility of the imagination, cf. E. Durkheim, *Suicide* (New York, 1951 [1897]); R.H. Williams, *Dream Worlds: Mass Consumption in Late Nineteenth Century France* (Berkeley, CA, 1982).

24. C. Mukerji, *From Graven Images: Patter of Modern Materialism* (New York, 1983), p. 12.

25. A. Appadurai, *The Social Life of Things* (Cambridge, 1985), p. 32.

26. M. Douglas and B. Isherwood, *The World of Goods* (New York, 1979).

27. D. Kuchta, 'The Making of the Self-made Man: Class, Clothing and English Masculinity, 1688–1832', in V. de Grazia with E. Furlough (eds), *The Sex of Things, Gender and Consumption in Historical Perspective* (Berkeley, 1996); F. Alberoni and G. Baglioni, *L'integrazione del immigrato nella societa industriale* (Bologna, 1965); D. Hebdidge, *Subculture: The Meaning of Style* (London, 1979).

28. B. Latour, 'Technology Is Society Made Durable', in J. Law (ed.), *A Sociology of Monsters: Essays on Power, Technology and Domination* (London, 1991).

29. L. Cohen, *A Consumers' Republic: The Politics of Mass Consumption in Post-war America* (New York, 2004); A. Marwick, *The Sixties* (Oxford, 1998).

30. L.R. Samuel, *Brought to You by: Post-war Television Advertising and the American Dream* (Austin, TX, 2001).

31. S.P. Miller, *The Seventies Now: Culture as Surveillance* (Durham, NC, 1999), p. 7.
32. A. Janson, 'The Mediatization of Consumer Culture: Towards an Analytical Framework of Image Culture', *Journal of Consumer Culture*, 2(1) (2002), pp. 5–31.
33. A.F. Firat and N. Dholakia, *Consuming People: From Political Economy to Theaters of Consumption* (London, 1998).
34. D. Cova, 'Community and Consumption: Towards a Theory of the Linking Value of Products and Services', *European Journal of Marketing*, 31(3–4) (1997).
35. R. Celsi, R. Rose and T. Leigh, ' An Exploration of High-risk Leisure Consumption through Sky-diving', *Journal of Consumer Research*, 20 (1993), pp. 1–21; T. O'Guinn and R. Belk, 'Heaven on Earth: Consumption at Heritage Village, USA', *Journal of Consumer Research*, 16 (1989), pp. 227–38; A. Muniz and T. O'Guinn, 'Brand Community', *Journal of Consumer Research*, 27 (2001), pp. 412–32.
36. M. Maffesoli, *The Time of the Tribes* (London, 1996).
37. A. McCarthy, *Ambience Television: Visual Culture and Public Space* (Durham, NC, 2001), p. 69; cf. F. Cochoy, *Une Histoire du marketing* (Paris, 1999); R. Marchand, *Advertising the American Dream* (Berkeley, CA, 1985).
38. L. Bogart, 'Inside Market Research', *Public Opinion Quarterly*, 27(4) (1963), pp. 562–77.
39. L. Bogart, Review: Bourdieu, P. 'Distinction', *Public Opinion Quarterly*, 51(1) (1987), pp. 131–4.
40. D. Yankelovic, 'New Criteria for Market Segmentation', *Harvard Business Review*, March–April (1964), pp. 80–8.
41. E. Dichter, *The Strategy of Desire* (New York, 1960); P. Martineau, *Motivation in Advertising* (New York, 1957). Despite the Freudian lingo of (in particular Dichter's version of) Motivation Research, what the method really produced was in-depth interviews that, for the first time, gave a detailed picture of consumer practice as a meaningful pursuit. As many of Dichter's critics pointed out, there were not many 'unconscious' motives that could be discovered in a single two-hour interview; cf. A. Politz, 'Motivation Research from a Research Perspective', *Public Opinion Quarterly*, 20(4) (1956), pp. 663–73.
42. H. Kassarjian, 'Scholarly Traditions and European Roots of American Consumer Research', in G. Laurent, G. Lilien and B. Pras (eds), *Research Traditions in Marketing* (London, 1994), p. 270.
43. Dichter, *The Strategy of Desire*, p. 63.

44. 'What the New Rich Americans Really Want to Buy', *Motivations* (July 1956), no pagination.
45. 'Something Must Be Added', *Motivations* (June 1956); 'The Emotional Plus in Suburban Living', *Motivations* (June 1957).
46. S. Levy, 'Symbolism and Life Style', in S. Geyser (ed.), *Proceedings* (American Marketing Association, December 1963), pp. 140–50, reprinted in D. Rook (ed.), *Brands, Consumers, Symbols and Research: Sydney J. Levy on Marketing* (London, 1999), p. 223.
47. Levy, 'Symbolism and Life Style', p. 149.
48. A. Arvidsson, 'The Pre-history of the Panoptic Sort: Mobility in Market Research', *Surveillance & Society*, 1(4) (2004); M.J. Weiss, *The Clustering of America* (New York, 1989).
49. D.W. Wells (ed.), *Life Style and Psychographics* (Chicago, 1974).
50. N. Koehn, *Brand New* (Boston, MA, 2001); A. McClintock, *Imperial Leather: Race, Gender and Sexuality in the Colonial Contest* (London, 1995); K.U. Hellman, *Soziologie der Marke* (Frankfurt, 2003).
51. B. Gardner and S. Levy, 'The Product and the Brand', *Harvard Business Review*, March–April 1955 (reprinted in D. Rook (ed.), *Brands, Consumers and Research*, p. 133).
52. S. Levy, 'Symbols for Sale', *Harvard Business Review* (July–August 1959) (reprinted in D. Rook (ed.), *Brands, Consumers and Research*, p. 205).
53. B. Gardner and S. Levy, 'The Product and the Brand', p. 134.
54. S. Levy, 'Symbols for Sale', p. 205.
55. P. Rutherford, *The New Icons? The Art of Television Advertising* (Toronto, 1994), p. 57.
56. C. Lury, 'Marking Time with Nike: The Illusion of the Durable', *Public Culture*, 11(3) (1999), pp. 499–526.
57. E. Provenzo, *Video Kids: Making Sense of Nintendo* (Cambridge, MA, 1991), p. 14.
58. J. Turow, *Breaking up America: Advertisers and the New Media World* (Chicago, 1997).
59. E. Joachimsthaler and D. Aaker, 'Building Brands without Mass Media', *Harvard Business Review* (January/February 1997).
60. J.H. McAlexander and J.W. Shouten, 'Brandfests: Servicescapes for the Cultivation of Brand Equity', in J. Sherry (ed.), *Servicescapes: The Concept of Place in Contemporary Markets* (Chicago, 1998).
61. A.L. Rodgers, 'Game Theory', *FastCompany* (January 2002).
62. T. Frank, *One Market under God* (Chicago, 1999); cf. S. Pollit, 'How I Started Account Planning in Agencies', *Campaign* (April 1979).

63. H. Rheingold, *Smart Mobs: The Next Social Revolution* (Cambridge, MA, 2003), p. 7.
64. A. Quart, *Branded* (London, 2003).
65. N. Rose, *The Powers of Freedom* (Cambridge, 1999).
66. D. Travis, *Emotional Branding: How Successful Brands Gain the Irrational Edge* (Roseville, CA, 2000), p. 10.
67. D. Aaker, *Managing Brand Equity* (New York, 1991), p. 15.
68. D. Keller, 'Conceptualizing, Measuring and Managing Customer Based Brand Equity', *Journal of Marketing*, 75 (1993), p. 1.
69. BBDO, *Brand Equity Excellence*, 2001, pp. 14–15.
70. D. Aaker, *Managing Brand Equity*, p. 16.
71. D. Aaker and R. Jacobson, 'The Financial Information Content of Perceived Quality', *Journal of Marketing Research*, 31 (1994), pp. 191–201.
72. J. Beller, 'KINO-I, KINO-WORLD: Notes on the Cinematic Mode of Production', in N. Mirzoeff (ed.), *The Visual Culture Reader* (London, 2002), p. 61.
73. D. Smythe, *Dependency Road: Communications, Capitalism, Consciousness and Canada* (Norwood, NJ, 1981), p. 39.
74. J. Pavitt (ed.), *Brand.New* (London, 2000), p. 23.
75. D. Holt, 'Why Do Brands Cause Trouble?', *Journal of Consumer Research*, 29(1) (2002), pp. 70--90; M. Ligas and J. Cotte, 'The Process of Negotiating Brand Meaning: A Symbolic Interactionist Perspective', in E. Arnould and L. Scott (eds), *Advances in Consumer Research*, Vol. 26 (Provo, UT, 1999).
76. M. Lazzarato, *Lavoro immateriale* (Verona, 1997); M. Weber, 'Politics as a Vocation', in H.H. Gerth and C.W. Mills (eds), *From Max Weber: Essays in Sociology* (London, 1948), pp. 102ff.
77. M. Hardt and A. Negri, *Multitude* (London, 2004), p. 212.

−4−

On the Movement of Porcelains

Rethinking the Birth of Consumer Society as Interactions of Exchange Networks, 1600–1750

Robert Batchelor

Pompey: Sir, she came in great with childe: and longing (saving your honour's reverence) for stewd prewyns; sir, we had but two in the house, which at that very distant time stood, as it were in a fruit-dish (a dish of some threepence; your honours have seen such dishes) they are not China-dishes, but very good dishes.
Escalus: Go too: go too: no matter for the dish sir.

William Shakespeare, *Measure for Measure*, Act 2, Scene 1[1]

It has become a commonplace to describe the seventeenth and eighteenth centuries as pregnant moments in the history of consumption in England and Holland.[2] Because of their role in a commercial society, everyday things seemed to have taken on a new importance. Subsequent scholarly labour drew attention to multiple and often unrelated births of this sort around the world, work that highlighted the anachronisms inherent in applying a term like 'consumerism' to the period.[3] Has it all been a tempest in a teacup? The dish mentioned above by Pompey, a tapster in a suburban brothel, was in the judgement of the 'ancient lord' Escalus a digression of 'no matter'. One would be hard pressed employing it to evoke the Baroque 'culture of curiosity', nor is its relation to the broader seventeenth-century porcelain craze clear, of which John Harold Plumb once wrote: '[n]o mania for material objects had ever been so widespread, so general to the rich of all nations'.[4] Yet Shakespeare has the value of the vulgar container and by implication the politics of the tavern and courtroom come into bizarre and comic juxtaposition with world-class 'China-dishes.' If longing for stewed prunes, the pregnant moment of consumption (and constipation), involves nothing extraordinary or even all that conscious, what about the mediation of the episode by a broad system of fashion (the 'Chinese'), one that moves objects vast distances between, across and through traditional social networks with their rather provincial questions of status and authority? Rather than searching for the birth of a consumer society in England or Europe as a precursor to modern mass 'consumerism', it may be more important to examine how the various habits of the self in this period, which no doubt emerged in complex regional hierarchies and networks of exchange, were also shaped and understood through markedly transcultural systems of fashion.[5] As part of this latter process, the global fashion system of porcelains between the late sixteenth and the mid-eighteenth centuries helped make sense of the interaction of expanding exchange networks, which bore unfamiliar textures, forms and images, as well as everyday things that performed mundane tasks.

The ubiquity of porcelain processes today makes the historical question of the way they highlighted problems associated with exchange in the seventeenth and early eighteenth centuries difficult to apprehend. Even the paper used to print this book contains kaolin or china clay (*gaolingtu*, ideal: $Al_2O_32SiO_22H_2O$) as both pulp filler and coating, ensuring a smooth, durable and white finish deemed appropriate for the business of scholarly exchange. This material along with some form of 'porcelain stone' (*cishi*, a pegmatite composed of feldspar [$Al_2O_32SiO_2K_2O$] and quartz [SiO_2]) and the development of high-temperature kilns formed the basis of a number of techniques now referred to under the general rubric of porcelains.[6] The results combined plasticity of form with remarkable hardness and durability, while high-temperature glazes allowed for surfaces of detailed texture, painting and writing. After a period of development from Shang dynasty high-fired stoneware (*c.* fourteenth century BCE) to pre-Tang dynasty white wares (*c.* 600 CE), porcelains became a significant medium in China from the Five Dynasties (907–60) to the Southern Song (1127–1279). The late sixteenth to early eighteenth century was a particularly important period in the history of porcelains as media not just because of their long tradition as objects that circulated transculturally, but also because as global bearers of fashions they began to mediate or gather together a large number of other media techniques and exchange processes. This allowed for the articulation of 'common differences' among a wide range of geographical locations.[7] Late Ming (1368–1644) production (as well as various regional imitations) also allowed for large domestic and foreign markets. Dutch imports into the Red Sea coffee emporium of al-Mukha for the year 1640 alone amounted to over 80,000 pieces, while conservative figures for the first half of the seventeenth century of imports into Amsterdam tally about three million pieces of Chinese and Japanese porcelain.[8] Especially in the Thames and Rhine estuaries and urban coastal China, the concurrent rapidity of urbanization, the global integration and exchange of currency (including cowries or '*porcelana*' as they were sometimes called), and the spread of printing all became intertwined with the development of exchange networks utilizing porcelains as a mass-produced and globally recognized medium, even if at times these ceramics served largely as the ballast for literally balancing the world silver, spice and textile trades.[9]

New patterns of circulation – 'modern' only in terms of the number of media involved, the extent of participation in exchange and the velocity of commodity movement – opened up performative possibilities for porcelains to articulate differences in a common medium. For a period they served as a visual medium for a wide range of social classes in diverse locations that could gather together more regionalized media like print, which circulated largely within language groupings, as well as coinage, painting styles, calligraphic writing, staple commodities and urban space itself. By the seventeenth and early eighteenth centuries, porcelains held power because they literally made sense of apparent ruptures in temporal and cultural continuity related to larger cities, new technologies and ever more rapid globalization of trade. Porcelains addressed three seventeenth-century ruptures in particular – incorporating into daily life the commodity that seemed to be a hybrid of nature and culture (materiality and inscription), comprehending the overlaps between various systems of symbols occurring because of exchange processes, and finally reconciling the multiple perspectives raised by the previous two ruptures. At stake in all three of these ruptures was a heightened sense of parallax, where everyday questions of exchange that should have been answerable through inherited tradition were constantly infused with visions of obscure, transcendent and disruptive systems of fashions, notably those of the 'Chinese'.[10]

The Hybrid Objects of Everyday Life

Porcelains circulated along with other commodities in the markets of Chinese coastal cities and the Eurasian, African and American emporia, but they had their own dynamic of difference. This held especially true in the new emporia of seventeenth-century Europe like Amsterdam and London, where widespread usage was relatively novel. Writers satirized and complained about problems emerging from repetitive encounters with porcelains, the way that their intrusions into everyday life could impinge upon the habits of the self in ways difficult to comprehend. Arbiters of taste demanded less opacity in porcelains, mixing a complex nostalgia for a former age of Venetian glass and commercial values with the optical and Enlightened pursuits of the new era. Porcelains, more than textiles, printing, coinage or stimulants (coffee, tea, sugar), both repeated and represented the movements of technical processes and fashion systems reaching beyond the boundaries of contemporary knowledge, the *episteme* itself.

Thus rather than simply being consumed or incorporated into domestic settings in these emporia at the western edge of Eurasia, porcelains engaged and even held bodies in the traces of past or unseen exchanges. In London Joseph Addison felt they almost mystically inverted the relation between owner and property, so that when a woman was 'visited' with a passion for '*China* ... it generally takes Possession of her for Life'.[11] Alexander Pope worried about the possibly infinite character of this problem. In his moral epistle 'To a Lady: Of the Characters of Women', dedicated to the famous collector of porcelains and lacquer-ware Henrietta Howard, he suggested that women should abandon sensual pleasure for virtue and character and remain 'Mistress of herself, tho' China fall' (l. 268). Jonathan Swift compared the fetish for porcelain to that for print, writing to Hester Vanhomrigh on 30 June 1711 that he had seen a bookseller purchasing an old library and his 'fingers itched, as yours would do at a china shop'.[12] Here the spatial lure of the fashion system replaced the temporal lure of the book as the record of past ages. In *The Ladies Visiting Day*, William Burnaby satirized the character Lady Lovetoy's love of 'monstrous' porcelain idols as a kind of polite slippage into pagan materialism:

> *China-woman*: These are Pagods, Madam, that the Indians Worship.
> *Lady Lovetoy*: I am so far an Indian.
> *Fulvia*: How ignorant they are, to make a God of a bit of China!
> *Lady Lovetoy*: Truly I think it is a genteeler deity than Beaten Gold.
> *Fulvia*: So should I, if Religion were a Fashion.[13]

More effectively than a Jesuit confessor, porcelains might even be converting the body – the female body and more generally the social body – away from Protestant textual obsessions through fragmented material repetition of difference (God as 'a bit of China'). Like money itself, the ability of porcelains to capture and preserve moments of exchange remote from the domestic setting through a system of fashion made them more genteel 'than beaten gold' and at least competitors with those massive silver services congealed from the efforts of slave labourers in the infamous American mines of the Spanish empire.

Arguably, the European interest in porcelain derived in part from its ability to resist classification within traditional schemes of objective knowledge (Aristotelian *episteme* or *scientia*), failing to be neatly contained within the 'natural' histories of the collection, curiosity cabinet or even the more ambiguous painterly still-life. Most sixteenth-century European commentators thought porcelain arose from some kind of natural process. The widely known account by Portuguese chronicler Duarte Barbosa suggested burying pulverized shells for long periods to produce porcelains.[14] Girolamo Cardano and Julius Cæsar Scaliger compared porcelain to Roman myrrhina, both thought to be congealed liquids shaped by the energies of the earth. They debated whether porcelain was a relic of ancient culture debased by mass production or a modern improvement on ancient practices.[15] All accounts initially assumed that Aristotelian natural order controlled the epistemic classification of technical processes rather than the technical processes themselves commanding the conceptualization of nature.

By downplaying the importance of porcelains as an imagistic medium and as objects of mass artisanal production, the burial theory suggested an early European resistance to broader questions about exchange raised by porcelains. One of the first English commentators on the subject, Francis Bacon, tried to sever porcelain from this realm of natural processes. Bacon called the transformation involved in burial 'induration', conceived of as 'a great alteration in nature'.[16] Comparable processes included the transformation or generation of earth apart from any human interference, but others used artificial heat such as brick-making or glassblowing. According to Bacon, porcelain was an 'artificial cement' or 'plaster' buried in the earth for several generations to create an 'artificial mine', a parallel to the natural deposits of silver possessed by the Spanish. Yet, because of artifice, the performance of durability did not transmit those properties to its possessor:

> So there is none of them ... but hath a double nature; inheritable and real while it is contained with the mass of the earth, and transitory and personal when it is once severed ... And this is not because it becometh moveable ... but because by their severance they lose their nature of perpetuity ... for by their continuance of body stands their continuance of time.[17]

Removal from the earth took porcelain from the realm of the pure thing, 'inheritable and real', to the hybrid natural–cultural object, 'transitory and personal'.[18] Porcelains, then, could only serve as a reminder of the durability and temporal continuity of the inherited natural order. This double nature of porcelain – connected self-making material thing and the deterritorialized, technical, consumed commodity object driven by the whims of fashion – required that aforementioned parallax view that was simultaneously everyday and transcendent, where two contradictory aspects are juxtaposed to achieve comprehension of the thing. For Bacon, the demand for a constant revaluation of the transitory and fashionable object's relation to natural order provokes a philosophical response that defines territory (land) and commodities as two distinct orders of value, even when the technical boundaries seem unclear as in the case of earthenware and especially porcelains.

Another approach, challenging the burial theory entirely, considered porcelain as a process of refinement related to the circulation patterns of Chinese urban commerce. Gonzales de Mendoza (1540–1617), whose book on China was translated into English in 1588 and became a standard reference, pioneered this approach. He described 'shops full of earthen vessels of divers making ... so good cheape that for foure rials of plate they give fiftie pieces'. As to the process, 'they make them of very strong earth, the which they doo breake all to pieces and grinde it, and put it into cisternes with water, made of lime and stone, and after that they have well tumbled and tossed it in the water: for the creame that is upon it they make the finest sort of them, & the lower they go, spending that substance, that is the courser'. The resulting production could be 'of what colour they please, the which will never be lost: then they put them into their kilnes and burne them'. But, explained Mendoza: 'The finest sort of this is never carried out of the countrie, for that it is spent in the service of the king, and his governours, & is so fine and cleere, that it seemeth to be of fine and perfect cristall.' The numerous porcelains 'made in that kingdome, and ... brought into Portugall, and carried into the Peru, and Nova Espania, and into other parts of the world' disproved the time-intensive burial theory, suggesting instead hierarchies of 'the best and the finest' defined by techniques of production and imperial tastes.[19] Instead of a parallax produced from a temporal break with nature, the split was cultural and global. Regionalized imperial order struggled against market overproduction and a diversity of exchange settings scattered across the planet. Positing spatial orders of exchange from the shop to the court to 'other parts of the world' could maintain the thingness of porcelain ('the finest sort' which is transparent), while appreciating that mass production and global exchange levelled the commodity into crude opacity, where through repetition 'forme and fashion [appear] as they do here'. Porcelain was not neatly 'severed', but instead a series of sometimes illicit exchanges carried it from its proper destination (the Ming court) and thus diluted its true performative power in a world governed by tribute and gifts. This imperial diffusion theory suggested that hierarchies of value for objects were created regionally, politically, so that true chinaware never really left China and the empire itself was the measure and source of value.

In general, a fashion system like porcelain from the late sixteenth to the early eighteenth centuries produced concerns about transcultural and translinguistic mediation by technical processes. Not surprisingly, in places where porcelains had circulated for centuries the process of comprehending the rapid expansion of these exchanges during the late sixteenth and seventeenth centuries was often subordinated in more general questions about culture, exchange and urbanization. The vast late-Ming and early-Qing accumulation and usage of ceramics in Beijing, the Yangzi Delta region and southern coastal cities of China raised questions there of how mass-produced artisanal commodities like porcelains should be distinguished. This occurred largely through contested notions of the unity and tradition of *wen* (writing/culture) and the manifold nature of *wu* (things/matter).[20] Such questions derived more from the techniques of circulation and exchange spurred by the rapid commercialization and the rising prominence of Chinese urban and suburban populations than the technical methods of porcelain production. Indeed, the distinction between *taoqi* (common earthenware) and *taoci* (high-fired wares, i.e. stoneware and porcelain) held less importance than the variety of uses for pottery products in urban settings and the criteria of their circulation. The 'Ceramics' chapter in Song Yingxing's encyclopedia of industrial craft, the *Tian gong kai wu* (1637), comments on the vast demand for ceramic products – from dishes to bricks. It then addresses how new designs and techniques help maintain a sense of coherent civilization:

> Sturdy earth crocks preserve wine to a good age, while clean pottery vessels are instruments for containing the sacrificial offerings of wines and bean sauces. The sacrificial dishes of Shang and Zhou times [*c.* 1700–700 BCE] were made of wood; was it not because the people then wanted to show great respect [towards ancestors]? In later times, however, ingenious designs began to appear in various localities, human craftsmanship exerted its talents, producing superior ceramic wares beautiful as a woman endowed with fair complexion and delicate bones, sparkling in quiet retreats or at festive boards, a concrete sign of civilized life [*wenming*]. It is hardly necessary to adhere [to traditions] forever.[21]

Ceramics here suggest concretized emblems of social processes, moments of time capturing various changes, with superior quality as the standard of judgement rather than slavish dedication to tradition. Thus while Europeans might perceive porcelains as the epitome of Chinese exchange relations, they were part of broader questions about fashion and civilized life in urban coastal China – precisely the kind of rupture or discontinuity that a fashion system moves objects across.

By the late Ming, porcelains were ordinary things that, like other objects, fed into and challenged standard distinctions about value. Song Yingxing makes less of the question of distinction than the everyday, noting that the majority of porcelains were made on the wheel to produce the 'wares' (*qi*) 'needed for everyday life' (*sheng ren ri yong bi*).[22] The ware was more prosaic than the thing (*wu*), a distinction embedded in practice and descriptive language. Craig Clunas has mined the literature of Ming literati collectors for various terms of judgement about things – *jiu wu* ('old things') often linked with the Shang, Zhou or Han period; *qi wu* ('rare things') such as those found in an elegant production centre like Suzhou with an air of antiquity to them; and *yun wu* ('charming things') having a certain degree of elegance. All were 'concrete signs of civilized life' and formed a web of distinctions and differentiations in *wen* used to comprehend 'things-in-motion'.[23] Enmeshing things in several levels of language addressed the question of change or tendency (their performative character), not unlike how Wang Bi (226–49) described the *Yijing* ('The [Ex]Change Classic') as designed, 'to treat exhaustively the true innate tendency of things and their countertendencies to spuriousness [*qingwei*] ... [to] let change occur and achieve free flow in order to exhaust the potential of the benefit involved'.[24] The *Yijing* in general, as most classical commentators noted, dealt with the production of both the images of heaven and the 'ten thousand things' (*wanwu*) of earth, the latter inspiring the Song dynasty neo-Confucian investigation of things (*kewu*), which carried on into the Ming. Thus, porcelains circulating in urban China also required a kind of parallax view, both everyday and transcendent, but one perceived explicitly through developing yet sophisticated languages of distinction among dense urban networks of changing fashions for various things, rather than the more specific difficulties raised by porcelains in particular as hybrid commodity objects that Bacon and Mendoza tried to confront.

Fields of Exchange and Pattern Recognition

As the production and distribution of porcelains expanded during the seventeenth century, new and multiple techniques developed in relation to them, exchange and circulation between trading emporia increased, relationships between porcelains and various media grew more complex, and their performative powers proved increasingly influential. The primary production centres at the time were the massive and rapidly expanding complexes at Jingdezhen in Jiangxi province, as well as those at Dehua in Fujian and various *min yao* (private or commercial kilns) sponsored by coastal merchant syndicates in Anhui, Jiangxi, Zhejiang, Fujian and Guangdong provinces. Production sites also existed in Korea, Vietnam and Hizen province, Japan, especially after the 1640s. Both Mandarin calligraphic and painting traditions, as well as writing practices related to local languages or 'dialects', notably Yue (Cantonese), Hakka, Min, Gan and Wu, and also Japanese, Korean and Vietnamese, inflected these production sites. But in many ways the most important forces shaping the development of the medium came out of urban fields of exchange. Fruitful interference among repetitive products allowed by mass artisanal production that nevertheless were adjusted for a wide range of audiences kept a language for porcelains from solidifying during the seventeenth century. As the Jesuit Louis Le Comte noted, '[t]hose that have Skill do not always agree in their Judgment they pass upon them; and I perceive that in *China*, as well as in *Europe*, Phancy bears a main stroke in the matter'. Each piece showed evidence of the various hands that had produced it, so that 'few Vessels but have some one of these defects; there must not only be found no spots, nor flaws, but notice must be taken whether there be some places brighter than others, which happens when the Pencil is unequally poised'.[25] Porcelains bore traces of uneven techniques of writing, preserving the efforts of hundreds of thousands of artisans to reimagine and to integrate various media in order to facilitate exchanges.

Rather than an essential difference between Europe and China in their approaches to porcelain (mapping versus distinction), three interrelated fields of exchange, each related to dominant forms of the reproduction of writing and the modes of commerce, emerged for porcelain by the end of the seventeenth century – the xylographic urban networks of coastal China (as well as Korea and Japan), the calligraphic emporia of Southeast Asia and Islamic trading systems, and the new typographic emporia of the European Atlantic coast (notably London and Amsterdam). Each field played a constitutive role in reshaping both the imagistic and environmental (form, usage) aspects of porcelains as media. In turn, these interactions pulled porcelains out of the older realm of the courtly tribute trade and into new roles as media that brought together symbolic practices from other seventeenth-century media and from a series of regions or fields of exchange around the world.[26]

The coastal cities of China had close connections with sites of porcelain production and deep cultural connections with traditions of calligraphy, painting and xylographic printing. In the late Ming, this first field of exchange linked porcelains with images from illustrated novels and other woodblock-printed texts. These were largely printed in urban areas like the Yangzi Delta and thus closer to sites of porcelain exchange rather than production. This convergence of print and porcelain occurred alongside three other related phenomena – the increased use of wage labour associated with the rise of urban commerce, the growth of private kilns and commerce more generally outside imperial supervision, and the rise of a significant population of cultured urban readers drawn from less cultivated merchant and gentry backgrounds who wanted favourite scenes from novels, plays, history, religious stories and folk culture on the surface of their household porcelains.

Thus the parallel developments of woodblock printing and porcelain painting became intertwined from the 1580s. For example, a Ming reprint of Su Shi's (1037–1101) *Chi bi fu* ('Rhapsody on Red Cliff'), a story about the pleasures of a wine-drinking party beneath the Red Cliffs near Wuhan, inspired a series of both high-end and low-end porcelain bowls (see Figure 3). Surviving examples have longer and shorter versions of the story inscribed in *kaishu* (regular script) and adapt with variations a woodcut showing the revellers' boat.[27] Certain aspects of these bowls suggest a Chinese audience, but they circulated as far as the Ottoman collections in Istanbul as well as Paris in the early seventeenth century, where Jacques Linard used one for two separate versions of his painting *Les Cinq Sens* (1627, 1638).[28] As the Linard painting indicates, the bowls might be read based on purely visual and sensual cues as well as in more site-specific cultural and literary ways. Examined more precisely by an urban reader of Chinese, the actual story text on the bowl and the image contrast the river's constant flow with the ephemeral objects it carries – whether boats filled with wine drinkers or fallen leaves – a contradiction embodied by the object itself, which can be seen either as one of many changing things or as part of the changeless aspects of the world. This was also an ambiguity about possession of the bowl and how the possessor (be they Chinese, Ottoman or French) might read it at one or many of these levels, given their degree of literacy and exposure to classical literature.

Chinese commentators were well aware that even readers and collectors in the sophisticated Yangzi Delta had complicated and by no means uniform sets of tastes arising from desires to emulate literati culture, lingering attachments to folk and popular forms, influences from designs used on exported wares, and participation in the urban social spaces of the brothel, the wine shop, the tea house and the Buddhist and Daoist shrine. They employed objects like porcelains to help define themselves and their situation or condition – *kuang* is the word used on the Red Cliff bowl – even if most porcelain did not have as many complex allusions and lessons as these bowls did. Some private kilns also adopted the *xieyi* ('write/desire') style of calligraphy and painting.[29] Sketchy but expressive and unrestrained, not careless but attempting a kind of innocence or naturalness, porcelain painting like this simultaneously tended towards the calligraphic and the popular in its iconic

Figure 3 Blue and White 'Red Cliff' Porcelain Bowl (*c*. 1620–44), Jingdezhen, British Museum, Asia F.811

Source: Copyright the Trustees of the British Museum.

reduction of brushwork and wide dissemination. Tensions remained during the Ming and early Qing between the traditional *gongbi* (lit. 'skilled writing') wares and the *xiyie* style, but porcelains did not generally fall into clear categories. Calligraphic, pictorial and material variation generated complex and ambiguous positioning of objects within networks of exchange.

Urbanization encouraged a studied virtual tourism among the elite through commodities like porcelains, landscape paintings and woodcuts, which could serve as a meditative replacement for Daoist nature – the virtuous qualities of a wild or natural landscape.[30] But porcelains also connected the household to the urban landscape – the 'floating worlds' of the outdoor drinking party, the wine shop (*jiulou*) and the courtesan districts in Beijing, Nanjing, Suzhou, Yangzhou and elsewhere. Haunted by the stereotypical *kuangshi* ('wild gentleman'), these sites served as informal meeting places for officials, literati and the scions of wealthy gentry and merchants, and social exchanges took place over and among porcelains. Here the narrow visual pleasure associated with objects (screen paintings, porcelain wine cups and decor, general furnishings and social spaces) merged with a broader sensual pleasure of the body made possible by courtesans, who participated both through managing an environment of objects and language (as the courtesan poets of this period suggest) and as objectified bodies valued in relation to their cultivation. These exchange-oriented spaces both defined the taste of the urban newly rich and in turn were defined by it, generating a demand for decorated interiors and commodified images reminiscent of their ephemeral pleasures.

The broadest cross-section of social groups participated in the markets and streets of urban centres. When Dutch ambassadors visited the Yangzi Delta in the 1650s, the extent of commerce amazed them, especially the public participation of women, and printed accounts included engravings of shopping districts.[31] The retail shop (*men*) and the vendor's stall or booth (*tan*) both fell under a special tax in 1425 – the *mentan shui* – to try to help paper currency circulate. This was lifted in core areas of the Yangzi Delta (Jiangnan) in 1528, spurring commercial growth. An unstable currency system and mass artisanal production made turnover less important than profit, and retail outlets remained ready to close and hoard inventory if necessary due to overvalued money.[32] Shopping architecture thus had a temporary feel, closely tied with the street or traditional market spaces and sensitive to fashions. This flexible and modular system of exchange made the transition to speciality porcelain for Islamic, Japanese, Southeast-Asian and European markets relatively easy. The shop was thus more of a locus of exchange than a stable environment, simultaneously organizing the chaos of things while remaining portable so that it could be set up anywhere and quickly in the spirit of Li Sung's famous painting of the *Knicknack Peddler* (1211), who carried the 'ten-thousand things' on his back.

The ceramic brick walls of the city or a temple yard allowed for this kind of temporariness. Architecturally, they proved of great advantage in setting up 'Chinatowns' in places like Manila and Bantam. Whole urban fabrics of markets, artisans, merchants, restaurants, shopping districts and labouring populations could appear rapidly, developing exchange relationships outside the mainland. These 'Chinatowns' helped define the second major field of exchange in which porcelains circulated – calligraphic emporia. Chinese sojourner merchants quickly built complex urban relationships with local scribal-based administrations. Manila, a silver entrepôt founded by the Spanish in 1571, accumulated 22,300 pieces of porcelain before the first trade galleons sailed to Acapulco.[33] By 1588 alongside the mestizo 'Spanish' population of 355 lived a permanent settlement of 600 Chinese merchants and artisans and a temporary population of about 2,000 more Chinese merchants and sailors. At Bantam the English and Dutch located their factories in a Chinese sojourner merchant community because of its brick (ceramic) architecture, dense network of artisans and services (from goldsmiths to brewers), well-established merchant connections and supply of wage labour. Typically in this pattern of merchant settlement, a Daoist altar was set up initially, followed later by larger Daoist and Buddhist temples that alluded to sites on the Chinese mainland. These not only pulled together the Chinese community but also helped establish ritual relations with locals.[34] Trade porcelains, often doubling as gifts, frequently used Daoist and Buddhist symbols as translatable signs of exchange, a characteristic inherited by the *kraak* wares carried by the Portuguese and Dutch. Certain designs would often take on roles in local religions, as was the case with the famous Malay kendi vessels.

Not only the sojourner Chinese but also trading middlemen and local buyers played important roles in what kinds of porcelains circulated in emporia and which were chosen for transshipment. Exchange frequently took place as 'point-for-point *ad hoc* settlements'.[35] In the seventeenth century, European factors also made key purchasing decisions in these contexts, often with only vague advice from the metropole. As the English East India Company directors wrote to their factors at Tonquin in 1681, 'that which will turne us best to accompt are cupps of all Kinds, Sizes & Colours and all sorts of small Toyes of severall figures & fashions, the more strange & novill the better and the more variety there is in your parcells the more acceptable they will be'.[36] Even then only 16 per cent of late-Ming exports of porcelain went to Europe, most going to Japan or Southeast Asia, which exerted significant pressure on the types of porcelains brought into the market.[37]

In this complicated transcultural atmosphere, porcelain held a prominent place as both a tribute gift and a trade good. The Malay Archipelago in particular became a nexus of South Asian and Chinese trade, traditionally drawing Southeast-Asian, Chinese, Gujarati, Chetti, Arab and Armenian and later European traders, all of whom had differing approaches to exchange media like coinage and script. Jacob Cornelisz van Neck (1564–1638), who visited Bantam from 1598 to 1600, noted in his journal that the two mosques at Bantam had walls of brick inlaid with porcelain. The Chinese gave a yearly gift of porcelains as part of the pepper and clove trade.[38] Money could be scarce, as the basic economy used a mixture of tribal and slave labour to gather pepper. The English would trade on credit with the Chinese from the earliest establishment of their factories, in part as a mutual measure to subvert the growing power of Dutch commerce in the region.[39] The English also had to give the Chinese credit during the period after the large junks from China arrived early in the year because of imbalances between Chinese copper 'Cashys' and silver *reals*. Before the junk arrived, few Chinese imperial 'Cashys' circulated in the economy but lots of Spanish *reals* ('royals') did. But since the Chinese sent to China all the *reals* they could obtain, cash was then cheap all year, 'wherefore we [the English] were forced to give them credit, or else wee must loose the principall time of yeare for our sales'.[40] A complicated network of gifts and debts between the Dutch, the Sultan, the English and the Chinese required constant negotiations over who owed whom what, who would pay whom when and who could purchase pepper at what price and with what form of money. It should come as no surprise, then, that when the Dutch felt they had finally circumvented such difficult exchanges, they commemorated the event in porcelain (see Figure 4). This cup design comes from a 1728 silver ryder struck at the Hoorn mint for use in Asia, with the Dutch VOC emblem and the caption 'Concordia res parvae crescunt' ('The concord of things from the smallest grows'). It was emblematic of the triumph of a uniform medium of exchange, as direct Dutch trade at Guangzhou began that year.[41]

Figure 4 Polychrome Porcelain Dish and Saucer (*c*. 1729), Jingdezhen, British Museum, Asia Franks 797

Source: Copyright the Trustees of the British Museum.

Calligraphic emporia tended to be scribal-oriented, often with a strong Islamic presence, but neither script nor coinage conveyed the image of stability and continuity that porcelains could. Like their namesakes the cowry shell, porcelains mediated across the worlds of gift and exchange as the more symbolic and more sublimated element of a process fraught with tensions and market instabilities. For example, standard *kraak* plate designs of the period (see Figure 5, which derives from these) often had eight petals surrounding a central circular design, which both alluded to Islamic seals such as those of the Mughal emperor and the Sultan of Aceh, as well as the Buddhist lotus flower and eight-fold patterns common to Malay, Hindi and Sufi religious traditions. Designs were both repetitive and closely linked with writing and brushwork – the paper-based world initially created by the spread of Islam as well as more regional palm-leaf writing traditions. Calligraphic elements also constantly called attention to the connection between writing and porcelain painting. Porcelains mediated between diverse script systems through iconic symbols, 'natural' and pattern-based ornamentation, and the actual inclusion of various sacred scripts (especially Arabic, Sanskrit, Latin and Chinese). Multiple visual readings linked together discontinuous scribal or exchange practices by juxtaposing sacred, dynastic and mercantile symbols and substituting the brushwork of painting for the authoritative demands of scribal writing. In this sense, porcelains acted as a force for equilibrium in exchange materially as a commodity, physically as ship ballast and imaginatively as a visual medium.

The currency and commodity exchanges of the Malay Archipelago fed into a broader network of emporia across Eurasia, Africa and even the Americas – the 'country trade' that channelled goods among scribal-based religious and dynastic communities. In many of the calligraphic emporia in Islamic and Christian regions without a Chinese sojourner presence, earthenware cultures developed independently and later supplemented and struggled to survive against imports of Chinese porcelain. Numerous examples of earthenware imitating Chinese porcelains exist from Southeast Asia, the Islamic Safavid and Ottoman empires, eastern Africa and even Mexico. There were also imitations of Islamic blue-and-white earthenware by Mediterranean majolica and Talavera potters and in the famous Medici porcelains of the late sixteenth century. Because most Islamic regions prohibited the representation of human figures, much of the symbolism was floral, along with stylized versions of Buddhist or Daoist emblems and Chinese and Arabic scripts. This older Islamic trade shaped the early parameters for *kraak* ware making up much of the Portuguese and initial Dutch trade.

A third field of exchange emerged during the seventeenth century, the typographic emporium, in which local porcelain and earthenware cultures (such as majolica or Delftware) developed in tandem with imports from China, only to be redefined by the expansion of typographic printing, copperplate engraving and commodity exchange. London and Amsterdam were classic examples. Traders sent designs taken from printed sources, as well as sculpted models designed for new commodity staples like coffee, tea, chocolate, sugar and tobacco, to Chinese and Japanese production centres as a counterbalance to the importation of vast amounts of new images and forms on porcelains.[42] In London, and to a lesser extent Amsterdam, a shopping culture developed around porcelains that paralleled developing networks of book and print sellers as well as textile shops. As containers of global staples from drinks to drugs, porcelains pulled together and defined the texture of much of the early culture of shopping, as well as social settings like the tea table or the coffee house. As much as by more parochial developments in typography and engraving, this was a field of exchange built out of and performed by the exchanges and global fashions for media like porcelains.

Compared with the cities of the Yangzi Delta, where this process had gone on since at least the Southern Song dynasty, both print and large-scale commodity exchanges were relatively new in London and Amsterdam. The china shop, or 'china house' as it was called in Ben Jonson's *The Silent Woman* (1609), became by the early eighteenth century the shopping experience *par excellence*. As Daniel Defoe wrote in 1710:

> We see the most noble shops in the City taken up with the valuable utensils of the tea-table. The china warehouses are little marts within themselves ... and the eminent Corner Houses in the chief streets of London are chosen out by the town tinkers to furnish us with tea-kettles and chocolate pots. Vide Catherine Street and Bedford Buildings. Two thousand pound is reckoned a small stock in copper pots and lacquered kettles, and the very fitting up one of these brazen people's shops with fine sashes, etc. to set forth his ware costs above 500 l. sterling, which is more by half than the best draper or mercer's shop in London requires.[43]

Unlike the stalls of Chinese metropoli, shops in late seventeenth-century London as well as in provincial towns were increasingly indoors, permanent and thus more capital-intensive establishments. Relatively unique practices of exchange characterized by increased amounts of capital, new forms of credit and debt, and London's emergence as a long-distance transshipment emporium, all allowed small businesses to invest in buildings as well as in more permanent stocks during the seventeenth century. Because of a lack of artisanal mass production, however, these permanent stocks had a certain hodge-podge atmosphere of collection, layered temporalities of the global exchange system that only in the 1720s and 1730s gave way to more uniform patterns and sets.

Porcelains in many ways converted London, but the results would of course be radically different from those in either the cities of the Yangzi Delta or the Chinatowns of the Malay Archipelago. As their own wares fell out of fashion, artisans turned to decorating 'white' unpainted china and started their own retail shops as 'toymakers' to supplement their income by reselling porcelain.[44] While enamellers, ironmongers and silversmiths carried on some of the china trade, 'china women' ran many shops. In the mid-1730s, for example, Dorothy Russel owned a shop at the Queen's Head and Anchor, Ludgate Hill, her bills explaining that she 'sells all sorts of Teas, Coffee, Chocolate, Snuff, & China Ware, Glasses & Lacquer'd Ware, Wholesale & Retail at Reasonable Rates'.[45] These entrepreneurs depended on fickle buyers untrained by advertising, who in turn often demanded the variety characteristic of 'old China' rather than the excessive uniformity of pattern allowed by regular shipments from the 1710s and 1720s. Even as early as 1708 Thomas Baker describes in his play *The Fine Lady's Airs* a retail operation resting on top of a pyramid scheme of debt dependent on overaccumulation:

> *Lady Rodham*: I'm overstock'd with China, and they say 'tis grown so common. I intend to sacrifice mine to my Monkey.
> *India Woman*: Nay, pray, my Lady, buy somewhat of me, you know I'm in great Tribulation, I trusted a couple of Trollops, that were turn'd out of the Play-House, for having too much assurance for the Stage, and set up a little Shop in Spring Garden; and the bold Jades are gone a strolling Fifty Pounds in my Debt.[46]

Attempts to unload inventories of unfashionable patterns pushed the boundaries of the market, encouraging the development of advertising and more aggressive sales to create buyers. In 1734 the East India Company wrote to their supercargo for the Grafton: 'Although there is still great quantities of chinaware left in Town it is only the refuse of many years, very bad patterns, and no variety, therefore could no ways turn to account, and still the loss as there has been such large quantities lately carried to England.'[47] Stores began to cater to distinctions in pattern, advertising and offering one-stop shopping for the world of the tea table. According to his trade cards, Benjamin Payne's shop on Fleet Street from the late 1730s into the 1750s offered 'Chinaware Old & New', glasses, tables, fans as well as a variety of teas and chocolate.

Buyers of porcelains in England used them to create interior spaces that had not previously existed – from the coffee house to the tea and dining table

– in addition to collections that decorated rooms, furniture and mantelpieces, alluding to the complexity of these new realms of sociability. From the 1720s the East India Company put an increasing emphasis on purchasing 'useful sorts' of wares, essentially sets designed to supply the markets for tableware and tea settings.[48] Local porcelain manufacturing from the 1740s and 1750s followed suit. From the materials available in a china shop, one could thus assemble an environment, as Elizabeth Montagu wrote to her sister on 3 January 1750 from Sandleford, Berkshire: 'I saw our friend Cotes the day before I left Town [London] … She has only a small lodging and I think she might afford a house of her own … She might furnish it in the present fashion of some cheap paper and ornaments of Chelsea China or the manufacture of Bow, which makes a room look neat and finished.'[49] This autonomy of a 'house of her own' may seem to be a kind of 'reprivatization' in which the setting becomes 'predictable and expected', as Henri Lefebvre has written of consumer culture in the 1950s, or to use Montagu's words 'neat and finished'. The creation of new environments through a process of 'globalization' seems to be 'achieved in the mode of withdrawal', in which control of distribution allows fashion systems to become controlled and predictable.[50] Yet the exchanges and the diverging repetitions of writing and picturing conveyed by porcelain as a technical medium did not end simply because both the emporia of coastal China and those of coastal Europe had the ability to produce their own imaginative 'floating worlds'. The process of differentiation and play with *chinoiserie* fantasies in the print emporia only raised further questions about the proper critical and cultural perspectives to bring to bear in relation to transcritical and transcultural fashion systems.

Perspective Problems and Dislocation

During the late seventeenth and early eighteenth centuries, images with hybrid forms of perspective began to appear on porcelains which did not simply weave symbols together as in the old calligraphic emporia. This was in large part due to the circulation in Chinese porcelain workshops of copperplate prints from Europe – a practice foreshadowed by a small number of Jesuit printing experiments in China during the early part of the seventeenth century. European observers often remarked that Chinese paintings and woodcuts lacked a sense of proper (i.e. Renaissance single-point) perspective, which distorted their human subjects. This critique did not extend to natural objects (flowers, plants, birds, etc.), which were accepted in their more calligraphic mode. In the early eighteenth-century plate shown in Figure 5, Chinese porcelain artists re-rendered Robert and

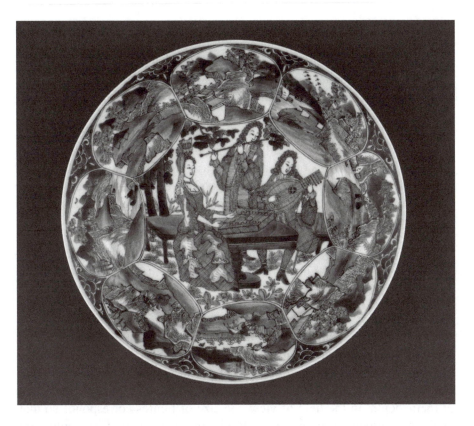

Figure 5 Blue and White Porcelain Dish (*c.* 1700–20), Jingdezhen, British Museum, Ionides Bequest, Asia 1963–4.22.18

Source: Copyright the Trustees of the British Museum.

Nicholas Bonnart's allegorical engraving about love entitled 'Symphonie du Tympanum, du Luth et de la Flute d'Allemagne', using traditional Chinese perspective techniques and framing it with various landscape and floral panels.

A piece like this highlighted the question of dual perspectives by juxtaposing traditional landscape technique with the redrawn European print. The human figures bend to adjust to the concavity of the plate and the lines of Chinese-style vertical perspective, while the transformation of the eyes calls attention to perception and difference. The surrounding panels, shaped like the petals of a lotus, move the eye through a series of landscapes framing the music. The original inscribed meaning of the engraving – about the superior pleasures of love to music – shifts towards an almost Daoist sense of harmony in relation to the landscape. Thus the reinscription and reframing on porcelain fundamentally changed how the French print would have been read both in terms of content and in terms of form.

When Erwin Panofsky argued that perspective was a kind of 'symbolic form', he did so on the basis of the difference between the way eyes actually perceive (two not one, in motion not fixed, upon a concave surface rather than a flat one) and the way that Renaissance perspective abstracted and constructed space mathematically.[51] Both European and Chinese painters in this period would have recognized painting as a visual technique of abstraction rather than a replication of the operations of the eye. Chinese painters were acutely aware that the medium shaped perspective, as in this passage from Cao Xuexin's eighteenth-century novel *The Story of the Stone*:

> The shape of the paper imposes its own perspectives. You have to make them into a composition. You have to decide which to bring into the foreground and which to push into the background, which to leave out altogether and which to show only in glimpses.[52]

Wu Hung has identified two traditional Chinese methods that create a sense of verisimilitude (*huan*) in painting. In the vertical method, two sets of lines drawn across the edge of figures and angled towards each other from opposite sides of the page create receding pictorial planes. Regardless of their 'depth' in the field of view, the size of figures corresponds so that, as the eye moves to the centre of the image, it feels as if one enters the picture. In the horizontal method, the eye either scanned across a continually scrolling picture (for which the vase is an ideal medium) or across a series of sequential cartouches that worked like the frames of a panel cartoon. This horizontal aspect gave the pictures temporality, while the vertical aspect implied motion.[53] Paintings were thus read visually (*du*, 'witnessed') according to the scanning movement of the eyes, rather than observed through the technique of single-point perspective.

Sir William Temple, writing in his 1685 'Essay on the Garden of Epicurus', called such images 'striking' – literally 'moving' if he followed Thomas Hobbes' theory of vision – in their 'beauty without apparent order'. *Sharawadgi* was the 'Chinese' word he coined for this method.[54] Arguably, their visual challenge to the sense of perspectival order in Europe also encouraged a kind of retreat into colour and more simple, iconic forms characteristic of *chinoiserie* designs in the eighteenth century. The central image increasingly took over from border and panel space to give a single scene or figure and focus rather than multiple images. Japanese porcelain exported from the port of Imari probably played a role in this simplification, as did so-called *Chine de commande* – the full maturity of cooperation between the Chinese export industry and the European trading companies that permitted orders for the direct copying of designs from copperplate prints using enamel paints. By 1734 the Dutch were systematically ordering porcelain designs (both shape and decoration) made in China to specification and others quickly followed.[55] Certainly not all porcelain coming from Canton was specifically designed for and by Europeans at this point, but it represented a much larger volume and much more predictable designs than had been the case in the seventeenth century. Moreover, in the 1740s, and especially the 1750s, new domestic porcelain manufacturing enterprises in London and subsequently across England, following upon earlier continental enterprises like Meissen, cut down further on the amount of transcultural 'experimentation'.

Displacing visual impact through *chinoiserie* and the strict regulation of production must have seemed a kind of solution to perspective problems generated out of the manifold collisions of scribal practices, exchange relations and visual techniques. Indeed, most scholarship tries to separate and distinguish this stage of *chinoiserie* as pure consumption abstracted from the process of translation and exchange, indeed from any kind of broader pattern of difference and repetition in fashions performed through the process of exchange of media like porcelains on a global scale. This approach reduces the mania for things Chinese to a purely 'Western' phenomenon of exoticism and views it as a kind of corruption once it subsequently returns to influence the xylographic field of exchange in urban China.[56] The mistake here is to ignore the relation between the development of *chinoiserie* fantasies and the broader problem of exchange. The parallax view and multiple perspectives generated by broadly transcultural systems of fashion like porcelains are thus sublimated into insignificant rococo play. Only during the eighteenth century does the field of exchange centred on the print emporia of Western Europe develop enough maturity of practice, density of writing, quality of technique and quantity of transaction to fully enter into the long-developing play of repetitions in porcelains. In ways not very different from how porcelains performed in the coastal cities of China or the calligraphic emporia of the Malay Archipelago, the cup and saucer with the Dutch ducatoon as an emblem of '*Concordia*' and the plate with the French engraving as an emblem of symphonic *harmonia* contract the movements of broader and deeper processes of exchange. They give record as unique snapshots in the complex history of exchange of illusory hopes for some stable privileged point or singular perspective. The primary question, then, should not be what these objects represent in terms of Europeans' fantasies about themselves and others, as if such views were possible without subjective illusions, but instead: what complex and dense movements of exchange produced such unbelievable things?

The three sections of this chapter have tried to answer this question by examining three overlapping roles that porcelains have performed in the history of exchange from the late sixteenth to the mid-eighteenth centuries. First, as porcelains circulated through urban exchange networks across Eurasia and the Americas from the late sixteenth century, they appeared to various possessors to embody hybrids of nature and culture or materiality and writing. The circulations of such hybrid objects raised the attractiveness of physical attributes of porcelains such as preservation, durability or concreteness. In this sense, they both participated in and promised respite from the seventeenth-century flux of things and scripts. Second, porcelains converted complex questions about exchange and the multiplicity of media into dream-like juxtapositions of symbols and calligraphic visions of nature. They turned the daunting task of engaging with the multifaceted transactions occurring among the great emporia of Eurasia into the more accessible question of pattern recognition across the shapes and surfaces of porcelains. The world in this sense became increasingly 'Chinese' in terms of fashion, while over time regional variations of media and commodity usage made such fashions relatively autonomous – fantastic *chinoiseries*. Finally, this kind of reduction in turn raised the question of proper perspective, not only upon the world of exchange and fashion but also upon the hybrid objects and shifting patterns of writing that porcelains embodied. By the early to middle eighteenth century, especially in Europe but even in China (as well as points in between), a demand for unbelievable things with a harmonious aesthetic took the place of an earlier fashion for hybrids that had been more 'concrete signs of civilized life'. Instead of offering an authoritative perspective and making the processes of exchange transparent, the now ubiquitous porcelains ultimately helped to render them invisible.

The very ambiguities of porcelains as things suggest that the historian cannot simply resort to either micro- or macro-histories to understand complex seventeenth-century processes of exchange, let alone to a particular birth or lineage of 'modern' consumption. Instead, approaching these problems requires not only a practice of translation but also methods both transcritical and transcultural. The meshing together of various exchange networks around the world through popular media like porcelains meant not only changes in the ways that exchanges took place, but also an increasing everyday sense of parallax – that sometimes disconcerting recognition, often embodied in the rather prosaic wares themselves, of a new reality exposed through a multitude of differences and transactions. Porcelains as a system of fashion in the seventeenth and early eighteenth centuries revealed through their textures, signs and perspectives not the birth of consumerism as a social phenomenon but more specific engagements with the challenges raised by new transactions and translations, reflecting upon the techniques, limits and measures of exchange.

Notes

1. *Mr. William Shakespeares Comedies, Histories and Tragedies* (London, 1623), p. 65.
2. For the birth metaphor see N. McKendrick, 'The Birth of a Consumer Society: The Commercialization of Eighteenth-century England', in N. McKendrick, J. Brewer and J.H. Plumb (eds), *The Birth of a Consumer Society: The Commercialization of Eighteenth-century England* (London, 1982), pp. 3–5.
3. For the concept of a 'fashion system', see R. Wilk, 'Miss Universe, the Olmec and the Valley of Oaxaca', *Journal of Social Archaeology*, 4(1) (2004), pp. 86–7, and K. Flannery, 'The Olmec and the Valley of Oaxaca: A Model for Inter-Regional Interaction in Formative Times', in E. Benson (ed.), *Proceedings of the Dumbarton Oaks Conference on the Olmec* (Washington, DC, 1968), pp. 79–117.
4. J. Plumb, 'The Royal Porcelain Craze', *In the Light of History* (Boston, 1973), p. 57.
5. The groundwork for the reworking of the narrative of the rise of consumerism can be found in F. Trentmann, 'Beyond Consumerism: New Historical Perspectives on Consumption', *Journal of Contemporary History*, 39(3) (2004), pp. 373–401. My reading of this essay as well as a rich mix of exchanges with the seminar participants at Caltech were greatly influential for this paper, as were more specific comments by John Brewer, Kirti Chaudhuri, Jessica Harrison-Hall, Robert Nashak, David Sabean, Haun Saussy, Nigel Thrift, Frank Trentmann and Richard Wilk.
6. The Jesuit d'Entrecolles (1664–1741), in letters dated 1712 and 1722, described the use of kaolin and feldspar in the production of porcelain. *Lettres édifiantes et curieuses, écrites des missions étrangèrs par*

quelques missionaires de la Compagnie de Jésus, v. 12 and 16 (Paris, 1717, 1724). Porcelain formulas, however, always vary in both technique and materials.

7. For the concept of 'common difference' see Wilk, p. 91.

8. C.G. Brouwer, 'Al-Mukha as a Coffee Port in the Early Decades of the Seventeenth Century', in Michel Tuchscherer (ed.), *Le Commerce du café avant l'ére des plantations coloniales: espaces, reseaux, sociétés (XVe-XIXe siècle)* (Paris, 2001), p. 282; T. Volker, *Porcelain and the Dutch East India Company as Recorded in the Dagh-Registers of Batavia Castle, Those of Hirado and Deshima and Other Contemporary Papers, 1602–1682* (Leiden, 1954), pp. 25, 39, 42, 59, 227.

9. On the coinage question see V. Godinho, *L'Economie de l'empire portugais au XVᵉet XVIᵉ siècles* (Paris, 1969), and R. von Glahn, *Fountain of Fortune: Money and Monetary Policy in China, 1000 to 1700* (Berkeley, 1996). For studying these phenomena in 'conjunction' see K. Pomeranz, *The Great Divergence: China, Europe and the Making of the Modern World Economy* (Princeton, 2000), pp. 191–4.

10. On 'parallax' see K. Karatani, *Transcritique: On Kant and Marx*, S. Kohso (trans.) (Cambridge, 2003), pp. 2–3, 44–8.

11. J. Addison, 'The Lover', no. 10, in T. Tickell (ed.), *The Works of the Right Honourable Joseph Addison*, vol. 4 (London, 1721). Since research has shown that men took part equally in the daily use and collection of porcelains, this stereotype of the female china consumer suggests a mythic dimension working to explain intrusions of transcultural fashions into everyday life. Cf. E. Kowaleski-Wallace, *Consuming Subjects: Women, Shopping and Business in the Eighteenth Century* (New York, 1997) pp. 52–69; L. Weatherill, 'A Possession of One's Own: Women and Consumer Behavior in England, 1660–1740', *Journal of British Studies*, 25 (1986), p. 140.

12. J. Swift and G. Aitken (eds), *The Journal to Stella* (London, 1901), p. 251.

13. W. Burnaby, *The Ladies Visiting Day* (London, 1701), p. 14.

14. G. Ramusio, 'Libro di Odoardo Barbosa', in M. Milanesi (ed.), *Giovanni Battista Ramusio Navigazioni e Viaggi*, vol. II (Turin, 1979), pp. 694–5.

15. G. Cardano, *De Subtilitate Libri XXI* (Paris, 1551), pp. 100v–101r; and J. Scaliger, *Exotericarum Exercitationum Liber Quintus Decimus, de Subtilitate, ad Hieronymum Cardanum* (Paris, 1557), pp. 135v–136r.

16. F. Bacon, 'Sylva Sylvarum or a Natural History', in J. Spedding, R.L. Ellis and D.D. Heath (eds), *The Works of Francis Bacon*, vol. IV (Boston, 1861), pp. 210–11.

17. F. Bacon, 'The Argument before the Judges in the Exchequer Chamber, Touching the Clause of Impeachment of Waste', in *Works*, vol. XV, pp. 37–9.
18. 'Hybrid' is borrowed from B. Latour, *We Have Never Been Modern*, Catherine Porter (trans.) (Cambridge, 1993), p. 117.
19. G. de Mendoza, *The Historie of the Great and Mightie Kingdome of China and the Situation thereof: Together with the great riches, huge Cities, politike government, and rare inventions in the same*, R. Parke (trans.) (London, 1588), pp. 22–3.
20. B. Elman, *A Cultural History of Civil Examinations in Late Imperial China* (Berkeley, 2000), pp. 45, 165.
21. Song Ying-Hsing [Song Yingxing], *T'ien-Kung K'ai-Wu [Tian gong kai wu]: Chinese Technology in the Seventeenth Century*, E-Tu Zen Sun and Shiou-Chuan Sun (trans.) (Univeristy Park, 1966), p. 145; Song Yingxing, *Tian gong kai wu*, Minguo 44 (Taipei, 1955), p. 185.
22. Song Yingxing, *Tian gong kai wu*, p. 196.
23. The phrase is from A. Appadurai (ed.), *The Social Life of Things: Commodities in Cultural Perspective* (Cambridge, 1986), p. 5, cited in C. Clunas, *Superfluous Things* (Urbana, 1991), p. 2. See also T. Brook, *Confusions of Pleasure: Commerce and Culture in Ming China* (Berkeley, 1998), pp. 129–38, 167–71, 222–8.
24. Wang Bi, 'Commentary on the Appended Phases [Xici zhuan], part 1', in R. Lynn (trans.), *The Classic of Changes* (New York, 1994), p. 67.
25. L. Le Comte, *Memoirs and Observations Topographical, Physical, Mathematical, Mechanical, Natural, Civil, and Ecclesiastical, Made in a Late Journey Through the Empire of China And Published in Several Letters* (London, 1697), pp. 155–6.
26. For this longer history see R. Finlay, 'The Pilgrim Art: The Culture of Porcelain in World History', *Journal of World History*, 9(2) (Fall 1998), pp. 141–87. On the role of the tribute trade see T. Hamashita, 'The Tribute Trade System and Modern Asia', *Memoirs of the Research Department of the Tokyo Bunko*, 46 (1988), pp. 7–25, and A.G. Frank, *ReOrient: Global Economy in the Asian Age* (Berkeley, 1998), pp. 113–17.
27. A. Spriggs, 'Red Cliff Bowls of the Late Ming Period', *Oriental Art*, n.s. VII(4) (Winter 1961), pp. 182–8. For a low-end bowl see British Museum OA F.810 and examples excavated in Sulawesi in S. Adhyatman, *Zhangzhou Ceramics: Sixteenth to Seventeenth Centuries Found in Indonesia* (Indonesia, 1999), p. 100. For the OA F.811 inscription see Jessica Harrison-Hall, *Catalogue of Late Yuan and Ming Ceramics in the British Museum* (London, 2001), pp. 366–7.

28. For the Ottoman pieces see J. Ayers and R. Krahl, *Chinese Ceramics in the Topkapi Saray Museum Istanbul*, vol. II (London, 1986), pp. 788–9, nos. 1529 and 1530. The Linard paintings are in the Musée des Beaux-Arts, Strasbourg, and the Musée des Beaux-Arts, Tours. Cf. Spriggs, figures 19–20.

29. B. Keguan, *Chinese Folk Painting on Porcelain*, Peng Ruifu (trans.) (Beijing, 1991), pp. 60, 93.

30. Wu Hung, *The Double Screen* (Chicago, 1996), pp. 129, 135–7.

31. J. Nieuhof, *Die Gesandtschafft der Ost-Indischen Geselschaft in den Vereinigten Niederlandern an den tartarischen Cham und nunmehr auch sinischen Keiser* (Amsterdam, 1666), p. 288. The first London edition appeared in 1669.

32. Brook, *Confusions of Pleasure*, p. 109.

33. W. Schurz, *The Manila Galleon* (New York, 1985), p. 27.

34. W. Gungwu, *The Chinese Overseas: From Earthbound China to the Quest for Autonomy* (Cambridge, 2000), p. 57.

35. The phrase is from descriptions of Jesuit translation practices in H. Saussy, 'In the Workshop of Equivalences', in *Great Walls of Discourse and Other Adventures in Cultural China* (Cambridge, 2001), pp. 31–2.

36. 'To Our Chief and Factors at Tonqueen', London, 12 Aug. 1681, British Library, India Office Records, E/3/89, f. 211.

37. C. Ho, 'The Ceramic Trade in Asia, 1602–82', in A. Latham and H. Kawakatsu (eds), *Japanese Industrialization and the Asian Economy* (London, 1994), p. 39.

38. J. Keuning (ed.), *De tweede schipvaart der Nederlanders naar Oost-Indië, onder Jacob Cornelisz. van Neck en Wybrand van Warwijck, 1598–1600: journalen, documenten en andere bescheiden*, v. 42 ('s-Gravenhage, 1938).

39. E. Scott, *An Exact Discourse of the Subtilties, Fashishions, Pollicies, Religion, and Ceremonies of the East Indians, as well Chyneses as Javans, there abyding and dwelling* (London, 1606), unnumbered, November 1604.

40. Scott, *Exact Discourse*, unnumbered, April 22.

41. See also the teapot in the same pattern described by D.F.L. Scheurleer, *Chinese Export Porcelain: Chine de Commande* (London, 1974), p. 149, fig. 267, and T. Volker, 'Early Chine de commande', *Bulletin Museum Boymans-van Beuningen* (Rotterdam, 1958), p. 18.

42. Broadly considered, word and image had different relationships in Chinese and European printing. Cf. C. Clunas, *Pictures and Visuality in Early Modern China* (Princeton, 1997), pp. 29–38.

43. D. Defoe, *Review*, v. 7, no. 43 (4 July 1710).
44. See, for example, 'Estimate of a Cargo to be provided in China for the Ship Townshend Burden 400 Tons', 17 November 1725, British Library, India Office Records, Despatch Book 1725, vol. 103, f. 132.
45. B. Horn, 'Ceramic Accounts Found among the Seafield Muniments', *Transactions of the English Ceramics Circle*, v. 18, no. 1 (2002), p. 190.
46. T. Baker, *The Fine Lady's Airs: Or, An Equipage of Lovers* (London, 1708), pp. 9–10.
47. 'Letter to the Supercargo of the Grafton', 18 October 1734, British Library, India Office Records, R/10/37, f. 83.
48. 'China Ware must be all of useful sorts, most Blue and White.' ['Estimate of a Cargo to be Provided in China for the Ships Caesar and Houghton Burden 880 Tons', 21 December 1724, British Library, India Office Records, Despatch Book 1724, vol. 102, f. 395.] But the orders go on to say that 'any other odd and useful pieces, the newer the pattern the better, but in this Article your own fancys must be chiefly rely'd on'.
49. Elizabeth Robinson Montagu to Sarah Robinson Scott, 3 January 1750, Huntington Library, MO 5716.
50. H. Lefebvre, *Critique of Everyday Life: Volume II Foundations for a Sociology of the Everyday*, J. Moore (trans.) (London, 2002), p. 90.
51. E. Panofsky, *Perspective as Symbolic Form* (New York, 1991), p. 31.
52. Cao Xuexin, *Story of the Stone*, vol. 2, D. Hawkes (trans.) (New York, 1977), p. 338.
53. Wu Hung, *Double Screen*, pp. 50–7.
54. W. Temple, 'Upon the Gardens of Epicurus', *Miscellanea II* (London, 1690), pp. 131–2.
55. T. Volker, *The Japanese Porcelain Trade of the Dutch East India Company after 1683* (Leiden, 1959), pp. 78–9.
56. The examples are too numerous to cite but consider these recent ones: 'For chinoiserie is western, it is a purely European vision of China; a fantasy based on a China of the imagination, the fabulous Cathay invented by the medieval world' (D. Jacobson, *Chinoiserie* (London, 1993), p. 27); 'Chinoiserie, in other words, was an aesthetic of the ineluctably foreign, a glamorization of the unknown and unknowable for its own sake' (D. Porter, *Ideographia: The Chinese Cipher in Early Modern Europe* (Stanford, 2001), p. 134).

–5–

Consumer Culture and Extractive Industry on the Margins of the World System
Richard Wilk

Scholars working on both historical and contemporary consumer cultures have focused their attention, with few exceptions, on the middle class, or those aspiring to join the middle class. The dominant scenarios of the origin of modern consumerism draw attention to the quest for respectability, comfort and the excitements of shopping in Europe and North America.[1] If we follow the familiar narratives of the role of consumption in western expansion, industrial revolution and the rise of modernity, there is little space for the poor and working classes, except as followers seeking to raise their social status or as the locus of resistant traditionalism. In *Distinction* Pierre Bourdieu relegates working-class culture to the position of an oppositional reflection, saying 'it must never be forgotten that the working-class "aesthetic" is a dominated "aesthetic" which is constantly obliged to define itself in terms of the dominant aesthetic'. Even the diversity of consumption recognized in the 'lifestyles' literature depicts the poor as making different aesthetic choices, rather than as having fundamentally non-middle class relationships with the material world.[2]

I do not have to move from my desk for evidence that there is more to class differences in consumption than resistance, imitation or aesthetics. Through my window in rural Indiana, I can see my neighbour's house, which is actually a prefabricated mobile home called a 'trailer'. When we built *our* house, we put every penny we had into it, knowing it would be a good investment, and indeed it has almost doubled in value in 12 years. Our mortgage payments are our single largest expense each month, and the next largest are our payments to pension funds and various kinds of insurance, and saving for our daughter's college expenses. We are prudent to a fault and avoid credit-card debts as much as possible.

My neighbour's home, on the other hand, cost less than a $1,000 down payment, and by the time the loan is paid off in 15 years the trailer will be worn out and almost worthless. My neighbours make less money than we do, but they spend more of what they earn. Parked next to their trailer are two large new customized four-wheel drive pickups, a twenty-eight-foot motor-home (with its own satellite dish) and a high-horsepower motorboat on a trailer. They also own four racing 'dirt bikes' (one for each child), two four-wheel ATVs, two lawn tractors, an above-ground swimming pool, two horses and three dogs. That is only what I have seen; I would be surprised if there wasn't a 60-inch widescreen TV and a home theatre system in the trailer. I have not asked about their family finances, but I expect that like many Americans they are deeply in debt, and that they are patrons of the shops around town that give weekly 'paycheck advance loans'.

It would be easy to sneer at my neighbour, following in the footsteps of innumerable middle-class critics who have condemned the wasteful, irrational or irresponsible consumption of the poor and working classes.[3] Instead I would like to use their style of consumption as the starting point to think more critically about the balance between responsibility and pleasure, social and domestic consumption, and consuming for the present and saving for the future, in different classes and occupational groups. Studies of consumer culture have been biased towards responsible, thoughtful and planned behaviour, relatively stable communities and ordered forms of social competition. Chaotic, dissipative consumption which is socially destructive or self-destructive has been marginalized as an aberration, a form of pathology or even a vestige of the premodern past.

The example of my neighbours, and millions of other individuals and families like them in the United States and elsewhere, demonstrates that a present-oriented hedonistic style of consumption-for-pleasure and immediate experience is still very much a part of consumer society and may actually be a growing and dominant influence, and that it is not fenced-off in a particular class or location but is quite generalized and widespread. In this paper I suggest that this hedonistic style of consumption, one variety of which I discuss here under the label *binge consumption*, has a long history, which should help us understand its place and status in the present.[4]

My initial assertion about binge consumption is that it must be understood in the specific historical contexts where it emerged. After establishing the circumstances surrounding binge consumption in one particular setting, I will discuss some of the other economic and social circumstances where varieties of bingeing can be historically located. Finally, I will suggest that there are some direct historical continuities through gender ideologies and romantic ideology between earlier kinds of binge economies and those found today, but I will also argue that binge-like behaviour emerges repeatedly when household institutions and family structures are weak, and working lives are highly gender-segregated. We therefore need to consider both cultural-historical and economic contexts in order to understand any particular historical manifestation of bingeing.

At the end of the chapter I move from specific examples to argue that the binge is also a particular kind of rationality, different from the bourgeois domestic rationality of saving and parsimony, which can be made understandable by economic and social instrumentalities. The short-term hedonistic qualities of bingeing are an important part of the ideological play in Western culture between the utilitarian and romantic, and the modern and anti-modern. The binge is also firmly emplaced in Euro-American constructions of gender and class that continue to carry deep political and moral significance. In this formal sense, the binge is always present in capitalist consumerism, for even if it is suppressed or concealed, it is always the logical complement, the 'evil twin' lurking in the background behind the ideology of thrift and reasoned, socially integrative forms of consumption.

Binges in the Caribbean

My first ethnographic introduction to the logic of the binge took place during my early fieldwork in the Central American (and culturally Caribbean) country of Belize, then called British Honduras. I was working on an archaeological project, and every weekend the men from a neighbouring Spanish-speaking village who worked for us invited me out to a dance or a bar. On Saturday night they would start off buying rounds of beer and rum for each other, and the drinking, dancing and sometimes fighting would last until everyone had passed out drunk or run out of money. Given how little the men were paid and the high price of drink, I was not surprised to see some of them go through an entire week's wages in a few hours.

Later, while doing ethnographic research with middle-class, English-speaking Creoles in Belize City, I also went out for a few Friday and Saturday nights of partying. These men were older, and all had children and lived with wives or girlfriends. While they all gave part of their paycheck to their household (and often some to mothers, ex-girlfriends and other relatives), they also kept a sizeable fraction aside for their 'sprees', to spend on drink or with new girlfriends. If they got home at all on a Saturday or Sunday, it was in the small hours of the morning, and their pockets were empty.

Most people saw this as a normal kind of male behaviour, though many also condemned it as irresponsible, wasteful and self-destructive. Many Belizeans, over the years, have expressed the opinion that regular bingeing breaks up families and makes it difficult for men to run businesses or keep jobs. Several people have told me that the economic development of the whole country is held back by binges, and one man told me:

> Belizeans don't think in the long term, they are not thinking about leaving something behind for their kids or the next generation. They just want to spend it and spend it now, on things they want and in partying. They see it in the shop window and they buy it. It's not like the Chinese. They save and save and buy house and shop, while we just spend everything. That's why they own the whole city now.

This is not an isolated sentiment. I have recorded many variations that focus on African-descended Creole people in particular as profligate and carefree spenders whenever they have cash. It's a consistent theme in Belizean descriptions of themselves, and in foreigners' commentaries about life in Belize for at least the last 200 years. The country closes down for long periods around the Independence and Christmas holidays, and merchants report that they do half their annual business in luxury goods during December, when the central bank usually reports a liquidity crisis due to high imports.

The empirical reality of Belizeans' wild spending and improvidence can be dismissed as a remnant of colonial racism aimed towards the class that was once enslaved, a particularly virulent form of 'blaming the victim'. Certainly there are many places in Europe and the United States where excessive drinking and wild spending are, if anything, more extreme than anywhere in Belize, where behaviour is at least restrained by poverty. The whole topic of how people spend their money is closely tied to class-based moral discourses about the irrational habits of the poor, which makes it difficult and contentious ground for scholarship. Belizeans are understandably sensitive about work (particularly by foreigners) that seems to blame the poor for their own poverty or express colonialist racial attitudes.

Nevertheless, other scholars working on Caribbean cultures have also noted how much money and time men spend on their own enjoyment, how little they contribute to their conjugal families, and their problems saving and accumulating property. Many have linked this to the dynamics of what has been called the Caribbean 'matrifocal' family structure.[5] The idea is that because of fragile conjugal ties and a lack of economic security, people quickly find their resources are dissipated among the competing claims of extended kin, so there is little incentive or ability to save money or accumulate property. One of the problems with this explanation is that even with this kinship system some people do manage to accumulate property and money. Moreover, the causality can be reversed, so the matrifocal family is a product, rather than the cause, of profligate spending habits. And this leaves open the question of the origin and persistence of the matrifocal family in a highly Christian society where the conjugal nuclear family is the acknowledged ideal.

The other major approach to understanding gender, kinship and money in Caribbean societies has been through the use of a dualistic structural approach, which posits two coexisting but contradictory cultural models, one derived from middle-class Europe and the other from the creolized cultures of African slaves. The opposing poles have been named 'reputation' and 'respectability', or in Miller's terms 'transcendence' and 'transience'.[6] Most scholars agree that within a single culture they represent two very different conceptions of freedom and the relationship between the individual and society, while sharing the goal of seeking social status through consumption and performance. Initially, the polarity was linked to class, with the idea that the middle class emulated European norms of respectability, while the working class created an opposing culture of reputation based on skill with words, sexuality and fertility.[7] This proved inaccurate in later ethnographic work, since both values were found in all classes and indeed in the same person. Others tried to tie the polarity to gender, so that women were the keepers of respectability and men sought reputation, but again this proved misleading.[8] In practice the two values appear to intersect in different ways in different cultural settings, to attach to different social groups, and to infuse (or collapse into) a variety of ethnic, religious and political divisions.

There are also subcultures of reputation that have few connections to respectable society. These might be occupational groupings like day labourers or criminal 'class fragments' like street gangs and drug smugglers. In some places membership in such a group is considered a normal stage of life; there are parts of the Caribbean where men and women seek reputation in their youth and then marry and pursue respectability in middle age. There are also intensely religious communities that deny all the values of reputation or seek to stand apart from the entire society, for example Jamaican Rastafarians.

The History of the Binge in Belize

While the dualistic models of Caribbean cultures are useful in ethnography, they present methodological and interpretive problems in historical analysis. How does one identify the specific ways reputation was constructed in eighteenth-century slave societies, or recognize the difference between emulation, enforced conformity or gentle irony in the dress of respectable nineteenth-century office clerks? Binges, however, are a relatively easily recognized kind of behaviour and were often noted in the historical record. Understanding the historical context of binge consumption in the Caribbean gives us a very different perspective on modern spending behaviour than does the comparative cultural analysis of reputation or speculation about the function of a 'type' of household. The case of Belize is a good demonstration, since it shows that binges were part of a particular kind of labour regime, embedded in a kind of extractive industry found very widely at the expanding margins of the international mercantile economy from at least the seventeenth century onwards.

The first non-indigenous settlers of Belize were buccaneers and their slaves, who came to the area then called 'the Bay' in the seventeenth and early eighteenth centuries to cut logwood, as an alternative to privateering, hunting and piracy. The people called buccaneers were a heterogeneous group of many nationalities, with a common background as sailors and adventurers or escaped indentured servants, slaves and transported criminals. Many began life in the European urban underclass or were displaced from farms.[9] There are many colourful and romanticized portraits of buccaneer life, but there are also some narrative first-hand accounts which say clearly that one of the characteristics of buccaneers and pirates was that they were free with money. At the end of successful voyages to steal and plunder, they returned to home bases like Tortuga, and later Port Royal and Providence, where they quickly spent their gains (rather than burying them) and then went looking for another ship when they were broke.

Those who settled along the Caribbean coast of Yucatan in the Bay to cut logwood were called Baymen. Captain Nathaniel Uring visited them in 1719 and reported:

> The wood-cutters are generally a rude drunken crew, some of which have been pirates, and most of them sailors; their chief delight is in drinking; and when they broach a quarter cask or hogshead of wine, they seldom stir from it while there is a drop left. It is the same thing when they open a hogshead of bottle ale or cyder, keeping at it sometimes a week together, drinking till they fall asleep; and as soon as they awake, at it again, without stirring off the place ... they do most work when they have no strong drink, for while the liquor is moving they don't care to leave it.[10]

The Dutch surgeon Alexandre Exquemelin (also spelled Esquemeling) visited the Bay a number of times in the late seventeenth century and made a similar report of the local drinking habits. Besides their provisions, tools and clothes, he reports, the buccaneers spent their money on drink, prostitutes and gambling:

> whenever they have got hold of something they don't keep it for long. They are busy dicing, whoring, and drinking so long as they have anything to spend. Some of them will get through a good two or three thousand pieces of eight in a day – and next day not have a shirt to their back ... My own master used to buy a butt of wine and set it in the middle of the street with the barrel-head knocked in, and stand barring the way. Every passer-by had to drink with him, or he'd have shot them dead with a gun he kept handy.[11]

And once back in port:

> their gains they spend prodigally, giving themselves to all manner of vices, and debauchery; particularly to Drunkenness, which they practice mostly with Brandy. This they drink liberally, as the Spaniards do Water. Sometimes they buy together a Pipe of Wine; this they stave at one end, and never cease drinking till 'tis out. Thus sottishly they live till they have no Mony left. And as freely gratify their Lusts, for which they find more Women than they can use.[12]

Exquemelin reports that most of the buccaneers were deeply indebted to tavern-keepers after being ashore for a short while and left for their next voyage in order to pay their debts, otherwise they were seized and sold into servitude. Besides their spendthrift ways, the buccaneers were famous for their generosity to comrades in trouble, and on board ship they practised an absolute (and often anarchic) democracy under elected leaders, and everyone shared risks, rations and rewards.

Initially, logging in the Bay's swamps and lagoons was just another way to raise cash in between voyages, like hunting turtles or feral cattle. But logging became the mainstay of the economy during the eighteenth century as piracy was successfully suppressed. An economy based on slavery and forestry developed, initially dependent on logwood, fustic and other dyewoods, but gradually mahogany became more important in response to European fashions in panelling, banisters and furniture, which shifted from domestic woods like oak to exotic tropical timber. At the end of the eighteenth century the settlement of the Bay, despite continuing harassment by Spanish authorities, had a population of about 200 whites, 500 free people of colour and about 3,000 African slaves.[13]

In mahogany work, the slaves and freemen spent ten months each year living on imported rations in small camps, the 'works' on river banks in the forest. At least twice a year they returned to Belize City, where most women and children lived year round. These periods of return, particularly the three weeks at Christmas, were marked by revelry among all classes. While the Europeans and 'free coloured' held and supervised balls, dances, parties, parades and sailboat, rowboat and horse races, the slaves were given special rations and money to supplement their own earnings (their Saturday labour was paid for).

A British army officer stationed in Belize in 1807 reported that 'they [slaves] are characterized by a random recklessness as regards the future, with, however, a keen sense of keeping the regular Christmas orgies in Belize, when their labour in the bush has expired'. And 'Christmas is the time of year that brings all ranks together. The master's house is a gathering place – all barriers are lowered.'[14] The different African tribes among the slaves would assemble for their own drumming, music and dance. He marvelled at their endurance in staying drunk and awake for days and even weeks at a time.

The editor of the *Honduras Gazette and Commercial Advertiser* wrote the following description of Christmas in Belize in 1827. The extravagance of the celebration was probably exaggerated to strengthen the author's point that slaves in Belize had a higher standard of living than the working classes in the mother country:

> Among the white, and more respectable people of colour, 'fun and feasting' prevail as much, (and pretty much after the same fashion,) as in Britain; but there is an amazing difference as to their manner of spending Christmas and their hilarity and comfort during its stay, between the Slave population of this settlement, and the labouring classes at home. Thousands, nay, hundreds of thousands of those last named, know of the comforts of the season, only by hearing others speak, or seeing their superiors partake of them, while almost all the slaves in this community, during the whole of the Holydays, neither labour, nor are called upon to do any labour whatever, but on the contrary, parade the streets during the day in large parties, preceded by Music and Flags – the males in better clothes than many respectable tradesmen in England can afford to wear, and the females in silken, or most gaudy attire, and very frequently with costly ornaments, such as genuine gold necklaces, ear and finger rings, silver mounted parasols, &c. &c. &c. In their progress they walk in a body, sans ceremonie, into the halls of all the merchants or respectable persons' houses, and commence dancing and singing, at the same time calling with the utmost sang froid for refreshments, which, we believe, are seldom if ever refused to them, however numerous their party may be; and as the owners of the slaves furnish each of them at every Christmas with wines, &c. (or money to the amount of at least £1 to procure them,) they club together, and at night, and generally in the open air, continue feasting, drinking, dancing, and singing, after their own fashion, very often enlivening their performances, or at all events, adding to the noise thereof, by the incessant discharge of guns; and the sun, in most cases, shines upon them the next day before they separate.[15]

The previous year the same newspaper published an account of the cost of keeping a slave in Belize that included both a Christmas box of 6 shillings 8 pence and a 'party and ball at Christmas: 1 gallon rum, beef or other butcher's meat, fish, turtle, liqiueurs [sic], sweet wine, &c.'[16] However exaggerated these accounts, the point is that Christmas was a time for a consumption binge by a large portion of the settlement, half of whom spent the rest of the year in privation and isolation, subsisting on a monotonous ration. The mahogany camps were isolated and populated almost entirely by men; the Christmas holiday included both conjugal settings where men and women could party together and events where male gangs were reconstituted for both celebration and competitive events like the *pitpan* (paddle boat) races.

The abolition of slavery in 1838 did little to change the basic rhythm of life in the colony, since the majority of workers were still engaged in the manual labour of logging, under the control of the same class of merchants and proprietors. Most of the freed slaves did not leave the logging economy for peasant farming for a number of reasons. Debt servitude was enforced by harsh labour laws that made it almost impossible to escape from an employer.[17]

The mechanism of debt as a substitute for slavery assumed that workers would engage in binge consumption over the Christmas holidays. Mahogany workers returned to Belize City in early December (an event called 'gang-broke') and were paid off for their year's work in a lump sum, with debts to the company deducted. What was left over was claimed by wives or other women who cared for the workers' children (some employers would pay wives directly), but men kept part of their pay aside for their own spree. Later, when this money was gone, agents would circulate in the community to 'engage' workers for the next year of work, offering advances, usually half in cash and half in goods from the company store. These advances financed the rest of the Christmas 'spree' but left the worker bound to at least five months of work just to pay off the debt. Over time, as employers added penalties and deductions to the worker's account, debts accumulated to the point where they could never be paid off (making savings almost completely pointless). The Christmas 'saturnalia', as contemporary witnesses clearly saw, was an essential element driving the whole system.[18]

As the settlement grew and became a colony in the later nineteenth century, the Christmas binge maintained most of the elements of the earlier festivity. Alongside the public celebration of parades, speeches, music and races, there was an intensification of domestic and individual consumption. On the one hand, most families cleaned their houses from top to bottom, painted the house, renewed the flooring and bought whatever new furnishings they could afford. Men gave expensive gifts to women, particularly clothing and perfume. At the public festivities both men and women participated equally. But after the domestic and public festivities, men congregated in 'crews' or 'sets' and treated each other to food and drink in rum shops, clubs and each other's homes, in a round of revelry that continued until none of the men in the group had money left. As import records and newspaper advertisements show, huge amounts of exotic European liquor and preserved foodstuffs, ranging from French cornichon to Indian curry powders, were imported during this time of year. Young men without families could participate longer, because after spending on their 'sweethearts' they had more left over for themselves. Older men with wives and children to support would have run out of money more quickly.

The mahogany logging economy began a steep decline at the beginning of the twentieth century. Machinery replaced much of the workforce, and the business was consolidated in the hands of a single company that maintained the workforce in more permanent settlements in the interior. While debt servitude and seasonal employment with rations continued, the country became more ethnically diverse, and the economy turned towards agriculture and urban services. The Christmas holidays became shorter and more domestic, and the street parades diminished and then disappeared. House cleaning and decorating became more central, and the main festivities took the form of the *Bram*. This was a neighbourhood party where groups of friends and relatives would dance for two or three hours in each person's house, eating and drinking everything in the house and then moving on to the next house and ending after two days.[19] Large amounts of baked goods and plenty of sweet local wines were provided at each stop. This was very much a co-educational family affair, largely supervised and controlled by women.

The Social and Historical Context of the Binge

This historical sketch depicts not a single binge economy, but rather a succession of at least three, each involving different groups. The first consisted of European buccaneers, the second of African slaves, and the third of a proletarian class that was truly Creole, in having a mixed and synthetic culture. This suggests that the context of binge consumption, the logic that defined it, was situational rather than simply a cultural pattern that was handed down historically or embedded in the social fabric of a single ethnic group. A comparative approach can therefore reveal the particularities that lead to binge-like behaviour in other times and places. While my larger comparative project is still under way, preliminary results suggest that the binge subcultures were particularly widespread around the world during the boom in the labour-intensive extractive industry during the nineteenth century.[20]

The most common context of bingeing was a workforce that lived and worked in an isolated space outside of conventional human communities, away from conjugal families and the kinds of open public life where workers could escape from the workplace when their labour was finished. The usually male workforce was sustained on some form of ration and had few or no opportunities to spend their earnings while working. When workers returned from isolation, they spent all or most of their wages, often in a context of social revelry and release, in ways that left them either broke or indebted. This kind of labour/consumption regime was common first in navies and among long-distance fishermen, sailors and pirate bands, but it was later widely found in logging, commercial hunting (including sealing and whaling), placer mining and commercial livestock herding on open ranges.

The isolation of men in single-sex groups seems to be a key to the most intensive forms of binge consumption. Men are wrenched out of the domestic context, where they are enmeshed in a network of constant exchange and interaction with their kin, and placed in a situation where they, their workmates and/or the institution they work for are providing the services that were previously provided by the domestic economy (for example cooking, sewing, laundry, cleaning, companionship). Cut off from the diverse social life of communities, most or all of their social and economic relationships are with workmates. If they have any kin, their connections to them become narrow and commoditized, since the only thing they can contribute to the domestic economy or the rearing of their children is their irregular income.

In the workplace there is no effective cash economy; instead there are rations and accounts. In isolated locations there is nothing to buy, outside of a limited range of personal goods that are usually disbursed on account. Employers try to control access to intoxicants, though alcohol and tobacco were usually part of the ration. The dependence of workers on tobacco and alcohol was an important aspect of labour control, since employers could punish workers by withholding them and profit by supplying them.

Workers, therefore, subsist in an economy without cash – and their pay appears as something apart from their daily experience of consumption, almost as an 'extra' that perturbs the daily rhythm of life (and may even appear to endanger it). Employers sometimes make arrangements to disburse part of a pay cheque to a worker's parents or spouse (this was the practice in the British navy), but some part of the pay ended up in his hands at the end of a pay period. One important variable among binge economies is how much of this pay is directed back into a domestic economy that ties the worker to a community or household, versus how much is kept for the worker's consumption with workmates.

Men on binges do not simply spend money directly on themselves. Belize woodcutters, for example, were sometimes thought stingy when it came to spending on clothes and personal possessions. Instead their character-istic mode of bingeing was through treating workmates to food, drink and entertainment, in a round of festive gift-exchange that has many of the compet-itive characteristics of the classic ethnographic example of the Potlatch. California gold miners, for example, would compete in buying drinks for hundreds of strangers at a time; crab fishermen in 1980s Alaska would put several ounces of cocaine on a bar in one long line for everyone to share.[21] Participation in festive competitive drinking parties was an obligatory part of the job, an essential way to build and maintain the social relationships that made dangerous, monotonous work in isolated places tolerable and relatively safe. Workers sometimes spoke of money as a burden to be thrown off as quickly as possible, putting everyone back into equality. 'If money did not go fast enough,' as one nineteenth-century text noted 'watches were fried, bank-notes eaten between bread and butter, and every practice resorted to for the purpose of its riddance'.[22]

Men in extractive work groups depended on each other to an extraordinary degree. One man's error could kill or maim an entire crew. Apprenticeship and entry into the crew were therefore not easy; testing was required that proved a new member's ability, and painful and humiliating initiations were common. But, once in the group, men treated each other with intense loyalty. While showing nothing but toughness and even violence towards outsiders, members of work crews were loyal and caring with each other, and they often claimed feelings of kinship closer than blood.[23] In Belize older men professed a tremendous attachment to their 'crew', and they took great pride in being mahogany workers. In fact, the reluctance of mahogany workers to take any other kind of work in town or on farms became a problem for colonial officials during the long decline of the forestry economy.

At some level the binge can be seen as a reasonable response to the working conditions of buccaneering and mahogany logging. But while the round of restraint and release that is so essential to binge consumption may build solidarity among work crews, it is often dangerous and damaging both to the workers themselves and to those who may depend on them for financial support. Deaths from drowning and fighting were common at Christmas time in Belize in mahogany days, and years of heavy drinking and smoking must have also taken a serious health toll. Ships on which the entire crew was partially intoxicated could hardly have been the most efficient. Accounts of men drinking up their salary and leaving their wives and children destitute and hungry were also common. Binge consumption is also a direct benefit to employers as the men's debt binds them in service. It is not hard to see how the intense solidarity of work groups and competitive relationships between such groups help discipline the workforce and reduce the costs of supervision. Logging, often a financially risky proposition, would probably have been unprofitable without this labour regime.

Binge consumption is therefore full of contradictions. Men look forward all year to being paid off and getting 'home', but then quickly consume the resources that, if saved, might eventually allow them to switch occupations and *stay* at home. Long periods of life in isolation leave them ill-equipped for the broader social life of established communities. They may have duties and obligations to kin, but feel strong obligations to their workmates as well. In order to maintain their standing in their peer group, they have to alienate themselves from their families, or vice versa. Yet despite these contradictions, and the hardship and danger of working life, contemporary narratives emphasize the intense subjective feeling of freedom of life in the forests and at sea. This is one of the most remarkable and lasting paradoxes of the binge economy, that such terrible exploitation and grinding misery could be transformed into an experience of freedom.

The greatest contradiction of the binge economy is that it is never clear whose interests are being served. In the Belize case, while mahogany workers were proud and independent, the whole system was in many ways highly exploitative. Under slavery, the binge could be seen as a way to allow limited rewards and incentives for loyalty and hard work. At the same time, the binges of the mahogany slaves were far more expansive and extravagant than those enjoyed by slaves elsewhere in the Americas, so in some sense they were an exercise of freedom and power. Later the advance system served the needs of employers for cheap, reliable labour under dangerous conditions; the binges kept the workers in debt. Its hard to see the mahogany workers' sprees as empowering, but on the other hand the local economy offered workers almost no alternatives. At least with the spree, there was one period of release punctuating a year of hard labour.

Other Binge Economies

Buccaneers and pirates constituted a small and relatively short-lived group whose importance has been far exaggerated by the romanticized image of freedom they came to represent. But they flourished in the context of a rapidly

expanding European mercantile economy, which extracted a huge variety
of new forms of commodities and goods from widely dispersed cultures
and natural environments. This extractive economy was built partially
through an unprecedented degree of gendered division of labour, building
on the pattern of early European navies and standing armies. Hundreds of
thousands of men voluntarily and involuntarily left their homes and families
and entered a global labour pool initially centered on the Atlantic world, but
then expanding to the Pacific and Indian oceans as well.

Extractive economies, by their mobile frontier nature, are poorly
documented. My primary research has focused on the forestry economy in
Belize, but comparative accounts from extractive economies in other parts
of the world disclose striking parallels with the Belizean case, which show
that each one is a variation on a common theme. Extractive economies were
heterogeneous and locally specific, each with unique characteristics. They
varied widely in their relationships to colonial and plantation communities.
In some cases they were seasonal, as with the *chicle* gathering in Central
America. Sometimes workers were only extractivists for a part of their lives,
as among modern crab fishermen in Alaska. In other cases they were lifelong
full-time specialists, like Belize loggers, Pacific-coast sealers, Georgia pine
tar tappers, and some New England whalers. In the North American fur
trade, or rubber tapping in South America, the industries appropriated and
intensified indigenous foraging and hunting economies. Yet each shared a
number of common social characteristics and had similar patterns of binge
consumption.

On the face of it, the major advantage of a specialist extractive workforce
is its low cost and mobility. To make extractive labour pay, a source of cheap
food was required, so the foundation of the global extractive economy was
a system for preserving and providing a low-cost reliable diet.[24] The second
advantage of a mobile extractive workforce, completely detached from the
social support of a subsistence economy, was its degree of specialization
and work discipline. Most extractive work required arduous labour and
high degrees of skill, gained through harsh training. In small spaces, such
as aboard ship or in hard-rock mines, it was possible to create the necessary
discipline through coercion and force. But in forests and frontiers, most
extractivists worked in gangs organized by entrepreneurs or acted as
independent contractors. Sometimes the prospect of high rewards and instant
wealth provided the incentive to accept privation and danger, so that work
itself became a gamble.

Another key aspect of the extractive economy was the insecurity of the
working conditions. Extractivists were constantly exposed to injury and

death due to natural forces, hostile indigenes, warfare and crime, and they were often subject to arbitrary authority and corporal punishment. Given the nature of the global markets for their products, extractivists were also subject to boom and bust cycles that left them unemployed and impoverished for lengthy periods, if not redundant for the rest of their lives. Industrial synthetic products gradually replaced many of the raw materials they produced; for example, the logwood that was extracted from the swamp forests of Belize in the eighteenth century was replaced by aniline dyes in the second half of the nineteenth century. Changes in metropolitan fashions for corsets or feathered hats could destroy the livelihood of an entire workforce halfway around the world, causing them to disperse and seek entry into other extractive work, or attempt to return to an agricultural or industrial economy. Different groups of extractivists often competed with one another in the same market, so the success of one led to the demise of another. New rich territories could open up, leading to gluts, price collapse and the displacement or idling of workers. The Belize mahogany economy endured at least five boom-and-bust cycles between 1840 and 1950. New technologies like steam tractors or harpoon guns could suddenly make a lifetime of skill and experience useless and redundant.

The insecurity of livelihood and the shifting location of capital made long-term resource management implausible. As others have noted, most extractivists have little incentive to conserve or ensure for the future; their approach to any resource is more like mining than it is like any form of cultivation. The lack of legal regulation at the margins of the expanding European world economy meant that property rights were impossible to enforce, so, with open entry, it made sense to exploit a common resource until it was gone. Some markets worked well enough to drive up prices when commodities were increasingly scarce, giving extractivists an incentive to press resources into extinction, as with sandalwood on the island of Vanuatu. Thus, the social characteristics and binge consumption of extractive workers played an important part in the ecological destruction wrought by Europeans on coastal and island areas around the world.

While I have focused this paper on extractivists, there are a number of other historical economic and social contexts which seem to promote binge behaviours. These include subsistence farmers and hunter gatherers who provide their own livelihood outside the cash economy. Historically, when these people made contact with capitalist economies, they were often willing to provide labour or valued local products in exchange for cash. Some of that cash was used to buy manufactured goods like steel tools, guns, iron pots and beads, which were initially luxury products but gradually became 'necessities'. In the early stages of this process, cash was often seen as having no intrinsic value and little use in daily life, and it could not be invested effectively. A great deal of it, in many parts of the world, was spent on liquor and in gambling, often in long dissipative bouts and binges that lasted until all the cash was gone.[25]

There are obvious similarities between contact-period aboriginal groups and extractive workers who are also only partially embedded in a cash economy, and in many parts of the world they were in close and intimate contact for long periods of time (e.g. European seal hunters and Tasmanian aborigines, or gold miners and Native Americans in the North American west). There were also important distinctions and differences reflected in the nature of the binges themselves.

Explaining Binge Consumption

From the vantage point of an educated middle-class academic, it is almost impossible to imagine living in the intensely male culture that developed among extractivist groups. These men developed their own argot, mostly unintelligible to outsiders and initiates (though it was a continual source of slang impressions in common speech). The work regimen required high degrees of physical strength and skill, and a physical adaptation that left a permanent mark on men's bodies. One could identify a logger, a sailor or a fisherman just by looking at their hands, their gait and posture. They adopted particular modes of dress, grooming and body modification that were themselves a lasting physical language of identification.

Some see the kinds of hyper-masculinity developed by these groups as an inversion of domesticity, based on the alienation of economically marginal men from the middle class.[26] This reduces their masculinity to being reactive. Yet sailors, sealers, trappers and others could go their whole lives without ever experiencing domestic life, and it is hard to explain the consistency of hyper-masculinity if it were only a reaction to forms of respectability that varied widely over time and space.

More satisfying explanations emerge from ethnographies of 'marginal people who live for the moment'. Comparing groups like gypsies, prostitutes and street people, the editors of a volume on this topic suggest that for people at the margins of society, with no prospects for entering the mainstream, living in the present transforms oppression into a subjective experience of freedom, a 'transcendental present'.[27] Future and past are denied them by poverty and prejudice, an absence they turn into a virtue by insisting that life only exists in the moment. As Astuti says of the Vezo people in Madagascar, they 'eat up all the food they have ... for lunch, without giving any thought to the evening meal', and they 'take pride in the fact that they ... are unable and unwilling to plan ahead'.[28] This freedom has to be taken seriously, as more than an illusion or 'false consciousness'. These ethnographers tell us that this is another way to experience the world, with profound effects on consumption and social life.

These comparative ethnographies suggest that an economy 'of the moment' can develop in other contexts besides the extractive economy. A larger comparative framework is clearly needed to better understand these different contexts. Another key question I have not addressed here is the way the ideals and experiences of the binge and transient consumption have been maintained and transmitted through time and across great distances, long after the working conditions that encouraged their origin had disappeared. How can my neighbour's trucks and road vehicles be connected in any way to the hunters or pioneering pig farmers of early nineteenth-century Indiana?

This also requires more research, but the two clearest and most obvious routes are through the medium of popular culture, and the compression of what was once a life-long state into one of many stages of life. For a variety of reasons, the cowboys, pirates and whalers who suffered in the extractive economy have been one of the most important sources of modern fiction and film. A major part of the appeal of the dramas built around these marginal characters is the way they satisfy 'the audience's twin desire for the security of the ordered world of the community and the freedom of unrestrained self-reliant individualism'.[29] This is exactly the conflict we would expect in a society where two contradictory social modes of consumption coexist, where I look at my neighbour (and my neighbour looks at me) with a complex mixture of contempt and envy.

In modern Belize, and to a large extent in the United States, the transient values of hedonistic consumption that I have associated here with professions and working cultures have been attached instead to the stage of life between the mid-teens and the mid-twenties. By the beginning of the twentieth century in Belize it was considered normal for most men, and some women, to leave home and travel, taking a variety of jobs and having a 'wild' period in their lives before eventually settling down to establish a family and take a place in the community. In a similar way, the rise of the concept of the 'teenager' in the United States promised the middle class a time of life free from responsibility and concerns for the future. Of course, the spring-break binge-drinking of American college students seems only a pale and attenuated reflection of the orgies of buccaneers after battle, but they ultimately draw on the same values and express a similar desire to live – and consume – in the present moment. Far from being the symbol of anti-capitalist values, in many ways one should see the cowboy on a bender as the ideal consumer, always ready to spend everything, work hard and then come back for more.

Acknowledgements

For support of my research in and about Belize I am grateful to the Wenner-Gren Foundation for Anthropological Research, the Fulbright Program and the College of Arts and Sciences of Indiana University, as well as the Energy and Resources Group at the University of California at Berkeley. Persephone Hintlian, Jennifer Eberbach and Katherine Metzo were all able research assistants. Thanks are also due to Anne Pyburn for numerous helpful conversations on these issues, to the many students and colleagues who have asked useful and important questions when I have presented this material at different universities, and to the editors of this volume for their suggestions for revision that improved the paper dramatically.

Notes

1. See the critique in L. Tiersten, 'Redefining Consumer Culture: Recent Literature on Consumption and the Bourgeoisie in Western Europe', *Radical History Review*, 57 (1993), pp. 116–59. The home has been a special arena for understanding bourgeois consumerism, as exemplified by V. de Grazia with E. Furlough (eds), *The Sex of Things: Gender and Consumption in Historical Perspective* (Berkeley, 1996); J. Frykman and O. Löfgren (eds), *Culture Builders: A Historical Anthropology of Middle-class Life* (New Brunswick, 1987); S. Schama, *The Embarrassment of Riches: An Interpretation of Dutch Culture in the Golden Age* (Berkeley, 1988). While the West End shoppers in E. Rappaport's *Shopping for Pleasure: Women in the Making of London's West End* (Princeton, 2000) venture out in public to buy, the context of consumption is always domestic. W. Smith's *Consumption and the Making of Respectability, 1600–1800* (New York, 2002) considers public forms of consumption in all classes, but the progenitors in his story are mainly in the upper and middle classes,

and their goal is to build and perpetuate what A. Clarke calls 'bourgeois values of social aspiration, material comfort, and lineage', 'The Aesthetics of Social Aspiration', in D. Miller (ed.), *Home Possessions: Material Culture behind Closed Doors* (Oxford, 2001).

2. Some of the work in cultural studies on popular culture and subcultures suggests that there really are resistant non-class based forms of consumption that represent real alternatives to the middle-class ideal, for example S. Thornton's *Club Cultures* (Hanover and London, 1996) and S. Winlow's, *Badfellas: Crime, Tradition and New Masculinities* (Oxford, 2001). The small literature on working-class industrial cultures of consumption does give us more to work with. D. Wight's *Workers Not Wasters* (Edinburgh, 1993), for example, gives a rich picture of an alternative form of social consumption from that of the middle classes, though his picture is complicated by widespread unemployment. See also R. Rosenzweig, *Eight Hours for What We Will* (Cambridge, 1983), and L. Cohen, 'The Class Experience of Mass Consumption: Workers as Consumers in Interwar America', in R. Fox and T.J. Jackson Lears (eds), *The Power of Culture* (Chicago, 1993), pp 135–60.

3. E. Chin, *Purchasing Power: Black Kids and American Consumer Culture* (Minneapolis, 2001), M. Weismantel, *Food, Gender and Poverty in the Ecuadorian Andes* (Philadelphia, 1988) and O. Lewis, *Five Families: Mexican Case Studies in the Culture of Poverty* (New York, 1962) provide rare sympathetic portraits of the consuming practices of truly impoverished people; these accounts contradict any notion that the poor have few choices to make through necessity. They also give the lie to the idea that poor people are always profligate, illogical or spendthrift.

4. My definition of a binge economy draws heavily on the papers in S. Day, E. Papataxiarchis and M. Stewart (eds), *Lilies of the Field* (Boulder, 1999), which generalize about groups of people who 'live for the moment' rather than saving and planning for the future.

5. See in particular N. Gonzalez, *Black Carib Household Structure* (American Ethnological Society, Monograph 48, Seattle, 1969), which prompted a considerable amount of research and controversy. I discuss these issues in reference to Belizean households in R. Wilk, 'Inside the Economic Institution: Modeling Household Budget Structures', in J. Acheson (ed.), *Anthropology and Institutional Economics* (Lanham, MD, 1994), pp. 365–90.

6. The literature on reputation and respectability in the Caribbean is large and ably discussed in D. Austin, 'Culture and Ideology in the English-speaking Caribbean: A View from Jamaica', *American Ethnologist*,

10(2) (1983), pp. 223–40, and K. Olwig, 'Defining the National in the Transnational: Cultural Identity in the Afro-Caribbean Diaspora', *Ethnos*, 58(3–4) (1993), pp. 361–76, and is reframed in D. Miller, *Modernity: An Ethnographic Approach* (London, 1994).

7. P. Wilson, *Crab Antics* (New Haven, 1973).
8. J. Besson, 'Reputation and Respectability Reconsidered: A New Perspective on Afro-Caribbean Peasant Women', in J. Momsen (ed.), *Women and Change in the Caribbean* (London, 1993), pp. 15–37.
9. A general description of the heterogeneous Atlantic sailing cultures of the era, and of groups like the buccaneers, can be found in P. Linebaugh and M. Rediker, *The Many-Headed Hydra* (Boston, 2000).
10. N. Uring, *The Voyages and Travels of Captain Nathaniel Uring*, with introduction and notes by Captain Alfred Dewar (London, 1928), pp. 241–2.
11. A. Exquemelin, *The Buccaneers of America*, translated by Alexis Brown (London, 1972), p. 68.
12. T. Esquemeling, *Bucaniers of America* (London, 1699), p. 28, another edition of the previous work.
13. G. Henderson, *An Account of the British Settlement of Honduras; being a view of its commercial and agricultural resources, soil, climate, natural history &c.*, 2nd edn (London, 1811), p. 85.
14. Henderson, *An Account of the British Settlement of Honduras*, p. 92.
15. *Honduras Gazette and Commercial Advertiser*, 1(12), 6 January 1827.
16. *Honduras Gazette and Commercial Advertiser*, 1(2) 16 September 1826.
17. N. Ashcraft, *Colonialism and Underdevelopment: Processes of Political Economic Change in British Honduras* (New York, 1973), pp. 35–6. On slavery in Belize, and the labour regime after emancipation, see N. Bolland, *Struggles for Freedom: Essays on Slavery, Colonialism and Culture in the Caribbean and Central America* (Belize City, 1987) and N. Bolland, *Colonialism and Resistance in Belize* (Belize City, 1988).
18. A. Gibbs, *British Honduras: An Historical and Descriptive Account of the Colony from Its Settlement, 1670* (London, 1883), p. 176.
19. G. Stuart, 'The Christmas That Went before', *Brukdown* (Belize), 3 (1978), pp. 10–12.
20. The working definition I am using in this project is that a binge is a stage in a temporal cycle of restraint and explosive release. Consumption during the binge episode is closely linked to the sense of deprivation or privation that arises during the period of labour, danger or restriction, so participants feel they have 'earned' their release. For this conception

I draw closely on the work on eating disorders by M. Nichter and M. Nichter, 'Hype and Weight', *Medical Anthropology*, 13 (1991), pp. 249–84.

21. A contemporary binge economy among Alaskan crab fishermen is documented by S. Walker, *Working on the Edge* (New York, 1991). Very similar binges are documented in the memoirs of a Texas oil-field worker, G. Lynch, *Roughnecks, Drillers, and Tool Pushers* (Austin, 1987).

22. Anon., *The Sea Book: A Nautical Repository* (London, *c.* 1866), p. 208.

23. For example, Esquemeling said buccaneers formed marriage-like pair bonds with each other; there is also disputed evidence that sailors and pirates formed sexual and romantic attachments to one another, as discussed by B. Burg, *Sodomy and the Pirate Tradition* (New York, 1983).

24. The provision of rations was a huge and important industry, arguably the first truly global food system, which drove agricultural and industrial development in parts of Europe and the rapid capital accumulation and western expansion of Britain's North American colonies. The full scale and importance of this early modern global economy have not yet been delineated.

25. The alcohol binges of aboriginal Americans, Africans and Australians were often seen as the result of 'racial' or cultural qualities, weaknesses or defects by early travellers and colonial observers. Robert Murphy and Julian Steward were among the first to argue that binges took place at the point of contact between intact subsistence systems and expanding capitalism in 'Tappers and Trappers: Parallel Process in Acculturation', *Economic Development and Social Change*, 4 (1956), pp. 335–53.

26. J. Belich, *Making Peoples: A History of the New Zealanders* (Honolulu, 1996).

27. S. Day *et al.* (eds), *Lilies of the Field*, p. 13.

28. R. Astuti, 'At the Center of the Market: A Vezo Woman', in S. Day *et al.* (eds), *Lilies of the Field*, pp. 84, 88.

29. S. Tatum, *Inventing Billy the Kid* (2nd edn, Tucson, 1997), p. 122.

−6−

'Flowers of Paradise' or 'Polluting the Nation'?
Contested Narratives of Khat Consumption
David M. Anderson and *Neil Carrier*

The study of consumption in the West has been dominated by a narrative of modernity. Consumption, the consumer and consumer cultures are usually seen to be a product of the progressive development of capitalist society. In this representation consumption itself is often presented as being a special process that subsumes or replaces older or more traditional practices. There is also an implicit assumption that the consumer society is a product of the West, as if it were one of the gifts of colonialism and empire that was exported to a non-European world. In this chapter we present evidence that challenges such a generalized representation. By looking at the consumption of an indigenous crop, we illustrate the ways in which narratives of consumption have developed quite different trajectories in their local and global formulations. We do not argue that these are entirely separate representations of consumption, but that the local and the global interact with one another in ways that are complex and often contradictory.

The commodity we will discuss is khat. This is the name by which the plant *Catha edulis* (Forssk.) is most commonly known; it is also known as the 'flower of paradise', *qat* (transliterated from Arabic), *miraa* (its Kenyan name) and *chat* (Ethiopian). The young stems and leaves of the plant are consumed by chewing, usually over the course of several hours and in the society of other consumers. The consumption of khat in Ethiopia dates back at least 500 years. The chewing of khat as a leisure pursuit has been historically associated with the elite Muslim communities of the region, but it has also been widely taken by farm labourers and others as an appetite suppressant.

With the migration of increasing numbers of Somalis, Ethiopians and Yemenis to the West in recent years, new markets for khat have opened up among communities in the diaspora. Cargo flights now bring khat to consumers in Europe and in North America, globalizing the trade and bringing good returns to those involved in the international market. At the same time, there is evidence that khat consumption has been increasing within East Africa and the Red Sea littoral, and that production has greatly expanded to meet this demand. Khat is now the single most important commercial crop in Yemen, Ethiopia's second most valuable export commodity, and the most valuable commodity traded through the entrepôt of Djibouti. In Kenya disputes over the control of the local and export markets have led to 'trade wars' between rival groups, especially between the Meru producers and the Somali exporters of the crop, and there is intense competition for cargo space on flights often full of other goods.

The khat economy is booming, then, but its success is now under challenge from the threat of international prohibition. This paper explores the contested narratives of khat consumption that underpin the campaign for regulation and control. Dominant amongst these at present is the now globalized discourse of the 'war on drugs': khat is labelled a 'drug', its use becomes 'abuse', and calls for its prohibition become frequent. However, there are other – more local – narratives of khat consumption, some also hostile to the substance, while others portray it in a more positive light. Such narratives, their interactions and the multiple meanings of khat that lie behind them are the themes of this chapter.

Khat and its Effects

Catha edulis grows in highland regions throughout much of Africa and also in Yemen and throughout west and central Asia. It favours an altitude band between 5,000 and 8,000 feet (*c.* 1,500–2,450 metres). Wild khat trees can grow as high as 80 feet, although the farmed variety is kept at around 20 feet with constant pruning. The actual harvested commodity varies from region to region in terms of what is considered edible, and how it is presented.[1] Thus, in Yemen often just the leaves are chewed, whereas in Kenya the small leaves and bark of stems are used. The stems are a mixture of green and purple hues depending on the variety; small leaves are normally quite dark, becoming greener as they mature. They can taste bitter, although the better the khat, the sweeter the taste. Differences in the provenance of the substance are likely to cause differences in the botanical and pharmacological properties, although 'it is still reasonable to assume an identity of essential chemical properties'[2] between Yemeni, Ethiopian and Kenyan *Catha edulis*.

Consumers are highly knowledgeable about the different varieties of khat, about their seasonal availability, and about fluctuations in price relating to quality and supply. In the main consumption areas of East Africa and Yemen, khat is graded in up to a dozen different qualities, correlating with the age of the tree, the time of harvest and the part of the tree from which the stems have been picked. In addition, the locality from which the khat derives has an effect upon market price; especially prized varieties attract a premium.

The stimulant effects of khat reputedly vary depending upon the variety and quality of the leaf. Research on the chemical actions of the constituent alkaloids of khat continues to reveal new effects, but none of these can be described as especially strong. The principal alkaloid is called cathinone, now known to be much more powerful than cathine (d-norpseudoephedrine), which was once thought to be the main active ingredient.[3] Cathinone releases dopamine in the brain and affects the central nervous system in a manner similar to amphetamine, 'that is, it increases heart rate, locomotor activity and oxygen consumption'.[4] Cathinone has been calculated as 'about half as potent as amphetamine',[5] hence the common description of its effects being rather like a mild form of amphetamine. While similar structurally, the comparison to amphetamine instantly makes khat sound powerful, but just as chewing coca leaves is different from taking pure cocaine, so chewing khat has a much more gentle effect than would taking isolated cathinone. Much of the pharmacological literature on khat speaks of the effects of cathinone *as if* they were the same as those of khat. They are not. Cathinone degrades rapidly post-harvest, and so the potency of khat is radically affected by the length of time it takes for the harvested leaf to reach the consumer. Trade networks delivering khat to the market must therefore operate extremely efficiently,[6] and the availability of speedy transportation is the most serious limiting factor on the extension of the market.

Cathinone and cathine are not the only active constituents. A further group of alkaloids – the cathedulins – was isolated in 1979,[7] and research has now identified more than 60 different cathedulin variants within khat samples. The psycho-activity prompted by the cathedulins appears to be very limited, although recent research suggests that they do play some role in the effects of khat as they, too, release dopamine in the brain.[8] Once again, although this can sound dramatic and potentially dangerous, it must be realized that many other substances also cause the release of dopamine. There is no evidence to suggest that the action of the cathedulins in this respect is any greater than that brought about by the drinking of a cup of coffee. One article in the pharmacologico-medical literature on khat describes its effects as follows:

> Khat consumption brings about a syndrome that arises from the central stimulatory action and from the sympatho-mimetic effects of the drug. The chewer feels elation and well-being together with increased levels of energy and alertness; his self-esteem

is enhanced. He becomes communicative and enjoys social interaction while having a sensation of heightened perceptive and imaginative ability as well as a ... greater ... capacity to associate ideas. For the observer, khat is seen to induce a state of mild euphoria and excitement accompanied by loquacity and, sometimes, hyperactivity and hypo-manic behaviour.[9]

In general, it can be said that chewing khat renders one alert and acts as a euphoriant. It also can be said to absorb the chewer into whatever activity he or she is doing when chewing and makes that activity feel 'right'. Thus, a chewer can become absorbed into even the dullest and most arduous of chores, as humorous tales in Kenya attest.[10] In Ethiopia, khat consumption is popular with university students in the examination season, to induce wakefulness and to 'sharpen' the mind. Other chewers may become absorbed in more tranquil pursuits: classically, khat consumption is associated in Yemen and Ethiopia with conversation, contemplation and relaxation in the company of friends. Ancient Yemeni and Ethiopic texts and Somali poetry extol the virtues of khat for those seeking religious enlightenment and devotion. Observation strongly indicates that the effect of khat is very much dependent upon the context in which it is consumed. It can stimulate farmers and other workers to persevere with arduous work or remain alert (it is used in East Africa by many night-watchmen and lorry drivers), and it can also relax and render the chewer sociably loquacious in recreational settings. Khat is associated with indolence by many, despite the fact that it is often consumed in work contexts. Associations with indolence derive especially from the labour time that is lost to 'qat parties' in Yemen, where it is popular to stop work after lunch to join friends to consume khat. The effects of khat – what might be colloquially termed 'the buzz' – are known by various terms in the main growing and consuming areas; in Kenya the term *handas* is used,[11] and in Somaliland *mirqaan*.

The medical side-effects of khat have been subjected to extensive research over the past fifty years, without any very significant result. Many of the side-effects appear linked more to the indirect effects of khat: some chewers do not sleep for long periods while chewing and sleep deprivation can obviously cause problems. Kennedy surveys the literature on khat and health. He mentions the research of Halbach, 'the most noted and cited medical authority on qat'.[12] Halbach 'asserts unequivocally that certain ailments are "common" among qat chewers: gastric problems such as stomatitis, esophagitis, gastritis, constipation, malnutrition, and cirrhosis of the liver'. Cases of anorexia, sexual problems and anemia have also been associated with khat consumption. Kennedy reports that other researchers have claimed that khat is linked to schizophrenia, and it has even been claimed that it may be carcinogenic.[13] The most frequently mentioned side-effect is insomnia. Kennedy's research team also conducted extensive surveys in Yemen on qat and health. The data collected led him to conclude that 'the argument that qat is responsible for the health problems of Yemen is exaggerated, but it also shows that they are not without foundation'.[14] Similar conclusions might be drawn from research on khat-related medical problems in Kenya. Kennedy also mentions potential health benefits of chewing: chewing khat might protect teeth – although the common practice of sweetening khat in Kenya can lead to dental decay – and even protect against diabetes.[15] Kennedy also states that Yemenis themselves 'are nearly unanimous in the opinion that qat is *not* an important threat to their health'.[16]

Most frightening to those unacquainted with the substance is its association with forms of psychosis. Such a link is often mentioned in the literature and is widely repeated in non-medical accounts of khat. There is in fact no clear empirical evidence to establish the existence of the condition that has sometimes been termed 'khat-psychosis'. Reports on individual cases – notably one from Ethiopia in the 1970s and other more recent examples from among the Somali immigrant population in the UK – are frequently mentioned, with those who wish to prohibit khat being only too ready to generalize from these examples.[17] Indeed, what is striking about the whole notion of 'khat-psychosis' is the lack of firm evidence supporting its existence. In the UK much talk of khat as a cause of psychosis is linked to the Somali community. There are no reports of khat-related psychosis among Yemeni, Ethiopian or Kenyan consumers in the UK. This suggests that social issues are behind the cases of psychosis amongst Somali consumers. High rates of unemployment and social exclusion might very well play a part, as might possible post-traumatic syndromes linked with incidents in their country of origin.

Khat and the West

Debate over the effects of khat consumption has recently focused upon a campaign to prohibit international trade in the substance, strongly influenced by the globalized values of Western institutions and lobbyists. Western attempts to bring in prohibition date back to the 1930s and 1940s, when, for brief periods, the French and British colonial governments tried to ban khat in Djibouti, Somaliland and Aden. In Djibouti and Aden prohibition led to social unrest, with street protests and strikes eventually forcing a reversal of the banning orders. In the late 1950s the World Health Organization (WHO) investigated the possibility of international prohibition but rejected the proposal on the grounds that no addictive narcotic reaction could be clearly established, and there was insufficient evidence of adverse medical side-effects.[18] Later enquiries by the WHO, in the 1970s and again in the 1980s, reached similar conclusions, and yet the United Nations (UN) Convention on Psychotropic Substances (1971) was amended in the 1980s to add khat's main active ingredients – cathine and cathinone – to its schedule list. This led to international moves to prohibit khat, and by 1993 khat was illegal in the United States by virtue of its containing cathinone and is now listed as a Schedule I drug in line with the UN Convention.[19] This was at a time when khat was a centre of much media attention due to the collapse of Somalia: US troops encountered Somali militia men who, it was alleged, were 'high' on khat. Media attention focused on khat consumption, presenting Somali militia men as drug crazed and trigger happy. In addition, it was reported that khat consumption was 'draining the Somali economy', and that trade in khat was controlled by a small cartel of 'traffickers' who had made their fortunes by its sale.[20]

Other Western countries have subsequently followed the United States in banning khat. These include Canada, New Zealand, Sweden and Switzerland, while several other European countries are now actively reviewing the status of khat. Australia allows restricted importation of moderate quantities of khat for permit holders. Within the region of East Africa and the Red Sea, khat has also been banned by Saudi Arabia, Eritrea and Tanzania, each seeking to prevent imports from neighbouring countries where khat is grown. In the UK khat is legal, and several tons are imported each week from Ethiopia and Kenya. Consumption in the UK is mainly restricted to the Somali, Ethiopian and Yemeni communities, and cities such as London, Manchester, Liverpool, Sheffield and Cardiff amongst others host chewing sessions, known as a *mafrish* by Somalis. A retail unit of Kenyan khat usually costs £2.50–3.00 in the UK, while the Ethiopian variety retails for £5. Much media hype surrounds the substance in the UK, as some blame it for many of the difficulties currently facing the Somali community, while others criticize it seemingly as part of an anti-immigration campaign. Khat has therefore become more controversial in the UK over the past two years. The Home Office is now engaged in new research on the substance, although they have been keen to downplay speculation that a ban is likely to be announced. The consensus among drug-awareness organizations in the UK is that such a ban would do more harm than good.

In the regions where khat is an important economic crop, there is also a deeper, local history of khat consumption that reveals contested narratives of consumption. These narratives are no less guilty of distortion, partiality and the selective deployment of facts than are global narratives of drug control, but they emphasize quite different aspects of khat consumption. Where Western discourse has increasingly politicized the debate about khat, emphasizing the potential dangers of the medical side-effects and the like as a route towards justifying the imposition of formal state regulation and control, local discourse has been more concerned with the themes of social responsibility, the family, public dignity and religion. Local discourses in Kenya, Ethiopia and Yemen stress the need of the individual to act in a socially responsible manner. In these debates, habituation and its impact upon behaviour is the principal problem, but there are also social and cultural aspects that reflect changing notions of identity and status. For some in Ethiopia, for example, khat consumption is viewed as a 'pollutant' – a symbol of the threat posed to Highland Christian hegemony by the rising tide of Islam in the surrounding lowlands. For others, including Muslims who themselves are khat consumers, the chewing of khat in public places represents a dangerous innovation, liberating khat from traditional chewing parties, where a host provides khat as a gift to his guests. The apparent increase in consumption among women and children has also prompted debate and public concern.

The international status of khat is therefore ambiguous and to some degree confusing, while within East Africa and Yemen there are also debates that focus upon consumption and its effects, drawing upon specific local issues, but at the same time being infused by the growing clamour of the international community for control and regulation of khat. There is a widespread assumption in the West, supported by the United States, that khat is an addictive drug that should be prohibited. Canada banned it principally in order to halt the smuggling of khat across its border with the United States. The UK is now under some pressure from the Canadian and US authorities to prevent khat being smuggled across the Atlantic. The American message – that khat is an evil and dangerous drug – is being widely promoted and feeds back into local debates within East Africa and Yemen.

Scenes from the Social Life of Khat

Scene 1: The Herb Garden

According to the drug enforcement authorities in the United States, Mrs MacGregor of Bristol, England, is a trafficker in a Schedule I drug. She runs a mail order business on the Internet, and among the items she sells are young *Catha edulis* plants. The plants, depending on size and age, sell, in a pot, for between £4 and £5.50, plus postage and packing. Mrs MacGregor's staff of green-fingered plant-potters will send these items by courier to any location within the UK. Fortunately for her, she does not at present export to the United States, but if she ever attempts to do so, she will be liable to arrest and prosecution under US law.

Mrs MacGregor doesn't exactly fit the image of an international drug trafficker. She runs a highly renowned herb farm in the west of England and is the author of a respected book on herb gardening. She started her herb farm nineteen years ago in the back garden of a house in Bristol. Two years later she moved out to a rural site on the edge of town. Her small herb farm has always been organic and has a certificate from the Soil Association to prove it. In fact, Mrs MacGregor was proud that hers was the first certified organic farm to be awarded a Chelsea Flower Show Gold Medal, back in 1995, and she has won seven further Chelsea gold medals since. It was around five years ago that she started selling khat plants and seeds. Always on the lookout for new herbs, she felt that khat's distinctive foliage made it attractive as a pot plant, and its exotic image gave the plant a little extra edge in the growing market for all things 'ethnic'. Playing to her market, her catalogue describes khat in simple but alluring terms:

> Catha edulis: Khat – Evergreen, Height 300 cm. Grow as a container plant in a very sheltered place. In Africa chewing the leaves is considered a potent aphrodisiac.

The idea that khat might be an aphrodisiac is not the only marketing ploy used to promote khat. On other websites advertising herbs and their uses, the aphrodisiac claim is repeated in connection with the Queen of Sheba and the River Nile, the inference being that khat has an ancient heritage, as well as a seductive image. But most of those who buy khat from Mrs MacGregor's herb garden are middle-aged gardening enthusiasts, more enamoured of the interesting red-green foliage than the supposed aphrodisiac properties of the leaf. While the US Drug Enforcement Agency gears up to smash the khat smuggling cartels in the international war on drugs, in middle England *Catha edulis* is becoming a popular houseplant.

Scene 2: Smugglers, Scientists, Sailors and Streatham's Somalis

David McCann, a seventeen year old from Deal in the English county of Kent, was arrested by US customs officials in 2003, when he was caught at New York's JFK airport with a suitcase full of khat. The story made it into the British press when it was featured in the BBC investigative programme *Inside Out*. Viewers were treated to a luridly sensationalized account of Britain's 'khat smugglers', who regularly took consignments in luggage on flights to the United States. Reporter Paul Ross bravely decided to chew some khat for himself – entirely in the interest of research, of course – under the 'close supervision' of a doctor. 'I feel trembly and a bit hyper, like I've had too much coffee', he said. 'Take it from me, khat tastes disgusting. My blood pressure has shot up and my head aches.'

Khat was described as a 'Class 1 narcotic'. Much was made of the suggestion – entirely uncorroborated by evidence of any kind – that 'profits from khat may go to terrorist groups'. It was claimed that khat fetched ten times its UK price in the United States, and that 'highly organized gangs are making £150 million a year smuggling khat into the States'. These claims were based upon an interview with Thomas E. Manifase, a special agent with the US Department of Homeland Security. Mr Manifase said nothing about his evidence, but he was keen to speculate:

> I can tell you we are taking a real hard look at the people who smuggle this into the US. We are trying to find out who these people are and who is behind this. We are looking at the funding, the money, where's it going? It could be being used to fund terrorism because it's being sent back to countries that support terrorism like Yemen and others.[21]

In February 2004 *The Guardian* newspaper lavished further hype on khat.[22] It carried a feature on khat in its science magazine, under a headline proclaiming: 'This has the same effect as ecstasy and cocaine: and its legal'. Drawing the deeply mistaken inference that all drugs categorized as Schedule I in the United States must be the same, *The Guardian*'s science writer did very little to enhance understanding of his topic and instead sowed the seeds of confusion in an article riddled with factual errors and mistaken assumptions. One can only reflect that any consumers who hurried to local stores to track down a bundle of khat after reading *The Guardian* must have been bitterly disappointed by the results.

Images of khat as a 'new drug' that might attract younger consumers sit uneasily with the reality of consumption patterns among the diaspora communities in the UK. Khat traders in London operate legitimate and open businesses, the Ethiopian traders even running their own association and producing a business card giving contact numbers for all their members. They supply regular customers, at a regular price. Their market depends upon stability and quality, and speedy and efficient delivery. Most of their regulars are middle-aged men – hardly the sort of consumers likely to foster a 'cool' image among the young. In Cardiff elderly retired seamen – originally from Hargeisa in Somaliland – gather at coffee shops for a chew and a hot spiced beverage, preferring Ethiopian to Kenyan khat as that is what they were accustomed to in Somaliland.

But not everyone in the diaspora communities in the UK takes a sanguine view of khat consumption. Somali community groups in London have recently launched a campaign to press for the prohibition of khat. The groups, which are mostly led by women, complain that too large a proportion of limited family incomes is being spent on khat by Somali males, and that khat consumption is undermining family life. The publicity given to these community groups has further heightened awareness of the potentially damaging effects of khat consumption and contributed to the most recent episode that brought khat into the media spotlight. In March 2004 police in the Streatham district of south London mounted an operation to arrest traders who were selling khat on the streets from their cars, without the appropriate hawkers' licence. The local newspaper, the *Streatham Post*, succeeded in attracting national interest to this essentially parochial story by headlining their report 'Crackdown on roadside drug trade'. Local residents were said to have applauded the police action against illegal traders. But this was only part of the story. The area of Streatham where the trade was taking place has, over the past three years, come to be dominated by immigrant Somalis. Somalis have opened several cafes and shops in the area, and many Somali asylum seekers have moved in. Tensions exist with other segments of the community, and within the Somali community itself between those with legitimate trading permits and those who are simply coming to the area to trade opportunistically. Many of the Somali shops in this area sell khat quite legally – a fact that was not reported in the *Streatham Post*.

Scene 3: The Death of Dr Tonelli

On 5 October 2003 a sixty-year-old Italian doctor and aid worker, Annalena Tonelli, was murdered in the Somaliland town of Borama. Tonelli was a respected and much loved local personality. She had worked in Somaliland for six years, running the TB hospital and raising awareness of communicable diseases, including HIV/AIDS. Her funeral and memorial service was attended by Somaliland's vice-president and several ministers, as well as representatives from the UN and other aid organizations. Among those present was Rakiya Omaar, director of the humanitarian agency Africa Rights. Writing in the *Somaliland Times*, Omaar explained that the Somaliland government had attended the ceremony 'in a show of force, both to express their appreciation for the work of Dr Tonelli, but also to send a message to the international community that her murder will not go unpunished'.[23] Two men had been arrested in connection with the murder, Omaar told her readers. Speculating as to the motive for the murder, she wondered about rumours that the killer was mentally deranged. 'Why are there so many mentally disturbed people walking on the streets of all our towns?' Omaar asked. 'We have as yet no statistics on the extent of the problem, but it is undeniably prevalent.' She continued:

Whether you live in Berbera, Hargeisa, Burao or Borama, you come across them every day. In fact you live in fear of them. They are mainly men, many of them in the prime of life, and often armed with knives, swords or heavy rocks. But there is a troubling increase in the number of women who are evidently in mental distress. And even more tragic are the far greater numbers we don't see – chained to beds in their homes by desperate relatives who do not know where to turn to for help. Some families are looking after more than one patient.

Every Somalilander who reads this article knows an individual with some form of mental health problem; they are our relatives, friends, colleagues, classmates and neighbours. We also know the terrible price each family is paying in the absence of even the most basic services – the psychological trauma, the economic burden and the social consequences of looking after disturbed and sometimes very violent people... This phenomenon is not only a tragedy for the individuals and families concerned, but is likely to undermine stability and growth on a national level.

In Somaliland the explosion in mental illness since the 1990s has customarily been blamed on the war that devastated the country, and the consequent social disruption of the multitude of Somali exiles in refugee camps in Ethiopia and Kenya. But Omaar had another explanation to offer: 'the surge in mental distress is a direct consequence of the dramatic increase in the consumption of *qat*'. Describing khat as 'a potent and addictive drug', Omaar chastised Somalilanders for their unwillingness to confront the harm that it was doing to their society. Unless khat was controlled, there would be 'many more senseless deaths on our streets'.

Warming to her theme, Omaar now provided a litany of evils associated with khat consumption – evils that hindered the social and economic development of the country:

You only need to look at the absurd economics of *qat*, with vast amounts of cash leaving our borders every day into Ethiopia. Don't expect to see civil servants, including senior officials, attend a meeting in the afternoon, no matter how important the subject under

> discussion is to the prospects of Somaliland. The dirt in our towns, littered with thousands of the multi-coloured plastic bags used to wrap *qat*, would be a sufficient reason to ban it. Not to mention the destructive impact on family life and our educational system where it is not uncommon to see secondary school students more interested in *qat* than in their studies. It is not, in fact, possible to measure the cost of *qat* to our society.

To underline the point, Omaar explained that young Somali males in Britain registered the second highest level of suicide among any immigrant group, 'no doubt while under the extreme and prolonged influence of *qat*'.

Calling for prohibition of khat in Somaliland was unlikely to gain much support, Omaar conceded, for the trade generated tax revenues for the government, was popular with the majority of people, and would be protected by 'powerful businessmen who have invested in this lucrative sector'. Indeed, in Somaliland's elections of 2003 shrewd politicians stockpiled khat for distribution to their potential voters. Both the government and its opponents 'literally chewed over their options while under the influence of *qat*'.

Khat consumption in Somaliland is therefore by no means restricted to deranged young men roaming the streets; but its use is all too easily deployed in any emotive discussion of the social and economic issues of the day. The questions that Rakiya Omaar wanted to ask were not really about the death of an Italian doctor, then, but about the death of a country.

Scene 4: Khat Busters and Barbarians

Mooryaan is a Somali word. Its original usage was in reference to a type of parasite that affects animals: 'un ver parasitant l'organisme humain surtout dans la saison des pluies'.[24] From these meanings, it is easy to see how the term came to be used pejoratively; nowadays it is commonly used to refer to young men in the militias of Somalia, those 'dispossessed ones' who are seen chewing khat and carrying weapons. Young, unemployed men in Somali cities were recruited in large numbers by warlords in the 1980s and they came to be known as *mooryaan*. According to Little,[25] 'they remain a powerful, well-armed force under different faction heads and warlords'. These young men carry out many functions in the 'stateless' country of Somalia, often acting as 'security escorts for the larger merchants and development agencies'. The destabilizing effect of these bands of young men is notorious. As a 'warlord's political power is generally based on an economy of plunder and violence',[26] they need recruits to carry out this plunder and violence, and such is the role of the *mooryaan*. Marchal refers to them as *pillards* ('looters').[27]

The term is said to have first entered common usage in reference to such men through Siyaad Barre (the former president of Somalia), who labelled as *mooryaan* those bands of youths attacking his own forces; Marchal states that it was used for the first time in official political discourse in 1990, when the chief of police, Ahmed Jilow, blamed Mogadiscio's troubled state on these marauding bands of 'delinquents'.[28] A current article on a Somali website gives the stereotype of a *mooryaan*: 'How do you tell a *Mooryaan*? Simple. Dirty, thief, killer, rapist, drug addict and drifter. A teenager who carries a fully-loaded AK-47.'[29] It was the *mooryaan* who caught and slaughtered the US Army Rangers in Mogadiscio in October 1993.[30]

In February 1993 cathinone, the principal alkaloid in khat, had been declared a Schedule I drug, effectively placing khat in the same category as heroin and cocaine. Until then supplies of khat had regularly reached the small but rapidly growing Somali and Ethiopian diaspora communities in New York, Washington and Minneapolis by air via London, Rome and Amsterdam. The war in Somalia had created a flood of refugees, the wealthier among them finding their way overseas to Europe and North America. The diaspora brought the khat habit with them, and in their wake more formal and enlarged export operations followed to supply the new consumers in the New World. The United States banned khat just as the demand for it in the international market was climbing sharply.

The result, of course, was the creation of a lively and lucrative black market, with khat being smuggled into the United States from neighbouring Canada. The Canadian government was then persuaded to follow suit, and they too banned khat. While the Canadian authorities have handled the khat issue 'with a light touch', making relatively few arrests and taking cultural factors into account when processing 'smugglers' through the courts, the US authorities have been more robust. That khat is not welcome in the United States is graphically – and comically – illustrated by a novelty uniform patch devised for customs officers; it makes a pun from the word khat to depict a snarling bulldog above the headline 'US Custom Service Khat Busters'. US seizures of khat have climbed steadily each year since 1995:

1996	17.6 tons
1997	21.1 tons
1998	27.6 tons
1999	22.1 tons
2000	33.8 tons
2001	37.2 tons[31]

In playing up the connection between khat and war in Somalia, the 'supporters of the US Border Patrol' are disturbingly graphic on their website.[32] There, a picture of a *mooryaan* holding an AK-47 is captioned 'Khat eater waiting for a new target'. A disturbing video clip on the same site shows the mutilated bodies of the American troops who were killed in Mogadiscio. The text that accompanies the clip tells Americans all that they need to know about khat:

> Almost all of the barbarians who attacked the UN peacekeepers and the barbarians who hacked them into chunks and the barbarians who attacked our troops and the barbarians who then – by the thousands – attacked our rescue forces all chewed a narcotic called khat.

> The number of violent aliens and illegal aliens in America at this moment from that part of the world can be calculated by the amount of this drug being smuggled into the country. The narcotic is an acquired taste and certainly not for an American palate.

And it doesn't stop there. The enthusiasm to prohibit khat exhibited by the US Customs Service has been taken up by its counterparts in other countries. Customs officers in New Zealand have discovered khat being sent to immigrants through the mail from both Melbourne and direct from East Africa. In 2000 New Zealand customs made thirty seizures of khat from the mail system.[33] Then, in 2003, two Somali men were prosecuted in Hamilton 'after they were seen stripping and trying to chew leaves from a khat tree growing on private property'. In reporting the story – on its crime page, naturally enough – the *New Zealand Herald* solemnly told its readers that khat leaves 'if chewed, can be hallucinogenic'.[34] For most New Zealanders, it seems, this was just another story about crazy immigrants.

Scene 5: 'Polluting the Nation'

> This place has the history of the whole town. It is the mother of Nairobi. And that is true, though some call it a two-shilling city because of those two-shilling women, others Majengo, Pumwani, Matopeni because of the mud buildings with brown rusted roofs, or Mairungi City or Miraa because of the drug... That is the Slums. A most corrupted city. A place where evil can be seen at any time of the day but worse in the night. A place with every kind of people. The richest and the poorest. A city of no shame. A place full of many bastards. Corrupt police too... Living here takes guts.[35]

In Kenya khat is known by the name *miraa*, or its older Swahili form *mairungi*. There are two very pervasive public perceptions about the use of khat in Kenya. The first is that the cultivation of khat trees was historically concentrated in the Meru district, and there is still a widely held view that consumption by the Meru people is 'traditional' and therefore somehow legitimate and acceptable, while consumption by other peoples in Kenya is a modern, and perhaps therefore dangerous, new innovation. Second, as the extract taken from Thomas Akare's novel about Nairobi's slums illustrates, Kenyans associate the consumption of khat with poverty. It is a substance taken only by those who cannot afford anything else. It is not a substance with which respectable people should be associated.[36] In recent years, Pentecostal churches in central Kenya – many of them under strong American influences – have therefore felt secure in condemning khat as an evil and unchristian commodity, dismissing it as an affectation of Islam and a polluting and unhealthy thing – even though those who grow it and sell it in Kenya are not generally Muslim. Among middle-class, respectable Kenyans, this message against khat strikes a cord, and especially so when khat is simply described as a drug. Evangelical Pentecostalists in Kenya generally set their face against all stimulants; there is no significant need to distinguish between cocaine, heroin, cannabis, khat, tobacco and alcohol. All are evil and should be banished. In this catalogue of prohibition, the distinctions between substances matter little. And it is within this broad categorization that much of Kenya's debate about khat consumption takes place.

Local discourse on khat consumption in Ethiopia has been moving in the same direction, though in Ethiopia the production and trade in khat have much deeper historic and economic roots. Historically, khat consumption is strongly identified with the Muslim community in Ethiopia, although its use is now very widespread. Consumption has never been solely restricted to males, although it is predominantly a male activity. It is customary for groups to gather to consume khat in a private home, in a room set aside for the purpose.[37] Ethiopian production is on a large and steadily increasing scale, and in the past decade the crop has become commercially important. The economic value of the crop as an earner of foreign exchange is a significant factor in local debates about regulation and prohibition.

The traditional heartland of Ethiopian khat cultivation is in the eastern province of Hararghe adjacent to the Somalia border. At present market prices, khat is considerably more profitable per acre than coffee or maize, and there is evidence that farmers are responding to this differential. Beyond the Hararghe district, the spread of khat cultivation into the southern highlands is already well established, and more recently farmers in the north have also taken up khat as a viable commercial crop. An example of the expansion of cultivation can be seen in the well-watered highlands of the Wondo Guenet area. Under irrigation, and with careful management, the yield of a khat plot here can be doubled from two harvests per annum to four. Without irrigation harvests are restricted by the timing of the rainy seasons. Despite the lack of statistics on acreages, there is much circumstantial evidence to indicate that khat cultivation is increasing rapidly in many parts of the country, and that it is now being cultivated in areas where it was not previously known.

There is currently a lively public debate in Ethiopia as to the social and economic impact of the increasing use of khat. There have been a number of academic studies that have sought to quantify consumption among schoolchildren and university students, groups believed to be among the most prominent of the new consumers. The results of this research indicate general widespread usage of khat among school pupils and tertiary students, but with some regional variations in the intensity of consumption. Among schoolchildren in Addis Ababa, around one-third appear to be khat users.[38] In areas to the south and southeast consumption is higher, rising to 60 per cent of all schoolchildren surveyed.[39] In other rural areas, for example Butajira, surveys indicate that 57 per cent of secondary schoolchildren have taken khat but do not distinguish the regularity of use. Among tertiary level students, principally those at Addis Ababa University, it is reported that 68 per cent of students take khat and that more than half this number are regular or heavy users. Both male and female students consume khat, but the frequency and intensity of use were found to be greater among males.[40] Use of khat by university students is associated with examination periods. In the Hararghe region consumption is believed to extend across 75 per cent or more of the population, children first taking up the habit from the age of ten.

The samples surveyed in these studies are all small, and it is difficult to draw general conclusion from the results. Nonetheless, the studies are usually presented within Ethiopia to reinforce concerns about the detrimental effects of khat chewing. Many health professionals, including those in the Ministry of Health Narcotics Unit, and senior academics in the Psychology Department of Addis Ababa University advocate prohibition, even though they admit that there is no substantive local evidence to show that addiction to khat has significant adverse effects upon physical or psychological health (interviews, Addis Ababa, February 1998).

Rather than health, current concern over khat appears to be located more in the domain of cultural representation and social behaviour, linked to anxieties about economic losses. It is argued that until recently khat was consumed by the Muslim community, and then only by men. Muslims represent between 40 and 50 per cent of the population, so this was already a significant consumer base, but it is generally held that consumption is now spreading into non-Muslim areas, particularly the north, where khat was previously unknown. In the towns of the north, notably Bahir Dar and Gondar, khat shops are now to be seen. It is apparent that the crop is now being marketed more effectively, and opportunities for export earnings have attracted farmers in many areas of the country where khat was not grown before.

Supply-side explanations are sometimes given to account for the apparent broadening of the consumer base, and there is some evidence to suggest this is indeed a factor. But the few available studies of consumers suggest that sociological factors are more important. Youths see khat consumption as a form of rebellion against parental control. In Ethiopia – as also in Kenya[41] – khat is becoming 'cool' among the young.

To some extent, present concerns about khat reflect anxieties about challenges to the previous dominance of a Coptic Christian highland culture, represented by the authority of the Coptic church. Khat, as a cultural symbol of Muslim influence, is viewed as a pollutant by many people in the Amharic and Tigrinya highlands, exposing young Christians to other aspects of Islam. Khat consumption thus represents a loss of parental control and undermining of cultural values for the people of the central and northern highlands. Paradoxically, the more liberal policies of the current government towards regional autonomy may also have played a part in fuelling the cultural defensiveness of those living in the Amharic and Tigrinya-speaking northern highlands. The debate about khat use is therefore infused with a number of religious and cultural issues which, though not directly related to concerns about drug use *per se*, can often serve to reinforce and justify prohibitionist views.

Through the Ministry of Health, a small but persistent media awareness campaign on drugs has been developed in an ad hoc manner since the mid-1990s, utilizing local radio and newspapers. Khat has featured very prominently in this public discourse. Emphasis is given to the potential for khat consumption to undermine the family: through the loss of the economic purchasing power diverted to khat, through the loss of productive labour time, and through the breakdown of family relationships among habitual khat chewers who neglect the social and conjugal needs of their wives. The journalists who promote such views have little sense of the need to support them empirically, and media reporting on khat tends to reflect only the cultural views of the highlands and not the traditional khat-consuming regions (interviews with journalists and broadcasters, Addis Ababa, February 1998).

While senior officials in the Narcotics Unit of the Ministry of Health and many other health professionals in Addis Ababa argue for the prohibition of khat, it is clear that this would not meet with general support in Ethiopia. The majority of people view khat as a relatively harmless substance and consider its effects to be less detrimental to society than alcohol abuse, for example. Moreover, the crop is economically important to farmers as a source of cash income and to the government as a valuable export earner.

In Ethiopia the local debate about khat has become ensnared in a wider, global discourse on drug abuse. 'Global' concerns about drugs have already penetrated Ethiopian 'public opinion'. There is a high degree of popular awareness of drugs, but this often contains inaccurate views about, and contradictory attitudes towards, their use. Views about drugs may sometimes become a vehicle for sentiments (of anxiety, fear, envy) generated by economic and social pressure, further fuelled by cynicism about official authority and its apparent failure to tackle a social problem which threatens to worsen. These attitudes are fostered by the globalized representation of drug use and abuse in sensationalized ways, both positively (through films and music) and negatively (official media, religious organizations, international and inter-governmental influences). Global influences amplify local concerns and provide a rhetoric that can be deployed in the local arena to empower arguments and to fuel anxieties.

Discussion

These scenes of khat consumption illustrate a vast array of meanings; from decorative houseplant to Schedule I narcotic, perspectives on the substance vary greatly. A multiplicity of motives and interests form and reinforce such perspectives, some global, some local, some invoking a discourse of modernity, others making claims upon tradition. For example, some perspectives on khat consumption are inflected by religious interests, as Pentecostal preachers urge their congregations to avoid the substance and as debate among Muslims continues as to whether khat is *halal* or not. Economic factors are clearly relevant too; the boost to the economy that khat gives producer countries like Ethiopia and Kenya dampens enthusiasm for prohibition, while calls for a ban are louder in Somaliland and Djibouti where khat is imported and consumed on a large scale. In the Nyambene Hills – Kenya's most intensive khat-growing region – the substance is held in high esteem as the bedrock of the local economy and as a consumption item of great cultural significance. Elsewhere in northern Kenya, where much khat is consumed, some lament it as a drain on the local economy and as the cause of marriage breakdowns and other social ills. While the young regard khat consumption as 'cool' and as deserving of respect, their parents regard it as an unseemly habit not suitable for respectable palates. Even amongst communities where khat is produced, traded and consumed, debates swirl around its social and economic impact, as well as its effects upon the health and morality of the consumer. Place, money, religion, ethnic identity and social class are all factors in the contested narratives of khat consumption.

From a global viewpoint khat is usually seen in more simplistic terms. Khat is infused with highly emotive and political significance in Europe and North America. In the imaginations of those who fear the unfamiliar, khat is connected with the troubles of immigration, the 'war on terror' and, most importantly, the 'war on drugs'. Its consumption by African and Yemeni diaspora communities has made it more conspicuous in the West, linking it firmly to the identity of alien communities. Behind social concerns about khat consumption, there often lurks a fear of race, as the 'Supporters of the US Border Patrol' website explicitly illustrates. In this instance, khat provides the 'politically correct' camouflage for 'politically incorrect' views. Although its trading network may reflect local and traditional practices, it seems opaque to international drug control agencies. Moreover, its consumers are largely Muslims from the Horn of Africa and the Arabian Peninsula, a fact that has prompted the tenuous link with the 'war on terrorism'. Most pervasively, by being labelled a 'drug', khat is now enveloped in the global rhetoric of another war, 'the war on drugs'. Viewed as 'drug abuse', khat consumption is all too easily stigmatized and laid open to campaigns for prohibition. Glib comparisons that link khat consumption with cocaine further assimilate what is essentially a mild social stimulant into a category of very different substances, ignoring the great differences between their respective effects and cultures of consumption.

This global discourse on khat consumption feeds back into a local discourse in East Africa and the Red Sea region. Those who wish to prohibit khat consumption in Ethiopia, Kenya and Yemen find support and justification in the global discourse of the 'war on drugs'. So powerful is this rhetoric that many khat consumers are themselves keen to know whether the substance should be classified as a 'drug'. The global spread of this rhetoric has resulted in a convergence of the discourse on khat consumption, whether in Nairobi, Minneapolis or Melbourne. Perhaps fearing the opposition of its international friends, the Kenyan government has never listed khat as one of its cash-crops, despite the foreign currency it brings in. Globalized values and reliance on donor money mean that Kenya would be uncomfortable in drawing attention to a crop illegal in several donor countries. Khat has hardly been celebrated despite its economic power.

But the global discourse of khat consumption does not hold sway everywhere. Local discourses of consumption vigorously defend the crop and its consumers, presenting alternative narratives that determinedly link khat to idioms of progress and modernity. Kenya's *Daily Nation* recently reported that Tanzanian members of the East African Legislative Assembly were being taken round the Nyambene Hills by their Kenyan counterparts to view the economically prosperous khat fields.[42] The purpose of the Nyambene tour was explained by a Kenyan MP: 'We want Kenyans to start selling the crop in Tanzania. That is why we brought the MPs to see the crop and how it benefits locals.' In Tanzania khat is illegal, and the government there has imposed strict penalties upon those caught with the substance. Several Kenyan traders are currently serving time in Tanzanian jails for their role in promoting the trade. Kenyan officials are surely well aware that khat is classified as a Schedule I substance in the United States, but this does not prevent them from mounting local resistance by promoting the sale of khat to their neighbours in Tanzania. Openly promoting the production and trade of what is a Schedule I substance in the United States is in itself a small victory of local resistance to the global discourse of the 'war on drugs'. Local narratives of khat consumption are not always traditional and affirmative, often invoking ideas of modernity and economic growth. These imperatives will continue to be resistant to a global discourse of consumption that is driven by quite different concerns. The narratives of khat consumption will long remain contested.

Notes

1. For a detailed look at the place of khat in the agricultural system of the Meru of Kenya's Nyambene Hills, see P. Goldsmith, 'Symbiosis and Transformation in Kenya's Meru District' (unpublished PhD thesis, University of Florida, 1994). For khat production in Ethiopia, see E. Gebissa, *Leaf of Allah: Khat and Agricultural Transformation in Hararge, Ethiopia 1875–1991* (Oxford, 2004).
2. J. Kennedy, *The Flower of Paradise* (Dordrecht, 1987), p. 178.
3. Kennedy, *The Flower of Paradise*, p. 181.
4. S. Weir, *Qat in Yemen: Consumption and Social Change* (London, 1985), p. 46.
5. A. Zaghloul, A. Abdalla, H. El-Gammal and H. Moselhy, 'The Consequences of Khat Use: A Review of Literature', *European Journal of Psychiatry*, 17 (2003), p. 80.
6. See N. Carrier, 'The Need for Speed: Contrasting Timeframes in the Social Life of Kenyan Miraa', *Africa*, 75(4) (2005).

7. L. Crombie, 'The Cathedulin Alkaloids', *Bulletin on Narcotics*, 32(3) (1980), pp. 37–50.

8. Research of a team at King's College, London, reported in *The Guardian*, 5 February 2004.

9. Zaghloul *et al.*, 'The Consequences of Khat Use', p. 80.

10. N. Carrier, 'The Social Life of Miraa: The Farming, Trade and Consumption of a Plant Stimulant in Kenya' (unpublished PhD thesis, University of St Andrews, 2003), pp. 3–5.

11. See Carrier, 'The Social Life of Miraa', chapter 6. For a humorous – and accurate – look at khat's effects, see P. Goldsmith, 'Computa Brain Supercharger', *Iko!*, October–December 2004, pp. 46–9.

12. Kennedy, *The Flower of Paradise*, p. 214.

13. Kennedy, *The Flower of Paradise*, p. 223.

14. Kennedy, *The Flower of Paradise*, p. 231.

15. Kennedy, *The Flower of Paradise*, p. 225.

16. Kennedy, *The Flower of Paradise*, p. 213.

17. A. Alem and T. Shibre, 'Khat Induced Psychosis and Its Medico-Legal Implication: A Case Report', *Ethiopian Medical Journal*, 35 (1997), pp. 137–41; S. Critchlow, 'Khat-induced Paranoid Psychosis', *British Journal of Psychiatry*, 150 (1987), pp. 247–9.

18. Weir provides a good account of WHO and other research into the effects and addictiveness – or lack thereof – of khat: Weir, *Qat in Yemen*, pp. 45–53.

19. *US Federal Register*, Volume 58, Number 9 (1993).

20. M. Goldstone, 'Cat – Methcathinone – a New Drug of Abuse', *Journal of the American Medical Association*, 269 (1993), p. 2508; T. Randall, 'Khat Abuse Fuels Somali Conflict, Drains Economy', *Journal of the American Medical Association*, 269 (1993), pp. 12–14; P. Little, *Somalia: Economy without State* (Oxford, 2003).

21. Thomas E. Manifase, 'Inside out', http://www.bbc.co.uk/print/insideout.

22. *The Guardian*, 5 February 2004.

23. Rakiya Omaar, 'The Murder of Dr Annalena Tonelli: What Questions Should We Ask?', *Somaliland Times*, 90(2), 11 October 2003.

24. R. Marchal, 'Les *Mooryaan* de Mogadiscio', *Cahiers d'Etudes Africaines*, 33 (1993), p. 313.

25. Little, *Somalia*, p. 150.

26. Little, *Somalia*, pp. 150–1.

27. Marchal, 'Les *Mooryaan* de Mogadiscio', p. 299.

28. Marchal, 'Les *Mooryaan* de Mogadiscio', p. 303.

29. M. Afrah, 'The Dark Side of Somalia', accessed online (26 March 2005): http://www.banadir.com/the_dark_side.shtml.
30. A. Simons, *Networks of Dissolution: Somalia Undone* (Boulder, CO, 1995), pp. 205–6.
31. Figures published on the US Drug Enforcement Administration website (accessed 26 March 2005): http://www.dea.gov/pubs/intel/02032/02032dt1.html.
32. http://www.borderpatrol.com/borderframe901.htm (accessed 26 March 2005).
33. R. Taylor, 'Drug Warning for Refugees to Chew on', *The New Zealand Herald*, 8 November 2000.
34. 'Somali Men Target Hallucinogenic Tree Leaves', *New Zealand Herald*, 21 January 2003.
35. T. Akare, *The Slums* (London, 1981), p. 139.
36. See Carrier, 'The Social Life of Miraa', chapter 7.
37. Gebissa, *Leaf of Allah*, pp. 7–14.
38. Z. Zein, 'Polydrug Abuse among Ethiopian University-Students with Particular Reference to Khat (Catha-Edulis)', *Journal of Tropical Medicine and Hygiene*, 91 (1988), pp. 71–5; M. Belew, D. Kebede, M. Kassaye and F. Enquoselassie, 'The Magnitude of Khat Use and Its Association with Health, Nutrition and Socio-economic Status', *Ethiopian Medical Journal*, 38 (2000), pp. 11–26.
39. F. Adugna, C. Jira and T. Molla, 'Khat Chewing among Agaro Secondary School Students, Agaro, Southwest Ethiopia', *Ethiopian Medical Journal*, 32 (1994), pp. 161–6.
40. See Z. Zein, 'Polydrug Abuse among Ethiopian University Students', pp. 71–5.
41. See N. Carrier, '"Miraa is Cool": The Cultural Importance of Miraa (Khat) for Tigania and Igembe Youth in Kenya', *Journal of African Cultural Studies*, 17(2), pp. 201–18.
42. *Daily Nation*, 29 June 2004.

–7–

Chewing Gum
Mass Consumption and the 'Shadow-lands' of the Yucatan
Michael R. Redclift

Few products in the twentieth century have proved as ubiquitous as chewing gum, and few have attracted so little scholarly attention. Chewing gum is an example of a new commercial product, which achieved iconic status in the United States during the early twentieth century and was 'exported' to the rest of the world. The history of chewing gum illustrates, among other things, how taste can be globalized. This chapter examines the political and social forces at work behind the globalization of taste, the difficult geopolitics behind chewing gum, and the contribution that it made to the forging of identity in both its consumers and its (largely invisible) producers. The 'shadow-lands' that lay behind the commercial product are revealed as spaces of social and political conflict, between the Mexican state and an insurgent civil society made up of heavily indebted forest workers, Mayan peasant revolutionaries, as well as labour contractors and transnational companies.

The Consumer Market

Chewing gum was a product of popular consumption in the United States by the early 1900s. Its early history was associated with the efforts of entrepreneurs, such as Thomas Adams, William White and William Wrigley, who developed new ways of processing, advertising, marketing and processing the gum base they imported from Mexico, *chicle*. By 1941 consumers in the United States alone accounted for sales in excess of $6.5 million (US).[1] During and after the Second World War chewing gum reached global markets as part of American GIs' rations. Gum became part of the standard ration ('C' and 'K' Ration) issued to combat troops and proved immensely popular among the three million stationed in the UK and (later) elsewhere in Europe and throughout the globe. In England the catchphrase 'Got any gum, chum' epitomized the relations between American troops and the local population.[2]

Within a few years sales in the United States increased enormously, to five times those of the pre-war period. This and the difficulties in sourcing *chicle* and Siamese jelutong during wartime, as well as the short supply of sugar and spearmint in the United States, provided strong incentives for the production of synthetic substitutes for natural gums, based on hydrocarbons. Most commercial chewing gums today are made of vinyl resins or microcrystalline waxes, similar to the vinyls used for the covers of golf balls. These technical innovations and the widespread use of bubble gum (for which *chicle* is unsuitable) were given a further boost in 1950 by the Korean War. The US military had learned how valuable gum chewing could be during combat. It freshened and cleansed the mouth when toothbrushes and paste were unavailable, it quenched thirst when water was scarce, it induced relaxation under fire, and it helped to keep the forces alert during manoeuvres. Most important of all, perhaps, chewing gum, most of which was withdrawn from the US domestic market in 1941, reminded the troops of home.

Chewing gum had already achieved popular 'iconic' status in the United States. In the 1920s and 1930s it became associated with movies, sports like baseball (especially through the issue of chewing gum cards) and popular music. Interesting parallels also exist with other products such as tobacco, bananas and chocolate.[3] In the UK chewing gum was a desirable product, especially during wartime and the period of post-war sweet rationing. At the same time, it was a key element in the growing Americanization of British culture.[4] Today over 500 companies produce chewing gum in ninety-three countries, most of which have no commercial base in the United States. The largest of these companies, and the one most closely associated with the product, William Wrigley's, has thirteen factories and sells its product in over 100 countries, representing global retail sales of over $2 billion (US).[5] The expansion and transformation of chewing gum is a very American story. In the course of the twentieth century chewing gum became not only a global product, but one that was identified as a quintessential and symbolic aspect of 'American' consumer culture.

Chewing Gum and the 'Shadow-lands' of Consumption

The history of chewing gum demonstrates that behind the mass advertising, branding and sophisticated marketing strategies that characterized chewing gum's early history lay an even more invisible process, that of *chicle* tapping in Mexico and the colonization of the tropical forests of Yucatan that followed. These were the 'shadow-lands' that provided the raw material for the mass consumption of a novel product in the first half of the twentieth century. The invention of synthetic gum and its widespread use in the second half of the century turned this product into an artefact and an icon of popular taste.

The 'boom' in *chicle* production, to meet North American consumer demand, began during the first two decades of the twentieth century and reached its peak in the early 1940s. *Chicle*, the raw material from which chewing gum was derived, came from the Yucatan Peninsula and Central America, where the *chicozapote* tree grew in the high, tropical forests. The demand for *chicle* from the United States served eventually to transform the landscape and ecology of the east and south of the Yucatan Peninsula of Mexico and paved the way for new land uses on the tropical frontier. It led to harvesting and production practices which are of contemporary importance, especially for protected tropical forest areas in which forest products represent a growing market activity.[6]

Most consumers in the twentieth century were doubtless oblivious of its origins, but nevertheless, by stimulating these distant commercial links, chewing gum illustrates the way in which 'nature' is actively produced as both material artefact and discursive construct. The history of chewing gum during this period has considerable significance for our understanding of the changing boundaries between local and metropolitan cultures, and the processes through which consumer cultures have become globalized. It also bears on current thinking about levels of personal consumption and international political economy in the United States, and elsewhere, as consumption is increasingly linked to cultural choices.

Recent research has emphasized the way in which consumer markets, especially for products of extractive industries, are linked in complex ways with environmental and other policies.[7] The areas from which raw materials are sourced have been described as 'the marginal spaces in, and through, which broader processes of socio-spatial order are worked out'.[8] Indeed, it is suggested that today these spaces are rendered even more marginal by the prospect of plenty: 'already rendered distant, shadowy spaces by the value of the commodity chains, these commodity supply zones are pushed further out of sight by the emergence of a post-scarcity discourse that celebrates material abundance'.[9] In the case of chewing gum, its close association with the values of the twentieth century – leisure, independence and private indulgences – seems almost to be a precursor of the 'post-scarcity' and 'post-material' age.

The Geopolitics of Chewing Gum: The Material and the Invisible

The impact of the enormous surge in the consumption of chewing gum during the 1930s and 1940s and the later depression in sales, when synthetics derived from hydrocarbons replaced the natural gum base, was felt particularly acutely in the east of the Yucatan Peninsula, today's state of Quintana Roo. Here, early production had been associated, like many extractive forest products, with transient labour working under onerous conditions and in an unregulated fashion, like so many 'informal sector' activities today.

The Yucatan was as remote from Mexico City as anywhere in Mexico; it was over a thousand miles from Merida, the colonial capital, to the Federal District. In another sense, too, Yucatan lay at the margins of the country. For a brief period after Mexican independence from Spain in 1821 the region had sought autonomy and even independence from Mexico. Its commercial links were with New York, Paris and London rather than Mexico City, and the trade in its primary products, dyewoods, copra and hardwoods such as mahogany, was with these centres. Later the rapid development of *henequen* (the sisal-like fibre which formed the basis of ropes and carpets) brought Europe and North America even closer and suggested even greater benefits from international trade.

The landholding system bequeathed Yucatan by the Spanish Conquest was in many respects one of the most unequal and oppressive in Latin America. Most of the best land was occupied by large landholdings (*latifundia*) which employed huge numbers of day-labourers and tenants. After the middle of the nineteenth century the rise of *henequen* production converted many of these estates into highly commercial enterprises, geared to the international market but still dependent on 'pre-capitalist' forms of labour mostly undertaken by Mayan populations living in the surrounding villages. The villagers, for their part, derived their non-cash livelihoods largely from the cultivation of corn and associated crops (chillies, beans and squash). Their religious ceremonies and rituals, and the structure of their political leadership, still owed much to the pre-Columbian forms of social organization which the colonial *encomienda* (estate/labour system) had exploited very effectively.

By the late nineteenth century, and the beginning of the *chicle* 'boom', the Mayan population of the region had been embroiled in what amounted to a prolonged ethnic struggle, the 'Caste War', for almost half a century. One section of the 'pacified' Maya was still working on the large *henequen* estates to the north and west of the peninsula. However, the rebel Maya (or '*Cruzob*') followed the cult of the 'Talking Cross', a symbol of resistance to the whites which had strengthened their sense of their own religious and

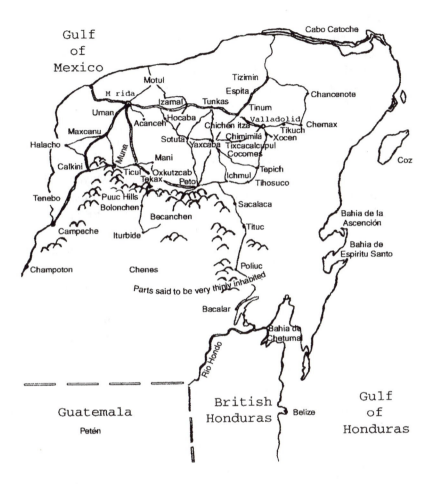

Figure 6 Map of the Yucatan Peninsula, 1847

Source: Museum of the Caste War, Tihuosuco.

political mission since the 1850s. They had retreated to the vast forests of the south and west, where they continued their struggle for independence even after the onset of the Mexican Revolution in 1910.

Most of the first commercial *chicleros* (tappers), on the other hand, were not ethnically 'Mayan'. They were natives of Veracruz on the Gulf coast, and they often arrived in the Yucatan Peninsula by boat after dangerous sea crossings. They worked under contract to men who provided the equipment for tapping gum and lived for six months of the year (the wet season from

June to December) in camps located deep in the mature tropical forest. Working in groups of about a dozen men in each camp, they tapped the milky white resin from the *chicozapote* trees within range of their camp. Using ropes and machetes, they climbed these trees, cutting zigzags in the bark and collecting the tasteless resin in cups underneath. This was then boiled in vats until it had congealed and could be transported in 'bricks' on mule-back. The contractors were allocated areas of forest for tapping or entered it illegally, for there were few workable laws in what was very much a frontier area.

The principal zone of production was a stronghold of rebel Maya chieftains, veterans of the Caste War between whites and Mayan followers of the 'Talking Cross'. Their leader in the south of the peninsula until 1931 was the notorious 'General' May, who had developed close relations with American gum manufacturers, such as Wrigley's, and whose revenues from *chicle* helped to fund armed opposition.[10] However, the containment and suppression of the rebel Maya and the enlarged role of the Mexican state, especially under President Cardenas in the 1940s, brought the harvesting of *chicle* within the compass of organized cooperatives and increasing measures of state regulation. In 1942 nearly four million kilos of *chicle* from Yucatan was sold to four large American-owned companies: Beechnut, Wrigley's, American Chicle Co. and Clark Bros. The commercial and strategic importance of these sources, at their height, can be gauged from the fact that in June 1943 representatives of *chicle* cooperatives travelled to the United States to 'discuss and defend the price of *chicle*, one of the most appreciated wartime materials in the United States'.[11]

During the 1940s and 1950s the Mexican government sought to control both the production and the export of gum through the Agricultural Ministry and the Banco de Comercio Exterior. *Chicleros* were encouraged to organize themselves into marketing cooperatives and greater controls were exercised over their production by the federal government, which was determined to 'settle' the forest frontier of Quintana Roo (and by the late 1960s to pave the way for mass tourism on the Caribbean coast south of Cancun). Most of the trees from which the resin was tapped grew on land held by *ejidos* (peasant communities) or on federal lands, making them a common property resource. Access to the forests, which was once governed by tradition and personal influence, became officially regulated. The production of *chicle* was increasingly managed through establishing production quotas and targets and using more competitive tendering. This period of state regulation, however, did nothing to reverse the fortunes of the industry. By the 1970s a forest industry that was potentially sustainable ecologically, and capable of providing livelihoods for poor families without causing large-scale

Figure 7 Juan Bautista May Tuyub tapping a *chicozapote* tree in Ejido X-Maben, Quintana Roo, Mexico, 2003

Source: Oscar Forero.

forest destruction, was in sharp decline and secondary to the demands of global tourism.[12] However, because *chicle* was sourced from the Yucatan Peninsula, several thousand miles from its main market in urban America, its origins were almost invisible to those who consumed it. It appeared, like other manufactured commodities, to have come into being to meet a need of consumers, rather than to provide a livelihood for producers. Few commodities were more material; but because of the distance (culturally as well as geographically) that separated consumers from producers, and the form taken by its commercial transformation into 'product', chewing gum was also invisible.

Chewing Gum and American Mass Consumption

The primary influence of Europe on American taste and culture was to change radically by the end of the nineteenth century. The congregation of large numbers of people in cities and in factories in late nineteenth-century America made the traditional entertainments of rural society impossible. What arose from within American society were forms of recreation and spectator sports that, while they owed something to Britain, were essentially made in America. This upheaval in popular recreation was made possible by technology, but not determined by it. As David Nye argues, national cultures were less technologically determined than technologically *determining*.[13] Together with much improved transportation and better business methods, urban America was embarking on a revolution in popular expectations.[14] 'All of the institutions that purveyed popular culture were being transformed.'[15] This was the crucible of both mass entertainments and popular spectator sports.

The rise of chewing gum was connected to new commercial forms of popular leisure and entertainment. One of the most important aspects of mass consumption and twentieth-century popular culture was the increased visibility of the 'product', and the increasing invisibility of the labour from which the product was drawn. Labour and production relations had often been invisible in the past, of course, but before the early twentieth century most of those who laboured were destined to consume very little, and most of the things they could buy were extremely expensive. The new century and the new continent changed all that. The era of mass production was also one of mass consumption, and it should hardly come as a surprise to find that many of the new products that were consumed became invested with meaning and importance by the new consuming classes.[16]

Similarly, it was not an accident that chewing gum became widely available in American society at a time when work itself was being reformulated, and workers were being challenged to accept a level of 'multi-tasking' that had few precedents in urban society. The workers who chewed gum often helped prepare food as well, but gum could be viewed as a substitute for food, at least in the short term. It filled a new space in the landscape of consumption.

The centrality of gum to people's lives was illustrative of both the changes in labour relations and the patterns of consumption that facilitated these changes.

Another key element in this evolving process was the centrality of spatial relations to the life of the new commodity. By 1918 sourcing from geographically remote areas was easier than ever before, and the resources that were necessary to the new consumer product were often so remote as to be invisible. As with many food products, so with chewing gum, the question few people considered was 'where on earth did this come from?' Few really knew the answer, and the ubiquitous product was wrapped in mystery.

Another aspect of chewing gum that requires some attention, and which rewards investigation, is that of the relationship between source and final product. It is clear that spatial scales do not exist independently of societies; they are socially produced and reproduced. The history of chewing gum provides evidence of the significance of spatial relations, and the way that spatial scales are linked to the evolution of capitalist economic relations.[17] The social and political struggles of rebel Maya and *chicleros* in Yucatan, as well as those of factory workers in the United States, served to transform these spatial relations. When it was difficult, or increasingly irrelevant, to source chewing gum from the tropical forests of Mexico and Central America, other avenues were explored. The technological changes that made synthetic gum possible by the 1930s (spurred on by the development of 'bubble' gum) held consequences for Mexican producers, and at a time when nationalism was reasserting itself south of the border. They serve to illustrate what some authors have termed the 'geographical embedded-ness of power relationships'.[18]

Spatial relationships are necessary to the commodity itself, to its production and consumption, but they are also necessary in another sense, since some products (and chewing gum is clearly one) achieve their iconic status from the fact that their origins cannot be easily identified. They serve to underline one of the most evident features of 'advanced' capitalist markets, that popular taste can elevate a product, sometimes making it a 'fetish' and often providing strong cultural associations which serve to deepen the consumer's attachment to it. In this sense popular taste and mass consumption are complements to each other, and it is difficult to explain one without explaining the other. The way in which chewing gum came to occupy a central role in the American psyche provides evidence of what Wittgenstein referred to as 'the mystery of appearances as they unfold in front of us'.[19]

Today chewing gum is an important part of the Mexican diet as well as that of many Americans. It plays an important part in children's parties, filling

Figure 8 Shop Selling Chewing Gum in Merida, Yucatan, 2003

Source: Michael Redclift.

plastic toys and playthings, and filling the shelves of major wholesalers, who in turn supply itinerant street sellers. The size of the 'informal sector' in Mexico, as in other Latin American countries, and the massive sales of cheap, sugar-based confectionery have ensured that chewing gum reaches every corner of the continent, although today it is not the *chicle*-based gum collected in Yucatan.

The Organization of Space

The history of chewing gum, then, serves to illustrate the way in which power relations are linked with spatial relations. In Mexico the itinerant workers who migrated to the forest frontier in the early twentieth century were part of a larger circle of transient labour in that country; and their counterparts in the United States were among those who consumed the gum. However, it was clear from the beginning of the century that power lay with those who could use natural resources and this itinerant labour to do business and make profits. The returns on *chicle* extraction were often spectacular for Mexican and foreign entrepreneurs, and the capital they accumulated was invested in the towns and cities of the United States. As Gavin Bridge has argued, commodity supply zones 'express a particular vision of socio-political relations as a form of power-knowledge'.[20]

In the case of Yucatan, the boom years for *chicle* production facilitated the transformation of the environment by bringing the Mexican state to bear on what had hitherto been seen as a remote jungle region. Later the gradual demise of the *chicle* economy provided another opportunity for the Mexican state to rework social relations in the zone. Having 'Mexicanized' the frontier through suppressing the Mayan resistance in 1901, thirty years later, under President Cardenas, the Mexican state sought to socialize production. In the United States chewing gum gradually became associated with all things American, and at a time when the United States was assuming political and cultural leadership of the West. Chewing gum communicated confidence in the repertoire of popular taste.

In Mexico *chicle* performed something more akin to a 'subaltern' role in the chronicle of relations between the two countries. Here, *chicle* held another kind of 'power/knowledge' association, and one that fitted more conveniently into a picture of economic dependence. *Chicle* production, in its social and geographical marginality, seemed to convey to a less confident civil society something of the 'mendacity' of popular taste. The chewing gum story in Mexico led to a darker side of history, much of which never found public acknowledgement.[21]

The ability to organize space in the chewing gum world was one that was dictated by the economic pre-eminence of the United States. Notwithstanding the 'power' of the commodity to elicit emotional attachments and cultural associations, its mass consumption was necessarily linked to capital penetration in spatially remote areas whose very 'remote-ness' did nothing to prevent them from being transformed overnight. Indeed, remoteness and the absence of controls often facilitated the process of extraction:

> The stretching and deepening of social relations and institutions across space and time such that, on the one hand, day-to-day activities are increasingly influenced by events happening on the other side of the globe and, on the other hand, the practices and decisions of local groups can have significant global reverberations.[22]

This forces us to reconsider space, and its relationship with power, as well as the limitations of 'territorial' divisions in explaining the relations between societies.[23]

Several things remain clear in assessing the bigger theoretical picture. First, globalization does not mean the triumph of the universal over the particular. 'The ways in which space and time are understood, and perhaps refashioned, are not universal', and we would be foolish to ignore 'the articulation/disarticulation of local space within globalizing economies'.[24] Local systems of production coexist with global brands and products, in the case of gum as in other cases.

Second, it is clear that, whatever the cultural weight acquired by a product in the course of its life, there can be little question that this is not historically dependent in a teleological sense on the economic and power relations that brought the product to the market. Primary commodity supply zones, such as the Yucatan in this instance, often play a key role in the wider histories of consumption and taste. But the full significance of the commodities concerned, to specific cultures and social formations, is constantly changing and being reconfigured. Chewing gum today is not the same commodity as it was in 1941, not only in its material composition but also in its cultural resonance. Patterns of mass consumption, together with popular taste, are capable of modification and adaptation to changing circumstances and economic conditions. Commodities require 'the libidinous, performative and novelty-generating potentialities of social life' to be re-imagined, their meaning taken from everyday life but recast over time.[25]

Examples abound of social institutions that enable commodities to adapt to popular taste, facilitating different patterns of consumption, in different locations, by different groups of people. The history of tobacco furnishes examples of a dominant tradition, in this case that of the nineteenth century bourgeois male, which influenced smoking cultures, but also provided opportunities for the penetration of new markets.[26] Another example is that of chocolate, which until the First World War was known largely as a beverage but is now principally a confectionery item of global proportions.[27]

At some point, of course, chocolate was *cacao* (and 'cocoa', the drink) rather than the confectionery bar we have grown to know and associate with specific global brands, like Nestle, Cadbury or Hershey. It was harvested from pods, which grow on trees in the tropics. Similarly, *chicle* needed to be transformed industrially into 'chewing gum' before it could be marketed successfully in the United States and later on the international market. The more that chicle became chewing gum, the more of a commodity it had become, and the more it developed into a *global* commodity, eventually made from hydrocarbons. Spatial relations then became fully subordinated to the demands of global commodity production and the promotion of global brands. In the case of chewing gum, popular taste provided the impetus, via branding and imaginative marketing, for a global product.[28]

Chewing Gum in the Age of 'Post-scarcity'

Chewing gum was once a strategically important product traded on global markets and deemed essential to the American war effort. The arrival of synthetics changed that status, and chewing gum, like so many other 'natural' products, left its legacy in specific histories of labour and capital that are largely untold and even unknown. In the case of gum, there is no 'post-scarcity discourse' to inform our view of the importance of the resource.[29] Chewing gum illustrates the way in which nature is produced as both material artefact and discursive construct, not primarily because discourse facilitates the acceptance (or rejection) of awkward political choices, as in the case of hydrocarbons, but because the commodity is itself discursively produced. Without marketing and branding it is difficult to see why anybody would chew commercial gum. Although originally sourced from 'nature', chewing gum is witness to the triumph of discourse over substance, to the fullest realization of an 'embodied social life', a life lived through the act of consumption itself.[30]

The process through which chewing gum has been redefined and naturalized has turned 'full-circle' in recent years, as authentic *chicle* has become a niche product, and the market for it has been widened through the Internet. At the same time, the sustainable production of *chicle* appeals to a new audience interested in promoting sustainable forest management in areas previously over-exploited for short-term gain. *Chicle*-based gum has entered a new market and a new set of consumer assumptions, perhaps closer to a 'post-scarcity' discourse than the early twentieth-century America from which it sprang.

There are several ways in which chewing gum forces us to reflect upon mass consumption and popular taste, as an exemplar and a test of theory. Chewing, like smoking or eating and drinking, is a primary bodily activity. It is associated with pleasure and contentment but also with denial (of food or liquids). Gum has acted as a substitute for what we do not have, as enjoyment realized and denied.

Within the history of its production and transformation from a raw natural product into a commodity, chewing gum also reveals the fault lines that demarcate the United States from its neighbour to the south. In Mexico the production of *chicle* was briefly associated with political struggles for the land and the resources it commands. The materialization of *chicle* into gum has a wider, and largely unacknowledged, role in mass consumption and popular taste. Through aggressive marketing and market opportunism, chewing gum was positioned, on the American market, as something necessary to life itself.

Its consumption has become near universal, and its links with the body have ensured that chewing gum will be seen as inseparable from those who chew it. Gum provides a way, and a discourse, through which 'external' nature can be integrated with 'internal', bodily nature and the 'embodied self'.

And the 'shadow-lands' which were the source of chewing gum are now the location of an entirely new form of mass consumption, as global tourism touches and transforms the Yucatan Peninsula. Most of the areas from which *chicle* was harvested and exported during the first half of the twentieth century have developed as tourist enclaves since 1970: Cancun, Isla Mujeres and Cozumel among them. The young men and women waiting at tables and working in bars along the Mexican Caribbean coast are the grandchildren and great-grandchildren of *chicleros*, whose labour underpinned the development of popular taste.

Chewing Gum's Ecological Footprint

One way of assessing the legacy of chewing gum is by assessing its 'ecological footprint' – what did chewing gum leave behind in the forests of Yucatan? The new Mexican government which came into being after the 1910 Revolution made little attempt to exert control over the extractive economies of the Republic, including the production of *chicle* in Yucatan. Through bribery and special dispensations, foreign interests were able to appeal to officials in Mexico City,over the heads of local power-holders. Moreover, with the start of the First World War, the global demand and prices for forest products increased dramatically. In 1916, when the United States entered the conflict, the demand for *chicle* accelerated, partly because of the US Department of Defence's policy of including chewing gum in soldiers' rations. By 1916 over ten million North Americans had become consumers of chewing gum. American companies, such as Adams and Wrigley's, began to replace London-based finance companies. They began to set up acquisition subsidiaries that operated in Belize and Mexico and managed to avoid any effective tariff or export controls or regulations.

The production and marketing of *chicle* involved large-scale capital and complex systems of distribution. Production was organized through a series of hierarchically linked centres. The producers' subsidiaries connected the foreign manufacturer with the source of primary material. They established overall administrative control of both production and export, establishing supply centres at Belize City, Cozumel, Santa Maria, Progreso and Isla del Carmen, Campeche. In the zones of production each *chicle* centre serviced a large number of bush camps called *hartos*, from which the *chicleros* worked.

The tapping season for *chicle* ran between June and February during the rainy season, when the *chicozapote* latex could be accessed. The workers were recruited from both Yucatan and Veracruz by means of advances in both cash and kind (*enganche*). In essence, the workforce was managed through debt to the companies and other labour-control mechanisms that left the workers poor and relatively powerless.

The harvesting of *chicle* was one example of a process of gradual global insertion, through which forest products in Mexico reached the world market via foreign capital. Timber, henequen and *chicle* were among the most important of these forest products. By 1919 the scale of officially recognized *chicle* production had risen to over a million kilos annually.[31]

It soon became apparent to some of the rebel Mayan (*Cruzob*) leaders that their separatist cause would gain from a conversion of the local economy from subsistence production to commercial *chicle*. Francisco May, one of the most important of the *Cruzob* guerrilla fighters, went to Mexico City to meet President Carranza in January 1919 and, after three months in which he was shown enormous hospitality, was invited to lead this process of economic development. Not the least important part of May's success was the official acknowledgement of his title of 'General' and the granting of a life pension.[32] May returned to Chan Santa Cruz and converted himself into a powerful and unscrupulous *cacique*, or traditional leader. The federal government was unable to control or manage the gum trade directly, and its accommodation to foreign capital left Quintana Roo, and *chicle* production, closer than ever before to the international market.

The conversion of General May from *Cruzob* leader to local *cacique* boss helped to 'pacify' most of the Mayan insurgents, and their political struggle was watched more closely from Mexico City. At the same time, the *Cruzob* entry into *chicle* production opened up new means of acquiring cash with which to continue the armed struggle. Agreements between Mexico and Britain had cut off supplies from Belize, and British lumber interests no longer paid rent directly to the *Cruzob*. The income from the sale of gum provided revenues that compensated the insurgents and seemed to open up new possibilities. The *Cruzob* involvement in the export trade brought changes that had not been anticipated. The cornerstone of Mayan subsistence was the *milpas* (corn) field, supplemented by gathering and hunting in the forests. These gradually became undermined by the need to secure income from the sale of gum.

The Mayan leaders, such as Francisco May and Juan Bautista Vega, used their revenues from *chicle* to amass armaments, but they soon found that guerrilla fighting and the gathering of gum were mutually exclusive activities. There was little point in hoarding gold coins when the 'army' spent most of the time tapping gum, and the revenues seemed to undermine the very idea of military insurgency.

In addition, the duties of the *Cruzob* guard, to protect the Holy Cross and to maintain military vigilance, conflicted with the *chicle*-gathering season. This served to weaken the relationship between the villages around Chan Santa Cruz (such as Xcacal Guardia, Chumpon and Chan Cah Veracruz), where religious observance was greatest, and the town of Santa Cruz itself. Gradually, *Cruzob* society lost much of its internal ideological cohesion, diluted by the presence of large numbers of non-*Cruzob* gum-tappers and a market economy that left little room for subsistence peasants.

By 1929 the *Cruzob* were being described in ways that drew attention to the malignant effects of frontier capitalism on subsistence producers; they were living in remote, miserable villages of ten to twelve *palapas* (huts), each with a church, a few fruit trees and a well. According to contemporary reports, the people no longer trusted their chiefs, who had become privileged contractors for the *chicle* concessions; they had lost their old theocratic discipline and were engulfed in a non-*Cruzob* population of up to 8,000 gum-tappers. Like many other indigenous peoples exposed to the onslaught of international capital, their society suffered from poor health, alcoholism and a lack of social cohesion.[33] The revenues that were derived from gum exports were largely expatriated; what remained in Yucatan was in the hands of local Mayan chiefs. By 1930 US companies had largely supplanted those of Britain, and chewing gum became an American fashion, one that was exported to the rest of the world through the US forces' rations.

The Maya in Yucatan: Indigenous Movements and Transnational Commodities

The attempted destruction of Mayan cultural identity, both before and after Mexican independence, and the transformative power of foreign capital were related processes. They stimulated an indigenous opposition in the Yucatan, and in the historical period known as the Porfiriato, in the second half of the nineteenth century, Mexico embraced modernity at considerable cost to its indigenous population. The subsequent revolution of 1910, although in the popular imagination fought on behalf of the landless and the peasantry, served to strengthen the power and influence of the Mexican state.

However, the position of the disempowered Mexican peasantry shifted. Land use no longer reflected the predominance of traditional landholding groups, but increasingly those of new economic groups closely associated with the Mexican state. In the drive towards 'modernization' much of the ecological understanding and awareness of the indigenous population was lost, and the repercussions of *chicle* harvesting were one important element in this loss. However, today the resurgence of interest in Mayan identity is closely associated with the systems of cultivation that pre-dated *chicle* in Yucatan. The interest in conserving sustainable systems of forest production, in which *chicle* has a role, owes much to the rediscovery of the practices and approaches to nature of the Maya.

There has been considerable debate about the ecological practices of the ancient Maya, and whether or not these were responsible for the eventual downfall of Mayan civilization. Until the 1920s the prevailing view was that the Mayan dependence on slash and burn agriculture had exhausted the fertility of the soil. The *milpas* (corn fields) could only be worked for two or three consecutive years before the land began to lose its fertility. In the two most important areas of Mayan settlement, the Peten and Yucatan, between four and seven years were needed for the fallow land to recover its fertility. The conventional argument was that this fallow period was shortened in the face of population pressure, and that it contributed towards soil erosion, crop failure and starvation.[34]

Difficulties arise, however, when the proponents of this theory project this view of 'carrying capacity' on to the modern Maya, whose conditions of existence are radically different from those of their ancestors, notably because of the importance of international markets and the Mexican state. At the same time, archaeological evidence that the ancient Maya were dependent on slash and burn agriculture has been challenged. There is now substantial evidence that the Maya 'developed a diverse system of agricultural production [which included] kitchen gardens for the production of vegetables and fruit trees, and raised fields' consisting of soil and organic waste.[35]

The interest in raised-bed agriculture, in which the Maya were pioneers, has convinced most archaeologists that the Maya were well aware of what we refer to today as 'sustainable' agronomic practices. The use of *milpas* (corn fields) for the production of the staple and of kitchen gardens and raised beds helped to ensure that the forests were not subjected to undue pressure. Far from seeing the forest as an unlimited resource, or 'free good', the Maya regarded the survival of forest lands as central to their own survival. The Maya successfully adapted to the exigencies of a tropical environment by achieving a balance between shifting and permanent agriculture, a successful example of adaptation that is frequently cited today.

In the Yucatan, as elsewhere, the environmental credentials of indigenous peoples have been questioned on the basis of historical evidence from areas in which they traditionally lived. This is a curious juxtaposition, if we consider whether populations in the developed world would be prepared to be judged by the behaviour of their ancestors. At the same time, however, indigenous peoples' access to modern technologies and means of communication is sometimes cited as evidence that they have lost their 'authentic voice'. History has displaced many millions of 'indigenous' people, whose survival is no longer necessarily connected with their place of origin.[36] Indigenous people, like the Maya, are frequently subject to romantic generalization that overlooks their own ambivalence to the environment, and their own history of mobility and change.

It is impossible to develop an 'objective' political stance on the contemporary Maya or the social movements in which they are involved, but the contemporary struggles of the Mayan peoples echo the conflicts between their leaders during the Caste War and the interests of the Mexican state. Today, as in the past, Mayan interests are being invoked within a discourse dominated by globalization. The economy of *chicle*/chewing gum can increasingly be placed in an historical context and its invisibility measured against that of the Mayan populations of the region.

Today Mayan political action is closely linked with other forms of global action. Writing about the Chipko movement in India, Rangan argues:

> Perhaps it is because we live in a world that is rife with debates over impending eco-logical catastrophes emerging from deforestation, global warming, desertification, and floods that so many people are drawn to the Chipko movement with such faith and hope. Chipko as myth touches all these problems in some way... It provides the symbolic weapons, the small ammunition, that fires the spirits of those who hope to save the earth, and who, perhaps, also nurture the romantic desire to see the meek inherit the earth one day.[37]

The example of the Chipko people, who sought to protect the forest, has immediate appeal to the developed world and to environmental activists. In the case of the Maya, much of the identification with their concept of nature and their cultural practices is based on imaginative links, and the supposed 'lessons' for the 'over'-developed north. Such associations are important in refuelling the discussion surrounding sustainability and the need to consider the interests of future generations as well as those of today.

The political resistance of the Maya, as depicted in 'Maya World' imagery, is confined to the pre-colonial and colonial periods, when the Maya are seen as sorcerers and warriors. The forest struggles of the nineteenth and twentieth centuries have largely been overlooked, and they fit rather awkwardly into the myths that have been built up about the Mayan 'affinity' for nature. As Goldmann writes:

> Is all knowledge common, generalizable and universally accessible, as the global discourse assumes? Are heritages, histories and interests necessarily common? Are the dynamics of ecosystems, and natural-social relations embedded in a commons site, really transferable, replicable or generalizable? In discovering or inventing the *global ecological commons* and its fragile future, elite Northern scientists and policymakers also gave birth to the appropriate method for their understanding (i.e. *global science*) and the character of its inhabitants (i.e. *global citizen*).[38]

Conclusion: From 'Shadow-lands' to Biosphere Reserves

The spatial relationships between producers and consumers are as important today in the Yukatan as they were in the early twentieth-century conflicts over chewing gum. The management of nature today is similarly undertaken in the name of the Maya, rather than by them. Its appeal to an expanding market of 'eco-tourists' represents another new avenue of contemporary consumption.

Few members of local communities are involved in the management of important biosphere reserves like *Xian-Kaan*, to the south of the Mexican Caribbean coast. There, as in other parts of the Yucatan Peninsula, international non-governmental organizations have also forged few links with local Mayan people. The environmental politics of much of the Mexican Caribbean coast, like that of most Mexican cities, is, however, taken up with much more mundane protests over important issues such as sewage disposal, electricity supply and land titles. Much of the 'global' discourse surrounding the environment involves moves to defend marine turtles or to protect endangered coral reefs, while for most local people the conflicts implicit in rapid urbanization between private developers, migrants and government are of more importance.

In assessing the role of chewing gum in the international geopolitics of the United States and Mexico, we can easily overlook the fact that at one point the secession of much of the Yucatan Maya population from Mexico was more than a threat. Today there are villages in the forest surrounding Felipe Carrillo Puerto (Chan Santa Cruz) where young men still protect their own 'Talking Cross' from the gaze of outsiders. In these villages the soldiers' barracks are recognized by the local population; but these are 'soldiers' of the

Cruzob not of the Mexican state. On the highways of the peninsula, a short distance from the remaining *Cruzob* heartland, cars are routinely stopped by the soldiers of the Mexican state and searched for arms, since elsewhere, in the adjacent state of Chiapas, where most of the population is also ethnically 'Mayan', the *Zapatistas* have forced the Mexican state into a more visible, and much resented, presence. They have partly succeeded by utilizing one of the major new portals for global consumption – the Internet.

To the south of the peninsula of Yucatan, in the forests of the *Gran Peten* on the borders of Belize, Guatemala and Mexico, approximately 5,000 workers still tap the gum of the *sapodilla* tree. This small 'army' of workers, some of them descended from the *chicle* workers of a century ago, supplies the main producers of chewing gum for the Mexican market. Like the more famous rubber-tappers of the Brazilian Amazon, they can lay claim today to a sustainable form of production, which helps preserve the forest and provides a livelihood for thousands of families. However, this very tangible example of 'sustainability' is much less known, and far less trumpeted, than the fashionable 'eco-hotels' in Playa Del Carmen on the coast nearby. As we scratch behind the glossy cover of the 'Mayan World', another world is revealed of conflicts over identity and the control of 'nature'. This world refuses to be incorporated within the commercial discourses surrounding the 'Maya' today. The history of *chicle* and the broader cultural chronicle of chewing gum may carry important lessons for the environment and for security, as well as the new consumer politics of 'eco-tourism'. The cultural and historical significance of chewing gum can only be revealed when we peel back the layers of celebration associated with its mass consumption and reveal behind them the stark and conflictual 'shadow-lands' of *chicle*.

Notes

1. L. Wardlaw, *Bubblemania: The Chewy History of Bubble Gum* (New York, 1997).
2. N. Longmate, *How We Lived Then: A History of Everyday Life during the Second World War* (London, 1971); D. Reynolds, *Rich Relations: The American Occupation of Britain* (London, 1996); A. Calder, *The People's War: Britain 1939–1945* (London, 1969); S. Briggs, *Keep Smiling through: The Home Front 1939–1945* (London, 1975).

3. M. Hilton, *Smoking in British Popular Culture: 1800–2000* (Manchester, 2000); V. Jenkins, *Bananas: The American History* (Washington, DC, 2000); B. Burford, *Chocolate by Hershey* (Minneapolis, 1994).
4. Reynolds, *Rich Relations*.
5. Wardlaw, *Bubblemania*.
6. R. Primack, D. Bray, H. Galletti and I. Ponciano (eds), *Timber, Tourists and Temples: Conservation and Development in the Maya Forest of Belize, Guatemala and Mexico* (Washington, DC, 1988).
7. L. Simonian, *Defending the Land of the Jaguar: A History of Conservation in Mexico* (Austin, 1995); G. Bridge, 'Resource Triumphalism: Post-industrial Narratives of Primary Commodity Production', *Environment and Planning A*, 33 (2001), pp. 2149–73; M.R. Redclift, 'Changing Nature: The Consumption of Space and the Construction of Nature on the Mayan Riviera', in M. Cohen and J. Murphy (eds), *Exploring Sustainable Consumption: Environmental Policy and the Social Sciences* (Amsterdam, 2001).
8. Bridge, 'Resource Triumphalism', p. 2149.
9. Bridge, 'Resource Triumphalism', p. 2153.
10. M. Ramos Diaz, 'La bonanza del chicle en la frontera caribe de Mexico: indigenas y empresarios 1918—1930', *Revista Mexicana del caribe*, 4(7) (1999), pp. 172–93; N. Reed, *The Caste War of Yucatan* (Stanford, 2001).
11. *Encyclopaedia de Quintana Roo*, Vol. 3 (Chetumal, Mexico, 1998).
12. Primack *et al.*, (eds), *Timber, Tourists and Temples*.
13. David E. Nye *Consuming Power: A Social History of American Energies* (Cambridge, MA, 1998).
14. Nye, *Consuming Power*.
15. H. Wayne Morgan (ed.), *The Gilded Age: A Reappraisal* (New York, 1963).
16. S. Mintz, *Sweetness and Power: The Place of Sugar in Modern History* (New York, 1986).
17. S. Marston, 'The Social Construction of Scale', *Progress in Human Geography*, 24 (2000), pp. 219–41.
18. J. Agnew, 'Mapping Political Power beyond State Boundaries: Territory, Identity and the Movement in World Politics', *Millennium*, 28 (1999), pp. 499–521.
19. N. Thrift, 'Afterwords', *Environment and Planning D*, 18 (2000), pp. 213–23.
20. Bridge, 'Resource Triumphalism', p. 2155.
21. Bridge, 'Resource Triumphalism', p. 2155.

22. D. Held, *Democracy and the Global Order* (Cambridge, 1995).
23. A. Amin, 'Spatialities of Globalization', *Environment and Planning A*, 34 (2002), pp. 385–99.
24. A. Herod and M. Wright, 'Theorizing Space and Time', *Environment and Planning A*, 34 (2001), p. 2089.
25. Thrift, 'Afterwords', p. 213.
26. M. Hilton, *Smoking in British Popular Culture 1800–2000* (Manchester, 2000).
27. W.G. Clarence-Smith, *Cocoa and Chocolate 1765–1914* (London and New York, 2000). Also B. Burford, *Chocolate by Hershey* (Minneapolis, 1994).
28. It has proved difficult for chewing gum manufacturers to penetrate markets where chewing other products is well established, such as betel nut in India and Quat in the Horn of Africa.
29. Bridge, 'Resource Triumphalism', p. 760.
30. J. Urry, 'Mobility and Proximity', *Sociology*, 36(2) (2002).
31. H. Konrad, 'Capitalism on the Tropical Forest Frontier: Quintana Roo 1880s to 1930s', in J. Brannon and G. Joseph (eds), *Land, Labor and Capital in Modern Yucatan* (Tuscaloosa, 1991).
32. Konrad, 'Capitalism on the Tropical Forest Frontier'.
33. Konrad, 'Capitalism on the Tropical Forest Frontier'.
34. M. Coe, *Mexico* (London, 1973).
35. Simonian, *Defending the Land of the Jaguar*.
36. Richardson, *Minds and Matter: Indigenous Consciousness and Nature* (London, 2001).
37. H. Rangan, *Of Myths and Movements: Rewriting Chipko into Himalayan History* (London, 2000).
38. M. Goldmann (ed.), *Privatising Nature: Political Struggles for the Global Commons* (London, 1998).

–8–

Japan's Post-war 'Consumer Revolution', or Striking a 'Balance' between Consumption and Saving

Sheldon Garon

Consumerism officially arrived in Japan in 1959. In its annual *Whitepaper on National Life*, the normally staid Economic Planning Agency declared Japan to be in the throes of a 'consumer revolution' in lifestyles and attitudes towards daily life. This was one revolution that would be televised, as millions watched on their recently purchased television sets – the very symbol of the dawning age of mass consumption. After years of austerity during the Second World War and its aftermath, Japanese households rapidly acquired a set of consumer durables that had theretofore lain beyond the imagination of most. Whereas wartime Japanese had been ordered to defend the imperial household's 'three sacred treasures' – a mirror, jewel and sword – the 1950s generation whimsically invoked the term to refer to the television, washing machine and refrigerator. A mere 5 per cent of Japanese households had owned black-and-white television sets in 1957. That figure soared to 89 per cent by 1963.[1]

This upsurge in consumption has not particularly impressed scholars of Japan until recently. Compared to the consumption-driven economy of the United States after 1945, the post-war Japanese political economy struck most observers as singularly oriented towards production, exports, saving and investment.[2] However, a growing body of scholarship highlights the role of the consumer in post-war Japan's economic and social development, while linking its consumer revolution to the transnational diffusion of American discourses of 'abundance' and a mass consumer society. By the end of the 1950s, notes Simon Partner, 'an elite consensus had emerged around the idea that [domestic] consumption was a key ingredient in the political economy of high growth'. Inspired by their American counterparts' success in creating consumer demand, 'some visionary Japanese business leaders saw the production of an American-style middle-class society as crucial to Japanese prosperity'. Other historians have written about early post-war Japanese economic planners who, influenced by Keynesianism and the contemporary American experience, promoted domestic consumption as the engine of economic growth. Though acknowledging the continuation of prewar appeals to frugality, Scott O'Bryan argues 'a competing language celebrating the "bright life" of consumption grew increasingly strong by the mid-1950s'.[3] Taken together, the new scholarship situates Japan within a more global context of the late 1950s, when American-style consumer societies are said to have simultaneously taken hold in Western European nations as well. In West Germany during those years, observes Erica Carter, the early post-war ethos of saving and rational consumption 'began to cede its place to a new ethic of consumption for leisure and pleasure'.[4]

Although recent studies of consumerism in Japan provide a welcome corrective, they also confront us with new challenges. Did the post-Second World War 'consumer revolutions' play themselves out more or less the same, regardless of where they occurred? Did 'consumer societies' in Japan and Western Europe uncritically embrace American-style cultures that privileged consumption and abundance over thrift and resource-conservation? And as Frank Trentmann warns, should we assume that those who bought the new commodities identified themselves, first and foremost, as self-interested 'consumers' – and not as producers, citizens or savers?[5]

Rather than examine Japanese consumerism as an autonomous development, this chapter profiles the ongoing tensions between consumer desire and the various discourses and practices of 'restraint'. Chief among these forms of restraint have been saving and economizing. In contrast to post-war consumption patterns in the United States, Japanese household savings rates rose steadily from the mid-1950s in tandem with expanding consumption. By the mid-1970s the nation had achieved a savings rate of 23 per cent, one of the highest in the world. Post-war Japan's 'culture of thrift' was more than a traditional artefact. State agencies, the media and various groups actively encouraged saving and economizing among the populace.

By analysing the relationship between savings-promotion and consumerism, this chapter cautions against interpreting Japan's 'consumer revolution' as evidence of modernity and Americanization, pure and simple. Most Japanese – from conservative officials to progressive activists – remained openly ambivalent about unfettered consumption. They took pains to distinguish between 'sound' consumption and 'wasteful expenditures'. To a remarkable degree, Japanese spoke of the need to strike a 'balance' between consumption and saving, and many still do. Moreover, consumerism was not the only modernist discourse to emerge after the Second World War. The impetus to *restrain* consumption flowed, as well, from explicitly modern movements to introduce science, rationality, improvements in daily life and the professional 'housewife'. Finally, the diffusion of 'Western' models is more complex than one might think. While images of American mass consumption had considerable appeal, Japanese were also influenced by European practices of austerity, rationalization and savings-promotion. And in the twists and turns of the US–Japanese relationship, consumerist America loomed sometimes as role model but often as the undesirable Other.

Rationalizing, Economizing and Saving before 1945

When the Japanese encountered the mass consumption of the 1950s, they brought with them a powerful set of attitudes and practices from the past. Under the reign of the Tokugawa shoguns (1603–1868), the authorities took a dim view of popular consumption that rose much above subsistence levels or that did not befit one's legally defined social status. Officials relentlessly exhorted their subjects to practise 'frugality' (*ken'yaku*). Conveying this message in more positive terms, peasant reformers and merchants advised commoners on ways to improve themselves by avoiding 'luxuries' (*shashi*) and engaging in 'diligence, thrift and saving' (*kinken chochiku*).[6]

In the years following the Meiji Restoration of 1868, Japan became a modern nation-state and rapidly emerged as a foremost exporter of manufactured goods. Fixated on expanding production for world markets, few influential Japanese considered domestic consumption to constitute an important facet of the economy. On the contrary, beginning in the late nineteenth century, the state mounted increasingly elaborate campaigns to encourage the people to save their money while limiting their spending. According to the regime's developmental strategy, popular consumption vied with industries and the state for scarce financial resources. If peasants and townspeople could be persuaded to spend less, their increased savings and tax payments could be invested in production, public infrastructure and military strengthening. The state's efforts to mobilize popular wealth were made more urgent by the leaders' decision to eschew all foreign loans between 1873 and 1897 and their wariness of relying on foreign capital thereafter. Because most Japanese in fact possessed little margin to buy the products of a modern consumer economy, the early savings campaigns targeted traditional 'wasteful expenditures' (*rōhi* or *kūhi*) on weddings, funerals and other ceremonial occasions.[7]

The term 'consumption' (*shōhi*) did not widely appear in Japan until the 1920s. Its advent coincided with the rise of a vibrant urban culture that offered a tantalizing diversity of commodities. Japan's economic boom during the First World War had created whole new groups of customers – from the notorious *nouveaux riches* (*narikin*) to white-collar 'salarymen', their wives and young working women. Stylish department stores began appealing to the broader middle class, and the cinema, baseball games and restaurants became affordable to many. Some Japanese scholars pinpoint the 1920s as the beginning of a 'mass consumption society'.[8]

To be sure, the inter-war years witnessed some standardization in urban consumer tastes. Yet consumption remained a problematic concept to most Japanese before 1945. From the start, state officials managed to define consumption in negative terms. The vast majority of the nation would have likely first encountered the word 'consumption' in the early 1920s, when the government launched a nationwide savings campaign for 'economy in consumption' (*shōhi setsuyaku*). In the coming 'peacetime economic war' in international trade, warned Home Ministry officials, Japan's competitive position was being eroded by rising prices, sharply declining savings and insufficient investment capital. The authorities left no doubt as to the culprit. The nation's economic boom in the First World War had given rise to 'habits of luxury and self-indulgence', as the 'people's consumption continues at its rapid clip'.[9] In this and subsequent savings campaigns, the government identified two types of 'unsound' consumption. One category comprised imported 'luxury' goods, which the campaigns portrayed as exacerbating Japan's trade deficits. Efforts to discourage the consumption of foreign goods culminated in two 'campaigns to buy Japanese products' (*kokusan aiyō undō*). In addition, the campaigns harangued villagers and poorer townspeople, as before, to cut back on the more traditional 'wasteful expenditures' associated with weddings, funerals, gift-giving, banquets and alcohol and tobacco.

These hortatory campaigns for economy in consumption may seem little more than reactionary throwbacks to the Tokugawa era, and liberal figures occasionally ridiculed them as anachronistic. More remarkable, however, is the extent to which progressive forces *cooperated* with the state in efforts to curb the consumer appetites of the masses.[10] Comprised of left-liberals, home economists and leaders of the burgeoning women's groups, the progressives adopted the modernizing goals of 'improving daily life' (*seikatsu kaizen*) and achieving 'cultured living' (*bunka seikatsu*). What brought progressives and officials together was their common recognition that most Japanese lacked the wealth to increase their consumption significantly. The champions of 'improvement' rarely argued for greater consumption. Like the bureaucrats, they insisted that the Japanese people could improve living standards only by engaging in the 'rationalization' of daily life and consumption – that is, consuming and saving within the constraints of household budgets. The modernity of their message was unmistakable. Well-educated urban men and women exhorted ordinary Japanese to practise household budgeting, 'scientifically' improve hygiene and nutrition, and eliminate wasteful expenditures on traditional ritual life. Beginning in 1920, educators, home economists, housing specialists and women's leaders joined government ministries in a series of 'daily life improvement campaigns', which intersected with the savings drives.

The campaigns to rationalize consumption would have appeared quite modern to contemporary Japanese in their appeal to changing gender norms. During the 1920s and 1930s both the state and influential women increasingly defined women as Western-style 'housewives' responsible for household finances and consumption. Large numbers of women worked in the savings and economizing campaigns at the national and local level. Mass-circulation housewives' magazines concurrently provided tips on economizing and issued hundreds of thousands of household account books (*kakeibo*) to encourage women to balance their families' consumption and saving.

The inter-war daily life improvement campaigns discouraged wasteful expenditures, but in a positive sense they did promote the 'sound' consumption of nutritious foods and hygienic, efficient kitchens. After 1937 consumption itself became a suspect act amid Japan's protracted war with China and then the Allied powers. Relentless savings campaigns strove to reduce domestic consumption to the bare minimum so as to boost national savings and check inflationary pressures. The nationalistic attack on consumption was best captured in the ubiquitous wartime slogan 'Luxury is the Enemy'.[11] As in the inter-war decades, women's leaders and housewives' magazines enthusiastically aided the state in instructing women to eliminate waste and be 'resourceful' in their consumption. For many middle-class women who had long struggled to abolish licensed prostitution, wartime austerity also offered unprecedented opportunities to control their husbands' 'extravagant' consumption of sexual services and alcohol.

The wartime savings campaigns bequeathed a complex legacy to post-war understandings of consumption and saving. On one hand, the campaigns drastically reduced popular consumption levels, as the regime compelled families to divert more and more of their wealth to war savings. By 1944 Japanese households were saving an extraordinary 40 per cent of disposable income, not including an additional 10 per cent in taxes and a host of communal exactions. At the same time, hundreds of thousands of Japanese assisted the regime in policing the consumption habits of those around them. In nearly every residential area, school and workplace, compulsory 'national savings associations' not only shook down members to make ever-increasing monthly contributions to national savings, they also thoroughly investigated the financial lives of their neighbours. With most men mobilized, large numbers of ordinary women served – often eagerly – as foot soldiers in the local struggles to reduce consumption. As we shall see, such collective approaches to regulating consumption did not die in the ashes of Japanese defeat in 1945.

The American Dream, the Japanese Reality and the European Model

Though nominally an Allied occupation under the Supreme Commander of the Allied Powers (SCAP), the occupation of defeated Japan (1945–52) was dominated by the United States. This was not the first time that Japan encountered American consumer culture. During the inter-war years ordinary Japanese had devoured 'America' in such forms as baseball, Hollywood and popular music. Nonetheless, the occupation provided the urban populace with an opportunity to gaze upon the rich consumer lives of Americans up close. American forces ranged from 600,000 troops initially to more than 100,000 throughout the occupation era. Within Tokyo, the areas around Roppongi, Harajuku and the Ginza became vibrant sites of consumption in part because that was where Japanese went to see how Americans lived, ate, drank and danced. Sex offered Japanese their most intimate encounter with American prosperity, notes John Dower. Tens of thousands of prostitutes, or 'panpan' girls, became 'exemplary pioneer materialists and consumers', directly benefiting from the cornucopia known as the PX.[12]

SCAP officials, for their part, were eager to convey images of American abundance in an effort to demonstrate the occupiers' unsurpassed power, while selling the virtues of American-style democracy. Under SCAP's direction, in 1947 Japanese national radio (NHK) began broadcasting 'Amerika tayori' (News from America), a popular programme that showcased American affluence and the many electrical appliances found in the typical home. Millions of Japanese also learned of American consumer life from the comic strip 'Blondie', introduced by the daily *Asahi shinbun* in 1949.[13]

These encounters with 'America' notwithstanding, the United States did not seriously attempt to export its model of mass consumption to Japan during the occupation era, nor were the Japanese in any position to embrace that model. With respect to the margin to consume, the gulf between post-war Japan and the United States was enormous. The Second World War, culminating in the American bombing of nearly seventy cities, had devastated the living standards of most Japanese. The nation suffered acute levels of homelessness, unemployment and the return of millions of soldiers and civilians from overseas. Hyperinflation wiped out families' life savings. Not until 1952 would per capita levels of consumption recover to their prewar high of 1934–6. In 1946 food accounted for fully 68 per cent of household expenditure, leaving little room to consume anything else. As late as 1955 households were still devoting 49 per cent of their consumption to food. Few Japanese could have afforded the vacuum cleaners or toasters depicted in 'Blondie' – not to mention many basic necessities. Prior to 1950 Japanese bought so little cloth and clothing that the nation's once vital textile industry had come to a virtual halt.[14]

Nor did the United States encourage the Japanese to expand consumption as a means of jump-starting the economy. Americans commonly overestimate their government's generosity towards occupied Japan. In Western Europe the United States financed the massive Marshall Plan in the late 1940s and 1950s. The plan aimed in part to create mass consumer markets based on the post-war American formula of consumer-driven growth and equality.[15] As much as Americans would like to believe otherwise, the United States never offered a Marshall Plan to Japan. Washington expected the Japanese people to tighten their belts not only to finance recovery and fight inflation, but also to pay for the enormous costs of housing and supplying the occupation forces. The Americans provided emergency food relief, but US aid totalled less than half of what the Japanese government was compelled to pay to maintain the occupation. Initially, expenditures on the occupation amounted to an onerous one-third of the Japanese government's regular budget.[16] US policy-makers demanded that Japan adopt an economic recovery strategy by which the people curbed their consumption to shift surpluses to export industries. In the words of Under Secretary of the Army William Draper in 1948, '[t]he Japanese people will have to work hard and long, with comparatively little recompense for many years to come'. Joseph Dodge, the banker whose famous US mission in 1949 forced the adoption of new austerity measures, called upon the Japanese government to hold the standard of living to levels prevailing *before* the early 1930s. Similarly, in their 'Program for a Self-sufficient Japanese Economy', SCAP officials insisted that the Japanese must sacrifice living standards to become competitive in exports.[17]

Confronted by runaway inflation and acute shortages of capital, Japanese officials in fact required little prodding from the Americans to revive the intrusive savings and austerity campaigns of wartime. In a letter to Prime Minister Yoshida Shigeru in March 1947, Supreme Commander General

Douglas MacArthur stated that Japan bore the ultimate responsibility for feeding its people and containing inflation, and the nation would have to draw sufficiently on its own resources. The Japanese government, Yoshida replied, was already tackling inflation by 'taking vigorous steps to augment savings'.[18] In November 1946 the Bank of Japan and Ministry of Finance had launched the first of nine National Salvation Savings Campaigns, which ran successively until the end of 1949.[19] In peacetime, as in war, the campaigns associated acts of saving and economizing with the very salvation of the nation. And like the wartime drives, the National Salvation campaigns mobilized youth and women's associations, enforced savings targets on prefectures, and reinvigorated the national savings associations.[20]

Japanese leaders exhorted their hard-pressed people to consume even less. Addressing the nation by radio in 1947, one finance minister urged listeners to 'reduce your daily living standard as much you can, economize, and above all save your unspent money'.[21] Another finance minister, Kurusu Takeo, turned to the time-honoured bureaucratic practice of blaming the consumers for high prices. Kurusu openly praised the wartime savings drives for imposing a healthy discipline on consumers. Regrettably, 'following the war, our people experienced a psychological liberation from these pressures [to save], and their sense of thrift hit rock bottom. Worse, *their desire to consume*, which had been suppressed during the war, burst forth with a vengeance and added fuel to the fire of inflation.'[22]

Vice-Minister of Finance Ikeda Hayato dramatically illustrated the government's low regard for consumption in a savings-promotion speech in Hiroshima. Ikeda has gone down in history as the Keynesian prime minister whose cabinet in 1960 initiated the successful Income Doubling Plan. Yet in 1947 he was no champion of raising consumption levels. A native of Hiroshima, Ikeda alluded to the city's devastation by the atomic bomb, praising residents for their extraordinary efforts at rebuilding. Yet without wasting any more words on the human toll, he explained that economic recovery would come about only if the Japanese people all engage in 'diligence and vigorous efforts' (*kinben rikkō*) and submit to 'lives of austerity'. The Japanese people would achieve a higher standard of living in the future only by increasing exports of manufactured goods: 'We will import as many raw materials as possible and then make as much money as we can processing them. Drawing on this income, we will import food and other commodities in short supply at home.' The people, insisted Ikeda, must save all of their unspent income, which the government and banks would then invest in industry. Standing in Hiroshima, a city that had endured more than its share of suffering from the last bout of mobilization, the future prime minister solemnly declared that only by continued austerity 'will our country exist in the future'.[23]

Occupation officials voiced uneasiness about the Japanese government's revival of wartime savings campaigns, but Washington's preference for austerity and anti-inflation measures in Japan overcame their reservations. SCAP supported the National Salvation campaigns throughout their four-year existence, touting the needs of saving over consumption. Lauding the savings drive's 'marked degree of success since its inception', one SCAP official praised the increased savings as 'a healthy sign and [it] provides a new reservoir from which vitally needed credit can be drawn for use in rehabilitation and expansion of the Japanese economy. It acts as a check to inflation and currency expansion and is a most commendable programme in all its aspects deserving the full support of the Japanese people.'[24] Joseph Dodge was a good deal blunter upon arriving in Japan in 1949. The American taxpayer would not maintain the Japanese people, who must themselves 'accumulate capital by producing more cheaply and by saving and economizing'.[25]

Whereas the American model of mass consumption struck both sides as inappropriate to occupied Japan, officials in the Japanese government expressed considerable interest in *European* models that promoted saving and restrained consumption. Japan was hardly alone, they insisted, in adopting austerity measures to recover from the war. All the former belligerents were doing so, 'whether victor or vanquished', noted Finance Minister Yano Shōtarō. The Soviet people, 'resigning themselves to austere living, are making spirited efforts at recovery' in the new Five-year Plan. The French and Belgians, he rightly observed, were mounting nationwide campaigns to reduce prices, and the Dutch had launched a savings campaign under the slogan 'Work Hard, Save Much'.[26]

Japanese economic bureaucrats were most influenced by Britain's National Savings Movement. During the 1920s, and again in the Second World War, the Japanese government had modelled their savings campaign organizations after the British government's National Savings Committee (NSC). Since 1916 the NSC had coordinated a national network of local savings committees and civic groups. Following the Second World War as well, Japanese officials lauded contemporary Britain's dedication to sacrificing consumption to the needs of recovery. Britain had won the war, yet as Vice-Minister of Finance Ikeda lectured his audience in Hiroshima,

the British have not chosen the easy path, but rather have austerely maintained wartime controls on the principal daily necessities... In the post-war era, they have even rationed bread, which had been freely sold in *wartime*. The British people ... have persevered, wearing extremely old and shabby clothes and eating small meals. Why must the victorious British maintain harsh lives of austerity? The answer, without a doubt, is that the money and material saved by lives of austerity can be applied, in full, to economic recovery... In the near future, free trade will be re-established in the world. These people are in a hurry to establish a favourable position that allows them to strut upon the stage of global economic competition.[27]

A Bank of Japan study elaborated on the lessons of British economizing for Japan. Like the Japanese, the British 'strive, first and foremost, for exports while severely constraining domestic consumption'. Britain had successfully negotiated an emergency loan of $3,750,000 in 1946 only because its citizens, 'who have little to spare', saved their money while 'living in destitution and austerity'. Japan, 'which desperately looks to assistance from other countries, should find much to study in the attitudes of these British', the survey concluded.[28]

These Japanese observations remind us that in the early post-war world the American model of mass consumption represented the exception, not the norm. From the Soviet Bloc to Western Europe, governments envisaged saving, investment and production – not consumption – as the key to economic recovery.[29] Post-war European leaders portrayed consumption (or at least unbridled consumption) as socially divisive and a 'diversion' from their nations' highest priorities – notably employment, price stability, social welfare and defence. British governments explicitly encouraged the populace to restrain or defer consumption during the first post-war decade. Labour's Chancellor of the Exchequer Stafford Cripps repeatedly urged Britons to limit their spending and eschew 'easy-going get-rich-quick' attitudes to life: 'If we consume too many of the goods which we produce ourselves, we cannot export them; and if, in the process, we force up our costs and so our prices, we shall lose our export markets.'[30] Aneurin Bevan, Labour's Minister of Health and an architect of the post-war welfare state, championed savings and the 'diversion of labour and capital from other purposes' to help finance several social targets – including care for babies and the elderly, improved housing and the new Health Service. 'If we are to enjoy these things,' declared Bevan, 'we have to deny ourselves other things now, in order that we may be able to accomplish them later on.'[31] Although some British Conservatives were less enthusiastic about continued austerity, Conservative cabinets similarly subordinated consumption to other priorities. When the incoming Churchill government embarked on rearmament in 1951, Chancellor of the Exchequer Richard A. Butler ordered a new savings campaign that 'would, by reducing spending at home, greatly assist us in attaining our twofold objective – to rearm in order to maintain world peace, and to produce enough exports to pay our way in the world'.[32] In the words of Prime Minister Winston Churchill, '[t]he defence programme requires a diversion of goods and services from the consumer – that is *from* you and me – to the national needs – that is *for* you and me'.[33] As late as 1955–6 the Conservative government mounted a 'Restraint in Spending Campaign', depicting the 'excess of demand as the main cause of our economic difficulties'.[34] Observing a world in which the saver – not the consumer – appeared sovereign, Japan's savings-promoters reported on like-minded savings campaigns in Britain, France, Belgium, Denmark and other European nations throughout the 1950s and early 1960s.[35]

Democratizing Thrift

Thanks to the economic stimulus provided by the Korean War, Japanese consumption levels began to revive in 1950. This is not say that Japanese households embarked on a spending spree during the 1950s. Rather, they responded to the better times by gradually spending more while saving a substantial portion of their disposable incomes. Household savings rates, which had been *minus* 2 per cent in 1949, abruptly rose to 15 per cent in 1950 and had climbed to 19 per cent by 1961.[36]

While families boosted their savings, the Japanese state redoubled its efforts to encourage saving and moderate increases in consumption. In 1952 the Ministry of Finance and Bank of Japan established the Central Council for Savings Promotion, charging it with the coordination of a national network of local committees, schools, civic groups, the media and local governments. The Central Council continues to this day, although it is now named the Central Council for Financial Services Information. Like Britain's National Savings Committee, Japan's Central Council for Savings Promotion endeavoured to reinforce a public consciousness that identified economizing and saving with bolstering Japan's 'international competitive power'. Alleging that Japanese had recently succumbed to 'excesses in consumption', the savings campaign of 1953 exhorted households to make 'thoroughgoing cutbacks in expenditures'. Campaign slogans were hardly subtle: 'Let's Save Ten Per Cent of Earnings', 'Let's Be Earnest about Conserving Money and Goods', and 'Let's All Change the Way We Live'.[37]

These campaigns may strike Americans today as reactionary, ineffectual attempts to stunt the inevitable flowering of Japanese consumer society.

However, we must note that the economizing and savings drives – like their inter-war predecessors – enjoyed considerable support from a wide array of popular organizations, including many progressive groups. In a sense, the early post-war campaigns democratized and modernized the consensus behind saving and the 'rationalization' of consumption. As in contemporary Britain, the non-communist left in Japan generally supported the restraint of consumption in the service of augmenting national savings. Several of Japan's Socialist Party leaders were Protestants, who along with middle-class reformers and women's leaders had cooperated closely with the imperial state in inculcating habits of thrift in ordinary Japanese before 1945.[38] In the post-war campaigns as well, the government subsidized Japanese Christian organizations to assist in savings-promotion. The famous Christian socialist reformer Kagawa Toyohiko was employed in 1947 to lecture at a national conference of savings promotion officers on the topic of 'Bringing Science to Daily Life'.[39]

Another Christian proponent of post-war austerity, Katayama Tetsu, became Japan's first Socialist prime minister in 1947. The Katayama cabinet emphatically continued the National Salvation Savings Campaigns, the prime minister himself observing that 'the beautiful customs of diligence, thrift and saving have long been fostered as a part of our national character'.[40] His government also revived the inter-war 'daily life improvement' movement. Under the post-war name of 'New Life Campaigns', these drives sought to teach households how to save and budget effectively as part of their central mission of 'rationalizing' and 'bringing science' to daily life. Katayama's first New Life Campaign exhorted the public to 'eliminate wastefulness in daily life and cut back on expenditures on luxuries'. His government cast this 'New Life' in explicitly democratic terms. The rationalization of daily life would not necessarily result in increased consumption in the short term, but continued austerity would promote a spirit of shared sacrifice. In 1955, when a conservative cabinet institutionalized these drives under the New Life Campaign Association, Katayama, Kagawa Toyohiko and other Socialist leaders proudly served as directors.[41]

Together with much of the labour movement, the Socialist Party embraced the restraint of consumption as beneficial to the working class and the Japanese people as a whole. No less than the economic bureaucrats, early post-war Socialists were shocked by the nation's hyperinflation, and they favoured soaking up purchasing power by persuading the populace to save more. They regarded saving, not consumption, as the most effective means of generating jobs by channelling the people's surplus into investment in production. In October 1946 the Socialist Party joined four centrist and conservative parties in the Lower House of the Diet in calling for a new savings campaign to stabilize the Japanese yen and fight inflation. Although Marxian economists denounced the conservative governments' attempts to weaken the labour movement by the 'rationalization' of production, several supported the bureaucracy's efforts to check inflation and boost production by fostering saving during the 1950s. Minobe Ryōkichi, the prominent Marxist economist and future governor of Tokyo, wrote widely used textbooks that instructed students in the importance of saving and the 'household management' of consumption. Household savings not only benefited one's family, but also become 'the capital for industry and the public good, and they function as the driving force in the national economy and the development of social life'. In 'our families', he noted, 'the mother or older sister keeps a household account book... Those who do this well [manage household finances] have relatively *rich consumer lives* even if their income is relatively low. Those who do it poorly will have poor consumer lives for a given income.'[42] In a primer for housewives, he reiterated that 'consumption can be rationalized just as production'.[43]

Within the workplace, wives of workers in large companies eagerly took part in employer-sponsored New Life movements from the 1950s to the 1970s. There, sometimes to the consternation of their husbands in the labour unions, they learned methods of household budget-keeping and cutting 'waste in daily life'. These experiences, Andrew Gordon concludes, were important to the efforts of business and the state to perpetuate anti-Fordist values. Rather than envisaging increased demand as the key to a vibrant economy, many working-class families continued to believe that improvements in daily life would primarily result from restraining consumption and boosting savings.[44]

Women became central to forging the consensus behind saving and the rationalization of consumption. Under the post-war National Salvation Savings Campaigns, officials relied most on residential women's associations to reactivate the wartime national savings associations – so much so that savings associations became known as 'mothers' banks'. In addition to collecting monthly savings, the women's associations distributed millions of government-issue household account books. Association leaders and other good housekeepers regularly instructed local women in how to keep the account books. Getting women diligently to record income, expenditures and surpluses has been a particularly effective means of instilling habits of saving and rationalized consumption in post-war Japan. In 1952 local women's organizations – with support from the state – coalesced into the National Federation of Regional Women's Organizations (Zen Chifuren). Claiming some 7.8 million members at its peak in the early 1960s, the federation provided the foot soldiers in the savings and economizing campaigns of the next several decades.[45]

The savings campaigns were much more than a state programme to control women's consumption. What gave the campaigns vitality was that large numbers of women sought to rationalize consumption for reasons of their own. Their motivations reflected the Japanese woman's evolving identity as the family member most responsible for financial management, child-rearing and safeguarding the family's morality. Whereas in the prewar order a husband or father-in-law headed the household under a legal system of patriarchy, the post-war era witnessed the rapid emergence of the 'housewife' as the mainstay of the typical family. Many women thus threw

Figure 9 'I'll Keep Planning Our Household Finances', Japan, 1955. This poster for postal savings depicts the seemingly Americanized, modern Japanese 'housewife' who was just emerging in the 1950s. Her modernity lay less in consumption than in her domestic role in rationalizing consumption and increasing savings

Source: Poster XD-C 50, Communications Museum, Tokyo.

themselves into the mission of saving and economy with an eye to elevating their position within the family and society.

Women activists took the lead, for instance, in popularizing the practice of keeping standardized household account books. By 1970 half of all households surveyed reported that they kept household account books (41 per cent of them regularly).[46] While this achievement resulted in part from official encouragement, it was the housewives' magazines and women's groups that most single-mindedly normalized the custom of account-keeping. The pioneer figure was the progressive educator Hani Motoko. As editor of the magazine *Fujin no tomo* (Woman's friend), Hani had since the 1910s exhorted housewives to keep account books in their capacity as rational managers of the home. She also spread the gospel of the 'budgeted life' by forming a nationwide network of readers' groups called 'friends' societies' (*tomonokai*). By the 1950s and 1960s, legions of self-described 'housewives' regularly kept household account books published by *Fujin no tomo* or the more commercial housewives' magazines, notably *Shufu no tomo* (Housewife's friend).

Women embraced the housewife's management of consumption as a sign of both her modernity and her growing power within the family. The major women's organizations actively participated in the New Life campaigns, equating the promised 'New Life' with science and progress. The 'elimination of waste' and 'rationalization of saving and household accounts' took their place alongside other objectives deemed progressive by women's groups – notably family planning, reducing prostitution and improving public health. The imperative to save also offered modern housewives a potent means of controlling their husbands' penchant for prostitution, hostess bars and other vices (see Figure 10). Among post-war families of salaried employees, it became the norm for the husband to tender his monthly earnings to his prudent wife, who assumed responsibility for spending and saving. Women's leaders delighted in advising housewives to dole out only small amounts of 'drinking money' to their men while saving the rest.[47] By the mid-1950s the wife's control of the purse strings had become a symbol of modernity. Even the relatively conservative Tokyo Federation of Regional Women's Organizations would denigrate communities where housewives were *not* the primary keeper of the household account book within their families. Such villages were simply 'preserving feudalistic intransigence'.[48]

We must also note the strong support for saving given by Japan's pioneer consumer groups. The Housewives' Association (Shufuren), which emerged as a champion of consumer protection, nonetheless enthusiastically worked with the government to persuade households to save and economize.[49] Led

Figure 10 'Success in the Bonus Rocket's Return', Japan, 1959. By gaining control of her husband's bonus, the clever housewife increases her family's savings in this cartoon. She also stops him from dissipating household income on hostesses and drink at the 'Cabaret Moon'

Source: *Chochiku* [Saving, newsletter of Central Council for Savings Promotion], no. 27 (1959), p. 1.

by Oku Mumeo, a prewar feminist with socialist leanings, the Housewives' Association became a member of the Central Council for Savings Promotion in 1954. Together with the Central Council, New Life Campaign Association and other women's groups, the Housewives' Association in 1959 began co-sponsoring the annual National Women's Meeting for 'New Life and Saving'. Oku, too, conceived of consumption as a behaviour that should be rationalized. Calling upon housewives to 'rationalize daily life and eliminate waste' in 1953, Oku advised them to apply 'efficiency' when spending on food, clothing, shelter and entertainment: 'In place of consumption, strive for a life with imagination and resourcefulness. Unless the clever housewife maintains her household, this country will not rise.'[50] For Oku and many other Japanese in the 1950s and early 1960s, too much consumption weakened the nation in the struggle to overcome 'economic dependence on the United

States'. Even as the 'consumer revolution' was being proclaimed in 1959, Oku insisted that 'we must thoroughly eliminate the waste in daily life and cultivate many people who will curb the dissipation of national power'.[51]

The 'Consumer Revolution' and the Language of 'Balance'

The late 1950s witnessed a cultural shift of sorts. After decades of devaluing consumption, agencies of the Japanese government began encouraging spending on consumer durables.[52] In 1960 the cabinet of Ikeda Hayato announced the Income Doubling Plan, which pledged to double national and per capita income by the end of the decade. The media went further and trumpeted the new catchphrase 'consumption is *the* virtue', replacing the traditional values of 'diligence, thrift and saving'. Even more than exports, the steady expansion of domestic consumption drove Japan's high economic growth from 1955 to the mid-1970s.[53] By many measures, Japan took on the trappings of a mass-consumption society. By 1970 per capita income had not doubled; it had quadrupled. Real per capita consumption increased at the impressive rate of 7.51 per cent per year from 1955 to 1973. Food's share of household budgets steadily declined from 50 to 20 per cent (1955 to 1988), enabling consumers to afford a greater array of goods and services.[54] At the same time, the rapid rise of installment buying and other forms of credit permitted less affluent Japanese to purchase the new mass commodities. An enormous advertising industry emerged to market consumption as the basis of the 'bright life'. By the mid-1960s nearly all Japanese families owned a washing machine, refrigerator and television. Over the next decade and a half consumers moved beyond the 'three sacred treasures' to acquire the 'three Cs' – the car, cooler (air conditioner) and colour TV. Thanks to substantial increases in housing loans, homeownership became the norm during the 1970s, as large numbers of Japanese were able to purchase houses for the first time.[55] In the ensuing years the conspicuous nature of Japanese consumption rarely failed to impress foreign observers. Attired in expensive clothes and armed with the latest gadgets, the Japanese appeared to worship at the shrine of mass consumption.

Appearances can be deceptive. The unmistakable rise in Japanese consumption levels was not matched by the advent of an American-style *consumer culture* that privileged consumption and abundance over restraint. Among the nation's households, the inculcated habits of thrift did not diminish noticeably but rather coexisted with the new consumption. As Japanese incomes grew, households became capable of significantly increasing *both* saving *and* spending. Far from spending freely, Japanese families saved greater portions of their income. Household savings rates soared from 14 per cent in 1959 to an extraordinary 23 per cent in 1976.[56] Consumers often afforded costly durables only by severely cutting back on other expenditures, including housing.[57] According to cross-national statistics for 1960, Japanese resembled Europeans more than Americans in expenditures on food and housing. Japanese households devoted 38 per cent of their consumption to food and only 10 per cent to housing and home-related expenditures. Similarly, in West Germany and France, respectively, food accounted for 43 per cent and 46 per cent and housing for 18 per cent and 11 per cent. In contrast, Americans spent only 32 per cent on food and an incomparable 29 per cent on housing, including furniture and household goods.[58] For most Japanese families, consumption continued to be something that had to be 'rationalized' within limited budgets.

Indeed, from women's magazines to government spokesmen, many Japanese persisted in distinguishing 'sound' or 'rational' spending from 'wasteful expenditures' and 'excessive consumption'. Assisted by the major women's organizations, the well-funded Central Council for Savings Promotion maintained its nationwide savings campaigns through the prosperous 1960s and beyond. Nevertheless, the much acknowledged 'consumer boom' did prompt the proponents of thrift to adapt their messages to the sensibilities of the new age. While they acknowledged the benefits of improved consumption, officials and many economists contested the formulation that consumption should be '*the* virtue' – that is, the highest priority for the Japanese economy. Instead they instructed the Japanese people to 'balance' consumption against other vital needs of the household and nation.

During the 1960s the critics of 'unbalanced' consumption most often spoke of the imperative to keep on saving. The economist Koizumi Akira recognized the importance of consumption in absorbing surplus production and raising Japanese living standards. Yet it would be a 'complete mistake', he warned, to interpret 'consumption is the virtue' as a repudiation of saving; Japan's high growth could only be sustained by the new investment generated by greater saving. Another economist, Okinaka Tsuneyuki, envisaged the balance as one in which consumption is 'the ultimate goal of the economy', while saving is, 'in the end, the means of achieving a more stable and better life'. Not only did saving protect families from life's emergencies, but also it financed increases in production, wages and ultimately consumption. The governor of the Bank of Japan, Usami Jun, was far blunter in 1966: 'The difference between a civilized country and a backward country is

Figure 11 'Keep a Balance in Life', Japan, 1955. An early version of the government's oft-repeated message to strike a 'balance' (*baransu*) between consumption and saving. This Japanese poster for postal savings mimics a popular British poster of the early 1950s that likewise featured a ballerina and the slogan 'Keep a Good Balance in the Post Office Savings Bank' (NSC 5/743, PRO, London)

Source: Poster XD-C 52, Communications Museum, Tokyo.

whether it accumulates capital in large or small amounts.' Japan boasted the world's highest personal savings rates, he granted, but the people's aggregate savings remained low because the Second World War had destroyed so much accumulated wealth. Japan had 'a long way to go before reaching the stage' enjoyed by American consumers. Thus, rather than spend freely, the people 'should endeavour to live rationally and save as the means of increasing the wealth of Japan as a whole'.[59]

From the start, officials admonished households against tilting too far in the direction of consumption. As Okazaki Kaheita, chairman of the Central Council for Savings Promotion, reminded women's leaders in 1961, the government's recently announced Income Doubling Plan did not promise immediate improvements in consumption. To develop the economy and raise living standards in the long term, the plan explicitly required 'high-level saving'. Saving remained essential to 'bring balance to Japanese life'. Okazaki reflected a wide range of Japanese opinion that criticized the nation's consumer life as 'unbalanced'. Such judgements were heavily influenced by contemporary American critiques of mass consumption, notably Vance Packard's *The Hidden Persuaders* (1957) and *The Waste Makers* (1960). *The Waste Makers*, noted Okazaki, revealed how American industry chronically overproduced for the consumer economy, and the book urged Americans to restore the 'balance' among factors in the economy. Like others at the time, Okazaki opined that Packard's diagnosis fitted Japan better than America, for it was the Japanese who spent most excessively on 'waste'. He charged his countrymen with frittering away their money on restaurants or consuming electricity in unoccupied rooms. And he cited a German friend's complaint that Japanese owned too many clothes and spent tens of thousands of yen on buying skis that they used only once or twice a year. By comparison, Okazaki observed, Americans generally bought only what they needed.[60]

Government officials did not stand alone in condemning unbalanced consumption. Oku Mumeo, the pioneer consumer advocate from the Housewives' Association, joined Okazaki in speaking to the national women's meeting on 'New Life and Saving'. She, too, exhorted younger Japanese, who had not experienced the hardships of the war and early post-war era, to eliminate 'waste' and engage in 'rational, sound consumption'. Like Packard in his own country, Oku took aim at the free-spending advertising industry, which had persuaded Japanese to buy anything marketed as a 'new brand'. Adopting the formulation used in the next several decades, Oku and the consumer movement urged Japanese to become 'wise consumers' (*kashikoi shōhisha*) who would 'rationalize how we buy and use things'.[61] Similarly, the economist Daimon Kazuki challenged advertisers' claims that their products advanced the 'rationalization of home life' and the 'modernization of life', when they were actually encouraging 'irrationality' and 'imbalance in consumption'. Whereas the French scrimped on household items to buy cars, which they truly needed, the Japanese wasted their money on appliances, expensive clothes and entertainment for the sake of 'appearance'. The Japanese, he sneered, 'are imitating America' in buying 'luxuries' on credit. Because Japanese could not yet afford 'what's really important in life' – notably quality housing – he advised people to remain tight-fisted (*kechi*). Daily rationalization, Daimon concluded, would permit the Japanese to 'achieve the greatest good', and 'isn't this the measure of the modernity of a modern people?'[62]

Moreover, Japan's 'consumer revolution' remained constrained by anxieties that too much spending would exacerbate yet another imbalance. During its first two post-war decades the nation suffered endemic deficits in its balance of international payments. This situation prompted the government to send mixed messages to the consumer. To support domestic industries, state agencies and Japanese manufacturers encouraged the consumption of 'national products', particularly electrical goods. Spending on imports was another matter. Even at the height of the 'consumer revolution', officials maintained nationwide campaigns that linked the consumption of imported goods to trade imbalances. In 1957 Japanese were exhorted to restrain their consumption and save more money in order to 'Promote Exports and Conserve Foreign Exchange'. Confronted by another 'crisis' in Japan's balance of payments in 1961–2, the government unhesitatingly identified the culprit: 'recently consumption has got out of hand'. The state unveiled a new savings campaign to make the nation aware of the need to 'economize on overall consumption, as well as consumption on company business'.[63] Speaking to women's groups throughout the archipelago, Bank of Japan officials explained that consumers bore some responsibility for the worsening trade imbalance, for they had 'unwittingly bought surprisingly large quantities of imported items like instant coffee and raisins'.[64] As conveyed by numerous pamphlets at the time, one's patriotic duty lay instead in increasing the nation's savings, which would finance the industrial production necessary to expand exports and pay for imported raw materials.[65]

Amid the booming economy of the 1960s, the warnings against excessive consumption would seem little more than a rearguard action against the surging consumer revolution. In the course of the 1970s, however, feelings of ambivalence gave way to the widespread criticism of mass consumption itself. Although several developments fuelled these discontents, the catalyst was unquestionably the 'Oil Shock' of 1973–4, when OPEC nations embargoed oil. Energy-dependent Japan experienced hyperinflation, shortages of necessities, and its first decline in GNP since the early post-war years. From conservatives to progressives, the Oil Shock served as the backdrop for a national morality play about the evils of 'affluence' and the opportunity for spiritual rebalancing. The government instinctively mounted a new anti-inflation campaign to encourage saving, economizing and the conservation of energy. National leaders became uncommonly philosophical in discerning a shift in public consciousness: whereas Japanese had prized 'material affluence' and 'mass consumption' during the high-growth era, they had now discovered 'a new form of affluence' by reducing expenditures.[66] The media, too, avidly reported on consumers' return to saving and 'stinginess', blaming

Japan's current economic woes on the high living of the recent past. 'It's undeniable', wrote a weekly magazine, 'that one of the main causes of rising inflation has been the motto "Consumption is the virtue".' The Japanese people, elaborated one market surveyor, had endured great deprivations in wartime and the post-war years, but during the 1960s they threw themselves into consumption and 'luxury-ism' (*gōkaishugi*).[67]

Independent commentators, women's leaders and consumer advocates joined in the condemnation of the recent consumer boom. Standing on the moderate left, they criticized personal consumption as out of balance with society's needs for a more generous welfare state and a cleaner environment. The social critic Higuchi Keiko seized upon the Oil Shock as an opportunity for consumers to move from 'material affluence' to a 'truly affluent society'. True affluence was not about being 'rich in goods or money', but required a society that neither destroyed the natural environment nor discarded the weak.[68] Like other national women's organizations, the consumer-oriented Housewives' Association actively participated in the state's mid-1970s campaigns for saving and conserving resources and energy. Rather than advocate improvements in consumption levels, the Housewives' Association castigated the government for having previously promoted the doctrine of 'consumption is the virtue' in its support of 'mass production' and 'mass consumption'. In late 1973 a survey of association members revealed the extent to which housewives blamed themselves for the rampant inflation. Some 29 per cent replied that 'consumers, too, are responsible' for the shortage of goods, and nearly half (48 per cent) agreed that 'consumers should refrain from buying goods and should economize' as the most effective solution (only one-third looked to the government).[69] Injunctions to economize filled the pages of housewives' magazines, as did the new catch-phrase '*economizing* is the virtue'. The language of 'balance' also appeared widely, illustrated in one instance by a cartoon of a scale that balanced 'spiritual affluence' against a heap of consumer goods.[70]

Fending Off the American Other

Ironically, the discourses of thrift grew stronger during the 1980s, a time of renewed economic growth and rising consumption. A great many Japanese came to regard thrift as a key marker of their 'national character' and a major source of Japan's seemingly unstoppable economic ascendancy in the world. These attitudes were as much a defensive response to American criticisms, as they were a sign of a new national confidence. As Japan amassed ever-increasing trade surpluses in the 1980s and early 1990s, the US government and OECD heatedly accused the Japanese of 'excessive saving' and under-consumption. Bowing to these pressures, the Japanese government in 1986 released the Maekawa Report, which promised to expand domestic consumption while curtailing programmes that actively promoted saving.[71]

Yet in both rhetoric and policy, Japanese leaders remained unpersuaded of the virtues of a consumption-driven economy. Joined by the media, officials instead took the offensive to condemn the *Americans* for having lost their balance in an orgy of consumption. Before authoring the report that bore his name, Bank of Japan Governor Maekawa Haruo had himself been an ardent defender of savings-promotion policies. High household saving had enabled Japan to subdue inflation, he observed in 1982, whereas double-digit inflation continued to dog the US economy as Americans turned from saving money to buying more and more.[72] In a 1987 bestseller extolling the Japanese spirit of hard work and thrift, the chairman of the Central Council for Savings Promotion depicted America as the degenerate Other – an image that widely persists to this day in Japan. Here was a land where the Puritan ethic of thrift had declined; 'excessive consumption' resulted from the rampant use of credit cards, and 'millions of households are indebted'.[73] By 1990 the Japanese government felt sufficiently confident to insist that the United States reduce its fiscal deficits by curbing 'excessive consumption' through tax preferences for saving and restrictions on credit cards.[74] At roughly the same time, Japanese agencies began aggressively exporting savings-promotion as an essential developmental strategy for poorer nations, particularly those in the rest of Asia.[75]

Looking back on Japan's past fifteen years, I am struck by the persistent ambivalence about consumption more than four decades after the 'consumer revolution' commenced. Japanese elites no longer lecture their American counterparts on the primacy of saving, of course. The Japanese economy has been mired in a state of recession or slow growth since 1991, and Japan and the United States have traded places. The US economic boom of the 1990s convinced American officials and economists of the brilliance of consumer-driven growth based on the massive expansion of consumer credit. Once again, US policy-makers pressed the Japanese to stop saving so much and instead to consume their way out of recession. Foreign observers thus welcomed the news that Japanese household savings rates had dropped sharply in 2001 to less than 7 per cent. 'Japanese households have lost their appetite for thrift', declared *The Economist*.[76]

However, the decline in Japanese savings rates has not been matched by a profound cultural embrace of consumption. The falling savings rate may be better explained by declining salaries and bonuses than by a national spending spree (and in 2002 and 2003 the savings rate began rising again). Recent statistics on real consumption per household tell a decidedly un-American story. Despite a dazzling array of new products and the proliferation of credit cards, Japanese consumer spending between 1993 and 2003 *fell* every year but one.[77] Although many more women now work outside the home, the post-war housewives' culture of closely monitoring spending has proved remarkably resilient. Monthly issues of women's magazines, notably *Shufu no tomo*, are filled with stories of resourceful housewives who cope with a bad economy by adopting the 'economizing lifestyle' (*setsuyaku seikatsu*). Moreover, because the media and government have been spotlighting the 'aging society problem' for more than two decades, Japanese have become sensitized to the tradeoffs between consumption and the imperative to support the elderly by saving and paying taxes.[78] The twentieth century ended with the government's savings-information agency still advising the nation to live a 'life that strikes a balance between saving and consumption'.[79]

Placing limits on consumption is, of course, not the same as opposing consumption. Unquestionably post-war Japan experienced a consumer revolution. Japanese today enjoy consumer choices and lifestyles that would have been unimaginable in the 1950s. Aggregate consumption has grown to constitute some 60 per cent of GDP, and policy-makers appreciate that increased consumption is essential to economic expansion. At the same time, this chapter argues against conflating all 'consumer revolutions' with each other and with the singular American experience. Decades of official and popular efforts to 'rationalize' consumption have moulded a Japanese consumer culture that remains quite different from its American counterpart.

Notes

Following East Asian practice, Japanese surnames precede given names.

1. Keizai kikakuchō, *Kokumin seikatsu hakusho, 1959* (Tokyo, 1959), pp. 1, 74–7; S. Partner, *Assembled in Japan: Electrical Goods and the Making of the Japanese Consumer* (Berkeley, 1999), p. 247.
2. See C. Johnson, *MITI and the Japanese Miracle: The Growth of Industrial Policy, 1925–1975* (Stanford, 1982).
3. Partner, *Assembled in Japan*, pp. 3, 5, 45; S. O'Bryan, 'Gotō Yonosuke, Statistical Knowledge and the Idea of Consumption in Post-World War

II Japan', paper delivered to the Annual Meeting of the Association for Asian Studies, 29 March 2003, New York.

4. E. Carter, *How German Is She? Postwar West German Reconstruction and the Consuming Woman* (Ann Arbor, 1997), p. 232, also pp. 3, 55–9.

5. F. Trentmann, 'The Evolution of the Consumer: Meanings, Identities and Political Synapses before the Age of Affluence', in S. Garon and P. Maclachlan (eds), *The Ambivalent Consumer: Questioning Consumption in East Asia and the West* (Ithaca, NY, forthcoming 2006). And see F. Trentmann's chapter in this volume.

6. D.H. Shively, 'Sumptuary Regulation and Status in Early Tokugawa Japan', *Harvard Journal of Asiatic Studies*, 25 (1964–5), pp. 123–64.

7. S. Garon, 'Fashioning a Culture of Diligence and Thrift', in S.A. Minichiello (ed.), *Japan's Competing Modernities: Issues in Culture and Democracy* (Honolulu, 1998), pp. 314–16.

8. T. Takemura, *Taishō bunka* [Taishō culture] (Tokyo, 1980), chap. 4.

9. Naimushō shakaikyoku, 'Shōhi setsuyaku ni tsuite' [Economy in consumption], *Shakai jigyō* [Social work], 6(7) (October 1922), pp. 1–2.

10. On state–society cooperation in the inter-war campaigns, see Garon, 'Fashioning a Culture of Diligence and Thrift', pp. 318–31.

11. S. Garon, 'Luxury Is the Enemy: Mobilizing Savings and Popularizing Thrift in Wartime Japan', *Journal of Japanese Studies*, 26(1) (Winter 2000), pp. 42, 57–60, 65–70.

12. J. Dower, *Embracing Defeat: Japan in the Wake of World War II* (New York, 1999), p. 136; see also S. Yoshimi, '"America" as Desire and Violence: Americanization in Postwar Japan and Asia during the Cold War', trans. D. Buist, *Inter-Asia Cultural Studies*, 4(3) (December 2003), pp. 433–50.

13. Yoshimi, '"America" as Desire'; Partner, *Assembled in Japan*, pp. 50–1.

14. H. Minami, *Zoku Shōwa bunka: 1945–1989* [Shōwa culture, part 2] (Tokyo, 1990), pp. 13–14.

15. L. Cohen, 'The Consumers' Republic: An American Model for the World?', in Garon and Maclachlan, *Ambivalent Consumer*; Sheryl Kroen, 'A Political History of the Consumer', *Historical Journal*, 47(3) (Sept. 2004), pp. 709–36.

16. R.B. Finn, *Winners in Peace: MacArthur, Yoshida, and Postwar Japan* (Berkeley, 1992), pp. 37, 332, n. 25; Dower, *Embracing Defeat*, p. 115.

17. L.E. Hein, *Fuelling Growth: The Energy Revolution and Economic Policy in Postwar Japan* (Cambridge, 1990), pp. 147, 158–9, 356, n. 7.

18. 'Yoshida sōri daijin-ate Makkaasa saikō shireikan shokan' [Supreme Commander MacArthur to Prime Minister Yoshida], 28 March 1947, Aichi bunsho, Chochiku: Chochiku zōkyōsaku, 2, doc. 15, Sengo zaiseishi shiryō [Post-war financial history archive; hereafter SZS], Ministry of Finance, Japan.

19. Chochiku zōkyō chūō iinkai, *Chochiku undōshi: Chozōi 30 nen no ayumi* [History of savings campaigns: 30 years of Central Council for Savings Promotion] (Tokyo, 1983), p. 15.

20. Garon, 'Luxury Is the Enemy', pp. 72–5.

21. S. Yano, 'Ōkura daijin rajio hōsō: Chochiku kyōchō junkan ni saishite kokumin ni uttau' [Finance Minister's radio address], 12 June 1947, p. 5, Aichi bunsho, Chochiku: Chochiku zōkyōsaku, 2, doc. 21, SZS.

22. Italics mine. 'Ōkura daijin kōen genkō' [Finance Minister's address], 16 Sept. 1947, Aichi bunsho, Chochiku: Chochiku zōkyōsaku, 2, doc. 36, SZS.

23. 'Jikan chochiku kōen shiryō' [Vice-Minister's address], 5 April 1947, Aichi bunsho, Chochiku: Chochiku zōkyōsaku, 2, doc. 1, SZS.

24. J.C. Smith (Chief, Money and Banking Branch, Finance Division, Economic and Scientific Section, SCAP), 'Statement for Release in Connection with Savings Campaign', *c.* Sept. 1948, Noda bunsho, Chochiku zōkyō taisaku (1945–52), doc. 42, SZS.

25. Quoted in Kokumin seikatsu sentaa (ed.), *Sengo shōhisha undōshi* [History of post-war consumer movement] (Tokyo, 1997), p. 61, n. 4.

26. Yano Shōtarō, 'Ōkura daijin rajio hōsō', p. 2.

27. 'Jikan chochiku kōen shiryō'.

28. Tsūka antei taisaku jimukyoku, *Chochiku to infureeshon* [Saving and inflation], pamphlet (Tokyo: Nihon ginkō, 1947).

29. On post-war French savings campaigns, see Caisse des Dépôts et Consignations, *Le Livret A: Une Histoire de l'épargne populaire* (Paris, 1999), pp. 217–27; for Polish campaigns for savings and 'enforced abstinence from consumption', see T.P. Alton, *Polish Postwar Economy* (New York, 1955), p. 291, also pp. 191, 220, 229.

30. 'The Economic Debate: The Danger of Inflation', *National Savings*, 7, no. 2 (1949), pp. 11, 14–15, NSC 3/14; also *National Savings*, 6, no. 3 (1947), NSC 3/13, Public Record Office (hereafter PRO), London.

31. 'Silver Lining Campaign', *National Savings*, 6, no. 2 (1947), p. 6, NSC 3/13, PRO.

32. National Savings Committee, 'Lend Strength to Britain Campaign: Notes for Speakers', Dec. 1951, p. 3, in 'Special Campaigns: Lend Strength to Britain Campaign, 1950–1952', NSC 7/183, PRO.

33. 'Lend Strength to Britain: The National Savings Campaign for 1951–1952', pamphlet to local committees, 1951, in 'Special Campaigns: Lend Strength to Britain Campaign, 1950–1952', NSC 7/183, PRO.
34. 'Restraint in Spending Campaign, 1955–56', in National Savings Committee, 'Special Campaign: Restraint in Spending Campaign – 1955–56', NSC 7/349, PRO.
35. For example, 'Kaigai chochiku posutaa, kyatchi fureezu-shū' [Foreign savings posters and catchphrases], *Chochiku jihō* [Savings times; hereafter *CJ*], no. 19 (Jan. 1954), pp. 67–71; 'Berugii, Oranda ryōkoku no chochiku undō' [Belgian and Dutch savings campaigns], *CJ*, no. 43 (March 1960), pp. 56–7.
36. C.Y. Horioka, 'Consuming and Saving', in A. Gordon (ed.), *Postwar Japan as History* (Berkeley, 1993), p. 283. Savings rates were calculated according to the Old System of National Accounts.
37. S. Garon, *Molding Japanese Minds: The State in Everyday Life* (Princeton, NJ, 1997), p. 155.
38. Garon, *Molding Japanese Minds*, pp. 163–6.
39. 'Dai 3-kai zenkoku chochiku jimu shokuin kōshūkai' [Third national savings officers' training course], 17 September 1947, Aichi bunsho, Chochiku: Chochiku zōkyōsaku, 3, doc. 1, SZS.
40. 'Kyūkoku chochiku tokubetsu undō ni kansuru Katayama naikaku sōri daijin dan' [Interview with Prime Minister Katayama on the Special National Salvation Savings Campaign], 1 Sept. 1947, Aichi bunsho, Chochiku: Chochiku zōkyōsaku, 2, doc. 46, SZS; Garon, *Molding Japanese Minds*, p. 154.
41. Garon, *Molding Japanese Minds*, pp. 164, also 163–72.
42. Italics mine. R. Minobe, *Keizai to seiji* [Economics and politics] (Tokyo, 1955), pp. 11–12, 199.
43. R. Minobe, M. Uno and H. Ujiie, *Kakei to seikatsu* [Household finance and daily life] (Tokyo, 1958), pp. 64–5.
44. A. Gordon, 'Managing the Japanese Household: The New Life Movement in Postwar Japan', *Social Politics*, 4(2) (Summer 1997), pp. 245–83.
45. On the role of women's organizations and housewives' magazines, see Garon, *Molding Japanese Minds*, chapters, 4, 6.
46. Chochiku kōhō chūō iinkai, *Chochiku to shōhi ni kansuru seron chōsa, 1996* [Public opinion survey on household savings and consumption] (Tokyo, 1996), p. 146.
47. See Ono Yoshisa (chair, Nishi-Tamagawa Women's Council), 'Dannasama no osake ni baketa' [Lest it be spent on the hubsband's drinking], *Fujin jihō* [Women's times], 21 (Sept. 1954), p. 1.

48. *Fujin jihō*, 34 (20 November 1955), p. 1.
49. For a history of the consumer movement, see P. Maclachlan, *Consumer Politics in Postwar Japan* (New York, 2002).
50. M. Oku, 'Shin seikatsu e' [Towards new life], *Shufuren tayori* [Housewives' Association news], 52 (15 August 1953), p. 1.
51. M. Oku, 'Kokusaiteki na chūritsu, kokunai de mo chūritsu' [Neutrality, internationally and domestically], *Shufuren tayori*, 119 (31 October 1959), p. 1.
52. Maclachlan, *Consumer Politics*, p. 94.
53. Johnson, *MITI*, p. 16.
54. Horioka, 'Consuming and Saving', pp. 261, 265, 268–9.
55. See Partner, *Assembled in Japan*, pp. 149–56, 168–70; A. Gordon, 'From Singer to Shinpan: Consumer Credit in Modern Japan', in Garon and Maclachlan, *Ambivalent Consumer*; Jordan Sand, *House and Home in Modern Japan: Architecture, Domestic Space, and Bourgeois Culture, 1880–1930* (Cambridge, 2003), pp. 374–5; A. Gordon, *A Modern History of Japan* (New York, 2003), pp. 249, 266–8.
56. Horioka, 'Consuming and Saving', p. 283. New System of National Accounts.
57. Partner, *Assembled in Japan*, pp. 163–5.
58. International Labour Office, *Year-book of Labour Statistics*, 1960, in *CJ*, no. 53 (Sept. 1962), inside back cover.
59. A. Koizumi, 'Keizai no antei seichō o sasaeru mono: Shōhi wa bitoku ka' [Factors supporting stable economic growth: is consumption the virtue?], *CJ*, no. 50 (Dec. 1961), p. 15; T. Okinaka, 'Chochiku to kokumin keizai: Chochiku no hitsuyō ni tsuite' [Saving and the national economy: on the necessity to save], *CJ*, no. 46 (Dec. 1960), pp. 2, 6–7; J. Usami, 'Seikatsu to chochiku' [Daily life and saving], *CJ*, no. 86 (July 1966), pp. 6–7.
60. K. Okazaki, in *Shin seikatsu to chochiku: Dai 3-kai zenkoku fujin no tsudoi kiroku* [New life and saving: Record of the third national women's meeting] (Tokyo, 1961), pp. 7–10; see 'Respecting the Eternal Balance', in Vance Packard, *The Waste Makers* (New York, 1960), pp. 274–93; Partner, *Assembled in Japan*, pp. 130–1, 188–9.
61. Oku Mumeo, in *Shin seikatsu to chochiku: Dai 3-kai*, pp. 12–13.
62. K. Daimon, 'Shōhi no baransu' [Balance in consumption], *CJ*, no. 45 (Sept. 1960), pp. 29–32.
63. Chochiku zōkyō chūō iinkai, *Chochiku undōshi*, pp. 44–5, 60–1.
64. *Fujin jihō*, no. 107 (Feb. 1962), p. 1.

65. See Chochiku zōkyō chūō iinkai, *Yasashii keizai no hanashi* [Economics made simple] (Tokyo, 1962), reprinted in S. Garon, 'Saving for "My Own Good and the Good of the Nation": Economic Nationalism in Modern Japan', in S. Wilson (ed.), *Nation and Nationalism in Japan* (London, 2002), p. 113.

66. Japan, Economic Planning Agency, *Whitepaper on National Life, 1975* (Tokyo, 1975), foreword, pp. 132, 136–7.

67. 'Infure ni kachinuku: Shin-chokingaku nyūmon' [Fighting inflation: a primer on the new savings school], *Shūkan sankei*, 28 December 1974, pp. 156, 158.

68. K. Higuchi, 'Kore kara no shōhi seikatsu' [Consumer life from now on], *Kurashi no chie* [Tips on living], 94 (1974), p. 1.

69. *Shufuren tayori*, 308 (April 1975), p. 2; 294 (February 1974), p. 2; Garon, *Molding Japanese Minds*, p. 192.

70. 'Atarashii yutakasa to sono jitsugen no tame ni' [Achieving the new affluence], *Kurashi no chie*, 118 (March 1978), p. 3.

71. K.B. Pyle, *The Japanese Question* (Washington, DC, 1992), p. 93.

72. *Kurashi no chie*, special issue (Feb. 1982), p. 3.

73. S. Toyama, *Nihonjin no kinben-, chochiku-kan* [Japanese views of diligence and saving] (Tokyo, 1987), pp. 163–4.

74. *Yomiuri shinbun*, 28 October 1990, p. 11.

75. S. Garon, 'The Transnational Promotion of Saving in Asia: "Asian Values" or the "Japanese Model"?', in Garon and Maclachlan, *Ambivalent Consumer*.

76. *The Economist*, 5 July 2003, p. 67.

77. Sōmushō tōkeikyoku [Ministry of Internal Affairs and Communications, Statistics Bureau], *Kakei chōsa* [Survey of household economy], July 2004, http://www.stat.go.jp/data/kakei/.

78. Garon, *Molding Japanese Minds*, pp. 222–7.

79. Chochiku kōhō chūō iinkai, 'Chochiku kōhō chūō iinkai undō hōshin' [Campaign policy of Central Council for Savings Information], 1997 (mimeo), p. 1.

–9–

Virtue, Responsibility and Consumer Choice
Framing Critical Consumerism
Roberta Sassatelli

A growing variety of discourses, both within the marketplace and outside it, in politics and civil society, is calling into being the 'consumer' not only as an active subject but also, and above all, as a moral and political subject. Institutional actors at the national and supranational level are particularly vocal in addressing consumers as a constituency and as a partner in checking the otherwise allegedly unhampered workings of international business. Examples abound, from the European Union Green Paper on business social responsibility which places the consumer alongside the citizen and identifies both as the main constituency for ethical business, to Amnesty International's *Human Rights Guidelines for Companies* which calls on consumers as well as business and citizens to consider the social responsibilities associated with economic activities, to a wide spectrum of local, national and supranational movements which are also increasingly concerned with mobilizing social actors as consumers, from traditional environmental movements and fair-trade campaigns to anti-sweatshop boycotts.

Efforts to explicitly link consumption with the pursuit of moral and political aims have a long history. At the turn of the nineteenth century in the United States, for example, the National Consumer League promoted the so-called 'white lists', a sort of labelling scheme which aimed at listing national companies that treated their employees fairly.[1] More generally, a host of mobilizations and boycotts called forth the consumer as a political actor, especially from the nineteenth century and more clearly in the twentieth century.[2] However, especially after the 1999 World Trade Organization protests in Seattle, which have worked as a catalyst and umbrella for a number of social and political movements concerned with 'critical' consumption, a variety of discourses about the 'duty' and 'responsibilities' of social actors *qua* 'consumers' have consolidated into an appealing and compelling narrative. People are increasingly and explicitly asked to think that to shop is to vote and that ethical daily purchases, product boycotts and consumer voice may be the only way that men and women around the world have to intervene in the workings of global markets.

In this chapter I will approach 'critical consumerism' as a normative frame which proposes a particular vision of the consumer, foreshadowing a shift in the way markets and politics may be conceived within liberal-democratic ideologies. I will use a variety of different sources – mainly documents produced by critical consumption transnational campaigns as well as interviews with activists in Italy and the UK – to bring discourses down to their institutional bases and provide a glimpse of both the transnational and local/national dimensions of the phenomenon. The movements which marshal the language of critical consumption have posed themselves as agencies for the representation of the consumer as a fundamental subject-category within public discourse, together with other more visible cultural agencies such as advertising, marketing and conventional consumer defence organizations. This chapter will only touch upon issues such as the competitive dynamics within the consolidating field of alternative and critical consumption mobilizations or the relations between activists and their constituencies. The primary focus is on the role that critical consumption movements ascribe to consumers. The particular model of the consumer they propose has to be problematized precisely because, like advertising and marketing, it works as a 'claim to truth' about consumers and codifies a series of practices which are tied to a particular vision of what they should do.[3] The moral and political discourses which surround critical and alternative consumer practices appear to draw on themes and tropes which cut across the different symbolic boundaries which have consolidated in the course of modernity.

Consumption and Politics

Within liberal and neoliberal discourse, consumption is conventionally aligned with the market, commerce and the family and pushed into the private sphere, opposed to the public and political spheres of the state and citizenship. The social sciences have shown, however, that the *de gustibus non disputandum est* which seems to make of consumption a space where subjects can and must freely express themselves is more a wish than a social reality. In reality, tastes are anything but indisputable. Judgements are made on the basis of taste, and people are preferred and rewarded because of their own tastes and those of others. This intrinsic political value is complemented by other more structural relations of power, which have to do mostly with the 'normality', 'legitimacy', 'fairness' or otherwise of certain goods and practices and with the identity ascribed to the consumer. The growth of 'alternative' or 'ethical', 'critical' or 'political' modes of consumer action – as manifested, for example, in the successful boycotting of global brands and chains, in the rising demand for organic food and Fair Trade goods, or in the flourishing of symbolic initiatives against multinational companies or in favour of simpler lifestyles – is often taken as an example of what is widely portrayed as a bottom-up cultural revolution touching upon both everyday lifestyles and the nature of political participation. 'Negative' and 'positive' forms of 'political consumerism', as Michele Micheletti has branded them, now seem to concern a wide sector of the population in developed countries.[4] Recent comparative survey data on Europe, for example, show that well over 30 per cent of the population of Denmark, Great Britain, Germany, Italy, Norway and Portugal are engaging in some form of consumer activism: boycotting products for political reasons, choosing specific items with a view on their ethical or environmental qualities, or participating in the activities of consumer-oriented associations.[5]

While boycotts draw on consumers' ability to refuse certain goods, alternative consumption practices critically address contemporary consumer culture from within. For all their diversity, alternative products are commodities which embody a critical dialogue with many aspects of commoditization as we know it (from rationalization to standardization, from lengthy commodity chains to the externalization of environmental and human costs). As such, they are presented by environmental organizations as occasions for 'political awareness', capable of 'stimulating democracy', bringing consumers 'closer' to 'products and producers' as well as to 'nature', 'humanity' and 'health'.[6] In terms of market share they are still to be considered niche products, taking up small fractions of pro-capita expenses among mainly middle-class people in Western countries; however, their market is soaring at the dawn of the new millennium, scoring annual rates of growth oscillating between 10 per cent and 20 per cent in most European countries.[7] What is more, their symbolic impact should not be underestimated, as the greening of even a tiny fraction of our daily consumption routines may enable the cultivation of utopias that are unrealizable in daily life.[8] Thus alternative products may come to represent bridges suspended not so much towards others as towards ideals that usually escape us, and which we do not want to renounce: even if a style of consumption that is entirely green might presently be difficult, through buying and using some organic, ethical or Fair Trade products consumers can gain proof of the importance of their aspirations, feel as if they have the capacity to contribute to change and claim a new kind of identity for themselves.

In recent years there have also been a host of *ad hoc* consumer boycotts which have helped consolidate the perception that consumers may be important as 'political' actors. Boycotts have a long history, notably in the Anglo-American world[9] – in the American Revolution sympathizers of the American cause would refuse to buy English goods.[10] Such anti-colonialist roots reverberate in today's global campaigns, which tend to stress global collective goods and the responsibility of the rich consumers of the north. Some campaigns have placed an emphasis on safety and the environment, such as the campaign against McDonald's; others have instead concentrated on the conditions of labour, for example campaigns against Nike; others still have stressed environmental and humanitarian issues, as in campaigns against Nestlé's distribution of artificial baby milk in Africa or the wider movement against GM foods.[11] These initiatives show that, besides entailing a sombre shift in everyday purchases, critical consumption is crucially sponsored on special occasions that take the shape of contestation and public denunciation. Bringing together a variety of critical discourses and making more visible the hegemonic criteria ordinarily marshalled for justifying choices, similar occasions may help to consolidate agreement on new and distinctive principles for the classification and appraisal of goods as well as for the definition of the role of consumers in the economy, culture and politics.[12]

Discursive strategies, in the form of symbolic protest campaigns and educational initiatives both at the cross-national level and at the local/national level, which use new communication technologies are also crucial forms of politically charged consumer activism. The target of similar symbolic campaigns may be the product itself (coming clean on its process of production or stressing its various externalities from environmental effects to costs in terms of human or animal rights), the advertising imaginary which surrounds it or, more widely, consumer culture as a way of life. Particularly relevant here is Adbusters, a global network of artists, activists, writers, educators and entrepreneurs which sponsors alternative information circuits and promotes various culture jamming activities as forms of social mobilization against multinational companies, commercial culture and consumerism.[13] Taking advantage of the public sphere created by the Internet, a variety of associations are promoting a host of activities of naming and blaming and an imagery of brand subversion which is the counterpart of the phenomenal development of branding and which deploys irony, pastiche and the carnivalesque[14] to contest the lifestyles associated with global brands that often encode sexism, racism, homophobia, disrespect for the environment and so on.

Political sociologists and political scientists working on new social movements have addressed these recent developments as essentially new forms of political participation. What Albert Hirschman[15] wished for in a well-known essay on market regulation mechanisms, they propose, is now finally coming true: the classical 'political' instrument of 'voice' appears to be working side by side with a politically inspired market 'exit', and 'choice' itself is being coloured with political shades. A number of voices have celebrated the political persona of the consumer. Beck and Gernsheim, for example, argue that today 'citizens discover the act of shopping as one in which they can always cast their ballot – on a world scale, no less'.[16] This development is related to two main abstract sociopolitical trends: the process of 'individualization', on the one hand, whereby social actors are increasingly reflexive about their everyday identities, values and actions, and, on the other, the process of 'sub-politicization', whereby politics is emerging in places other than the formal political arena (sub-politics) because citizens no longer think that traditional forms of political participation are adequate.[17] Thus Beck has famously argued that if modernity is a democracy oriented to producers, late modernity is a democracy oriented to consumers: a pragmatic and cosmopolitan democracy where the sleepy giant of the 'sovereign citizen-consumer' is becoming a counterweight to big transnational corporations.[18]

The enthusiastic tone of such ideas notwithstanding, it would be mistaken to *always* attribute a deliberately political finality to consumer choices. Equally, it is debatable whether all practices of consumption are indeed conducted by social actors who self-reflexively constitute themselves as consumers. Many of the practices which come under the umbrella of alternative and critical consumerism might be conducted by consumers who have in mind meanings and objectives other than strictly political ones. What they are doing, both in form and content, cannot be easily equated with the expression of a 'vote' on collective goods such as justice, equality, nature, etc. It may be true, as Mary Douglas has observed in a much-quoted essay on shopping as protest, that 'the consumer wandering round the shops is actualizing a philosophy of life',[19] but much of this happens *despite* his or her intentions. Each purchase decision is not perceived, nor practically organized, as a consequential and eventful action like a political vote. More generally, Douglas's approach tends to confine social actors to a rational and cognitive dimension instead of a more practical one which would situate them in time and space, considering consumption practices as situated learning practices which are co-productive of consumers' desires and objectives and thus escape that neat separation between means and end which underlies liberal democratic models of choice as well as Douglas's view.[20]

When social and political scientists embrace and reproduce slogans which are common currency back into the reality they are studying, they run the risk of missing both the social limits of similar slogans and the particular configuration of power–knowledge–subjectivity on which they are built and which they call into being.[21] For example, the work of political scientists has often focused on the fact that different institutional settings are more or less conducive to consumer collective action, rather than exploring how and why the consumer has become a viable and helpful category for mobilization in different national contexts.[22] If we concentrate mainly on such aspects as the socioeconomic determinants of political consumer action, the way it may or may not correspond to different political orientations, degrees of participation, levels of societal or interpersonal trusts, we prepare the ground for a normative rather than a critical analysis. Even if we study the discourses promoted by the variety of associations promoting critical consumption without a critical awareness of the particular view(s) of the consumer encoded, we are bound to transform their visions of the consumer into that which Eco defines as a 'fetish concept': an instrument which has 'a particular ability to obstruct argument, strait-jacketing discussion in emotional reaction',[23] rather than a shifting historical code for defining and promoting a particular social identity, either being a total rejection or an unconditional apology.

There are a number of other reasons why it is important to problematize the equation between alternative and critical consumerism and political action. An obvious problem has to do with the fact that the different practices which are usually collected under this banner are fragmented and potentially conflicting, thus rendering rather difficult the formation of viable collective identities and initiatives. If we consider only alternative products, it is clear that they mobilize different meanings and promote different world-views. The growing body of work on vegetarianism, green consumption, alternative green consumption, organic food and Fair Trade indicates that different themes and issues typically contribute to each specific form of alternative consumption and that they all are far from being internally coherent.[24] For example, alternative distribution networks (from second-hand shops to farmers' markets to box schemes) not only respond to a politically conscious middle-class consumer, but also attract urban disadvantaged groups which might not be able to afford to shop via formal channels.[25] Likewise, the demand for organically grown vegetables typically mixes private health concerns with some degree of environmental consciousness and is coming from diverse sources, from a large vegetarian movement as well as health-conscious or gourmet carnivores.[26] Indeed, different practices and issues may converge or not – just like green consumers may or may not sympathize with the redistributive concerns which inspire Fair Trade. Contradictions of this kind might be acknowledged, and yet they are not easy for activists themselves to tackle. For example, *Enough!*, a magazine published by the Centre for a New American Dream which campaigns for a more healthy and sustainable lifestyle, celebrates the rise of organic food consumption and the fact that major multinationals are getting into organic business, while recognizing that organic food is still too expensive for many consumers.[27]

This clearly shows the extent to which alternative consumer practices, with all the ordinariness which accompanies daily consumption, cannot be easily translated as 'means' of political participation.[28] They can be easily absorbed by the market precisely because they are often routine and polysemic practices situated within the market. Ethical and political dimensions are perhaps now entering the market more explicitly than at previous times, but this does not mean that purchase decisions become a form of political practice *tout court*, a practice which subjectively and institutionally targets the functioning principles of the entire economic and political system. For one thing, 'the market' is composed of many different institutions with different interest and powers; the marketing and advertising industries are well aware of the interests in ecological, ethical and political themes among certain strata of Western populations and long ago started to promote their own versions of the 'greening of demand'.[29] Indeed, if we consider the whole cycle of production-distribution-consumption of any particular ethical or green commodity, we will see that it is punctuated by market and political institutions which all contribute to define and entrench a particular vision of ethics and politics. Codes for ethical business and for socially responsible management are becoming widespread and are typically self-administered by industries themselves. While cause-related marketing is responding to boycotting, a variety of labelling schemes, often set up by *ad hoc* organizations variously linked with either business or political institutions, play a crucial role. This does not mean that ethical claims can be easily used in a pure instrumental fashion, as ethically oriented consumers may demand proof of standards and may pressure companies much further than expected. But it does suggest that it is unrealistic to imagine that there is a simple demand/supply relation between consumers and producers.[30]

Finally, considering consumption as politics, as a new but powerful means of political participation, we may both underestimate the role that the 'political' has to play in translating ordinary practices into politically consequential ones and lose sight of the politics of consumption, ranging from social distinction to the realization of intimate aesthetic experiences.

Today's political mobilization of consumers is probably related to how national markets are organized and reorganized while globalization proceeds. International commerce grew by nearly 50 per cent in the 1990s, while economic inequality grew more than ever before during the 1970s and 1990s.[31] Indeed, as is now widely acknowledged, globalization and standardization have in turn stimulated localization and heterogeneity, contestation and resistance, helping to make ecological implications more visible and more clearly linked to issues of global equality.[32]

However, it would be mistaken to simply suppose that the 'consumer' now realizes a new 'global citizenship', working on pure universalistic, cosmopolitan and humanitarian grounds.[33] Certainly in post-colonial times such as ours, overt nationalistic uses of goods may come under attack, but this does not mean that our consumer identities are truly cosmopolitan. Politically charged consumer actions often have a national orientation (as Michele Micheletti has demonstrated in her recent survey of 'political consumerism'),[34] being entangled in national public debates, rather than representing a real form of transnational citizenship embedded in a global public discourse. Today's politically charged consumer activism often articulates and embodies the local/global contradiction. Humanitarian justice and respect for local traditions may run into conflict in Fair Trade protocols. Fair Trade protocols may themselves work as instruments of cultural hegemony and economic domination, especially where societies such as China, which have productive systems often irreconcilable with workers' rights as defined in the West, are becoming more competitive than Western countries might like. A global humanitarian consumer-citizenship may also require further economic disembedment, as it commands growth rates and volumes for green and ethical products which are at odds with small-scale local production. It may therefore run against the re-embedment of economic action in local environments, which is also one of the aspirations of alternative and critical consumer practices.[35]

While alternative consumer practices cannot be equated with political participation as such, they do signal that consumption and the consumer are being problematized by drawing on political repertoires. Taken together, the discourses surrounding and promoting alternative and critical consumer practices amount to a particular discourse or frame which not only politicizes consumption and promotes new principles of commodity qualification and visions of 'quality',[36] but also does so by mobilizing social actors as 'consumers' and by bestowing on them particular qualities.

Framing Critical Consumerism

Instead of considering ethical, critical and political forms of consumption as a panacea which responds to the failure of other political means typical of participatory democracy in a global world, we may consider them as a normative frame. This frame is sustained through discourse and practice by a host of different actors – from labelling institutions to alternative producers and distributors to critical consumption associations to individual social actors themselves – which call into being a particular type of consumer.[37] Critical and alternative consumption associations and movements are political entrepreneurs and legitimate themselves by constructing a particular consumer identity. Consumer choice is not taken for granted as necessarily good or as a private question. Rather, it is framed as a consequential and momentous practice, capable of expressing consumer sovereignty only if consumers do not lull themselves with the sirens of the Smithian tune, but take full responsibility for the environmental, social and political effects of their choices.

Despite their diversity, many forms of alternative and critical consumption articulate the notion of 'nature' and share some kind of interest in environmental values.[38] As stated by the magazine *Enough!*, it appears 'absolutely vital' that 'products and commodities be produced and harvested differently – with a long-term focus on resource conservation, labour and community impacts, and limiting waste production'.[39] For this reason Mary Douglas has branded green and environmentally-friendly consumer attitudes as instances of a 'movement of renunciation' or 'non-consumption', akin to that of Ghandi or early Christianity, which puts public or collective goods before one's own individual desires, or, in other terms, 'a rejection of the world as we know it'.[40] Still, as narratives aimed at bringing forward the political potentialities of the consumer, the discourses thematizing critical consumption go far beyond an ethic of renunciation.

Let us look at the minimum common denominator of the many voices which come together in a major event that specifically aims to critically address Western consumer culture – the so-called 'Buy Nothing Day' (BND). This is a day of boycotts, events and abstention from purchase which is now celebrated in over fifty countries around the world – the day after Thanksgiving Day in the United States and Canada and the last Saturday of November in Europe. It was initiated in 1992 by Adbusters. Activists themselves may consider the actual shift in everyday purchasing patterns 'far more important' and regard BND as a 'fairly low profile event which presents an opportunity to focus on anti-consumerist issues', as one organizer of BND in York, England, put it, or as a 'media event which can be used to diffuse a mentality, a concern, a type of consumer', as the Italian editor of *Altraeconomia*, the main alternative economy magazine and sponsor of BND in Italy, states.[41] Yet, for the social analyst BND is important on at least two counts. First, there is the form of protest. With its reliance on Internet connections as well as a host of local environmental, consumer and development associations, BND exemplifies the mixture of globalization and localization and the preference for protest techniques which try to get the message across through surrealistic actions, an important feature of new social movements.[42] Second, there are the themes which are articulated in the protest. BND campaigners ask each individual to be 'a consumer-hero' rather than a 'consumer-zero', by 'standing up against the pressure to buy'. This is presented as a 'simple idea': 'challenging' consumer culture by 'switch(ing) off from shopping for one day' with the hope that it will provide a 'lasting experience' and a moment for redressing our lifestyles: 'you'll feel detoxed from consumerism and realize shopping is less important'.[43] The organizers of BND in the Italian city of Bologna, for example, stress that this is not 'against shopkeepers nor against the government', as these would be 'limited targets'; the real target is 'people themselves, their own way of life as consumers'.[44] Reversing the well-known rhetoric which links private vices to public virtue and which has had so much success in the Western world, the organizers of the BND protest in Birmingham, England, declare that 'overspending on credit cards may indeed improve the economy in the short term, and therefore seem to be patriotic. But over-consumption is the root of global disaster that has already started to crop up: climate change is only one of the many problems it causes. And we all know it doesn't really make us happy.'[45] What seems, at first glance, an invitation to give up consumption and its excesses is indeed a melting pot for the amalgam of many forms of alternative consumption. Environmental, humanitarian, ethical and political motives are all present in the discourses that accompany the Canadian web resources: 'the rich Western countries, only twenty per cent of the world population, are consuming eighty per cent of the earth's natural resources, causing a disproportionate level of environmental damage and unfair distribution of wealth. As consumers we need to question the products we buy and challenge the companies which produce them.'[46]

Most of the themes deployed in the initiative are only superficially close to an ascetic rhetoric of renunciation. While there are attempts to expose 'shopaholicism' as a condition that is reaching epidemic proportions, it is very clear that it is not shopping in itself that is harmful, but rather the fact that people typically shop without considering issues such as the environment and poverty in developing countries. There is a wide variety of themes articulated by the campaigners in this 'anti-consumerist' syndicate – from negotiation of the notion of necessity with respect to the north/south divide, to the environment and sustainable agriculture, to new patterns of consumption relying on self-production. In particular, the separation between consumption and production is exposed and various ways of re-embedding consumer practices in the local natural environment, in communal social relationships and in the production process are recommended. This is mirrored by the idea that product labelling, as advocated by traditional consumerist campaigns, is not enough. 'Ethical consumers' ought to know the 'sustainability cost' of their choices, i.e. how much pollution has been created and how many non-renewable resources have been spent in the manufacture and distribution of any chosen product. Here consumer sovereignty is something other than consumer choice as predicated on the variables singled out by neoclassical economics and free-market ideologies alike (i.e. price and quantity). The value-for-money logic does not hold when the target is not only individual satisfaction but also a set of public goods. Consumer sovereignty itself is predicated not on hedonistic premises but on responsibility. In many forms of alternative consumption there is, to different degrees, an attempt to re-establish a direct relation to goods. Such attempts may be aimed at countering 'risk' and the perception that one is no longer controlling one's material world, as an expanding material culture has led to a separation between the spheres of production and consumption.[47] However, they also signal that the symbolic boundaries that have come to define the 'consumer' as a specific economic identity who lives in a private world removed from production are being destabilized.

Ethical shopping guides offer a fascinating insight into the moral and political problematization of the consumer. On the surface, ethical shopping guides look like catalogues or inventories of where to find information about ethical producers and products. As such they can be considered intrinsic to a larger trend within modern culture which foregrounds the relevance of expert discourse on commodities as articulated by cultural intermediaries for the promotion and legitimatization of (certain) visions of consumption.[48] However, they also turn upside down conventional and well-established discourses of use and recommendation, subverting hegemonic lifestyles and dominant views of consumption. For example, *Ethical Consumer* – a major association for ethical and responsible purchases in the UK – offers its constituency a magazine which professes to be a guide to 'progressive products', helping to avoid unethical products and providing a list of 'ethical

Best Buy' options.[49] Best buys are indeed defined through a variety of ethical criteria, i.e. criteria exceeding short-term, self-oriented hedonistic consumer action and embracing long-term effects on a variety of third parties. They include the impact on the environment (pollution, nuclear power, etc.), on animals (animal testing, factory farming, etc.), on humans (oppressive regimes, workers' rights, irresponsible marketing, etc.) and 'extras', which involve more than one party, such as the use of GM. In the case of food, ethical shopping guides entail a shift in the way food is classified as 'good to eat': issues most conventionally related to food quality, such as safety and health, taste and aesthetic pleasure, are very marginal while the environment, human rights or workers' labour conditions become primary concerns.[50] Ethical shopping guides provide a set of specific criteria of choice drawing on political and ethical codes and principles. As explained by the Editor of *I CARE*, an alternative consumption magazine based in Pisa, Italy, which has also published a best-selling critical consumption guide, 'the first pages of our guide are extremely important, there we explain which criteria we base our choice of products on ... distinguishing features are essentially referred to the social question in a broad sense, peace, environment and democracy: these are, as it were, the four cardinal coordinates for all products'.[51]

Similar guides are typically concerned with more than offering a set of ethical criteria for the evaluation of products and producers. The discourses surrounding ethical shopping have to do with 'orders of justifications' which have been pushed outside the dominant mode of legitimatizing markets in Western culture, i.e. the redistribution of resources and the role of demand. They promote a particular image of the consumer as correct, i.e. truthful and right. Reference to the conditions of labour in general and child labour in particular, as well as to the north/south divide, are the main codes marshalled for reframing the role of the consumer. Proposing that consumers are 'raising consciousness' and 'becoming aware' of what 'consumption really is', a recent guide to ethical shopping, for example, constructs its readership as one made up of 'consumers concerned about the working conditions under which the products they buy are produced in developing countries'. Once consumers realize that what the Western world consumes is 'subsidized by the poor' in the form of unsafe and underpaid labour and the exploitation of natural resources, it assumes, they will 'pressurize' retailers, producers and governments to change their practices and bring about an 'equitable world trading system'.[52] Free trade and globalization are said to have removed the protecting influence of the nation-states and the local communities; it is consumers themselves who are presented as uniquely having the power and duty to safeguard both fair economic distribution and the natural environment.

The 'Consumer' as a Subject of Power and Duty

The moral and political discourses which define the frame of critical consumerism play with different orders of justification. They can be conceptualized as drawing on repertoires of evaluation or 'orders of worth' and 'justification' which exist prior to the individual and are available across situations, even if they are realized, made salient and transformed by individuals in particular settings and circumstances.[53] Critical consumerism is intrinsically oppositional. Organized through practices and episodes of contestation, it reveals how these repertoires work and attain wider relevance. Whether successful or not, these discourses make explicit what in normal circumstances is implicit and taken for granted. Critical consumerism may thus be seen as a multi-level phenomenon which involves different classification processes – some of which are identified as practical, others as discursive. Considered as a normative frame, critical consumerism engages directly with the hegemonic legitimatizing rhetoric which emerged in the eighteenth century to justify market societies and modern cultures of consumption. Such rhetoric entailed a particular political morality, epitomized not so much by the supposed de-moralization of luxury, but by the entrenchment of a new sphere of action and order of justification for commodity consumption. Consumption became a private matter, constructed in opposition to production and envisaged as the pursuit of private happiness linked to virtuous mechanisms in the public sphere – as in Mandeville's famous motto 'private vices, public virtues'.[54] As a frame, critical consumerism takes issue with the idea that consumers are and should be private economic hedonists, preoccupied with individual pleasures, and proposes, both for the good of the consumer and society, that the former be virtuous so as to offset the vices of both the market and politics.

The identity which is thus bestowed on consumers draws on themes which cut across the different symbolic boundaries and orders of justification which have consolidated in the course of modernity. Themes prevalently associated with the promotion of consumption as a legitimated sphere of action *per se* – 'taste', 'good taste', 'pleasure', 'fantasy', 'comfort', 'distinction', 'happiness', 'refinement', and so on – are substituted by themes prevalently associated with the definition of a democratic public sphere and rationalized production. The political and moral discourses informing critical consumerism in Italy, the UK and the United States portray the consumer as essentially *active*. They often resort to a vocabulary which draws either on social and political activism (to purchase is to 'vote', 'protest', 'make oneself heard', 'change the world', 'help the community', 'mobilize for a better future', and so on) or on production (to purchase here becomes

Figure 12 Bilanci di Giustizia, 2004, 'Reform your lifestyle' (www.bilancidigiustizia.it), elaboration on US War Poster, US Army, 1942, Minneapolis Public Library

Source: Bilanci di Giustizia.

'work you do for the community', 'effort done for yourself and the other', 'effective', 'productive', and so on).

These metaphors of political activism and production also emerge in visual representations, as in a recent image created by Bilanci di Giustizia, a radical association for the promotion of frugal lifestyles and critical consumption in Italy. Drawing on an American Second World War poster that itself had been influenced by socialist iconography, the image portrays consumers as well-organized worker-soldiers who, armed with pencils, march together to change the world.[55] More generally, the discourses addressing critical and ethical consumption all tend to stress various strategies which consumers can adopt either to shorten the commodity chain and get closer to producers – relying on various alternative, more direct and informal, forms of distribution – or to reappropriate the process of production itself – baking at home, freezing at home, growing vegetables, collecting wild berries, DIY, and so on, thus implicitly contesting the neat separation between production and consumption which is normatively and institutionally sustained in the global economy. The focus on the consumer as a producer and a political actor on the global scene often passes through a reappraisal of that separation between production and consumption which is associated with the entrenchment of the public/private divide.[56] The production–consumption distinction is denaturalized and exposed as a complex political and ethical relation rather than a neutral mechanism which each consumer can exploit to his or her (supposed) benefit. To this end, the Worldwatch Institute report *Vital Signs* is widely quoted in the various web resources of critical consumption associations in Italy, the UK and the United States. Consumers are invited to 'take action' by considering 'alternative combinations of production and consumption'. Contrary to the classical free-market rhetoric, only more integrated forms of economic life – localized and community based – are deemed capable of giving consumers more control over their choices. The lengthening of the commodity chain is criticized for limiting consumer sovereignty instead of enhancing it: consumers' 'range of choices becomes controlled' by supermarkets and many other intermediary actors, which amount to an often 'transnational' and characteristically 'unelected elite'. Thus consumers must widen the scope of their purchases, asking for more: '[e]ven when a product label is frank, it is not complete. Ethical consumers ought to know how much waste (i.e. pollution) has been created, and how many un-renewable resources have been consumed, in the manufacture of a product, and also in its distribution. A lettuce that has been transported to New York from California costs a lot of "food miles". To be ethical consumers, we need to know the sustainability-cost (the real cost) of what we consume'.[57]

The consumer is posited as active, productive and political. As a political actor, he or she is seen as directly responsible not only for him or herself but also for the world. Blame, far from being just externalized and placed on companies and authorities,[58] is internalized and placed on the self as a consumer. As a consequence, the dominant attitude is that of a re-evaluation of how to consume and what place consumption should take up in daily life.

For the Ethical Consumer group, individual consumers are all powerful if only they 'decide' to be so: with their consumption they will thus encourage 'sustainable businesses that don't exploit or pollute'.[59] Consumer choice becomes a concentrated and influential act: we can 'make a difference with every cup' of coffee, as a well-known book on Fair Trade coffee puts it.[60] As one organizer of the main Fair Trade cooperative in Bologna has noted, 'we may say that, starting from consumption, each of us may come to think, to interrogate many other choices which are connected to it. Thus Fair Trade is a powerful lever, which starts from a small, banal thing, something which we all have to do – like buying coffee – and from there a whole world of decisions is put into question.'[61] It is precisely as such a powerful practice that consumer action is symbolically assimilated to the vote, political action par excellence in parliamentary democracies. While, as Ethical Consumer insists, consumer choices are sometimes said to offer a 'powerful additional tool' to traditional political action which is 'both practical and accessible', more often dominant political tropes are directly evoked to stress the power of the consumer. In the United States, even organizations such as Oneworld, which promotes what it describes as 'an elegant sufficiency', place emphasis on consumer choice as political action. We are invited to consider that 'to buy is to vote': 'we vote "yes" with every purchase we make – a pound of bananas, a tank of diesel fuel – and we vote "No" with every purchase we turn down, forcing the companies to diversify into products we prefer'.[62]

While versions of such a slogan are also present in Italian moral and political discourses promoting critical consumption, the emphasis here is more clearly placed on the possibility of working from within the market in search of locally based alternative economic forms that offer new ways of expressing human creativity. The editor of *ConsumiEtici*, an ethical consumption magazine which cuts across different political groups, for example, offers 'methodological tools rather than ideological ones'. He proposes a 'model of the consumer who reflects on what he or she does but who also knows that one must not always reflect, otherwise reflexive behaviour becomes just depressing. We must be capable of enjoying things ... and for this surely we refer to all those movements which are looking for new forms of expression.' He emphasizes the importance of acting 'through the market': 'I want to say I am in favour not against, we must win not protest, even if it is more difficult.'[63]

Such a proactive and pragmatic attitude, which celebrates micro-subversions possible and enjoyable at the interstices of everyday life, often goes hand in hand with a picture of the 'enemy' constructed in discourses about critical consumption. This enemy includes not only transnational trade institutions, global brands or conventional advertising companies; the enemy is also a certain 'mentality' or 'cultural attitude': a 'culture' of 'waste' and 'profit' in fact, which generates 'indifference' and 'lack of awareness' among consumers and which is responsible for their disempowerment. 'It is not just a matter of practically demonstrating how things may work differently', one of the organizers of Rete di Lilliput, an Italian Catholic network of associations working in the alternative economy stresses, 'but also of hitting that collective imagery which prevents each of us from being bothered.'[64] By working on themselves as 'consumers', social actors can thus act 'from within the system', modifying the terms of economic exchange rather than simply ameliorating its functioning.

Many of the themes that have become marginal in traditional consumer movements are thus once again moving to the fore in 'critical consumerism'. The particularistic, self-interested and instrumental logic of conventional comparative tests – witness the 'value for money' approach of successful magazines such as *Which?* in the UK or *Altroconsumo* in Italy – is exposed as missing the point: consumers are brought into life very much like 'citizens', emphasis is placed on choice as a public, community-oriented and therefore moral and political action, rather than as a self-interested, private and therefore apolitical affair.

Whatever their scope or particular configurations, the model of the consumer endorsed by conventional consumer associations translates the instrumental and numerical mentality typical of private capitalist enterprises for the domestic sphere. Product-testing organizations and conventional consumer-protection movements not only provide rules of choice, establishing themselves as channels for identifying issues and handling complaints, but also entail a particular view of the consumer.[65] They tend to embrace a hegemonic notion of the consumer as guided by instrumental rationality. This notion implies the idea that everything can be compared and leads to the 'exclusion of those dimensions which are not measurable'; value is consequently reduced to just one unit of measurement. What emerges is the 'possibility of formalizing an ultimate principle of choice' based on quality–price analysis.[66] *Which?*, the influential comparative testing magazine in Britain, provides an example of how it constructs its audience as made up of rational self-interested consumers – forward-looking, risk-averse, time-consistent and ascetic. Claiming to supply consumers with 'objective' information on whose basis readers can make their own choices, *Which?* 'both attributes and cultivates in its readers a set of virtuous character traits that constitute the rational consumer. For *Which?*, the value of design is purely functional. It is axiomatic that no rational person would buy a pair of trainers because of the prestige of the manufacturer's label, or a car because of its sleek appearance.'[67] Like other expert risk-reducing discourses, product-testing magazines assume that quality may be translated into objective quantities and that the rational consumer will seek expert advice. 'Objective' information is information that concentrates on use-value as defined by price and quantity, responding to puritanical self-interested consumers.[68]

The discourses which surround alternative and critical consumption indicate a shift in the definition and evaluation of consumer choice as related to its specific location within wider cultural boundaries. As individual consumer choice is charged with power, it appears to be defined less in terms of rights and more in terms of duties. Consumption is seen less as the sphere of negative freedom par excellence and more as a sphere for the exercise of positive freedom, less as a private sphere where the consumer can think only of him/herself and be freed from the constraints, worries and burdens of political and productive imperatives, and more as a public domain defined by consumers' freedom to voice their own moral commitments in order to change politics and the economy. Furthermore, when the consumer is defined as a public and political character, his or her happiness may not be directly correlated to increases in private commodity consumption. Indeed, consumption is often weighted *against* happiness. 'Almost any consumption', Oneworld emphasizes, 'uses up resources. But since one can't live without some consumption ... how could I live just as satisfying with less? People are increasingly experimenting with living simply but more fulfillingly.' Underlying such themes is the idea that the 'growth of material culture does not translate into more happiness' and that people's well-being could be 'reformulated on other grounds', as a concern with 'quality of life' gradually replaces the negative vision of individual choice with community-oriented contents.[69] Far from being seen through the lens of a modernist project, happiness is conceived to involve a re-embedding of people in locality and social relations of direct reciprocity. The framing of the consumer within political consumerism thus comes full circle: it codifies a series of practices which are bound up with a particular vision of what consumers should do for the common good as well as their own happiness.

Concluding Remarks

The literature on consumer practices is full of examples of how social actors use commodities to place moral and political weight on to the world.[70] As consumers people can be deemed normal or deviant, fair or unjust, innocent or corrupting, articulating hegemonic views of consumption, choice and identity.[71] All in all, consumption is a contested moral and political field and, indeed, it is discursively problematized as such; it raises issues of fairness both within and beyond the human community. It is imbued with a set of crucial binaries such as immediate versus delayed gratification, private versus public, nature versus culture, necessity versus luxury, body versus mind, etc. These moral and political issues do not arise after the fact as justifications; they are part of the way we consume, but they also draw on specific repertoires which are sustained by a number of social institutions, from the family to the state, from marketing to consumer associations, from international business to supranational organizations and global social movements. There is a growing historical awareness that consumers 'did not arise as an automatic response to the growth of material culture or commercial society, they had to be made ... through mobilization in civil society and state as well as the commercial domain'.[72] Our analysis of the current framing of the consumer as a political actor suggests that consumers today, perhaps more than ever, are continuously turned into key social figures via symbolic processes which can cut across some of our firmest cultural boundaries.

The discursive problematization of the consumer should thus become an important object of critical analysis; in order to document and to understand contemporary consumer practices and cultures we also have to understand – to paraphrase Max Weber[73] – the 'good reasons' that actors give for their own and others' practices of consumption and the 'type of person' they want themselves to be if and when they do indeed posit themselves as consumers. Of course, this does not mean that we, as social scientists, have to proclaim this or that moralist or political view of consumption or of the consumer. Daniel Miller has recently exposed the temptation to criticize consumption long prevalent among social scientists, showing the poverty of a moral critique which typically holds a deeply ethnocentric view, an ascetic and conservative vision of consumer culture and a pessimistic, elitist theory of consumer identity whereby the 'superficial persona who has become the mere mannequin to commodity culture is always someone other than ourselves'.[74] These comments epitomize what is now a widespread tendency within consumer studies, namely to consider consumers as active and creative subjects that de-commodify goods, de-coding the meanings conveyed by commercial culture. While the emphasis on consumption as resistance and transgression is important, we risk losing its full cultural and historical meaning if we transform it into an ontology of the consumer. In other terms, we should not take what Miller himself considers today's task for consumption studies at face value, i.e. 'to rescue the humanity of the consumer from being reduced to a rhetorical trope in the critique of capitalism'.[75] We rather should consider that such a task is co-terminus with a set of political and ethical discourses which are articulated in the world of consumption in specific practices and institutions. By looking at the discourses accompanying new forms of consumption such as ethical and critical consumption, the adoption of a frugal lifestyle or the preference for Fair Trade goods, we can start asking *when* and *how*, under *which conditions* and to *what effect* consumption might be the means people use to create the identity they feel they have lost as labourers or use mass goods to counter the homogenization of capitalist production, rather than suppose that this is precisely what consumption is *per se*.

If we should leave moral criticism to the philosophers, we can and indeed should as social and cultural analysts consider very closely the ways in which consumer goods and practices are moralized and the consumer posited as a particular social actor. Moral and political discourses about consumption and the consumer offer a perspective on the processes of classification which are coextensive with consumer practices and otherwise remain taken for granted. In this view, discourses about consumption are best taken as a set of diverse situated practices, which are assembled in specific contexts and which reflect more or less directly the consumer practices they describe and/ or the moral and political order they take for granted, promote or otherwise qualify. While considering consumers' experience as ordered and patterned, and material culture as a means to fix the categories of culture or objectify people's values,[76] the sociology and anthropology of consumption have not been very keen to pursue the study of discourse in this way. To proceed in this direction and strike the right balance between due consideration of the discursive and parody of the semiotic fallacy, we need further examination of discourse as a reflexive and normative practice. Actions and accounts are mutually constitutive; accounts construe and support the reality of those situations which they comment upon, while they are reflexively linked to the socially organized occasions of their use.[77] As they address consumption and consumers, accounts offer a normative vision, drawing on discursive repertoires and working as a frame orienting action and constituting subjectivity. Just as the notion of consumer sovereignty has worked as a normative claim which helped construct a specialized sphere of action, so the political framing of the consumer, which builds on and promotes his or her capacity to resist market disentanglement, constructs an ideal image of consumers.[78] In both cases, the consolidation of a normative frame draws on practices and has an effect on them; and in both cases practices also engage with other framings and repertoires in such ways as to reproduce or tease wider cultural boundaries. In this chapter, looking at 'critical consumerism' as a particular framing of both consumption and the consumer, I have tried to show how consumer culture is constituted as a culture both *for* consumers and *of* consumers, both a set of commodities for people to consume and a set of representations of people as consumers, with the latter working as an intrinsically normative way of encoding the varieties of meanings associated with consumption practices.

Notes

1. K. Kish Sklar, 'The Consumer White Label Campaign of the National Consumers' League 1898–1919', in S. Strasser, C. McGovern and M. Judd (eds), *Getting and Spending: European and American Consumer Societies in the 20ᵗʰ Century* (Cambridge, 1998). At the time consumer concerns were not as separate from labour interests as they became later on during the Naderist phase in the 1960s; on the contrary, the ideal was that of 'citizen consumers' rather than of the 'consumer customer', see E.A. Cohen, *A Consumers' Republic: The Politics of Mass Consumption in Postwar America* (New York, 2003); L.B. Glickman, 'The Strike in the Temple of Consumption: Consumer Activism and Twentieth Century American Political Culture', *Journal of American History*, 88(1) (2001), pp. 99–128; C. McGovern, 'Consumption and Citizenship in the United States, 1900–1940', in Strasser *et al.* (eds), *Getting and Spending*, pp. 37–58. An excellent discussion of the development of the consumerist movement in Britain, which shows the shifts of consumer protection initiatives from working-class preoccupations with necessity to middle-class management of affluence, can be found in M. Hilton, *Consumerism in Twentieth Century Britain: The Search for an Historical Movement* (Cambridge, 2003). For the changing interface between the social identities of the citizen and the consumer, see M. Daunton and M. Hilton (eds), *The Politics of Consumption: Material Culture and Citizenship in Europe and America* (Oxford and New York, 2001), and F. Trentmann and P.L. Maclachlan, 'Civilising Markets: Traditions of Consumer Politics in Twentieth-century Britain, Japan and the United States', in M. Bevir and F. Trentmann (eds), *Markets in Historical Contexts* (Cambridge, 2004), pp. 170–201.
2. On boycotts see in particular N. Craig Smith, *Morality and the Market: Consumer Pressure for Corporate Accountability* (New York, 1995);

M. Friedman, *Consumer Boycotts: Effecting Change through the Market-place and the Media* (New York, 1999). Generally on the history of consumer mobilization and the framing of the consumer as a political actor, see F. Trentmann (ed.), *The Making of the Consumer: Knowledge, Power and Identity in the Modern World* (Oxford and New York, 2005). See also M. Micheletti, *Political Virtue and Shopping: Individuals, Consumerism and Collective Action* (London, 2003); M. Micheletti, A. Follesdal and D. Stolle (eds), *Politics, Products and Markets: Exploring Political Consumerism Past and Present* (New Brunswick, 2004); Y. Gabriel and T. Lang, *The Unmanageable Consumer: Contemporary Consumption and Its Fragmentation* (London, 1995).

3. M. Foucault, 'The Subject and Power', in H.L. Dreyfus and P. Rabinow (eds), *Michel Foucault: Beyond Structuralism and Hermeneutics* (Chicago, 1983).

4. According to Michele Micheletti, political consumerism includes 'actions by people who make choices among producers and products with the goal of changing objectionable institutional or market practices ... Political consumers are the people who engage in such choice situations. They may act individually or collectively. Their market choices reflect an understanding of material products as embedded in a complex society and normative context.' While acknowledging historical precedents, Micheletti conceives political consumerism essentially as a 'new' form of 'political participation', which indicates that 'citizens are looking outside traditional politics and civil society for guidelines to help them formulate their more individualized philosophy of life and live as good citizens' (Micheletti, *Political Virtue and Shopping*, pp. 2ff.). The emphasis in her work, as in most political scientists' work, is not on consumption but on political participation. Thus critical and alternative consumer practices are equated with political actions and considered against the background of other forms of participation rather than in the context of consumer cultures, identities and lifestyles. To open up this equation and prioritize consumption as the focus of analysis I prefer to use the term 'critical' consumerism.

5. The survey was conducted during October–November 2002 as part of the EU research project 'Trust in food'. See C. Poppe and U. Kjaernes, *Trust in Food in Europe: A Comparative Analysis* (Oslo, 2003). See also www. trustinfood.org.

6. Worldwatch Institute, *State of the World 2004: A Worldwatch Institute Report on Progress toward Sustainable Society* (Washington, 2004, chapter 1).

7. For data on Fair Trade see EFTA, *Fair Trade in Europe* (EFTA, 2002), and www.efta.org; on organic produce see M. Youssefi and H. Willer, *The World of Organic Agriculture 2003, Statistics and Future Prospects* (IFOAM, 2003), and www.ifoam.org.

8. This view is borrowed from G. McCracken, *Culture and Consumption: New Approaches to the Symbolic Character of Consumer Goods and Activities* (Bloomington, 1988), which applies it to luxury objects. Consumption in this guise is profoundly ambivalent because it enables people to carry on living in an imperfect world, believing that perfection can eventually be reached through the accumulation of objects.

9. Micheletti, *Political Virtue and Shopping*, especially chap. 2; M. Friedman, *Consumer Boycotts*.

10. L.B. Glickman, 'Born to Shop? Consumer History and American History', in L.B. Glickman (ed.), *Consumer Society in American History: A Reader* (Ithaca, 1999), pp. 1–16. Glickman indeed considers that consumption and its political aspects are crucial for the formation of American identities and ideologies. See also Cohen, *A Consumers' Republic*, and D. Vogel, 'Tracing the American Roots of the Political Consumerism Movement', in Micheletti *et al.* (eds), *Politics, Products and Markets*, pp. 83–100.

11. See Y. Bar and N. Bromberg, 'The Nestlé Boycott', *Mothering* (Winter, 1995), pp. 56–63; W.L. Bennett, 'Branded Political Communication', in Micheletti *et al.* (eds), *Politics, Products and Market*, pp. 101–25; J. Peretti (with M. Micheletti), 'The Nike Sweatshop Email: Political Consumerism, Internet, and Culture Jamming', in Micheletti *et al.* (eds), *Politics, Products and Market*, pp. 127–44; A. Ross (ed.), *No Sweat: Fashion, Free Trade, and the Rights of Garment Workers* (New York, 1999); J. Vidal, *Mclibel: Burger Culture on Trial* (New York, 1997).

12. For a similar perspective see what Luc Boltanski and Laurent Thévenot suggested in more general terms about the market and the consolidation of different 'orders of worth' in modern society, in L. Boltanski and L. Thévenot, *De la justification* (Paris, 1991).

13. Adbuster is a non-profit organization based in Vancouver that publishes an 85,000 circulation magazine (60 per cent in the US) concerned with the 'erosion of cultural and natural environment by commercial forces' and adopts a 'fun approach' to protest. An example of how Adbusters culture jammers work is to try to disclose 'who is behind some of the world's most popular brands', inviting people to put up in offices, coffee shops or local supermarkets a poster illustrating a set of familiar food items which are in fact produced by tobacco companies. See www.adbuster.org.

14. These subversive strategies may be described as a 'semiotic guerrilla warfare' (U. Eco, *Travels in Hyperreality* (New York, 1986)) and are considered increasingly typical of contemporary social movements; see K. Nash, *Contemporary Political Sociology: Globalization, Politics and Power* (Oxford, 2000). They can be traced back to the Dada and the Surrealist movements and their aesthetic practices of collage which articulated the anarchic idea that a new 'surreality' would emerge through the subversion of common sense, the collapse of dominant categories and dichotomies and the celebration of the forbidden and the abnormal.

15. A.O. Hirschman, *Exit, Voice and Loyalty* (Harvard, 1970).

16. U. Beck and E. Gernsheim, *Individualisation* (London, 2001), p. 44.

17. See in particular U. Beck, *The Reinvention of Politics: Rethinking Modernity in the Global Social Order* (London, 1997), and A. Giddens, *Runaway World: How Globalisation is Reshaping Our Lives* (London, 1999). These observations build also on recent political science scholarship on citizenship. The increase in individual skills, as a consequence of the improvement in educational levels and in the information available to the public, is seen as creating citizens who are more aware of the possible causes of social malfunctioning and have greater capacities and means to articulate their dissatisfaction; see R.J. Dalton, *Citizen Politics* (Chatham, 1996). The rise of new forms of political participation is often associated with a growing distrust among citizens of traditional political institutions, particularly regarding the ability of political institutions to control new uncertainties; see P. Norris, *Critical Citizens* (Oxford, 1999).

18. U. Beck, *The Reinvention of Politics: Rethinking Modernity in the Global Social Order* (London, 1997).

19. M. Douglas, *Thought Styles* (London, 1996), p. 86.

20. For further discussion see R. Sassatelli, 'Trust, Choice and Routine: Putting the Consumer on Trial', *Critical Review of International Social and Political Philosophy*, 4(4) (2001), pp. 84–105, and R. Sassatelli, *Consumer Culture: History, Theory and Politics* (London, Forthcoming).

21. This develops Foucauldian themes that I considered in R. Sassatelli, *Fragments for a Genealogy of the Consumer Society: History in Perspective* (Norwich, Discussion Papers in Public Choice and Social Theory, Discussion Paper 25, University of East Anglia, April 1996).

22. See Trentmann and Maclachlan, 'Civilising Markets'.

23. U. Eco, *Apocalypse Postponed* (Bloomington, 1994 [1964]), pp. 17 and 20.

24. On vegetarianism see A. Beadsworth and T. Keil, 'The Vegetarian Option: Varieties, Conversions, Motives and Careers', *The Sociological Review*, 40(2) (1992), pp. 253–93; K. Tester, 'The Moral Malaise of McDonaldization: The Values of Vegetarianism', in B. Smart (ed.), *Resisting McDonaldization* (Sage, 1999), pp. 207–21; on green consumption and environmentally friendly products see W. Belasco, *Appetite for Change* (Ithaca, 1993); A. James, 'Eating Green(s): Discourses of Organic Food', in K. Milton (ed.), *Environmentalism* (London, 1993), pp. 205–18; on organic and 'natural' products see M. Miele and D. Pinducciu, 'A Market for Nature', *Journal of Environmental Policy and Planning*, 3 (2001), pp. 149–62; J. Murdoch and M. Miele '"Back to Nature": Changing "Worlds of Production" in the Food Sector', *Sociologia Ruralis*, 39(4) (1999), pp. 465–83; on the promotion of local traditions and especially as related to the Slow Food movement see A. Leich, 'Slow Food and the Politics of Fat', *Ethnos*, 68(4) (2003), pp. 437–62; J. Murdoch and M. Miele, 'The Practical Aesthetics of Traditional Cousins, Slowfood in Tuscany', *Sociologia Ruralis*, 42(4) (2002), pp. 312–28; on Fair Trade see I. Hudson and M. Hudson, 'Removing the Veil?', *Organization & Environment*, 16(4) (2003), pp. 423–30; M. Levi and A. Linton, 'Fair Trade: A Cup at a Time?', *Politics & Society*, 31(3) (2003), pp. 407–32; M.C. Renard, 'Fair Trade: Quality, Market and Conventions', *Journal of Rural Studies*, 19 (2003), pp. 87–96.
25. C.C. Williams and C. Paddock, 'The Meaning of Alternative Consumption Practices', *Cities*, 20(5) (2003), pp. 311–19.
26. S. Lockie and L. Kristen, 'Eating Green', *Sociologia Ruralis*, 42(1) (2002), pp. 23–40.
27. See www.newdream.org.
28. For an attempt to consider both the ordinariness and the ethical dimension of alternative consumption see C. Barnett and P. Cloke, 'Consuming Ethics: Articulating the Subjects and Spaces of Ethical Consumption', *Antipode*, 37(1) (2005), pp. 23–45.
29. M.G. Zinkhan and L. Carlson, 'Green Advertising and the Reluctant Consumer', *Journal of Advertising*, 24(2) (1995), pp. 1–16. For a more critical approach see P. Kennedy, 'Selling Virtue', in Micheletti *et al.* (eds), *Politics, Products and Market*, pp. 21–44.
30. For the crucial and contradictory role of labelling schemes, see A. Kolk and R. van Tulder, 'Child Labour and Multinational Conduct: A Comparison of International Business and Stakeholder Codes', *Journal of Business Ethics*, 36 (2002), pp. 291–301; A. Jordan, R.K.W. Wurzel

and A.R. Zito, 'Consumer Responsibility-taking and Eco-labelling Schemes in Europe', in Micheletti *et al.* (eds), *Politics, Products and Market*, pp. 161–80.

31. IMF, *World Economic Outlook* (Washington, 2003); UNDP, *Human Development Report 2003* (Oxford, 2003).

32. See A. Appadurai, *Modernity at Large: Cultural Dimensions of Globalization* (Minneapolis, 1996), and R. Robertson, *Globalization: Social Theory and Global Culture* (London, 1990). An example of this is the development of Slowfood, an Italian-born eco-gastronomic organization which has rapidly become an international actor in the global promotion of the local (www.slowfood.org). Movements for the safeguarding of local produce and territories have also developed elsewhere in the world. A well-known example is Navdanya ('nine seeds'), founded in India in 1987 by Vandana Shiva (www.navdanya. org); see Sassatelli, *Consumer Culture*, chap. 8.

33. See L.W. Bennett, 'Branded Political Communication: Lifestyle Politics, Logo Campaigns and the Rise of Global Citizenship', in Micheletti *et al.* (eds), *Politics, Products and Market*, pp. 101–26.

34. Micheletti, *Political Virtue and Shopping*, esp. chaps 2 and 3. See also F. Trentmann and P.L. Maclachlan, 'Civilising Markets', and especially F. Trentmann (ed.), *The Making of the Consumer*, which contains many contributions that detail the translation of the consumer into a political subject within various national traditions and socioeconomic spheres.

35. The reaching of global markets may imply an emphasis on efficiency and promotion which can transform green and Fair Trade (FT) products into fetishes. This shows the antinomy between commercial aims and ethical aims. Such antinomy is also the fundamental mechanism of value creation within the FT field, at least as it emerged in the interviews conducted in Italy: activists have stressed the importance of keeping these values synergic to make FT viable and meaningful; they have used this antinomy as the basis for distinguishing between 'real' critical consumers ('activists' and 'committed') and 'lifestyle' or 'fashion-oriented' consumers ready to jump on the bandwagon of FT. The different actors occupying different positions in the field of alternative and critical consumption in Italy display different attitudes with respect to this dichotomy. Activists that work on the commercial end of FT (shops, import organizations) place an emphasis on the positive role of commercialization as 'cultural vector'; those concerned with labelling schemes stress the role of 'good principles'; and the cultural and political entrepreneurs emphasize the risks of commercialization and the role of 'education and awareness'.

36. See M. Harvey, A. McMeekin and A. Warde (eds), *Qualities of Food* (Manchester, 2004).
37. The notion of frame adopted here develops from Goffman's concept which was used to indicate the 'principles of organization which govern events – at least social ones – and our subjective involvement in them', E. Goffman, *Frame Analysis: An Essay on the Organization of Experience* (New York, 1974), pp. 10–11. A frame is a set of 'organizational premises – sustained both in mind and in activity' (p. 247), a 'context of understanding' and a 'membrane' which orientates our perceptions within it (p. 3, and E. Goffman, *Encounters: Two Studies in the Sociology of Interaction* (London, 1961), p. 71). See D. Tannen (ed.), *Framing in Discourse* (Oxford, 1993). Political scientists in particular have often treated it as a way to analyse ideology (see D.A. Snow and R.D. Benford, 'Ideology, Frame Resonance and Participant Mobilizations', *International Social Movements Research*, 1 (1988), pp. 197–217), thus forgetting the interactional and institutional anchoring of the original Goffmanian concept.
38. See D. Goodman, 'Agro-food Studies in the "Age of Ecology": Nature, Corporeality, Bio-politics', *Sociologia Ruralis*, 39(1) (1999), pp. 17–38, and J. Murdoch and M. Miele, 'A New Aesthetic of Food? Relational Reflexivity in the Alternative Food Movement', in Harvey *et al.* (eds), *Qualities of Food*, pp. 1656–75.
39. B. Taylor, 'Buy Different: Building Consumer Demand for Sustainable Goods', *Enough!*, 12, available at www.newdream.org/newletter/buydiffernt.pdf.
40. Douglas, *Thought Styles*, p. 11.
41. Respectively, email interview held in November 2001, telephone interview held in January 2004. For more information see www.adbusters.org; www.buyingnothingday.co.uk; www. Giornatadelnonaquisto.it
42. Adbuster runs a website which celebrates pluralism and the positive side of globalization with links and material from several countries which have taken up the initiative. The variety of local traditions which are accommodated in this 'global' network is evident, for example, in the fact that the emphasis on self-control which is an important theme in the US is not found in the same way in the corresponding UK or Italian context. Comparing US and Italian materials, we find different pictures; in Italy there is a stronger emphasis on no-profit activity and cooperatives and the political and associational landscape is more fragmented. This has obvious effects. On the same day of the BND 2001 there were two competing initiatives: the Organic Breakfast Day and the Food Bank Day

(with activists in front of supermarkets collecting food items to donate to the poor).

43. BND-UK, press release, 23 Nov. 2001.
44. Email interview, November 2001.
45. Email interview, November 2001.
46. BND-UK, press release, 23 Nov. 2001.
47. R. Sassatelli and A. Scott, 'Trust Regimes, Wider Markets, Novel Foods', *European Societies*, 3(2) (2001), pp. 211–42.
48. On the role of knowledge flows in the consolidation of a modern culture of consumption see A. Appadurai, 'Introduction: Commodities and the Politics of Value', in A. Appadurai (ed.), *The Social Life of Things: Commodities in Cultural Perspectives* (Cambridge, 1986). On cultural intermediaries and consumer culture see P. Bourdieu, *Distinction* (London, 1984); M. Featherstone, *Consumer Culture and Postmodernism* (London, 1991).
49. www.ethicalconsumer.org; see also Gabriel and Lang, *The Unmanageable Consumer*.
50. In the paradigmatic case of food, conventional issues of health and safety are still relevant in so far as they offer alternative themes the opportunity to reverberate in larger social circles. The most important competing narratives are indeed themselves often related to episodes of breach of trust in the market brought about by health risks associated with industrial food production and globalization. The BSE crisis, in particular, has been incorporated into the wider movement against McDonald's. In Italy, for example, a 'boycott day' against McDonald's arrived after a case of BSE was discovered in cattle raised for use by McDonald's itself. To broaden their reach and penetrate new sections of the public, the organizers of the campaign can therefore count on a very sensational theme. This is then articulated through the usual environmentalist arguments, such as that meat production entails an inefficient use of resources, as well as criticism of aggressive advertising and fears of globalization and homogenization; see R. Sassatelli, 'The Political Morality of Food: Discourses, Contestation and Alternative Consumption', in Harvey *et al.* (eds), *Qualities of Food*, pp. 176–91.
51. Telephone interview, March 2004.
52. W. Young and R. Welford, *Ethical Shopping* (London, 2002), p. ix.
53. See Boltanski and Thévenot, *De la justification*; see also M. Lamont and L. Thévenot, *Rethinking Comparative Cultural Sociology* (Cambridge, 2000).

54. See further R. Sassatelli, 'Consuming Ambivalence: Eighteenth Century Public Discourse on Consumption and Mandeville's Legacy', *Journal of Material Culture*, 2(3) (1997), pp. 339–60, and Sassatelli, *Consumer Culture*, chapter two.

55. Bilanci di Giustizia (Balances of Justice) is a missionary-style organization, which operates mainly in the centre and north of Italy. Families keep a constant diary of their expenses and publish every year an overview of the social and environmental cost of their lifestyles. See www.bilancidigiustizia.org.

56. Historically, this separation has been coded by gender, with women being mostly confined to the private sphere as the perfect consumer; see V. de Grazia with E. Furlough (eds), *The Sex of Things* (Berkeley, 1996). However, as shown by Matthew Hilton's work on the gendering of consumer politics in twentieth-century Britain, an increasingly gender-neutral category has emerged following the 1950s image of the consumer-housewife. This has been promoted by business groups and an affluent consumer movement which has inscribed consumerism with the values of a male professional class; see M. Hilton, 'The Female Consumer and the Politics of Consumption in Twentieth-century Britain', *The Historical Journal*, 25(1) (2002), pp. 103–28. For a discussion of the continuing relevance of gender in contemporary political consumerism see M. Micheletti, 'Issues of Gender and Political Consumerism', in Micheletti *et al.* (eds), *Politics, Products and Markets*, pp. 245–65.

57. WorldWatch Institute, *Vital Signs 2001* (Washington, 2001), p. 11.

58. Douglas, *Thought Styles*, p. 161.

59. www.ethicalconsumer.org.

60. L. Waridel, *Coffee with Pleasure: Just Java and World Trade* (London, 2002).

61. In-depth interview, June 2004.

62. www.oneworld.net.

63. In-depth interview, October 2004. Historically, Anglo-American and southern European views of how market and personal relations intertwine have differed. In both cases, from the Enlightenment onwards, the market is conceived as making possible a society of horizontal relationships. However, if we consider friendship or genuine reciprocity, Smith believed that the market was the place of instrumental relationships which allowed for the conditions for experiencing true friendship *outside the market*, while Genovesi and the Neapolitan School saw market relationships themselves as relations of reciprocity, see L. Bruni and R. Sugden, 'Moral Canals: Trust and Social Capital in

the Work of Hume, Smith and Genovesi', *Economics and Philosophy*, 16 (2000), pp. 19–46.

64. Telephone interview, September 2004.

65. For a review of the issues and organizations which are part of conventional consumerism with particular reference to the US, see D.A. Aaker and G.S. Day, 'A Guide to Consumerism', *Marketing Management*, 4(1), 1997, pp. 44–8. For a more comparative outlook see R. Sassatelli, *Power Balances in the Consumption Sphere* (Florence, European University Institute, Working Paper 5, September 1995, pp. 1–74). For a perspective on the development of the British consumer movement see Hilton, *Consumerism in Twentieth Century Britain*.

66. L. Pinto, 'Le Consommateur: agent économique et acteur politique', *Revue Française de Sociologie*, 31 (1990), pp. 179–98.

67. A. Aldridge, 'The Construction of Rational Consumption in Which? Magazine: The More Blobs the Better?', *Sociology*, 28 (1994), pp. 899–912, 901. This is in striking contrast with specialized magazines dedicated to particular product categories such as fashion, wine and cars. In opposition to depersonalized authority, scientific analysis and asceticism typical of product-testing magazines, they promote charismatic authority, connoisseurship and a hedonistic outlook; see M. Featherstone, *Consumer Culture and Postmodernism*.

68. It may be possible to suggest some continuity between the 'form of life' of some sectors of the middle class, and in particular the traditional middle class living on a fixed income, and the development of the 'rational consumer'. The traditional middle class on a fixed income is different from the lower classes who are pushed by their precarious status towards a pattern of negative choices with desultory wasting-off expenditure and far from rational calculation (see Pinto, 'Le Consommateur'). They are well distinguished from the entrepreneurial middle class, for whom it is capital which can be stretched and which requires rational calculation. They are also distinct from the new middle class in the media and fashion professions for whom the promotion of self-indulgence in consumption is clearly a means of self-expression (see Bourdieu, *Distinction*, and Featherstone, *Consumer Culture and Postmodernism*).

69. Worldwatch Institute, *State of the World 2004*, pp. 53–4. There is a wide academic literature on this, from *The Joyless Economy* by T. Scitovsky (New York, 1976) to the more recent *An All-consuming Century* by G. Gross (New York, 2000), as well as articulated interdisciplinary discussions on the notion of 'quality of life' and 'welfare' such as M. Nussbaum and A. Sen (eds), *The Quality of Life* (Oxford, 1993).

70. See Douglas, *Thought Styles*, Bourdieu, *Distinction*, and, for an emphasis on the subversive strategies of consumers, M. de Certeau, *The Practice of Everyday Life* (Berkeley, 1984).
71. See R. Sassatelli, 'Tamed Hedonism: Choice, Desires and Deviant Pleasures', in A. Warde and J. Gronow (eds), *Ordinary Consumption* (London, 2001), pp. 93–106.
72. F. Trentmann, 'Knowing Consumers: Histories, Identities, Practices', in Trentmann (ed.), *The Making of the Consumer*, p. 8.
73. M. Weber, *Gesammelte Aufsätze zur Wissenschaftslehre* (Tübingen, 1922); Eng. trans. *The Methodology of the Social Sciences* (New York, 1949), *passim*.
74. D. Miller, 'The Poverty of Morality', *Journal of Consumer Culture*, 1(2) (2001), pp. 225–44.
75. Miller, 'The Poverty of Morality', p. 234.
76. M. Douglas and B. Isherwood, *The World of Goods: Towards an Anthropology of Consumption* (New York, 1979); D. Miller, *Material Culture and Mass Consumption* (Oxford, 1987).
77. Rather than considering consumers as reflexive actors, this perspective develops the ethnomethodological notion of reflexivity as applied to accounts, H. Garfinkel, *Studies in Ethnomethodology* (Cambridge, 1984 [1967]), and brings it closer to Foucauldian concerns, i.e. considering that accounts are embodied practices which sustain the reality of a situation but emphasizing conflict, history and power and discourses as repertoires for mutual understanding and justification which cannot be reduced to situated accounting practices. This allows the consideration of how people from different institutional positions may act differently and, especially, how certain themes and evaluation criteria get entrenched and become hegemonic throughout history: that is, how power and history shape the conditions for mutual understanding. See also R. Sassatelli, 'The Political Morality of Food'; for a discussion of Garfinkel and Foucault see also A. McHoul, 'The Getting of Sexuality: Foucault, Garfinkel and the Analysis of Sexual Discourse', *Theory, Culture and Society*, 3(2) (1986), pp. 65–79.
78. Here I take a position different from both Callon and Miller on the role of mainstream economics wisdom and its various ramifications for public discourse. Callon considers that markets are indeed disentangled realities, disciplined, as it were, by economic expert discourse; Miller considers that neoclassical wisdom offers only a virtual picture of consumption, its ideological function being resisted in practice. Certainly, there is ample evidence that no matter how much market exchanges try to

shut themselves off from other spheres of life, they are, as Polanyi said, 'embedded' in social networks; likewise, we witness daily to what extent the instrumental picture of the consumer is institutionally reinforced and frankly hegemonic in a number of key institutional contexts. Much more research is needed on how these competing views of the consumer and consumption are promoted by a number of institutional actors and indeed mixed and mingled in daily practices. See M. Callon (ed.), *The Laws of the Market* (Oxford, 1998), esp. Callon's 'Introduction', pp. 1–57, and D. Miller, 'Turning Callon the Right Way up', *Economy and Society*, 31(2) (2002), pp. 218–33. See also A. Barry and D. Slater, 'Introduction', *Economy and Society*, 2 (2002), pp. 175–93, and B. Fine, 'Callonistics: A Disentanglement', *Economy and Society*, 32(3) (2003), pp. 478–84.

–10–

Negotiations with the American Way
The Consumer and the Social Contract in Post-war Europe
Sheryl Kroen

In 1989, when the Berlin Wall was dismantled (and sold all over the globe), the world watched anxiously as the two halves of Germany began to reunite. Among the many issues that presented themselves was how the once communist East Germany would be integrated into the consumer democracy of West Germany. The spectacle of East Germans spending their welcome money on jeans was coupled with serious discussions on both sides of the disintegrating wall about the relationship between democracy and consumer capitalism, and in particular about the ability of the West's consumer culture to strengthen and sustain, or to pervert, democracy. The official policy of West Germany envisaged democratization of the East through financial assistance and the active promotion of consumer capitalism. Meanwhile critics, such as Günter Grass, called the West German intervention in the East 'colonization'.[1] Others saw the events of 1989 as an opportunity to offer an alternative to consumer democracy in the form of true socialism, as the founding manifesto of Democracy Now declared: 'Socialism must now find its true, democratic form, if it is not to be lost to history. It must not be lost, for threatened humanity ... needs alternatives to Western consumer society, the prosperity of which is paid for by the rest of the world.'[2] These debates have been reopened in recent years around the enlargement of the European Union and globalization.

It was in the immediate aftermath of the Second World War, in the context of the Marshall Plan, that the framework for these contemporary debates was established. The reconstruction of Western Europe after the Second World War aroused many of the same critical concerns and hopes about the role that consumer capitalism could play in the stabilization and democratization of Europe, again with Germany at the centre of the debate. While productivity and economic recovery were the terms used to mobilize the massive rebuilding of Western Europe under the Marshall Plan, the assumption of the positive and sustaining role of consumption in the solidification of democracy was everywhere apparent.[3] In the words of Ludwig Erhard, the so-called father of the economic miracle in Germany, mass consumption was the keystone of the new social market economy; the informed consumer was the linchpin of freedom and democracy. In the 1950s consumer democracy became a byword of parliamentary rhetoric, and the citizen-consumer was the new subject around whom the new social and political order would be built. Critics also attacked the American conflation of consumer capitalism and democracy; in France, for example, the communist daily *L'Humanité*, rather than crediting the Marshall Planners with 'democratization', accused them of 'Coca-colonization'.[4]

The Marshall Plan is well known as a diplomatic and economic initiative by the United States to rebuild Western Europe after the Second World War. Less well appreciated are the cultural initiatives that were tied to this economic aid package. As historian David Ellwood has explained, 'all European countries accepted a clause which allowed for the dissemination within their borders of information and news on the workings of the Marshall Plan itself. From these premises, barely noticed at the time, sprang the greatest international propaganda operation ever seen in peacetime.'[5] In addition to dispersing funds to rebuild housing, transportation networks and factories, Marshall Plan administrators used 2 per cent of all counterpart funds to organize exhibitions and mobile film shows; they produced pamphlets, radio shows and documentaries; they sponsored concerts, essay contests and photography competitions. American houses were erected to bring American culture to Europe; 'missions' were organized to bring Europeans to witness the American way of life first hand. More influential in some countries than in others, this cultural project everywhere initiated a conversation among Western Europeans and Americans about the ideals and practices on which the social and political order of the post-war period should be founded.

Imagining Europe in the aftermath of the Second World War as a *tabula rasa*, Americans offered a new social contract on which to found a stable, prosperous and democratic political order.[6] In the liberal tradition stretching back to John Locke and Adam Smith, the consenting individual at the heart of this political order was an economic actor; but rather than a property owner, a trader, a merchant or a labourer, the political subject of the post-war order was the consumer. The consumer as a building block of the social and political order had been steadily gaining ground since the eighteenth century, but it was not until after the Second World War, in the context of the Cold War, that the consumer came to be seen as the fundamental historical agent around which a stable, democratic order was to be erected.[7] Certainly this is the vision that gained dominance in the United States at this time;

the consumer came to be seen as the quintessential citizen, and free market capitalism as the necessary medium to ensure democracy. In the thirty years after the Second World War this ideology, of what Lizabeth Cohen has dubbed the Consumers' Republic, became 'almost a national civil religion' and 'provided the blueprint for American economic, social, and political maturation, as well as for export around the globe'.[8] It was to Western Europe that this conception of democracy was 'exported' most aggressively, on the wings of the Marshall Plan. But the Consumers' Republic arrived on a continent that was not a *tabula rasa*, and the social and political ideals propagated by information officers butted up against competing ideals tied to the specific historical experiences of the different nations receiving Marshall Plan aid.[9]

As a result, neither the message of the information campaign nor the methods by which it was propagated were uniform across Europe. If the consumer was presented everywhere as the fundamental building block of a new and stable democratic political order, who that consumer was, who the consumer was meant to replace, how that consumer should act, and the social and political order that could be imagined around the consumer depended on both the agendas of American information officers in different countries as well as the local social and political traditions to which they were responding. As a report presented to the American Congress in 1950 by the Administration of Economic Cooperation in Europe explained: 'The diversity of economic situations, of political organizations and national traditions made it necessary to adapt the information programme to each of the countries of Europe.'[10] The analysis that follows examines three instances of this information campaign, in France, West Germany and Britain, and attends precisely to the ways in which the campaign was adapted in each of these settings. In so doing, it offers a glimpse of the multiple Euro-American negotiations about the consumer and his/her place in the social and political order that began in the immediate aftermath of the Second World War and continue to this day.

France, Germany and Britain: Variations on a Theme

In France, Marshall Plan information officers found themselves in hostile territory and with a clear ideological mission: to counter the active pro-paganda of communists, they had to project a clear and unequivocally positive portrait of what the French had to gain by learning the lessons of American-style consumer capitalism. French men and women questioned the motivations behind the Marshall Plan. They worried about their economy being taken over and controlled by the United States, and about becoming pawns in an inevitable confrontation between the United States and the Soviet Union likely to take place on their soil. After their recent experience under the Vichy government they were also inclined to distrust all 'information' propagated by state officials. The Communist Party and Union (the CGT) actively encouraged these views. All of this put the American information officers in a defensive posture and led the French government to minimize its efforts on behalf of the Marshall Plan propaganda campaign.[11] Unlike their counterparts in West Germany (who enthusiastically cooperated with and helped to transmit the message of the Marshall Plan administrators) and in Britain (where the government led the information campaign), French government officials walked a fine line between fulfilling their obligation to assist in disseminating information on behalf of the Marshall Plan and avoiding the appearance of speaking on behalf of the American government.[12] Handling most of the propaganda effort themselves, American officials tried to be sensitive to their audience. They were respectful of French pride. They relied upon humour and tried to make their radio shows, travelling exhibitions and brochures as entertaining as possible. Their representation of America demonstrated that they were mindful of the critical assumptions and expectations that they had to battle.

One exhibit, *Le Vrai Visage des U.S.A.* (The Real Face of the USA), beautifully illustrates both the message and the methods adopted by the Marshall Plan information officers in France.[13] Between late spring and early autumn of 1951 *Le Vrai Visage* wended its way around France, stopping in Avignon, Paris, Bordeaux, Marseilles, Lille, Montpellier and Clermont-Ferrand. The exhibit was not very large. Constructed for easy transport, to be dismounted and reassembled quickly, the whole thing could fit into four carriages of a train. It did not, for all that, look ramshackle. Surrounded by a neat picket fence, with a large sign announcing the name of the exhibit, it looked like a temporary fairground, designed to entice local inhabitants with an afternoon to kill. Comprised primarily of posters, the exhibit had a portable movie theatre and boasted some modest special effects, like the illuminated Statue of Liberty and an electric billboard with moving text. The exhibit opened with an overview of the United States, described statistically:

> In the United States today:
>   150,000,000 inhabitants
>   65,000,000 wage-earners
>   37,000,000 families
>   15,000,000 union members

Union dues are regularly paid (–3% of wages)
Unions are absolutely independent:
> From employers
> From the state
> From political parties.

The progressive narrowing from all inhabitants of the United States to workers, to members of labour unions, to the nature of those labour unions makes it clear that the 'real' face of the United States presented in this exhibit is that of working-class America. That this was designed to counter a 'false' face of working-class life is made clear in the next triptych, which opens with an image of a worker brandishing a tool, over which is printed in bold type: 'SLAVE OR FREE MAN?' The rest of the exhibit is devoted to illustrating and explaining the secrets of capitalism that allowed American workers to be both free and extraordinarily prosperous, enjoying a standard of living unimaginable in war-ravaged Europe.

The false face of the United States, as well as the reasons why most French men and women shared this misguided view of working-class life in America, are presented only subtly in the exhibit. The radical juxtaposition of 'slave or free man?', for example, is echoed in another poster entitled 'Bluff or reality?', which features images of cars travelling on a multi-lane superhighway. The monthly, glossy, richly illustrated *Rapports France-Etats-Unis*, put out by the Marshall Plan information officers and handed out at the exit of the exhibit, was more direct in its assessment of the French population's assumptions about America. In articles such as 'Voyage to the Land of Productivity' and 'Marx and America' authors brought home the message again and again that Europeans – 'communists and non-communists' alike – shared the fatalistic view propagated by Marx in the nineteenth century that 'capitalism must necessarily reduce the masses to misery'. What the example of the United States proves is that *'Capital* is dépassé'.[14] 'Contrary to what Marx predicted, the rising standard of living [in America] is widespread, and is accompanied by economic and social security for all.'[15] Far from producing class struggle, American capitalism was erasing class difference altogether. The 'level' and 'classless' nature of American society was brought home in articles depicting workers' homes, the homes of servants and regular surveys touting how many Americans owned which kinds of commodities over time. The first triptych of the *Vrai Visage* imparts precisely this message. In answer to the question 'Is he a slave?', a second poster responds 'NO!' and explains: 'He earns time and money for family leisure, and cultural and athletic activities. [His] gains include a reduction of hours worked and an increase in wages.'[16] Supplementing this text are images of workers enjoying consumer prosperity and leisure: workers are pictured in their homes (with 'one television for every six families'), in public facilities such as libraries, and with their families bowling ('20 million Americans are fervent bowlers'). A majority of the exhibit is devoted to underscoring this message about consumer prosperity: image after image depicts workers shopping in fully stocked supermarkets, sitting in their comfortable new houses, walking from the factory to car parks full of cars. The final posters in the exhibit feature several iconic American commodities (a full refrigerator, a washing machine and, of course, a car); these are accompanied by statistics explaining how few hours of labour were required to buy such goods in the United States as opposed to in other countries, in particular in the Soviet Union.

How did American capitalism avoid the misery predicted by Marx and instead deliver this astounding level of prosperity to its workers? What 'new

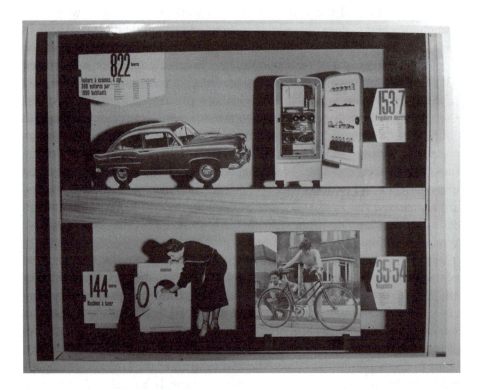

Figure 13 'The Promise of Commodities for All': The Real Face of the USA, France, 1951

Source: Document conserved in the Archives Nationales, Paris, F60ter 394; photograph by the author.

stock of ideas about capitalism' did Americans have to offer Europeans, and especially Europeans such as the French, who clung tenaciously to the dépassé assumptions of Karl Marx?[17] The *Vrai Visage* offers three answers.

First, employers and employees are not adversaries; class struggle has been superseded in the United States by an alliance between workers and their bosses. Only three posters are devoted to this theme: one asks whether employees and employers are enemies or allies; the second asks if the worker has a say in the running of his firm; the third depicts workers and employers around a table, engaging in direct negotiations (where employers speak and write, and workers listen). This final poster also lists the specific means by which workers participated in the running of their firms; these include regular meetings with employers (pictured), suggestion boxes and union representatives. Labour unions or union representatives are, in fact, never shown. When pictured collectively, workers are not striking. Crowds of workers form the backdrop for text explaining the increase in their buying power over the past thirty years. But it is not collective action that has earned these advantages. That point is made indirectly through statistics: only 15 million wage earners out of 65 million even belong to unions (a number inferior to the 20 million workers who are avid bowlers). The same point is underscored in the final three posters featuring commodities along with the labour hours required to purchase them; it is in the countries with the weakest, least organized labour unions where workers benefit most from the prosperity ensured by capitalism (see Figure 13).[18]

The second secret of American capitalism is that its worst abuses have been eradicated – anti-trust legislation has eliminated monopolies, and 'the old-fashioned conception of accumulating wealth for one's individual pleasure has been transformed into a new belief, that wealth entails social obligations, that the head of a company not only owes to his employees, but to society as a whole'.[19] Thanks to an alliance of the government and reform-minded employers, workers enjoy the fruits of public works (one library for every 2,000 inhabitants); they receive unemployment and disability insurance (paid for by the state and by employers), and every worker and young couple receives loans to finance their own home.[20] While the *Vrai Visage* touches upon those aspects of American labour politics and government intervention that ensure that '[t]he worker receives a fair share of the wealth he produces', the overwhelming message of the exhibit is that this is the result of the third and most important secret of American capitalism, namely its organization around the principle of productivity.

At the heart of the exhibit's principle of 'productivity' is not production, but consumption. While Adam Smith argued as early as 1776 that 'consumption is the sole end and purpose of all production; and the interest of the producer ought to be attended to, only so far as it may be necessary for promoting that of the consumer', it took the Keynesian revolution to fully subordinate production to consumption in thinking about capitalism.[21] That revolution took place in post-war America, where in Lizabeth Cohen's words, 'consumers were becoming responsible for higher productivity and full employment, whereas a decade earlier that role had uncontestedly belonged to producers'.[22] The *Vrai Visage*'s focus on productivity offered the opportunity for the United States to signal this shift from production to consumption, from workers to consumers, as the basis for healthy capitalism.

What is striking about the representation of productivity in this exhibit is its complete divorce from the production process. Never, in the course of the entire exhibit, is production represented visually, and when it is invoked in text, it is always in relation to the consumption that makes it possible. The wheel of productivity demonstrates that 'the secret to American prosperity' is increased consumption: for it is increased sales that lead to higher wages and fuller employment, higher production at lower cost, lower prices and therefore more consumption. As consumption fuels production, so are producers, or workers, always transformed into consumers when the exhibit tries to explain their role in the economy. The first poster devoted to productivity contains two captions: first, 'In the U.S.A. one can buy more having worked', and, second, 'The American worker earns more quickly and can buy more'. In poster after poster it is the American worker's buying power that is highlighted. 'His buying power has doubled over the past 30 years'; 'he has the greatest buying power in the world'. What is important is that workers receive 'a fair share of what they produce' and therefore can buy more. The images of the exhibit do even more to erase the production process, and the worker as someone who works.

Of all the images in the exhibit, only one actually depicts something being produced: that is the picture of the house being constructed, with the text explaining that government loans make such a house accessible to workers and young couples. Of the thirteen images depicting workers, only five hint at or directly involve work. Collective shots never show them working, only standing; it is their hard hats and work clothes that mark men as workers, not their labour. By contrast, workers are depicted once leaving a factory to reach a car park full of cars, once at a conference table with their employers, once in a library, once bowling, once in a supermarket, and three times in their well-furnished houses. If workers in America do not apparently work, commodities seem to appear without being produced. Of all the commodities featured in this exhibit, only cars are depicted once near the factory that might have produced them. But this one image is counterbalanced by the three which feature them on highways, on a freight-boat, in the car park of a factory and free-standing in the final poster, connected to labour only abstractly. For the numbers alongside the car indicate the number of hours it would take an average labourer to earn the money to buy it, not to produce it (see Figure 13).

The *Vrai Visage* conveyed a political vision that followed naturally from this portrait of consumer capitalism. The Statue of Liberty and its accompanying moving text ('only in democratic nations do workers have freedom') are the only explicit references to the political order included in the exhibit. But implicit in this economic order is a very specific kind of democratic political order. In the tradition of Adam Smith, the main constituent of the all-inclusive, and therefore democratic, political order is an economic actor; but as the exhibit clearly demonstrates, that economic actor is not a worker, but a consumer. What makes the order 'democratic' is that 'each worker gets a fair share of the wealth he creates'; each worker has 'increased purchasing power'; each worker has the 'right' to a certain level of consumer affluence. Capitalism in France would have to be 'reformed' in many ways: employers and employees would have to learn to cooperate; the economy would have to be reorganized around the principle of productivity. But once these changes were made, French workers – like their counterparts in the United States – would no longer need to rely upon militant (and especially communist) trade unions. They would simply enjoy freedom, security and democracy.

In France the consumer – the new 'rights'-bearing individual at the centre of the democratic social contract – was defined against the worker and all of the political organizations and practices by which he had been defending his rights. In Germany the consumer also took centre stage in the vision of the future propagated by Marshall Plan officials. But the figure it was designed to replace, and the means by which the vision was propagated, were quite different. West Germany, a country that was 'occupied, utterly destroyed by the war, having no "usable" past traditions upon which to draw and resist the "American Way"', was according to many historians 'arguably the perfect breeding ground for consumer democracy. Consumer society was ushered in as a way of rebuilding society in the wake of the war, [making] West Germany more dependent on consumerism in providing meaning and orientation than almost any other nation.'[23] Certainly the message of the Marshall Plan information officers in West Germany and the enthusiasm with which they were aided by German government officials corroborate this view. Unlike France and Britain, which boasted long democratic traditions, West Germany was faced with the prospect of building a new nation and a democratic political order in the wake of National Socialism. That it would embrace an economic definition of both citizenship and the nation, and the consumer-citizen as an alternative to the fascist subject, makes perfect sense in this regard.[24] This, combined with the material devastation of the war and West Germany's position on the front line of the Cold War, made the Marshall Plan and its message both welcome and urgent.

Unlike in France, the Marshall Plan information campaign in Germany was embraced and assisted by government officials in different ministries; its message was propagated far and wide. While there were plenty of exhibits, for example, organized solely by American officials, more commonly Marshall Plan information officers worked closely with German officials and added small stands on the Economic Recovery Programme (ERP) to trade shows and exhibits spearheaded and primarily organized by the Ministry of Finance or local, regional and national organizations.[25] When American information officers took the initiative, the voices and portraits of key German officials were integrated into their presentation; far from remaining distant, as they were in France, government leaders such as Ludwig Erhard continuously gave their official imprimatur and support to these efforts. That the Americans could count on not only official support but also popular support for their campaign is implied by their reliance on participatory activities; photography contests, drawing contests and essay contests invited Germans to represent 'What the Marshall Plan does for you', 'You and the Marshall Plan', 'You and a united Europe'.[26] The photographs, drawings and essays produced by these competitions were themselves turned into exhibitions. Of course the winners were chosen because their message conformed to that of the information officers; but it is important that it was their voices, their representations of the Marshall Plan that were presented all over Germany. (In a more hostile context such as that which prevailed in France, such efforts were attempted rarely and were largely unsuccessful.)[27]

The basic message of the Marshall Plan information officers in Germany involved a representation of American capitalism, and especially consumer capitalism; but unlike in France, its vision of productivity was not pitted so aggressively against production, or the producer. The German National Barge, which travelled to various cities in 1951, illustrates the subtle variations in message that defined the German information campaign.[28] As with most exhibits on the Marshall Plan in Germany, this one opens with a photomontage picturing the country in ruins: cityscapes are covered with rubble; war-damaged factories stand idle and deserted; bedraggled, despairing men and women wait in line for bread. Having tried, unsuccessfully, to rebuild on their own, the Germans in 1947 'stood on the brink of chaos' when America stepped in and offered assistance. The process of reconstruction is explained directly to Hans and Gretchen, prototypical 'free' Europeans who 'want a better life'. Housing is the first thing Hans and Gretchen desperately need, and the exhibit works from this example to demonstrate how American aid is facilitating a full revival of the industrial economy in Germany. From the basic materials necessary to construct the frame of the house (steel, iron and coal), to the glass for windows, to the porcelain and carpets to furnish the house, to the electricity, water, and gas to service it, to the telephone, radio and television that connect it up to the modern world, to the food that the couple needs to survive, the exhibit marches through the stages of industrial and agricultural redevelopment that Germany is experiencing on its march towards 'a better life' for all. If the exhibit initially addresses Hans and his wife as consumers (who want housing and a better life) and production as a means to enable consumption, it shifts gear midway and focuses first on the revival of industry, or production, and then on Hans (but not Gretchen) as a worker, and a union member at that.[29] The text explains: 'Industry benefits – and so does Hans. Because he belongs to a Union.' The 'free, democratic Trades Unions' ensure that Hans gets his fair share of the wealth being produced, higher wages and better work conditions. It is not by striking that workers gain these benefits; as in the *Vrai Visage*, unions are visually represented only through their officials, who negotiate and cooperate with management.

Unlike in the *Vrai Visage*, where workers are never depicted working and commodities appear as if by magic, a large part of this exhibit is devoted to illustrating the production process and, interestingly, the way in which the ERP is enabling not only Germany, but Western Europe as a whole, to resume its economic position in the world. Indeed, in addition to underscoring the reconstruction of industry (one sector at a time), this exhibit is typical of the information campaign in Germany in its continual reference to Hans not only as a consumer and a worker, but as a European. The statistics explaining the revival of industry are European statistics: 'We, the people of Free Europe, mine 32.3% of the world's coal. We own 46.5% of the world's Merchant Fleet. We grow 15.6% of the world's wheat, etc.' This section ends with the flags of countries participating in the Organization of European Economic Cooperation (OEEC), with pictures of their heads of state, and the explanation that 'ALL this wealth, ALL these talents are OURS if we are willing to work together'. Economic cooperation between the eighteen countries of the OEEC will allow Western Europeans to benefit economically; they will get higher wages, more employment; they will fight inflation. And as a result, the political consequences of security and freedom naturally follow. The final image accompanying the caption 'By working together we find security and freedom' features Hans and Gretchen in their fully furnished, modern home with their children. Hence while the reconstruction of various industrial sectors, the unification of Europe and the evocation of Hans as a worker constitute important parts of this exhibit, it begins and ends with Hans and his family enjoying 'security and freedom' defined by the comforts of a modern home. Given the extraordinary housing shortage in Germany after the war, this is not surprising. But as other exhibits sponsored by Marshall Plan information officers in Germany demonstrate, the home became a space for projecting a utopian vision of private consumer prosperity.[30]

The German National Barge exhibit hints at other peculiarly German aspects of the Marshall Plan information campaign. Like the Marshall Plan train and the Europe Train before it, the German National Barge demonstrates the predilection to use forms of transportation to carry but also to house exhibitions. Devices installed within the exhibit also emphasized the wondrous, technological dimension of modern industrial society; visitors did not passively look at photographs and read text, they had to activate displays mechanically by pushing buttons and switches. One exhibit that travelled around Germany in 1953 went a bit too far in this direction; called the 'gadget exhibit', it featured not the kinds of necessary, and much-desired, commodities that showed up in the *Vrai Visage* (like full refrigerators), but totally useless gadgets, supposedly designed to make life easier. Newspaper coverage of the exhibit poked fun at the 'press-a-lite', a gadget that hands you lighted ready-to-smoke cigarettes while you drive, the doggie bell that you put at dog level so he can tell you when he needs to go out, and the goggles you wear in the shower when you wash your hair. One journalist noted ruefully that 'those who want to buy such things will be disappointed, at the moment one can get such things only in the land of limitless opportunity'.[31] While most of the articles laughed at the useless objects and expressed doubt that housewives' lives would be improved by them, this exhibit clearly defined a new consumer horizon for Germans, a world of 'limitless opportunity' and technological marvels that they were not yet in a position to appreciate. 'Alle sollen besser leben' (we will all live better), which appeared in Düsseldorf in the same year, was much more successful; its whiff of the future included an ultra-modern house and a vision of rationalized domestic life organized around packaged, processed foods.[32]

One other feature of the Marshall Plan information campaign in Germany deserves notice: if everywhere in Europe Americans were determined to showcase the fact that capitalism was superior to communism by demonstrating that it afforded 'prosperity' and consumer satisfaction for all, that message was transmitted with particular urgency in West Germany, and especially in West Berlin, which stood on the front line of the Cold War. While Marshall Plan information officers organized special exhibits in West Berlin to be seen as much by East as by West Berliners,[33] the goal of turning the economic miracle in the West into a political lesson for those living in the East was absolutely at the heart of the German government's efforts in these years. In other words, nowhere was the inevitable connection between consumer capitalism and democracy more enthusiastically broadcast than in West Germany. Indeed, as Katherine Pence has argued, '[w]hile the development of mass consumer cultures throughout Europe and in the US featured similar models of consumer-citizenship, ... the problems created by the Cold War ideological struggle across the border heightened the politicization of consumption as each German state claimed to offer its populace the most successful "Economic Miracle"'.[34]

Whereas in France, a country with an active, outspoken and critical communist presence, the prosperous consumer was projected as an alternative to the organized and militant worker, and in Germany the consumer was conceived as the basis for a stable and democratic political order on the front line of the Cold War, in Britain the post-war social and political order was imagined around an austere, self-abnegating consumer. This is because in Britain it was the socialist Labour government which orchestrated the information campaign for the Marshall Plan, and in so doing it articulated its own vision of post-war economic and political reconstruction based on productivity, austerity and fair shares (rather than prosperity) for all.[35] Conceived as a government-sponsored economic education programme that was a natural outgrowth of efforts initiated during the war, ERP information was simply integrated within the framework of propaganda issued by the Labour government. Various divisions of the Central Office of Information organized exhibitions, lectures series, radio shows, film productions and a wide range of publications, which included weekly newspaper reports, richly illustrated brochures and special pay slips placed in the pay envelopes of workers. 'On Our Way', an exhibit that originated in London in 1949 before being sent out to provincial cities, illustrates the basic social and political message of the information campaign in post-war England.

'On Our Way' opened in London in 1949 and was seen by almost 50,000 people within its first eleven days; it shared the *Vrai Visage*'s focus on productivity, although, unlike its French counterpart, what its organizers meant by that was real production, not consumption.[36] Like most of the propaganda put out by the Central Office of Information in these years, this exhibit was explicitly didactic. It was designed to demonstrate that Britain was definitely 'on [her] way' to economic recovery. But the secret to that recovery was based on a combination of production and the abstention from consumption. 'The Four-Point Plan for Britain', the opening installation that gave an overview of the steps Britain was taking towards recovery, gives a taste of the dry, economic principles the exhibit was designed to convey. This installation explained that Britain must: '1) Export more, especially to dollar countries; 2) Supply ourselves; 3) Help the non-dollar countries to recover; and 4) Import less from dollar countries.'[37] In the four life-sized dioramas that constitute this opening installation there is only one visual representation of consumption. Under the rubric 'Supply ourselves', there is a scene of a family in a modest house. But visually this scene occupies a minor place compared to the range of activities depicted in the other three stalls. There is no question that what is fuelling the economic recovery is not this one modest representation of domestic consumption, but the work taking place in adjacent stalls (where men are tending machines) and the preparation of goods for export (men are handling cartons of finished goods). 'Export,' 'Supply ourselves' and 'Import less' all rely upon increased production, and that process is represented quite literally in whole installations that feature workers, machines and the products of their labour. Hence the display on agricultural production, entitled 'More wheat, barley and potatoes', features a man on a large tractor; the display entitled 'more production of textiles' has two women tending to a loom.

Even the displays that represent production more abstractly always emphasize the manufacturing process and real and tangible products. Hence the display illustrating 'Production of Rolling Stock – to improve transport – to sell abroad' does not feature workers but machinery. An oversized, two-dimensional diagram of a machine invites viewers to peer into three windows that reveal its complicated, three-dimensional inner workings. The 'Production of Iron and Steel' features a large poster with cartoon-like drawings of cars, sewing machines and trains. These flat, two-dimensional representations of products stand behind a large, real-life, dirty vat of the type that would have been used to make the materials from which they were manufactured. In the display focusing on 'The Production of Vehicles – to improve transport – to sell abroad' ten larger-than-life, three-dimensional tools are affixed to a poster with flat, industrial drawings of two cars. The tools of the production process are thus given primacy over the cars they produce. A smaller poster next to this one translates this process into statistics, demonstrating in tangible terms the improvement in Britain's productivity over the last year. There were 17 per cent more passenger cars and chassis, 10 per cent more commercial vehicles and chassis, 12 per cent more locomotives, and 20 per cent more wagons produced in 1948 than in 1947. A quick comparison with the representation of the desirable, finished car in *Le Vrai Visage*, next to the statistics translating hours of labour into consumption of this commodity, makes it clear how much 'On Our Way' reinscribes labour and the manufacturing process in its representation of 'The Production of Vehicles' (see Figure 13).

Just as 'The Production of Rolling Stock' and 'The Production of Vehicles' installations emphasize the goal of selling these tangible products abroad, the display of textile production more clearly articulates the point that if British production is making consumption possible, it is for foreigners not for Britons. The 'Production of Textiles' section of the exhibition is comprised of four separate installations, which look like department store windows without glass. Three of the displays form a line and share the same basic design; richly woven fabrics and feather boas are enticingly hung from the wall; above each 'window' is a caption defining its products' composition: 'Rayon, Wool and Silk'. Shelves with spools of thread separate the three contiguous stalls; the manufacturing process by which these fabrics were made is thus evoked by the presence of the raw materials. The fourth stall is set apart and is the only one with a mannequin, with finished products as opposed to fabrics, and no allusion to the process by which the featured clothing was actually produced. Here a dark-haired female mannequin stands gracefully, wearing a flower-print evening gown; she is framed by a curtain and looks like an actress on a stage. Clearly this is the only one of the four stalls explicitly displaying an enticing commodity; just as clear is the exclusion of British viewers as potential consumers of this commodity, for the caption below the mannequin's feet reads 'Textiles for Export' (see Figure 14).

Another display, featuring the exterior of a shop, defines the austere vision of British consumption more overtly. On the door is a sign marked 'Open', but the viewer is not invited to enter, nor is he or she able to see any of the products that are within. Rather, the title of the installation invites the viewer to consider 'How shall we manage in 1952?', and a chalkboard, leaning up against the shop front, explains ominously: '1952 (or sooner) MARSHALL AID ENDS. Now about ⅛ total imports – food + raw materials – come from dollar countries + are not paid for with exports. After 52 we shall have only what we produce or can pay for ourselves.' At the front of the shop, where one would expect to see a window displaying goods available for purchase, one sees a printed sign that reads: 'We shall grow still more at home. But we shall import only what we can pay for ourselves.' If this display invites the

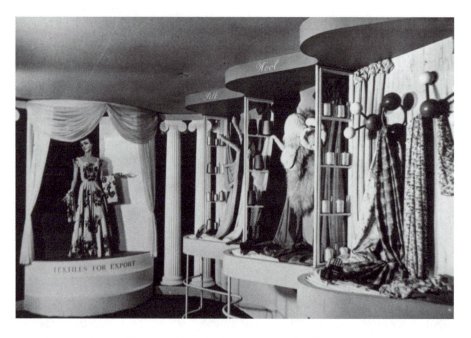

Figure 14 'Commodities for Export': On Our Way, London, 1949

Source: Document conserved in the Archives Nationales, Paris, F60ter 393; photograph by the author.

British viewer to imagine him/herself as a consumer, it is a consumer who must accept continued austerity in order to ensure the healthy recovery of the economy (see Figure 15). (Again, the contrast with the images of full supermarkets brimming with happy consumers in the *Vrai Visage* and the futuristic displays of packaged and processed foods in *Alle sollen besser leben* highlights the austere vision of consumption represented here.) There is only one installation that directly represents the consumer in Britain. This is the final display of the exhibit, which features a shady looking rat, with its too-fancy clothes and beady, suspicious eyes. The text above identifies this rat as engaging in the wrong kind of consumption that would hurt the recovery project in Britain, namely consumption on the black market.[38]

Far from projecting a vision of consumer prosperity, 'On Our Way' anticipated continued austerity, a few more years of working hard and making do. If not addressed directly in this exhibit, the Labour government's view that sacrifice in the short term was the price to be paid for 'fair shares for all' later on was articulated repeatedly in its wide-ranging information campaign.[39] This socially democratic conception of consumption emerged in Britain towards the end of the First World War, when the basic regulation

Figure 15 'The Shop: Austerity and Fair Shares (Not Prosperity) for All': On Our Way, London, 1949

Source: Document conserved in the Archives Nationales, Paris, F60ter 393; photograph by the author.

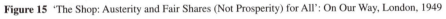

of foodstuffs became a central political problem and reached its apogee during the 1940s; accounts of rationing during and after the war and the general consensus regarding fair shares that historians have found in personal accounts of the black market all help to explain the central social and political significance of the austere consumer represented in 'On our Way'.[40] This frugal, self-sacrificing, socially conscious consumer was represented along with the all-important producer, whose dignified and essential labour offered the basis for economic recovery, political stability and democracy in the post-war period.[41]

Negotiations with the 'American Way'

As the undisputed leader of the capitalist world after the Second World War, the United States was in a position to set the terms of the debate regarding the social and political order that could and should reign in war-torn Europe. The massive aid they provided to Western Europe and the 2-per cent clause requiring dissemination of information about the Marshall Plan gave them the means to propagate a vision of a new social contract organized around the consumer, of democracy as inevitably tied to and sustained by free-market capitalism. But as this newly consolidated American vision of consumer democracy made its way to Europe on the wings of the Marshall Plan, it was adapted to specific local circumstances. When French, West German and British men and women came to exhibitions like *Le Vrai Visage des U.S.A*, the German National Barge and 'On Our Way' to get a glimpse of their future, the vision they were offered was inscribed in time and place and was far from perfectly consonant with the ideals of the Consumers' Republic. Long-standing social and political traditions, the specific recent experience of the two world wars and of fascism, and the local engagement in the Cold War gave Europeans in different countries very different ways of imagining the social and political order after the Second World War. In the immediate aftermath of the war, just as the United States was abandoning the New Deal order and putting its faith in capitalism itself instead of in the interventionist state, Western Europe was solidifying its commitment to the welfare state, a state whose responsibility it was to ensure social rights as well as democracy for all European citizens. In that sense one can speak of a socially democratic 'European Way' that countered the 'American Way' in the decades after the war. Certainly many scholars have stressed this basic opposition between Western Europe and the United States.[42] Yet if one can speak generally of the European commitment to social democracy, the specific ways in which different countries imagined and institutionalized a new social and political order in this new age of consumer capitalism were quite different.

In the case of France, domestic sympathy for communism and a long history of working-class activism and organization inspired Marshall Plan administrators to use the *Vrai Visage* and magazines such as *Rapports France–Etats-Unis* to proffer the prosperous, satisfied consumer as an antidote to and replacement for the militant worker. The producer gave way to the consumer; production was fully subordinated to consumption; commodities were represented as fully independent, magical mediators of the social order. The same representation of the benefits of consumer capitalism could be found in other countries where communist sympathy was an ongoing problem, countries such as Italy.[43] But in France the unilateral presentation of consumer capitalism by Marshall Plan information officers inspired aggressive criticism; exhibits such as the *Vrai Visage* were physically attacked by communist union members.[44] Trade unions and political parties on the left continuously struggled to maintain freedom of action for workers and the real representation and influence of labour.[45] In

France the post-war period also saw a confrontation with the easy conflation of consumer capitalism and democracy, and the merging of the categories of the consumer and the citizen. Intellectuals and political figures criticized not only the message of the Marshall Plan, but also the means of modern consumer capitalism (the extensive use of advertising and public relations as a suspicious alternative to real, democratic practices). This negotiation about the substance and methods of the Consumers' Republic gave rise to some of the funniest artistic representations of American-style consumer society, as well as to some of the most influential critical theory to date on the relationship between consumer capitalism and democracy.[46] Building on a tradition that dates back to the late nineteenth century, France also saw the emergence of vibrant political movements that insisted upon the active and critical role of the consumer in curbing the dangerous tendencies of capitalism, ensuring social rights and protecting a way of life threatened in an age of the American challenge; these movements continue to shape debates today in Europe, but also worldwide in relation to globalization.[47]

The recent experience of fascism and the post-war position of West Germany on the front line of the Cold War rendered its citizens and leaders more susceptible to the appeal of a social order imagined around the prosperous consumer. But even here, where the public support of officials such as Ludwig Erhard seemed to echo the ideals of the Consumers' Republic and especially its faith in the essential link between consumer capitalism and democracy, one finds negotiations with basic features of the American Way. As in France and Britain, one sees the continued insistence upon the importance of the worker and the dignity of labour in the post-war social order. Also, if the affluent consumer could be imagined as a panacea for social and political problems, it was also because the state was called upon to protect consumers and defend and ensure the rights to which all would be entitled. The recent experience of fascism led many in Germany to be rightly suspicious about the ease with which democracy could be re-established by the mere creation of a free-market economy or even a new social-market economy; here economic reform and modernization were important, but so too were extensive efforts to rewrite constitutions, to reform the educational system, to understand what it took to de-nazify and truly democratize these societies. Also, if the utopian vision of private consumer prosperity, associated in particular with the beautiful, high-tech home, gained prominence in West Germany, it was in competition with views and habits akin to those which were dominant in post-war Britain and related to the many years of privation, rationing and a moral economy around restrained consumption.[48] These did not disappear overnight; indeed debates involving labour unions, government agencies and consumer groups articulated these competing visions of the healthy consumer as the building block for West Germany and Europe as a whole in the ensuing decades.[49]

Britain under the leadership of the Labour Party government witnessed the clearest articulation of a social-democratic alternative to the 'American Way', insisting as it did upon the dignified productivity of workers and 'fair shares' rather than prosperity for all. 'On Our Way' imagined a social order that was democratic and just because Britons worked, saved and avoided rather than indulged in consumption. In that sense it was the nation whose post-war political culture came closest to the consensus Sheldon Garon found in Japan in the 1960s.[50] Yet widespread as these views were, even as early as 1944 attacks on this socially democratic, welfare-state consumerism were being issued, most famously by von Hayek, whose *Road to Serfdom* slowly but surely gained adherents, especially among Conservatives.[51] The Conservatives' victories in 1951 and 1955 have been attributed by many historians to their promotion of the competing ideal of the affluent consumer of precisely the type represented in *Le Vrai Visage* and typical of the American Consumers' Republic.[52] Yet the British dedication to the more social-democratic conception of consumption did not simply disappear. Since the 1950s struggles about the state, economic policies, even consumerist politics itself bear traces of these fundamental debates about the consumer and what kind of social and political order can and should be erected around him or her.[53]

In the decade after the Second World War fundamental ideas were open to debate: the role of the consumer as opposed to the worker in post-war society and politics, the role of consumption as opposed to production in economic recovery, the role of the state and labour unions as opposed to capitalism itself in providing freedom, security and prosperity, the relation-ship between the consumer and the citizen, between consumption and democracy. Marshall Plan information officers were important participants in this post-war negotiation, but in the ensuing decades they were joined and supplanted by many others. Governments and their ministries, political parties in power and in opposition, labour unions, employer organizations, housewives' associations, new consumer groups, intellectuals and artists all offered visions of society and politics imagined around these competing principles. The details are extremely interesting and far too complex to treat here, but, like the initial information campaign itself, a close analysis of these debates has lots to teach us both about the peculiarities of these different countries and also about the overall fate of the Consumers' Republic in Western Europe.[54]

The economic success of the Marshall Plan and the full incorporation of Western Europe into the consumer capitalism represented in the late 1940s by the United States – especially since 1989 – have combined to erode our appreciation of the various European alternatives to the American Way. By the 1980s powerful forces in England, Germany and France (in that order) began to attack the social welfare state; they began to articulate (and act on) a vision of society that sounds more and more like the social contract at the heart of the American Consumers' Republic at the moment of the Marshall Plan. Since the 1980s it has become axiomatic to use the language of free enterprise and consumer goods to describe the rights and benefits of citizenship and the process of democratic politics. This is a position that has been proclaimed ever more triumphantly since the collapse of communism in 1989. Now the ideals of the Consumers' Republic are being broadcast more widely: first reaching East Germany, in the context of its reunification with West Germany, then all of Eastern Europe as it was folded into the European Union, and now the whole world as it is integrated into the consumerist West via globalization. But as in the aftermath of the Second World War, the basic premises of the Consumers' Republic are up for negotiation in what is now a global debate. What are the benefits and costs of imagining the consumer as the quintessential citizen, of forgetting, erasing and failing to organize politically around the worker, and of relying upon capitalism alone to provide the basis for democracy? The various European alternatives to the American Way, hinted at in the information campaign associated with the Marshall Plan and inscribed in various institutions and practices across Western Europe over subsequent decades, offer relevant lessons in this urgent contemporary debate.

Notes

1. H. James and M. Stone (eds), *When the Wall Came Down: Reactions to German Unification* (New York, 1992), 'Introduction', p. 4.
2. James and Stone, *When the Wall Came Down*, p. 25.
3. The following historians have addressed the ideological dimension of the Marshall Plan, and in particular its message about capitalism and democracy, although the emphasis on the consumer is not central to their analyses. A. Carew, *Labour under the Marshall Plan: The Politics of*

Productivity and the Marketing of Management Science (Berkeley, 1987); D. Ellwood, *Rebuilding Europe: Western Europe, American, and Postwar Reconstruction* (London, 1992); M. Hogan, *The Marshall Plan: America, Britain, and the Reconstruction of Western Europe, 1947–1952* (London, 1987); C. Maier, 'The Politics of Productivity: Foundations of American Economic Policy after World War II,' in P.J. Katzenstein (ed.), *Between Power and Plenty: Foreign Economic Policies of Advanced Industrial States* (Madison, WI, 1978), pp. 23–49; A. Milward, *Recovery of Western Europe* (Berkeley, 1984).

4. *L'Humanité*, 8 November 1949, 'Will We Be Coca-Colonisés?', cited in R. Kuisel, *Seducing the French: The Dilemma of Americanization* (Berkeley, 1993), p. 55. R. Wagnleitner pursues this line of thinking in his analysis of the Marshall Plan, and especially its propaganda campaign, in Austria: *Coca-Colonization and the Cold War: The Cultural Mission of the United States in Austria after the Second World War* (Durham, NC, 1994).

5. D.W. Ellwood, 'Italian Modernisation and the Propaganda of the Marshall Plan', in L. Cheles and L. Sponza (eds), *The Art of Persuasion: Political Communication in Italy from 1945 to the 1990s* (Manchester, 2001), p. 23.

6. 'Americans are inclined to believe that the period at the end of the war will provide a *tabula rasa* on which can be written the terms of a democratic new order.' Council on Foreign Relations: Studies of American Interests in War and the Peace, Memoranda of Discussion, Economic and Financial series, E-A 36, 27 October 1942. Cited in Maier, 'Politics of Productivity,' p. 35.

7. S. Kroen, 'A Political History of the Consumer', *The Historical Journal*, 47(3) (2004), pp. 709–36; J.O. Appleby, *Economic Thought and Ideology in Seventeenth Century England* (Princeton, 1980); J.O. Appleby, 'Consumption in Early Modern Social Thought', in J. Brewer and R. Porter (eds), *Consumption and the World of Goods* (London, 1993); I. Hont and M. Ignatieff (eds), *Wealth and Virtue: The Shaping of Political Economy in the Scottish Enlightenment* (Cambridge, 1983); C.B. MacPherson, *Political Theory of Possessive Individualism: Hobbes to Locke* (Oxford, 1964); J. Brewer, *Error of Our Ways: Historians and the Birth of Consumer Society*, Working Paper 12, June 2004, www.consume. bbk.ac.uk; F. Trentmann, chapter in this volume.

8. L. Cohen, *The Consumers' Republic: The Politics of Mass Consumption in Postwar America* (New York, 2003), p. 127.

9. Kroen, 'A Political History of the Consumer', treats the divergent experiences of Europe and the United States from the late nineteenth

century to the Second World War that help to explain the precise context in which the Marshall Plan arrived after the war.

10. Archives Nationales (AN), F60ter 438, Extrait du 5ème rapport présenté au congress par l'Administration de Cooperation Economique, Chapter IV, 'Le Programme d'Information en Europe Occidentale'. Translation my own.

11. The problems that information officers faced in France were regularly discussed in their memoranda. See, for example, 'Connaissance du Plan Marshall en Europe: France', especially pp. 7–11, 'Les Difficultés qui font obstacle a l'information en faveur du Plan Marshall', 14 October 1949, AN F60ter 393.

12. G. Bossuat, *La France, l'aide américaine et la construction européenne, 1944–1954* (Paris, 1992), pp. 394–402; G. Bossuat, *L'Europe Occidentale à l'heure américaine: Le Plan Marshall et l'unité Européen, 1945–1952* (Brussels, 1992), esp. chapter 8. See also Ellwood, *Rebuilding Europe*.

13. AN F60ter 394 contains photographs depicting the exhibit presented below, as well as correspondence and reports regarding its organization and reception.

14. *Rapports France–Etats Unis*, 41, August 1950, 'Voyage au pays de la productivité,' p. 11.

15. *Rapports France–Etats-Unis*, 51, June 1950, Georges-Genri Martin, 'Marx et l'Amérique,' p. 38.

16. AN F60ter 394, 'Le Vrai Visage des U.S.A.'.

17. *Rapports France–Etats-Unis*, 41, August 1950, 'Voyage au pays de la productivité,' p. 11.

18. AN F60ter 394, 'Le Vrai Visage des U.S.A.'.

19. *Rapports France–Etats-Unis*, no. 49, April 1951, 'La Transformation du capitalisme américain,' p. 13.

20. Just as it failed to refer to the Taft-Hartley Bill that hindered the organization of labour, the exhibit glossed over the fact that post-war legislation actually marked a decline in the kind of progressive legislation typified by the New Deal era. As Lizabeth Cohen has shown, measures such as the GI Bill and government loan programmes marked a turn away from the activist, reformist state of the New Deal era that did so much to redistribute the wealth produced by capitalism. Depending on existing educational and banking institutions, these post-war programmes systematically favoured white middle-class men and increasingly excluded women, African Americans and workers from achieving the American dream. Far from creating a classless, uniformly prosperous society, such measures hardened class divisions and increased racial and

sexual inequality. Cohen, *Consumers' Republic*, pp. 112–65. Exposing this reality (or 'vrai vrai visage') was one of the goals of the critics of the Marshall Plan in France and elsewhere in Europe.

21. A. Smith, *The Wealth of Nations* (New York, 1994; orig. 1776), p. 715.
22. Cohen, *Consumers' Republic*, p. 55.
23. K. Jarausch and M. Geyer, *Shattered Past: Reconstructing German Histories* (Princeton, 2003), 'In Pursuit of Happiness: Consumption, Mass Consumption, and Consumerism', p. 313. Much the same argument is made in the introduction and several contributions to P. Betts and G. Eghigian (eds), *Pain and Prosperity: Reconsidering Twentieth-century German History* (Stanford, 2003).
24. This is the central point of the excellent introduction to E. Carter, *How German Is She? Post-war German Reconstruction and the Consuming Woman* (Ann Arbor, MI, 1997).
25. Bundesarchiven Koblenz (BAK), B146 387, a carton devoted to the exhibitions of Marshall Plan information officers, demonstrates how often the Americans simply integrated their own displays into trade shows and exhibitions organized by German officials.
26. See, for example, BAK, B146 396, Photo-Wettbewerb 'Mach das beste Bild vom Marshall plan!' from 1952.
27. AN F60ter 438, 1950, drawing contest in France on inter-European cooperation represents a rare effort by French Marshall Plan administrators to elicit popular participation in its information campaign.
28. All references to this exhibit are taken from BAK, B146 387, in which a full script for the German National Barge is included.
29. The gender dimension of this exhibit, as with the whole negotiation about the principles of the Consumers' Republic, is of central importance and has been taken up in the German case by Carter, *How German Is She?*, and K. Pence, 'From Rations to Fashions: The Gendered Politics of East and West German Consumption, 1945–1961', PhD dissertation, University of Michigan, 1999, and in the British case by I. Zweiniger-Bargielowska, *Austerity in Britain: Rationing, Controls and Consumption, 1949–1955* (Oxford, 2000); it is yet to be studied for the French case, although K. Ross offers some interesting ideas which can be applied to this in *Fast Cars, Clean Bodies: Decolonization and the Reordering of French Culture* (Cambridge, MA, 1995).
30. BAK, B146 390, Wohnungsausbau exhibit from 1951 and 1952, is particularly overt in this regard. See also P. Betts, *The Authority of Everyday Objects: A Cultural History of West German Design* (Berkeley, 2004).

31. BAK, B140 73, folder, 'Gadget Exhibit', article from *Hamburger Abendblatt*, Wednesday 17 June 1953.

32. BAK, B146 1138, folder on Rationalisierungsausstellung 'Alle wollen besser leben', which the correspondence describes as extremely popular and successful.

33. BAK, B146 387, Ausstellung in Berlin; the correspondence about this exhibit is explicit about hopes that East as well as West Berliners will visit.

34. K. Pence, 'Shopping for an "Economic Miracle": Gendered Politics of Consumer Citizenship in Divided Germany', Colloque International Paris, 10–11 June 2004, 'Au nom du consommateur', p. 23. Her splendid dissertation plays out the battles over consumer-citizenship in East and West Germany in the ten years after the Second World War: 'From Rations to Fashions'.

35. On the basics of Labour Party ideology, see M. Francis, *Ideas and Politics under Labour, 1945–1951: Building a New Britain* (Manchester, 1997). On ideas about consumption in particular, see Zweiniger-Bargielowska, *Austerity in Britain*.

36. Public Records Office (PRO), Kew Gardens, INF 8/22, report from March 1949.

37. The following analysis is taken from photographs and reports on this exhibit included in AN F60ter 393.

38. Katherine Pence's work on Germany underscores the important efforts by government officials to get the black market under control there as well, by a wide variety of propaganda efforts focused mainly on women. It would be very interesting to do a full-scale comparison of the two representations of this kind of bad consumption. Also see Zweiniger-Bargielowski, *Austerity in Britain*, and M. Roodhouse, 'Popular Morality and the Black Market in Britain, 1939–55', in F. Trentmann and F. Just (eds), *Food and Conflict in Europe in the Age of the Two World Wars* (Basingstoke, 2006).

39. For example, 'Fair Shares of Scarce Consumer Goods', Labour Discussion Series, No. 2 (London, 1946); see discussion in Zweiniger-Bargielowska, *Austerity in Britain*, p. 206. Here the author demonstrates how the Cold War ideological battle was played out in debates between Labour Party and Conservative Party pamphlets around consumption.

40. F. Trentmann, 'Bread, Milk and Democracy: Consumption and Citizenship in Twentieth-century Britain', in M. Daunton and M. Hilton (eds), *The Politics of Consumption: Material Culture and Citizenship in Europe and America* (Oxford, 2001), pp. 129–63; F. Trentmann, 'Civil

Society, Commerce, and the "Citizen-Consumer": Popular Meanings of Free Trade in Modern Britain', in F. Trentmann (ed.), *Paradoxes of Civil Society: New Perspectives on Modern German and British History* (2nd edn, Oxford, 2003), pp. 306–31; Zweiniger-Bargielowska, *Austerity in Britain*; Roodhouse, 'Popular Morality and the Black Market'.

41. Francis, *Ideas and Politics under Labour*, treats the centrality of a masculinist discourse regarding the dignity and central importance of work in the post-war period; he also hints at some of the tensions between the labourer and the consumer, as well as their gender dimension.

42. For an excellent summary of this argument that reviews recent books on the subject, see T. Judt, 'Europe vs. the United States', *The New York Review of Books*, LII, 2, 10 February 2005, pp. 37–41.

43. Ellwood, *Rebuilding Europe*; Ellwood, 'Italian Modernisation'.

44. Kuisel, *Seducing the French*; AN F60ter 394.

45. For a discussion of the debates about labour provoked by the Marshall Plan in France and other European countries, see A. Carew, *Labour under the Marshall Plan: The Politics of Productivity and the Marketing of Management Science* (Manchester, 1987).

46. Here I refer to the veritable arsenal of critiques of consumer capitalism produced in France in the post-war period, which are most profitably understood as part of a negotiation with the 'American Way'. The films of Jacques Tati, especially *Mon Oncle*, mock the vision of individual consumer prosperity and the replacement of real social relations with those mediated by commodities such as high-tech kitchens and cars; novels such as G. Perec's *Les Choses* treat many of the same themes. Most important among the theoretical critiques of consumer culture in relation to democracy are those by Roland Barthes, Jean Baudrillard, Guy De Bord, Henri Lefebvre.

47. The French movements, such as Jose Bové's campaign in favour of small farmers in France and worldwide, and ATAQ, are both domestic and global in their orientation. Both draw upon a tradition of the activist consumer that dates back to André Gide in the late nineteenth century, who imagined the consumer would be the most important political actor of the twentieth century. See R. Williams, *Dream Worlds: Mass Consumption in Late Nineteenth-century France* (Berkeley, 1982).

48. Daunton and Hilton (eds), *The Politics of Consumption*; Trentmann, 'Bread, Milk, and Democracy'; Betts and Eghigian (eds), *Pain and Prosperity*; Belinda Davis, *Home Fires Burning: Food, Politics, and Everyday Life in World War I Berlin* (Chapel Hill, NC, 2000).

49. Pence, 'From Rations to Fashions'.

50. S. Garon, chapter in this volume.

51. On the original reception and progress of von Hayek's ideas in theory and in practice in the post-war period, see R. Cockett, *Thinking the Unthinkable: Think Tanks and the Economic Counter-Revolution, 1931–1983* (London, 1994).

52. Zweiniger-Bargielowska, *Austerity in Britain*; Francis, *Ideas and Politics under Labour*; M. Francis and I. Zweiniger-Bargielowska (eds), *The Conservatives and British Society, 1880–1990* (Cardiff, 1996); H. Jones and M. Kandlah (ed.), *The Myth of Consensus: New Views on British History, 1945–64* (New York, 1996).

53. T.H. Marshall and T. Bottomore, *Citizenship and Social Class* (London, 1992); M. Bulmer and A.M. Rees (eds), *Citizenship Today: The Contemporary Relevance of T. H. Marshall* (London, 1996); M. Hilton, 'Consumer Politics in Post-War Britain', in Daunton and Hilton (eds), *The Politics of Consumption*; M. Hilton, *Consumerism in Twentieth Century Britain: In Search for a Historical Movement* (Cambridge, 2003).

54. These details are the focus of three chapters of a book I am currently writing, entitled *Capitalism and Democracy: The Lessons of the Marshall Plan Era*.

–11–

Emerging Global Water Welfarism

Access to Water, Unruly Consumers and Transnational Governance

Bronwen Morgan

Introduction

Water is a paradoxical good. Just as water itself exists in the natural environment in several different states, so water as an object of consumption is both ordinary and special at the same time. It is ordinary in the sense that it forms part of the background infrastructure of daily life, a necessary facet of ingestion and hygiene without which life itself would not continue in any sense of everyday normality. Precisely for this reason, however, it has a special status when compared with other goods; the urgency of its place in our range of consumptive needs and practices means that, as a good, water stands out. It subsists within a different frame from other goods. While within this frame, water has multiple meanings, connecting to life and death, change and transformation, visions of collective existence, health and pollution, purity and spirituality, and conceptions of order or disorder,[1] its status as a basic or essential good has a particular salience for public policy and public discourse, especially for debates about access to water. In this respect it is not unique; the notion of 'necessity' and basic needs has a long historical tradition, but water is perhaps more than anything else 'the first necessary of life'.[2] Whenever a good has been drawn into the net of 'life's necessaries', there has been a tendency for notions of special state responsibility to develop: responsibility for providing or protecting access to the necessary good. This may be exercised directly by the state, as with the great public administration reforms advocated (after his call for central state intervention failed) by Chadwick in Victorian Britain in respect of urban water and sanitation,[3] or indirectly, as with, for example, the courts' exclusion of 'necessities' from the ordinary operations of the debtors' law.[4] But while the role of the state in relation to necessaries is central, it is not exclusive; the underlying core is collective responsibility rather than the state *per se*. Where goods are necessaries, their consumption invokes broader civic values, so that consumers can be as individuals 'informed, ethical users of necessaries, performing important civic roles',[5] or galvanized into collective civil society forms such as cooperatives.[6] In all these situations, collective action is motivated by the goal of providing access to a basic good only partly because of the good itself, but partly too because of its significance for civic freedom. Water is a quintessential example of just such a good, where lack of access quite literally devours the practical time, sense of personal dignity and good health necessary to participate in collective life.

In the nineteenth and twentieth centuries, at least in what we now think of as the developed world, water's links to civic solidarity and legitimacy were mainly institutionalized within the nation-state, with the public provision of access to clean water being a crucial incident of citizenship, understood in the social Marshallian sense.[7] In recent times, the public policy salience of water's special valorization has developed contours that go beyond the role of a national government. 'Global governance', so pervasive a trend in respect of more traditionally untethered goods than water, from coffee to banking services, is coming of age in the water sector. The transnational dimensions of legal and regulatory politics in relation to water over the last fifteen years or so have reinjected an intensified appreciation of the role of civil society into debates over the state's responsibility *vis-à-vis* the provision of basic goods and essential services.[8] The main focus of this chapter is to analyse the political and legal struggle over the growing trend of supplying urban drinking water[9] on a commercial, for-profit basis, often by multinational corporations. Private sector participation in domestic water service delivery links the prominence of the corporate private sector in recent developments in governance with a contested view of access to water as a consumer service to be provided on a market basis. In developing countries, in particular, the link between market-based consumption and drinking water is one that has to be forged, but even in developed countries the economic implications of full cost recovery spark resistance to the notion that water is an object of 'ordinary consumption'. An oft-repeated trope of the debate over private sector participation in the delivery of water services is to pose a challenge: is water a human right or a commodity? While this is, as we shall see, much too blunt a conceptualization of the tensions generated by the special valorization of water, it is nonetheless at the heart of an interesting process of 'constructing consumers' that is implicit in some of the practices of consumption later examined in this chapter. This process is at an early stage: at present, the private sector provides water to less than 10 per cent of the world's population and the public sector provides the remainder. But even this level of private sector involvement has generated considerable controversy, and the resulting attempts to diffuse the controversy through various strategies of routinization are at the forefront of this analysis.

Routinization

Routinization is an aspect of the patterns of global governance that are emerging around the delivery of water services, which have both substantive and procedural dimensions. Substantively they are constructed by conflicts over social justice and access to basic goods. These conflicts accord a political salience to consumption practices that has implications for civic freedom, political participation and citizenship. Because of the underlying substantive conflicts, procedural attempts to institutionalize routinized practices of 'ordinary consumption' around water come into conflict with a variety of perceptions of the scope of the special responsibility of the state in relation to access to water. For example, charging on an individual volumetric basis is an 'ordinary' practice of consumption in relation to bottled water, but may seem quite extraordinary to citizens who have always had water from the tap delivered either for nothing or for a flat fee.

Such shifting assumptions are part of a familiar conflict over the appropriate limits of market systems of distribution. In other words, the politics of global governance today still focuses, as did national politics in the post-war period in industrialized democracies, on piecing together 'a grand social bargain whereby all sectors of society agree to open markets ... but also to contain and share the social adjustment costs that open markets inevitably produce'.[10] This chapter focuses less on the substantive policy dimension of the conflict, such as the costs and benefits of market-based water service delivery, and more on the routinization of procedures and institutional interactions. This refers particularly to the introduction of legislative and regulatory rules and practices that make certain kinds of consumption practices (such as volumetric payment) an ordinary part of the process of consuming water.

Substantive issues are of course by no means unimportant. They provide an arena for effecting compromises between winners and losers, and such compromises are necessary preconditions for actors to move forward through 'high politics' to a more incremental series of adjustments in solving the problems that generate the conflicts. But the *means* of thus moving forward are made possible by the routinization of procedures and institutional interactions. Some of the bitter conflicts of recent years over the privatization of water services have led to severe stand-still or counter-productive policy see-saws, at least in terms of the narrow but vital goal of getting clean affordable water through the taps to people. Routinization is important because it builds bridges between 'regulatory space' and 'citizen space'. It stabilizes expectations and provides limited predictability, ideally enough to establish a basis for ongoing engagement between actors with diametrically opposed views of how to proceed.

The routinization effected by modern administrative law, as by practices of 'good governance' generally, is never just a technocratic exercise in problem-solving at the margins, but a political process that selectively opens space for some to participate in setting the basic rules and others not to. Understanding the routines of governance in a political way has three advantages. First, it alerts us to their potential to effect structural change, for the detail of their repertoires, strategies and techniques has a significant bearing on the *future* dynamics of conflict over substantive issues of social justice and access to water. Second, it helps us understand that such structural change can be effected by surprising means. A rich hybrid of strategies are currently employed in pursuit of both the view of access to water as a fundamental human right and a view that water, at least in its anthropic cycle, is little different from ordinary commercial services – and in either respect consumer rights can be as useful to the human rights activists as human rights can be to business actors. Finally, insisting on the political stakes in routinization also reminds us of the *limits* of routinization. Routinization defines itself against the stakes articulated by disruptive protest, and the global water field is marked by sustained social protest in many (though importantly not all) of its sites.[11] In comparison, say, to the routinized forms of 'network governance' that typify European social policy formation,[12] private sector participation in water provision at the global level is much more like a 'formative episode of the [global] welfare state, where social divisions and ideological clashes' dominate.[13] In the current flux, it is important to chronicle the dialectic between routinization and disruption, to explore not only the emergence of regulatory frameworks but also the challenges to those frameworks by activists. The figure of the 'consumer' is capable, as we shall see, of being mobilized by both sides of this dialectic, and it is for this reason that consumption practices figure centrally in trajectories of public policy formation. The next two parts of the chapter explore the dialectic between routinization and disruption, first at the level of 'global water welfarism' and then in two particular national settings where water has become a legal and political flashpoint and a focus of consumer activism: South Africa and New Zealand.

Global Water Welfarism

The modest sketch of the global context that follows extrapolates current trends that are, in my view, cumulatively constructing a global field of 'water policy', where, over time, a bounded set of actors repeatedly interact in relation to a finite universe of institutions, procedures and routines. I identify an emerging skeletal architecture that is being constructed at the global level by key actors involved in funding, managing, regulating and consuming water services. I contend that this architecture supports a policy of corporate welfarism in water provision at the global level. The reference to welfarism is intended neutrally, simply to convey the fact that these developments at a global level are portrayed by their proponents as policies that will, amongst other goals, alleviate the plight of those who lack access to water or the means to pay for such access. The likelihood of succeeding in this goal, or even the sincerity of the motivation, is bitterly contested by those who challenge the trajectory of commodification of water.

The debate can be seen as an echo of older debates on the question of whether national welfare state policies established in post-war industrial democracies served merely to legitimate the basic structures and results of capitalism, or to genuinely modulate it as a form of political economy. In contrast to debates over the form and extent of national welfare states, however, the special responsibilities of states are supplemented and at times almost replaced by a sense of the importance of both business and non-business civil society organizations. A series of United Nations conferences and gatherings dating from the 1970s[14] and the so-called 'International Drinking Water and Sanitation Decade' during the 1980s have since the 1990s taken an increasing interest in the role of a private sector perspective on water, with an important 1992 UN conference endorsing for the first time the principle that water be treated as an economic good.[15] After private sector investment in water between 1990 and 1997 increased 7,300 per cent on 1974–90 investment levels,[16] intergovernmental activities in relation to water have intensified,[17] and are increasingly incorporating the private sector as a key partner in their vision.[18]

The private sector's interest in the economic potential of providing water services on a transnational basis continues to increase,[19] in the face of growing resistance and criticism from non-business civil society organizations. The criticism arises in part because of the absence of structures of representation and accountability that typically characterize state institutions. The potential legitimacy deficits that result are important aspects of the struggles over consumption practices in relation to water at the grass-roots level.

But analogies with state institutions in a global context, while they can temporarily anchor the readers' institutional imagination, are often strained. The deeply politically divisive nature of water issues has already led to what some have hailed as the first true institutional innovation in global governance, the World Commission on Dams (WCD),[20] a hybrid institution that put government, NGOs, activists and corporations on a level playing field in an institutional context unmoored from standard representative and accountability mechanisms, and tasked them with generating general principles to guide the funding and building of dams. More recently, a Global Water Scoping Review[21] has been established to explore the possibility of establishing another, similar, global institution on the issue of private sector participation in domestic water service delivery.

In essence, global water welfarism entails a vision of a regime where public aid supplements the private investment of multinational corporations to solve the social and environmental problems of global water provision, catalysed by a hopeful mix of corporate social responsibility and the probing eye of government and civil society monitors. In what follows, I elaborate this vision by reference to three dimensions: the fiscal capacity, the administrative capacity and the ideological character of this emerging 'regulatory space'. The 'welfare goal' that animates the field of global water welfarism can be envisaged succinctly by reference to the water-related Millenium Development Goals that aim to halve the numbers of people in the world who lack clean drinking water (1.5 billion) or sewage (2.4 billion) by 2015.

The fiscal capacity of global water welfarism is provided by an inter-meshing of private investment capital and official development aid (ODA). Multilateral development banks have for some time imposed loan condition-alities that require private sector participation in the water sector, and this continues to be the case.[22] Further, since 1999, when the high 1990s level of private sector investment in the water sector began to fall,[23] there has been a trend towards *mixing* aid with investment. This mixing underpins a particular model which is widely disseminated: public–private partnerships where all partners share the goal of efficiently delivered basic goods and services bolstered by a subsidy framework that will facilitate universal or affordable access. This has been specifically endorsed in the water sector by the World Bank,[24] and a regional lending facility in Africa (the Africa Water Facility) has recently been established along similar lines.

Such fiscal arrangements have been labelled by civil society critics as 'a franchising model for global water corporations'.[25] They certainly leave open the question of what kind of organizations will provide the administrative capacity for actually delivering water services, and this is obviously crucial for developing countries with limited resources. In water, direct provision via multinationals is an important carrier of such administrative and technical capacity. The global water market is growing[26] and is dominated by three firms in particular from France and Britain: Ondeo, Veolia and Thames Water.[27] Furthermore, efforts are increasingly being made collectively by those with the administrative capacity to deliver water services to shape the environment in which they operate in several dimensions: standard-setting, policy, advocacy and implementation. France spearheaded the formation by the International Organization for Standards of a Technical Committee on Water and Wastewater Standards in late 2001, with the objective of developing standards on service activities relating to drinking water supply and sewerage. Many major companies in water (including construction and engineering as well as water service delivery and management) are members of the World Water Council (WWC), as are the major multilateral development banks. The WWC, legally incorporated in France as a UNESCO-affiliated NGO, describes itself as 'an international water policy thinktank dedicated to strengthening the world water movement for an improved management of the world's water'.[28] It functions as a forum for policy and advocacy and hosts a tri-annual World Water Forum which includes a formal Ministerial Meeting, despite the fact that it is not sponsored directly by the United Nations. Finally, the private sector has also taken a lead in fostering a more implementation-oriented kind of support for building administrative capacity, via technical assistance and capacity building. The Global Water Partnership, a network that complements the work of the WWC, funds a wide range of water-related activities globally, at twelve regional levels, and develops and promotes management norms and principles applicable at practical implementation level.

Ideologically, the activities of this web of primarily non-governmental actors are underpinned by broadly neoliberal views regarding the merits of market efficiency and competitive pressures. But the promotion of 'raw' market-driven reforms is also mixed with a concern for poverty reduction goals, both at the level of policy[29] and in a range of water-specific documentation.[30] This emergent 'social face' of the neoliberal consensus poses a growing dilemma for opponents and activists. Private sector provision of water services has become an increasingly contentious aspect of the World Water Forum, and disruptive civil society protests at the second forum in 2000 resulted in the inclusion of formal NGO panels at the third in 2003. But the dichotomous cleavage in water access politics that energizes the political divide ('water as a commercial service or a human right') does not sit comfortably with the welfarism increasingly inflecting the rationale of global water policy. The notion that human rights and commercial services are inherent opposites is a perspective that dissolves if in fact the ideological and practical effects of human rights strategies reinforce and support the structure of global markets precisely *because* they ameliorate their harshest effects. To illustrate the potential for this compatibility, consider remarks made by a member of the United Nations Committee on Economic, Social and Cultural Rights in 2000 which give to human rights the task of redistributive politics characteristic of national welfare states but transposed now to a global level:

> [T]he Covenant [for Economic, Social and Cultural Rights] – and other international human rights treaties – can be used as a shield to protect the state's poorest citizens from the policies of powerful, global non-state actors ... NHRIs [National Human Rights Institutions] can show how the Treasury's negotiators can use the Covenant in negotiations with [international financial institutions]. They might offer human rights training for the Treasury's negotiators ... [Moreover] just as the Covenant can be used to tackle unfair inequalities within a state, so it can help to address the grossly uneven distribution of power between the economic north and the economic south.

This sounds admirably progressive, but his concluding words show how this use of human rights is also compatible with the long-term *persistence* of the market reforms they seek to temper or dilute:

> Economic re-structuring still occurs. But it does mean that the reforms are introduced in ways which minimize avoidable suffering, for instance by the introduction of safety nets for vulnerable groups – *thereby contributing to the reform's longterm sustainability*.[31]

The legitimation of global water welfarism is thus intimately linked to its fiscal and administrative dimensions. Indeed, the three dimensions of global water welfarism can be linked by projecting them to a 'shadow water state' at the global level. In this ghostly image, legislative potential haunts the WWC, the UN Committee on Economic and Social Rights and ISO Technical Committee 224 on Water and Wastewater Services. Loan conditionalities from the multilateral development banks intersect with the activities of the Global Water Partnership to flesh out these developments in executive fashion, while intergovernmental investment treaties adjudicate the inevitable conflicts. While each of these tendencies is real, even on a hypothetically extended basis their cumulative effect is insufficient support for the actual execution and implementation of water service delivery. In practice, emergent global water welfarism piggybacks significantly on national-level rule structures.

From Global to National Levels

Institutions and practices at local and national levels, embedded in their own histories, intersect with global water welfarism in varying ways. The most important filter of global water welfarism is the legislative and regulatory framework established at national (and sometimes local) level. It is useful to contrast political and transactional frameworks for the provision of water services. Transactional frameworks minimize political discretion (for example over tariff-setting processes) and emphasize the allocation of property rights and protection against risk (primarily for those funding infrastructure operation and investment), value for money, affordability and open procurement procedures. In essence, transactional frameworks seek to establish a framework for market-based exchanges that will in the process deliver access to water for individuals. Political frameworks, by contrast, either consciously modify market-based exchanges or directly specify redistributive outcomes that could not or would not be achieved in a market setting. In the process they preserve political discretion (especially on key issues such as tariffs) and prioritize participatory mechanisms for consultation with labour and consumers over the structure of water services.

Political and transactional frameworks are not incompatible alternatives, but their coexistence tends to generate tensions between the competing policy goals of equity and efficiency implicit in the 'human right versus commodity' dichotomy. Political and transactional frameworks provide different degrees of opportunity and responsiveness for the key actors in the water policy networks. In particular, transactional frameworks prioritize the relationship between funders, governments and water operators (producers), whereas political frameworks have more space for the voice of labour and of 'end-users' whether conceptualized as consumers or as citizens. Furthermore, the evolution of legislative and regulatory frameworks at national level is periodically disrupted – at least in South Africa and New Zealand – by social protest and civil society resistance. The emergent shape of the field is as much a product of this disruption and protest as of repeated political negotiations or legal strategies.

But there is no simple correlation either between political regulatory frameworks and the use of human rights strategies, or between transactional frameworks and commercial strategies. Rather, activists challenge commodification by using – both legally and politically – human rights, consumer rights, informal administrative mechanisms and budgeting processes, and hybrid amalgams of all of these. And while commercial providers of water, especially but not only corporate ones, are indeed more

Figure 16 A Fire Engine Parks over a Water Meter to Prevent Disconnection, New Zealand, 2001

Source: Water Pressure Group, New Zealand.

likely to use 'commercial' strategies (e.g. investment treaties, property rights, competition law), these intersect with activists' practices in ways that lead to unpredictable results, as the New Zealand case study will demonstrate.

Each case study narrative will highlight two dimensions: the character and evolution of the legislative and regulatory framework for water services, and the range and type of challenges made by ordinary citizens. I will seek to highlight bridges between regulatory and citizen space: that is, mechanisms that respond to disruption and protest in ways that routinize their impact while remaining responsive to the concerns expressed by the protestors. The links with the architecture of global water welfarism are rarely direct or formal. But the influence of that regime nonetheless will, I hope, become evident, albeit inflected by the different histories and traditions of each country.

South Africa

South Africa is an instance of a developing country context that is a particularly interesting case for exploring the relative salience of national and international dynamics in its governance of water services. With its relatively high level of state capacity and fiscal autonomy, it is fiscally much less dependent on foreign aid than many other developing countries, having only taken out one World Bank loan since its transition to democracy in 1994. This is by no means to say that it is immune from pressures in favour of market-led governance. In the immediate aftermath of winning power, the ANC government effected a policy shift from an electoral platform of state-driven redistribution in the social democratic mould, fed by extensive local consultation and participation (RDP or Redistribution and Development Policy), to a market-led strategy that prioritizes economic growth and provides redistribution later and residually (GEAR or Growth, Employment and Redistribution). This shift, which was significantly influenced by a deliberative process in which international capital interests played a critical role,[32] had direct implications for water services policy. It included a policy commitment by the government to keep the non-tradable input costs of economic production for industrial consumers (electricity and water primarily) as low as feasible for the purpose of attracting foreign investment. At the same time, GEAR also constrained government borrowing, limiting intergovernmental transfers, crucial for local government delivery of water services.[33]

These pressures fed directly into the new democratic government's legislative framework for water services, which faced the immense challenge posed by a mere 34 per cent of its citizens having access to piped water. The resulting turn to private sector investment as a response to these pressures has produced over time a legislative framework that one interviewee characterized as 'schizophrenic'.[34] The schizophrenia has arisen from tensions poignantly illustrated by the jarring transition in this 1996 speech by the Mayor of Johannesburg:

> Transformation has a price. Our country has been liberated into an era governed by the fundamental principles of non-racism, non-sexism and justice for all. But please understand the particular conditions of government which require resources to give people the basic services which are their fundamental right as citizens of this country ... Businessmen from the US are used to fast services. It takes us six months to find out who owns a piece of land. There are danger signals when our councillors and administrators do not meet the investors' aspirations. Some administrator tells the investor to go to such a room and there they find a woman painting their nails. This is the way to rule ourselves out of international global competition.[35]

In South Africa water welfarism has see-sawed between a focus on human rights and universal access, and the needs of investors. On the one hand,

South Africa, almost alone in the world, has made a formal constitutional commitment to a human right to water.[36] And this legal commitment is backed by a genuine political will to effect major redistributive change in this crucial area of basic socioeconomic need. On the other hand, over the decade 1994–2004, in tandem with the more general shift from RDP to GEAR, three principal trends can be observed: first, the overlay of an initially political framework for the delivery of water with a transactional one; second, a distinct muting of an initial preference for public sector provision; third, marked decentralization to municipal governments mostly stretched very tightly for resources and expertise.

South Africa has so far explicitly avoided creating an independent regulatory agency to oversee the delivery of water services, preferring to maintain direct political control at least over the framework for provision, even if not always over service delivery itself.[37] Initially, regulatory oversight was located in a Community Water Supply and Sanitation division of the Department of Water Affairs that, in tune with the social democratic spirit of RDP, also worked directly with communities in a participatory fashion to provide water supply. Over time, however, this quintessentially political framework has shifted to an increasingly transactional framework. One important institution in this shift has been the Municipal Infrastructure Investment Unit (MIIU), a unique institution for providing technical support to local government. The MIIU's ascendancy illustrates well the interpenetration of national and international personnel and knowledge. Structured in a hybrid fashion that bridges the public and private sectors,[38] the MIIU's capacity to provide both funding and expertise means that it has a powerful influence in shaping the terms of any deal for which it provides support. Thus despite its lack of formal political authority, and the existence (at least initially) of an explicit statutory preference for public provision in the regulatory framework,[39] the MIIU's influence encouraged the adoption of the models, techniques and norms promoted by the World Water Council and the Global Water Partnership that support commodified delivery of water services.[40] Over time, the MIIU's policy-based influence has been supplemented by greater legal controls given to the Treasury,[41] by dilution of the statutory preference in favour of public provision,[42] and by the negotiation of arrangements with the private sector that sidestep the legislative mandate to involve affected groups in the political policy-making process over water.[43]

The supplementation and partial displacement of a political framework by a transactional one is a general trend[44] that has three particularly interesting features. The first is that it has been accompanied by a steady increase in the extent of private sector participation in delivering water services, at least as measured by population coverage. In the decade from 1993 to 2003, foreign private sector operators in water services[45] now serve, from a base of zero, 7 million (roughly 15 per cent) of the total population. Second, transactional regulation is increasingly embodied in either 'hard law' at the national level or powerful policy conditions at the international level which the national government is not in a position to ignore. The third feature is either the correlative of the second (i.e. political regulation is increasingly embodied in 'soft law' or 'mere policy' initiatives), or it is given 'hard law' status but confined to *procedural* entitlements only.

Take, for example, the important power to disconnect consumers for failure to pay. The regulatory framework in the early 1990s reserved powers over collection and disconnection to local governments only,[46] but when private banks withdrew their financial support in 1997 for a major concession contract as a result, the legislative framework shifted over the next few years to intensify Treasury control from the centre and clarify that water service providers (including private companies) could be directly involved.[47] At the same time, the government introduced a Free Basic Water Policy in 2001, and a 'credit control code' animated by principles of due process and compassion in its 2003 Strategic Framework – important measures, but carefully confined to the arena of 'soft law'.[48]

The overall result of this can be summed up as a hard law framework that is increasingly transactional and relatively neutral to the identity of the provider, combined with 'soft law' (policy-based, non-statutory) measures to legitimate this approach. The soft law measures do not reinscribe opportunities for political participation and influence into the regulatory framework, but rather ameliorate its harshest side-effects. It is the impact of social activism at the local level, including important activism around consumption practices, that performs such a reinscription. Organized labour, partly through its role in the governing ANC coalition, partly through lobbying, but also through strike and protest action, has played the most important role in bringing the legislative and regulatory framework to its current uneasy mix of contradictory signals. But in the townships and peri-urban areas, consumer resistance to the move towards greater cost recovery and marketization in the delivery of water has had equally important implications for the viability of the framework changes. In these areas, there have long been severe problems of mass non-payment for services, the result of collective political action taken by township residents in protest against apartheid. Apartheid has ended, but now cost-recovery principles applied to previously badly underserviced areas, even in diluted form, have raised tariffs very significantly from the low base flat rate that was charged (but not paid) under apartheid. Township residents continue to boycott payment and, in relation to water, have employed a wide mixture of strategies to disrupt the policies of the government, including marches, protests, payment boycotts, illegal reconnections, political education and test case constitutional litigation.

There is a broad and important contrast (and tension) between strategies that seek to build political agency on the one hand and, on the other, strategies that are aimed at fostering responsible consumer behaviour, such as consumer education programmes, as a means of diffusing conflict over structural reform. Tensions between these strategies create barriers to productive interactions that otherwise might build bridges between regulatory and citizen space.

At present, strategies focused on political agency have more mass support and undermine the goals of 'responsible consumer behaviour'. Building political agency, for example, is a goal of mass mobilization strategies, both cooperative peaceful ones and adversarial violent ones that coexist in a pattern one participant calls 'popcorn politics'.[49] This activism aspires to establish vaguely specified alternatives to capitalism and rejects the current models premised on private sector participation altogether. The aim is to harness the current 'politics of sheer refusal'[50] into a more proactive, mundane, sustainable political education that will create a sense of collective identity for those excluded not just from basic provision in water, but also in health, education and shelter.[51] Some of these activists seek to build an alternative political party, but whether or not they aspire to this level of representation, they are motivated by pragmatic service delivery issues – such as service standards or the cost of water – only because of broader goals to change the structural agenda of neoliberalism and privatization.

The starkest contrast with this level of social activism is provided by 'tri-sector partnership initiatives', such as the 'consumer education' programmes run by Durban Metro Water Services in partnership with Vivendi (Veolia) Water. Seeking to build social and political consensus in support of current reforms, the partnerships employ local young people to work with their neighbours on paying bills, managing debt schedules, water conservation techniques, the proper operation of sanitation systems and the like. The structural questions that are the concern of the more disruptive activists are part of the taken-for-granted background for this work. Early conceptions of this work as primarily technical have more recently shifted, as illustrated by a change in job description for those liaising between citizens and the two partners in service provision. These were initially known as 'Customer Service Agents' but in the second phase of the project were renamed 'Community Development Officers', reflecting the early inefficacy of the technical, problem-solving approach and the realization by the partners that the preconditions for securing consensus required a less instrumental approach to this mode of responding to affected interests. More recently, some water service providers in South Africa have sought to bridge regulatory and citizen space by subcontracting not foreign multinationals but a local South African firm that has more experience of working with local township communities, and which builds into its strategies some attention to structural issues (e.g. hiring only those in the local community who have been unemployed for a certain amount of time).

There is no necessary link, however, between individualized assistance and consumer identity, on the one hand, and collective strategies and political agency on the other. For example, citizens also mobilized in what became known as 'ten-rand marches', converging in large crowds on the offices of the water service provider with ten-rand notes (£1) in their hands to symbolize what they were willing to pay per month for water. This was a strategy that melded political agency and consumer responsibility, while still making a strong appeal for addressing the structural forces that lead to a situation where ten rand is the maximum affordable amount an individual can pay.

Legal actions also blend collective and individual strategies in interesting hybrids. Activists' use of legal strategies in South Africa to try to ameliorate the impact of market-based water service delivery on poor consumers has so far met with only limited success. Of the two cases so far brought, neither succeeded in eliminating disconnection for non-payment of bills as an option for the state or the private water provider, though the second[52] provided some temporary relief by mandating a range of procedural protections for the consumer before disconnection. Insofar as the first case appeared to withhold a remedy because the plaintiff had illegally reconnected to the network,[53] the cumulative effect of the two cases is to provide important but purely procedural protection to citizens who pay what they can afford, and who refrain from civil disobedience in their broader demands to the political decision-makers. The litigation has no effect on the principal issue that divides the stakeholders in the broader structural conflict: the justice or appropriateness of a cost-recovery approach to the delivery of water services. It softens the impact of that policy approach, but in a way that accords more dignity to responsible consumers rather than giving more voice to political participants.

Arguably, South Africa's passionate commitment to a human rights approach has developed over time, in the context of the imperatives of transactional risk and commercial service delivery that dominate the fiscal and administrative support for the emerging strategy of global water welfarism, into a type of soft consumerism, encapsulated in the following remarks by a senior municipal official:

> You've got to be able [to] provide the free basic services, cut the damn thing off when the person's consumed that amount and be able to bill in a reliable way. [But] your credit control policy must include – as opposed to the hard-line 'forcing people' kind of approach – a customer relations function, a complaints centre, a mechanism of incentivizing payment … It's all about creating new systems, new management capacity, and we're saying, really, that whilst you're doing that, pay attention to *the human consumer issue stuff* because if you don't do that, you've got very little chance of success.[54]

Cutting 'the damn thing off', however, inflames social activism at local levels that continually destabilizes the fragile bargain of soft consumerism described above. Yet attempts by activists to harness the guarantees of basic human rights encoded in the formal legislative framework do not necessarily reinforce the identity of active political agent either; rather, they buttress the model of 'soft consumerism' which leaves broader questions of collective representation and responsiveness to be determined by political institutions that increasingly adopt the transactional model favoured by the regime of global water welfarism. Thus, activists who seek to assert a collective political identity are pushed to do so in oppositional and unruly forms that are both unrecognized and increasingly repressed by the formal political system.

New Zealand

The very different economic and social context of New Zealand, where access to water is already almost universal, might be expected to facilitate the logic of commodification, or at least to be a context relatively impervious to framing water as a human right. In fact, the public policy framework for water service delivery in New Zealand has during the 1990s been shaped by vigorous consumer activism that does appeal (albeit recently) to the notion of human rights, additionally invoking a range of other arguments and strategies that draw on the special status of water as an essential good or service. The role of consumer activism has been institutionally effective only in combination with two other crucial features of the institutional environment: small political parties and autonomous (and fragmented) local government. Arguably, an unorthodox use of the courts by the activists has also played an important role. The combined effect of these institutions and actors has been to secure recent legislative change that constrains both the scope and the extent of private sector participation in water services, as well as prohibits the disconnection of citizens who do not pay their bills.[55]

The significance of this should be seen in the wider context of New Zealand's reputation, established between 1984 and 1999 on an international basis, as a particularly marked case of textbook application of market-strengthening reforms. Many state-owned sectors, from electricity, telecommunications, airports and postal services to banking were first corporatized, and then privatized, with the result that New Zealand's highly protected, welfare state economy was transformed into an open economy with extensive private sector involvement.[56] These changes were deeply unpopular at citizen level, but their rapid imposition was made possible nonetheless by the unicameral, non-federal nature of the first-past-the-post parliamentary system then in place. In no small part because of the unpopularity of the imposed changes, however, a mixed member proportional (MMP) voting system replaced first-past-the post in the mid-1990s, and by 1999 New Zealanders had elected a minority Labour government, which ruled, in coalition with green and further-left parties, on a platform that promised to temper and even reverse the intensity of market-led changes to the social and economic system.

The public policy framework for water service delivery became a flash-point in the first half of the 1990s in this struggle. Pressure to expand the role of the private sector in delivering water came from both local and foreign business interests.[57] But water in New Zealand is a responsibility of regional and local government, which has strong autonomy both traditionally and in terms of financial capacity, and each council had the discretion to make separate governance arrangements for the delivery of water. Although two major reforms of the 1974 Local Government Act during the first half of the 1990s increased pressure on local governments to demonstrate value for money in all their activities and to justify explicitly decisions *not* to use the private sector in providing services to local communities, few extended this logic to water services. Indeed, in the political climate of the mid-1990s, public determination to establish water as a kind of 'final frontier' of marketization policies helped contribute to the formation of the Alliance Party, a radical left party that won electoral success at *regional* government level in the capital city, Auckland, on a platform of anti-privatization. In the political battle between local and central government that followed, the Alliance Party succeeded in passing legislation that explicitly prohibited the privatization of the *bulk* water supplier for Auckland (Watercare).[58]

Although the Alliance Party does not operate at local government level, where retail water delivery takes place, private sector participation has taken very little hold there either. This is true even in the Auckland metropolitan region, which after 25 per cent growth over the last 5 years is under pressure to find economies of scale in infrastructure services, despite the barriers posed to this by the existence of six fragmented councils. There is substantial citizen opposition to taking a commercial or private route to gaining such economies of scale. The Auckland Water Pressure Group (WPG) was formed in 1998, and since then has had a fluctuating membership of as many as 2,000 people, mainly from lower-working-class families, to fight both private sector participation and commercial restructuring of public water services.[59] In 1997 Papakura District Council – the smallest of the six – signed a thirty-year concession contract with the foreign private sector,[60] and in the same year Auckland City Council corporatized its water services, creating Metrowater.[61]

These developments catalysed a trajectory of consumer activism that not only derailed other councils' plans to corporatize but also resulted, by 2002, in legislative constraints on privatization at the level of local government, supplementing the outcomes secured at regional level by the Alliance Party. In essence, the WPG's small-scale but rambunctious social activism created a political space for the minority party members of parliament upon whom the Labour government depended to pass legislation,[62] allowing them to insert – into the otherwise open-ended and facilitative 2002 Local Government Act – restrictions on the involvement of the private sector in water service delivery.[63] While this was an intentional outcome of the activists' activities, a further unintentional but equally important legislative amendment was also secured: water disconnections were prohibited and water restrictions allowed only where they would not create unsanitary conditions.[64]

The WPG challenged the commodification of water through an unorthodox mix of civil disobedience, legal strategies, savvy use of the media and political lobbying. Their approach mixed a practical reliance upon (some would say distortion of) administrative law and consumer rights litigation with a rhetorical public emphasis on human rights and environmental and social justice issues. The interesting feature of this mix is that, in relation to the 'hard law' regulatory framework, the activists used their status as consumers of a commercial service to press their objectives, but combined this with 'soft' activities that vigorously rejected this commercial framework. Moreover, while their strategies of direct action exposed them to some degree of public censure for undercutting norms of responsible consumer behaviour, their capacity to air their arguments in court (even while losing) legitimized their cause and, at the same time, amplified the publicity they received about their civil disobedience. In this way, the activists simultaneously routinized the conflict over water delivery and redisrupted the political arena.

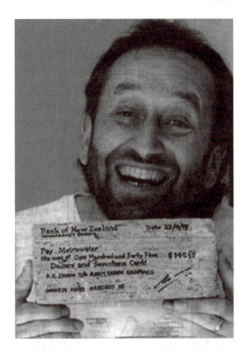

Figure 17 A Protestor against Water Price Rises Sends His Legal Payment on a Brick to the Privatized Water Company, New Zealand, 2001

Source: Water Pressure Group, New Zealand.

The WPG's approach employs the cumulative interaction of at least five strategies: i) using consumer rights instrumentally against the water companies; ii) employing civil disobedience as an enforcing tool; iii) appealing to socioeconomic human rights as a rhetorical justificatory frame; iv) litigating civil and political rights to legitimize the negative implications of civil disobedience in the wider community (in particular softening the image of unruly bandits acting in frank dismissal of the shared community norms of paying one's bills); v) leveraging political action by using media exposure and political lobbying of minority party members who hold the balance of power as the key implementing tools. Their principal strategy initially was civil disobedience: a subset of up to 500 members of the WPG refused to pay their bills or in some cases withheld only the waste treatment charges. Their main justification was rooted in claims of distributive social justice; they argued that the charges were an illegitimate commodification of an internationally recognized socioeconomic human right,[65] and that the shift from property rate-based flat tariffs to volumetric user-pays methods of charging for both water and sewage treatment was regressive, damaging the capacity of large poor families to provide for their basic needs.

After a year or so, Metrowater began to pressure the boycotters to pay by disconnecting their water supply. An early claim lodged by one of the founding members of the WPG in the Disputes Tribunal (an alternative dispute-resolution venue for small claims) pleaded the boycotters' case in terms of the old common law doctrine of 'prime necessity', in particular the principle that monopoly suppliers of essential services must charge no more than a reasonable price. Although the legal case was lost,[66] the boycotters persisted in and expanded their use of the Disputes Tribunal as a forum for pressing their claims, shifting to a more explicit (and strategic) reliance on their status as consumers of a commercial service. They claimed, for example, that Metrowater's pricing strategy breaches the Consumer Guarantees Act,[67] and that its claims regarding water quality do likewise. Over time, these strategies became increasingly routinized: over fifty separate cases in the last three years have been lodged in the Disputes Tribunal, and the 'letter of dispute' lodged by boycotters with Metrowater and kept on file by the WPG was recognized in 2001 by Metrowater as a legitimate basis for not disconnecting customers who refused payment. Although they later withdrew this recognition, the boycotters then shifted venue yet again, this time to the Competition Commission, demanding continued abeyance from disconnection in light of the ongoing unresolved legal status of their objections.

Although the boycotters relied on commercially founded bases for some of their litigation, they also lodged claims more directly founded in civil and political rights. These claims range from defending the free-speech right of their members to drape their houses in protest banners[68] to challenging the validity of a local election because candidates who promised not to back privatization ultimately did back public–private partnerships in water services.[69] These actions highlight their entitlement to participate in the political process that shapes the public policy framework for water service delivery and thus bolster their more direct and sometimes illegal activism. The judge's remark in the election case rather ironically highlights the ways in which their efforts to push consumerism to its limits continually fail. He says:

> some might say that it is of the very nature of politics that candidates will promote their policies in a way [that] takes advantage of knowing that different interpretations might be put on the meaning of his or her words, unrestrained by any political equivalent of the 'misleading or deceptive conduct' provisions of the Fair Trading Act relating to commerce (para 47).

The activists have in a sense tried to bring *both* private providers and politicians to account with arguments grounded in assumptions that the provider–citizen (and the politician–citizen) relationship is a commercial one of consumer and provider. In all cases, they have failed at the legal level. But the curious resulting combination of routinization and disruption arises from the frank disregard of the activists for the coherence and consistency of their strategies *in legal terms*. Most of their legal arguments would, if successful, at most have tempered the commercial provision at the edges, in ways not dissimilar to the South African constitutional litigation. What they cared about was the ability to mobilize politicians to vote, asserting repeatedly that 'it's not the court of law that counts but the court of public opinion'.[70] The imbrication of direct action, media exposure, political lobbying and litigation enlarged the space for political participation of ordinary citizens in policy-making, not only in respect of the technical aspects of the public policy framework for water specifically, but also in respect of broader issues of civil and political rights to participate in governance, even if the language and style of the contribution is jarring for the 'usual' participants. The link between direct political action and legal arguments based on the status of water as a commercial service is interestingly reflexive, in that the combination actually facilitated resistance to commercialization. Just as the 'ten-rand' marches in South Africa also demonstrate, the subjective identity of the consumer here can clearly be mobilized to pursue something more than the individualistic, self-maximizing path of the economic market actor. Rather, consumer identity here encompasses a range of collective political goals that impinge directly not only on the terms of water's consumption but also on the regulatory framework for the production of water services, and the public sphere spaces that mediate the two.

Conclusion

The two case studies can be extended to draw some conclusions about how different practices of consumption *vis-à-vis* water give rise to different implications for public policy frameworks, especially in the light of its status as a basic necessity. Overall, there is no monolithic status, whether of consumer or subject of human rights, that can be ascribed even to the narrowest subgroup of activists focused on the most urgent of issues, such as affordable access to the minimum volume of water necessary for survival. In particular, there is no stark dichotomy between citizen and consumer; rather, there is a degree to which aspirations to social citizenship are necessarily bound up with the norms of consumerism. Consequently, we see, in both case studies, a web of social activist strategies that allow for multiple shifts in the discursive frameworks in which protest is located. These shifts, ranging from political rights to legal rights to consumer education to consumer protection, make a difference to the range of available justifications for action, the scope of potential allies and the scale of the issue that gets defined as 'the problem' to which the public policy framework should respond. Broadly speaking, one can identify three varying (non-exclusive) emphases in the implications for the role of the state, each of which is more explicitly political than the last. The first is that the state functions as a kind of technocratic handmaiden supporting a governance structure in which the 'corporate connection' plays a significant role. The second is a more constitutional vision, with sovereign state action at its centre, the limits and goals of which are shaped by a legally mandated vision of the collective priorities of the community. The third is a blend of civil society activism and parliamentary legislative politics.

We find aspects of all three emphases in both case studies. Pressures towards the first have a stronger impact in South Africa than in New Zealand, which may be at least in part due to New Zealand's relative insulation from the regime of global water welfarism. Unconstrained at the national level by either explicit or implicit conditionality from international lending institutions, and marked at local government level by unusually strong financial autonomy, water services in New Zealand remain a political arena over which national collective choice can still be effectively exercised. The global regime of water welfarism bears more heavily upon South Africa than upon New Zealand as a consequence of their different levels of socioeconomic development, albeit not necessarily in an obviously visible institutional fashion. Rather, the network of corporate actors so central to global water welfarism transmits knowledge-transfer-based governance routines at the international level, and over time these shape the evolution of distinct national institutional frameworks in ways that appear as an indigenous trajectory of local change.

This pressure may possibly account for the relatively muted effects of the second strand, constitutionalism, in South Africa – muted relative to the expectations engendered by South Africa's history of powerful politically organized civil society, constitutionally embedded legal commitments to universal access to essential services and the strong political will in the wake of apartheid to reverse its legacy. This history creates an apparent opportunity for social movements to play a coequal role with powerful market actors in debates over how to embed markets in broader social policies that temper their harshest distributive effects. Yet what eventuates in the South African case is not productive collaboration, but instead fractious parallel trajectories of legislative change and social protest that occasionally intersect but largely coexist in uneasy tension. Within this environment, the practices that constitute a responsible consumer run against the grain of political agency, at least when focusing on the consensus-oriented, 'problem-solving' approach that characterizes the tri-partite partnerships focused on consumer education. Yet consumer identities are not necessarily confined to playing a marginal role within the sphere of technocratic governance; the ten-rand marches urge a different vision of 'responsible consumer behaviour' that is at the same time explicitly part of a practice of collective representation, and one linked to the history of anti-apartheid activism. Such actions could potentially alter shared understandings of what the key public policy problem is, by focusing attention away from the irresponsible (in terms of service delivery expectations) consumer behaviour towards issues of political representation – highlighted because those who fought with the township poor against water cut-offs in apartheid now sit in offices exacting payment through oppressive responses to resistance. While a service delivery perspective would generate the question 'how much pressure can an individual legitimately put on the public fisc?', a focus on political representation might ask instead 'how much pressure can a democratically elected government legitimately impose on specific social groups such as the poor?'

Of course, South Africa has responded to such a question, not least through its Free Basic Water Policy, but, as argued above, that response has been made in such a way as to ease its fit with the technocratic governance strand of responses to water's necessity as a public good. Moreover, legal strategies in South Africa have so far failed to live up to hopes of leveraging the third strand of civil society activism and legislative politics, arguably contributing more to a stabilization of the technocratic compact than to a disruption of it. By contrast, in New Zealand a more 'low-politics' version of the constitutional vision, one that uses informal dispute resolution rather than constitutional courts, does succeed in surprising ways in impacting on the public policy framework via legislative politics. This bridge-building across regulatory and citizen space is possible in part because the urgency of access to water is much more attenuated as a public policy problem in New Zealand, a longer history of stable democratic government facilitates more space for unruly protest by relatively small minorities, and the presence of multi-party coalition government makes possible the translation of that protest into legislative change. None of those conditions subsists in present-day South Africa, where boycotting payment of bills and illegally reconnecting to the network engender an oppressive reaction from the state.

This is not a conclusion that dictates clear lines – we see webs of coexisting consumption practices interlinking with multiple variations of possible state responses to the essential quality of water as an 'ordinary' good of extraordinary importance. What is clear is that attempts to establish a relatively uniform approach to the public policy problem of access to water at a global level are highly variable in their outcomes, in part because of their dependence upon nationally specific institutional configurations. That said, the global model of water welfarism tends to become embedded more firmly in frameworks for production and the organizational routines of state institutions than in the practices of the consumers of water services. As producer and national state politics are increasingly reoriented to, and even become accountable to, extra-national actors, practices of consumption play an increasingly important role in redirecting at least attention (and sometimes also choices and decisions) downwards again in a traditional 'democratic' sense. Understanding how grass-roots consumer politics in the struggle to access water feed into and shape national regulatory frameworks increasingly influenced by global pressures is a story that integrates consumption and production in interesting and unpredictable ways. It is perhaps ironic that the political force of consumer activism in both case studies rests hardly at all upon notions of legitimate consumer entitlement, and much more upon notions of basic needs, fundamental human rights and the demands of social justice and protection from risk. Multifaceted as it can be, the figure of the consumer is a powerful resource at a technocratic level but continues to lack resonance at the broader political level, at least in the context of one of life's necessaries.

Acknowledgements

The research project on which this chapter is based is funded by the ESRC and the AHRC under Research Grant 143-25-0031, in the Research Programme on Cultures of Consumption, and their support is gratefully acknowledged.

Notes

1. V. Strang, *The Meaning of Water* (Oxford and New York, 2004).
2. See F. Trentmann in this volume.

3. C. Hamlin, *Public Health and Social Justice in the Age of Chadwick: Britain 1800–1854* (Cambridge, 1998).

4. M. Finn, *The Character of Credit: Personal Debt in English Culture 1740–1914* (Cambridge, 2003).

5. F. Trentmann, 'Beyond Consumerism: New Historical Perspectives on Consumption', *Journal of Contemporary History*, 39(3) (2004), pp. 373–401.

6. F. Trentmann, 'Bread, Milk and Democracy: Consumption and Citizenship in Twentieth-Century Britain', in M. Daunton and M. Hilton (eds), *The Politics of Consumption* (Oxford and New York, 2001).

7. T.H. Marshall, *Citizenship and Social Class and Other Essays* (Cambridge, 1950).

8. As with the salience of 'necessary goods', this too has a long historical trajectory and the role of civil society actors and private corporations in collective action in relation to basic goods has been cyclically important (Trentmann, 'Beyond Consumerism', pp. 384–5).

9. The project focuses on both the international level and on national-comparative case studies, which have been carried out in South Africa, Chile, New Zealand, Bolivia, Argentina and France. The case studies vary along a number of different dimensions that explore a cross-section of possible governance contexts. They all involve one or more of the three largest multinational water companies. They include both developing countries and OECD countries, and a full range of different legal structures. The project limits do not extend to rural water supply nor – except tangentially where they have special salience for end-delivery politics – to the larger terrain of water resources.

10. J. Ruggie, 'Taking Embedded Liberalism Global: The Corporate Connection', in D. Held and M. Koenig-Archibugi (ed.), *Taming Globalization: Frontiers of Governance* (Cambridge, 2003), p. 1.

11. A recent survey by the InterAmerican Development Bank (IADB) identifies, for almost half those surveyed, social resistance as either a critical issue or one that is both significant and hard to solve (IADB, 'Obstacles and Constraints for Increasing Investment in the Waste and Sanitation Sector in Latin America and the Caribbean', Survey, November 2003, www.iadb.org).

12. C. Sabel and J. Zeitlin, 'Networked Governance and Pragmatic Constitutionalism: The New Transformation of Europe', unpublished 2003 paper, on file with author.

13. Sabel and Zeitlin, 'Networked Governance', p. 6. The dominance of French and British companies in the sector arguably echoes the older and equally formative episode of colonization.

14. United Nations, *Water Development and Management*, Proceedings of the United Nations Water Conference Mar del Plata 1977, Argentina, Volume 1, Part 1 (Oxford, 1978); *The Dublin Statement on Water and Sustainable Development*, International Conference on Water and Environment, Dublin, Ireland, 1992, available at: www.wmo.ch/web/homs/documents/english/icwedece.html.

15. *The Dublin Statement*, Principle No. 4. The other three principles recognize the importance of participatory approaches in water development and management, the importance of the role of women, and the status of water as a finite, essential and vulnerable resource.

16. G. Silva, N. Tynan and Y. Yilmaz, 'Private Participation in the Water and Sewerage Sector – Recent Trends', *Public Policy for the Private Sector*, 147 (1998), pp. 1–8, published by the World Bank Group: Finance, Private Sector and Infrastructure Network.

17. The Millenium Development Goals set at the UN Summit of 2000 include a commitment to halve the 1.5 billion people in the world without access to safe drinking water. The 2002 World Summit on Sustainable Development in Johannesburg extended this goal to the 2.5 billion lacking sewage, also to be halved by 2015. The United Nations Commission on Sustainable Development has chosen water, sanitation and human settlement as the focus of its implementation cycle for 2004 and 2005. In January 2004 the European Commission launched the EU Water Facility: http://europa.eu.int/eur-lex/en/com/cnc/2004/com2004_0043en01.pdf.

18. See United Nations, *Guiding Principles for Partnerships for Sustainable Development ('type 2 outcomes') to Be Elaborated by Interested Parties in the Context of the World Summit on Sustainable Development (WSSD)*, 7 June 2002, available at: http://www.un.org/esa/sustdev/partnerships/guiding_principles7june2002.pdf. Although less than 10 per cent of all water in the world is currently managed by the private sector, by 2000 at least 93 countries had partially privatized water or wastewater services: G. LeClerc and T. Raes, *Water: A World Financial Issue*, PriceWaterhouseCoopers, Sustainable Development Series (Paris, 2001).

19. Thus *Fortune* declared water to be the oil of the twenty-first century (*Fortune*, 15 May 2000); Schwab Capital Markets hosts global water conferences for investors and publishes market analyses of the sector; the 2004 World Economic Forum in Davos launched a Water Initiative, see http://www.weforum.org/site/homepublic.nsf/Content/The+Water+Initiative.

20. World Commission on Dams (WCD), *Dams and Development: A New Framework for Decision-Making* (London, 2000). The novelty of the WCD may be disputed if a longer historical perspective is taken that encompasses the growth of many international bodies in the late nineteenth century such as the Danube River Commission.

21. P. Urquhart and D. Moore, *Global Water Scoping Process: Is There a Place for a Multistakeholder Review of Private Sector Participation in Water and Sanitation?*, ASSEMAE (Brazilian Association of Municipal Water and Sanitation Public Operators), Consumers International, Environmental Monitoring Group, Public Services International, RWE-Thames Water, and WaterAid, April 2004, available at http://www.wateraid.org/documents/Full%20report%20MSR.pdf.

22. See the analysis of proposed loans for 2003 in Public Citizen, *World Bank Watch*, Vol. 1 (January 2003), available at www.wateractivist.org.

23. D. Hall, 'Water Multinationals in Retreat', Public Services International Research Unit, January 2003, available at www.psiru.org/reports/2003-01-W-Suez.doc. The causes of the decline are not yet well established, but the political risks engendered by the widespread social protests against private sector participation in water are thought by many to be an important factor.

24. See D. Hall, 'Public Solutions for Private Problems – Responding to the Shortfall in Water Infrastructure Investment', Public Services International Research Unit, available at http://www.psiru.org/reports/2003-09-W-strats.doc, for a discussion of the recommendations of the influential 2003 Camdessus Panel on Financing Water Infrastructure (*Financing Water for All – Report of the World Panel on Financing Water Infrastructure*, available at http://www.worldwatercouncil.org/download/CamdessusReport.pdf) and the World Bank's response.

25. Karl Flecker, Polaris Institute, Canada, quoted in 'Civil Society Delegations Break from World Water Council Consensus', 20 March 2003, http://cupe.ca/www/news/3827.

26. See *Water Utilities: Global Industry Guide* (Datamonitor, 2003).

27. Ondeo (previously Suez and before that Lyonnaise des Eaux) serves 110 million people in more than 100 countries. Veolia (previously Vivendi Environnement and before that Générale des Eaux) serves 96.5 million people in 90 countries: see P. Gleick, G. Wolff, E.L. Chalecki and R. Reyes, *The New Economy of Water* (Oakland, 2002), pp. 24–5. Thames Water serves 22 million people: see D. Yaron, *The Final Frontier* (Ottawa, 2000).

28. See http://www.worldwatercouncil.org/about.shtml.

29. World Bank World Development Report 2004, *Making Services Work for Poor People* (Washington, DC, 2003). See also K. Jayasuriya, 'Workfare for the Global Poor: Anti Politics and the New Governance', Asia Research Centre, Murdoch University, Australia, Working Paper No. 8, September 2003.

30. Examples can be drawn from high-level reports like that of the Camdessus Panel on Financing Water Infrastructure as well as contractual documentation such as concession agreements.

31. Paul Hunt, Rapporteur of UN ESCR Committee, statement made at the Fifth Annual Meeting of Asia-Pacific Forum of National Human Rights Institutions, August 2000, p. 4, at http://www.asiapacificforum.net/activities/annual_meetings/fifth/Hunt.pdf, emphasis added.

32. See the process described in Chapter 9 of A. Sparks, *Beyond the Miracle: Inside the New South Africa* (Chicago, 2004).

33. The Department of Finance in real terms cut intergovernmental grants which pay for municipal service subsidies by 85 per cent between 1991 and 1997: Financial and Fiscal Commission of South Africa, *Local Government in a System of Intergovernmental Fiscal Relations in South Africa: A Discussion Document*, (Midrand, 1997), p. 18.

34. Senior Official, Municipal Infrastructure Investment Unit, interview, 16 September 2003.

35. Tokyo Sexwale, Mayor of Gauteng Province, September 1996, quoted in Matthew Burbidge, 'Non-payment End to Democracy: Sexwale', *The Citizen*, 11 September 1996.

36. Section 27 of the 1996 Constitution reads, as relevant: 1) Everyone has the right to have access to ... b) *sufficient food and water*; (2) The state must take reasonable legislative and other measures, within its available resources, to achieve the progressive realization of each of these rights. Uganda makes a constitutional commitment to a right to water, and Gambia, Ethiopia and Zambia include constitutional aspirations endeavouring to provide clean safe water.

37. Interview with official from Department of Water Affairs and Forestry, 17 September 2003.

38. The MIIU is a government department structured as a non-profit company, with the objective of facilitating private sector investment in infrastructure, including water and sanitation. It reports to the Department of Provincial and Local Government and relies on its accounting and employment systems, but it operates at arms length from that department with considerably more flexibility and autonomy as a result of its company structure.

39. Water Services Act 1997 (SA), s10(2)(b).
40. Though there is no personnel overlap between these institutions, USAID funds expatriate advisors who work for MIIU locally and have facilitated extensive knowledge transfer about approaches to water services from all over the world, though as the MIIU stressed: 'USAID doesn't have any say over what we do, in the South African context ... there's very very little leverage over the decisions of government here' (interview with senior official of MIIU, 16 September 2003).
41. Municipal Financial Management Act 2003 (SA).
42. Municipal Systems Act 2000 (SA).
43. For example, the five-year management contract signed in 2000 between Suez Water and Johannesburg does not trigger the requirements of the Municipal Systems Act to carry out public and labour consultation.
44. While the general trend is visible over time, it has developed in a see-saw pattern of 'action and reaction', where both the extent of legal delegation the government has been willing to commit to private companies and the orientation of the legislative and policy framework have see-sawed abruptly in response to the political controversies generated by involving the foreign private sector in water service delivery.
45. The major actors in this private sector provision are almost all members of the World Water Council, with the exception of Saur. It should be noted that where a contract or concession is made 'with' a global water company, it almost always participates as a partner in a consortium of companies that includes local South African companies, thereby leading to a different name for the local subsidiary (for example, Water Services South Africa for the Suez Ondeo subsidiary).
46. This was only one interpretation of the Local Government Transition Act 1993 (Act 209 of 1993 SA), but although there was not a clear consensus within the legal community about this interpretation, the doubt it raised was still sufficient to change the banks' position: Ross Kriel, 'Facing Local Government Post-demarcation: Impact of the Regulatory Framework on the Private Sector – Case Studies and Analysis', paper prepared for the Development Bank of Southern Africa Symposium on Risk Management, 1 September 2003, p. 3, on file with author.
47. Municipal Systems Act 2000 (SA), Municipal Financial Management Act (2003).
48. See *Free Basic Water Policy* (Government of South Africa, 2001), establishing a universal right to access 25 litres of water per person per day within 200m of their dwelling; *Strategic Framework for Water Services* (Government of South Africa 2003), Clause 4.5.8 (principles

governing credit control include communication, fair process, warnings, compassion, restriction rather than disconnection as a last resort).

49. A. Desai, *We Are the Poors: Community Struggles in Post-apartheid South Africa* (New York, 2002).

50. Richard Pithouse, interview, 11 September 2003.

51. The South African 'Social Indaba' hosts cross-sectoral forums that encourage networking across different areas of social activism and also fosters international connections with anti-globalization activists overseas.

52. *Residents of Bon Vista Mansions v Southern Metropolitan Local Council* 2002 (6) BCLR 625, requiring fair and equitable procedures, reasonable notice of intent to disconnect, and provision of an opportunity to make representations before disconnecting anyone from their water supply as a matter of constitutional right.

53. The explicit reason for denial of relief was a technical ground because the plaintiffs had neglected to plead the direct constitutional obligation and the relevant statutory provisions did not yet contain regulations specifying the minimum amount of water to which each citizen has a right. But when the transcript of the hearing is read with the decision, it becomes clear that the judge considered that the plaintiff's illegal reconnection to the system had deprived her of the benefit of the rights accorded by the Water Services Act: *Manqele v Durban Transitional Metropolitan Council* 2002 (6) SA 423.

54. Senior Official, Municipal Infrastructure Investment Unit, interview, 16 September 2003.

55. Local Government Act 2002 (NZ), ss130–137 and s193(1).

56. According to the 2000 UNCTAD World Investment Report, New Zealand is the most transnationalized economy in the OECD, with productive, financial, retail, energy, transport, media and communications sectors all primarily owned by transnational corporations: cited by B. Curtis, 'Third Way Partnerships, Neo-liberalism and Social Capital in New Zealand', Research Paper No. 4, Local Governance and Partnerships Research Group, University of Auckland, New Zealand, www.lpg.org.nz/publications/, p. 4.

57. For example, through a 1995 conference on the water sector run by the investment bank First Boston, a series of impassioned speeches by the director of the New Zealand Business Roundtable, Roger Kerr, imploring the national government to 'finish the business' [of privatizing core government services], and background lobbying of local officials by multinational water companies: L. Harre, ex-leader of the Alliance

Party, interview, 15 December 2003; see also New Zealand Business Roundtable, *Reform of the Water Industry* (Auckland, 1995).

58. The Local Government Act 1974 as amended in 1998 prohibits Watercare's six local authority shareholders from selling their shares. The simultaneous restructuring of Watercare into corporate form imposed social obligations that constrain profit-making from water service delivery: viz. a statutory duty to work in the best interests of those who live in Auckland, to maintain prices at the *minimum* levels consistent with the effective condition of its business, and a prohibition on paying dividends to its local authority shareholders.

59. Sister groups in other districts of Auckland were later formed to protest the privatization of Papakura Water and the planned corporatization of Manakau Council Water. The WPG also worked closely with Citizens against Privatization, an environmental community group in Waitakere Council that had fought the initial water privatization initiatives in the early to mid-1990s.

60. The franchise was awarded to a private multinational consortium comprised of Veolia Water (Vivendi), Thames Water (RWE) and Halliburton KBR. There is only one other concession for water services with the private sector thus far in New Zealand, which is an equally small contract with a rural council in a ski tourism area. Vivendi has a concession for a waste treatment plant in the capital city, Wellington.

61. Metrowater is a local authority trading enterprise fully owned by the local council but must conform to company law governance structures.

62. By the late 1990s the Alliance Party had won seats at the national level under the MMP system and formed, with the support of the Green Party, the coalition that enabled the 1999 minority Labour government to govern and that held crucial leverage over the reform of the 1974 Local Government Act. The Minister for Local Government was an Alliance member, and the Chairman of the Select Committee overseeing the legislative reform was the leader of the Green Party.

63. See *Local Government Act* 2002 (NZ), Sections 130–37: the effect is to prohibit local governments from divesting themselves of water supply and wastewater services within their areas, unless it is to another local government authority. Contracting out of water service operations is limited to a maximum of fifteen years, and it is illegal to delegate control over water pricing, water services management and the development of water policy. These restrictions prohibit some public–private partnerships (such as a future version of the Papakura franchise) and significantly dilute the commercial scope and attractiveness of other forms of PPPs.

64. See *Local Government Act* 2002 (NZ), s.193(1), inserted by a last-minute intervention by the Department of Health, who used the WPG for leverage in support of a longer-term aim of imposing compulsory drinking water standards upon local authority water providers.

65. The human rights dimension to their argument developed more recently, recharacterizing what was initially a purely distributive justice argument, as a result of growing links between the water activists and other activists involved in advocacy of social and economic rights.

66. The court agreed that this doctrine applied to water but held that the common law rule was displaced by Part IV of the Commerce Act on price control, which precluded private enforcement and restricted regulatory intervention solely to the 'lighthanded touch' of the Commerce Commission on the motion of the Minister: *Metrowater v Gladwin et al.*, High Court of New Zealand, 17 December 1999, unreported judgment of Salmon J. Metrowater regarded this as a confirmation of the legitimacy of treating water delivery as a commercial service.

67. The nub of this claim is that a fixed charge from the bulk water supplier is passed onto the customer as a volumetric fee calculated at 75 per cent of the water used that month. The protestors argue that not only does this breach consumer guarantee laws, but it also breaches the obligation in para. 27 of the international right to water expressed in the UN General Comment, which stresses: 'Equity demands that poorer households should not be disproportionately burdened with water expenses as compared to richer households.'

68. Auckland City Council ordered the removal of these banners under local by-laws, resulting in a chain of events that first jailed the occupant of the house for refusing to comply with the court order, then reversed the order in embarrassment at the resulting publicity (*Auckland City Council v Finau*, District Court of Auckland, unreported judgment of Joyce J, 28 February 2003), and eventually amended legislation to clarify that the Human Rights Act does apply to local government.

69. *Bright v Mulholland* [2002] DCR 196.

70. Penny Bright, Water Pressure Group spokesperson, interview, Auckland, 2 December 2003.

Index